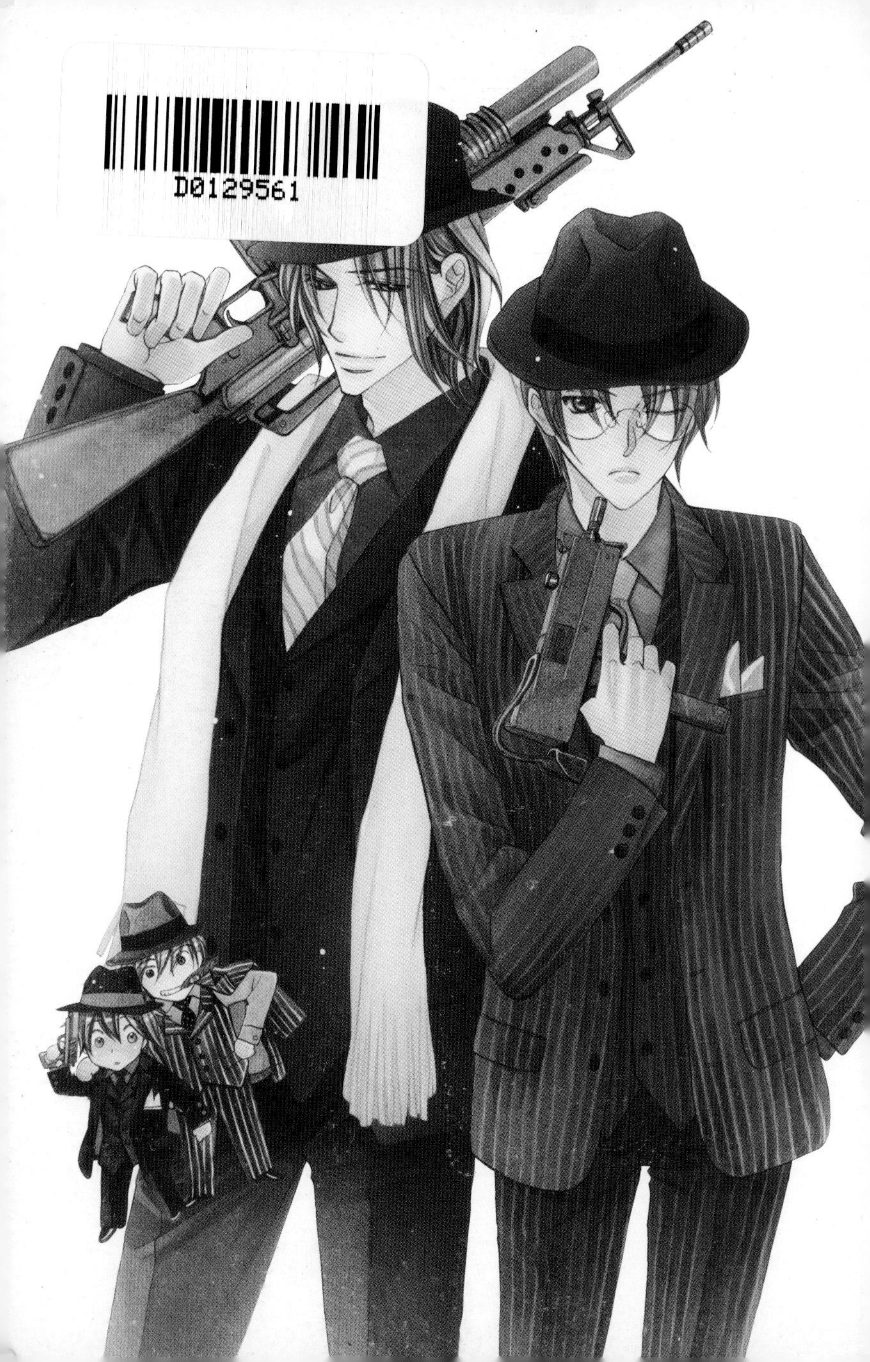

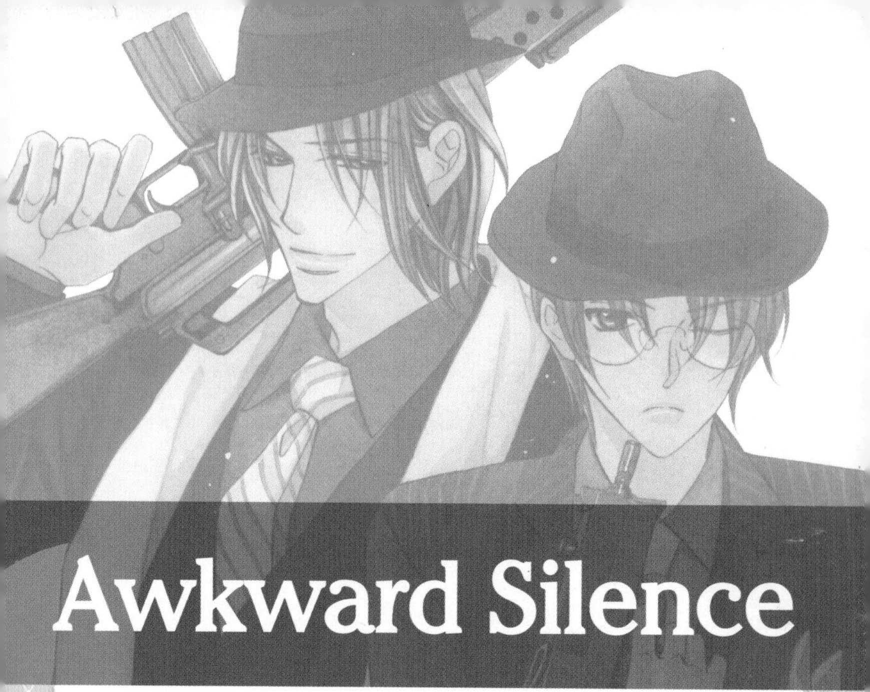

Awkward Silence

Story and Art by Hinako Takanaga volume 3

CONTENTS

SUBLIME
SuBLime Manga Edition

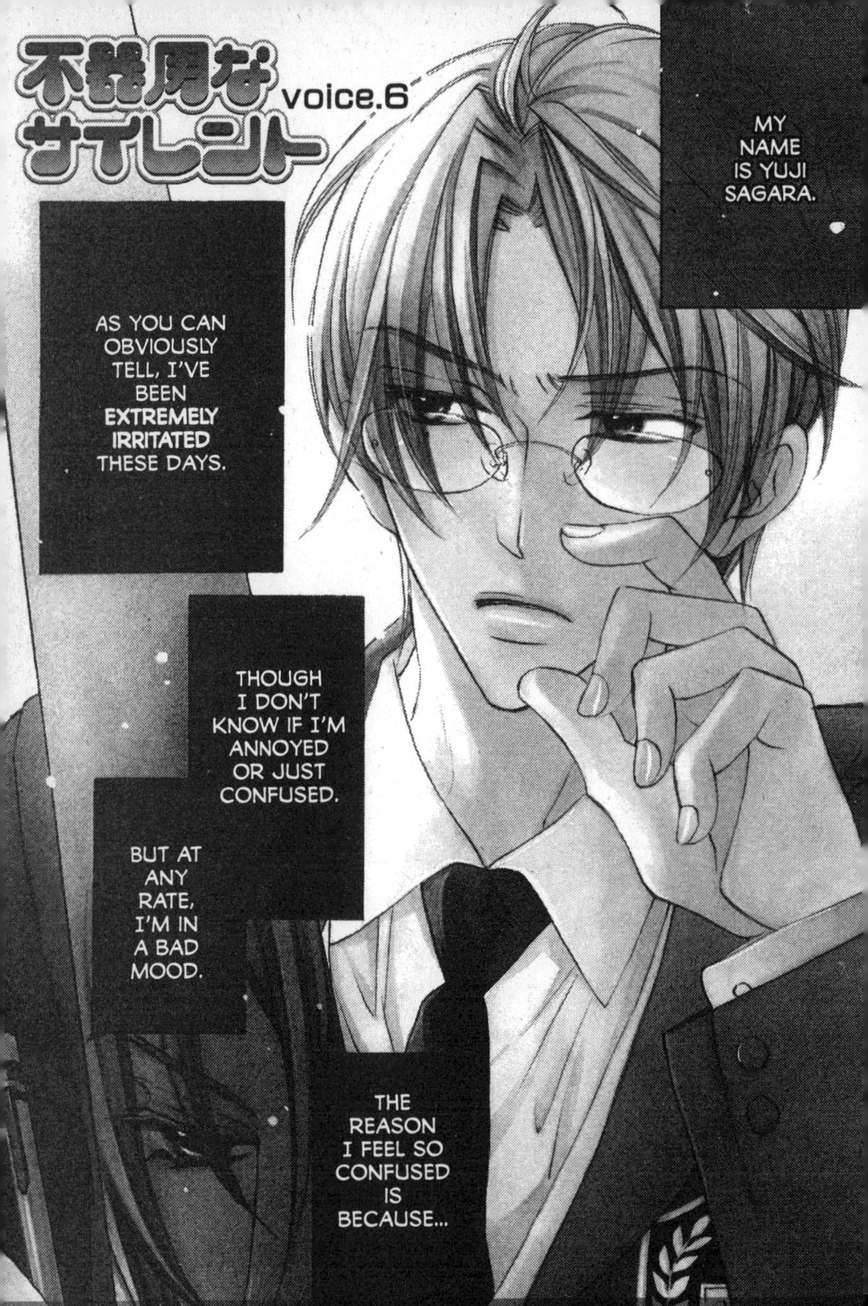
MY NAME IS YUJI SAGARA.
不器用なサイレント
voice.6
AS YOU CAN OBVIOUSLY TELL, I'VE BEEN **EXTREMELY IRRITATED** THESE DAYS.
THOUGH I DON'T KNOW IF I'M ANNOYED OR JUST CONFUSED.
BUT AT ANY RATE, I'M IN A BAD MOOD.
THE REASON I FEEL SO CONFUSED IS BECAUSE...

Awkward Silence: Voice 6

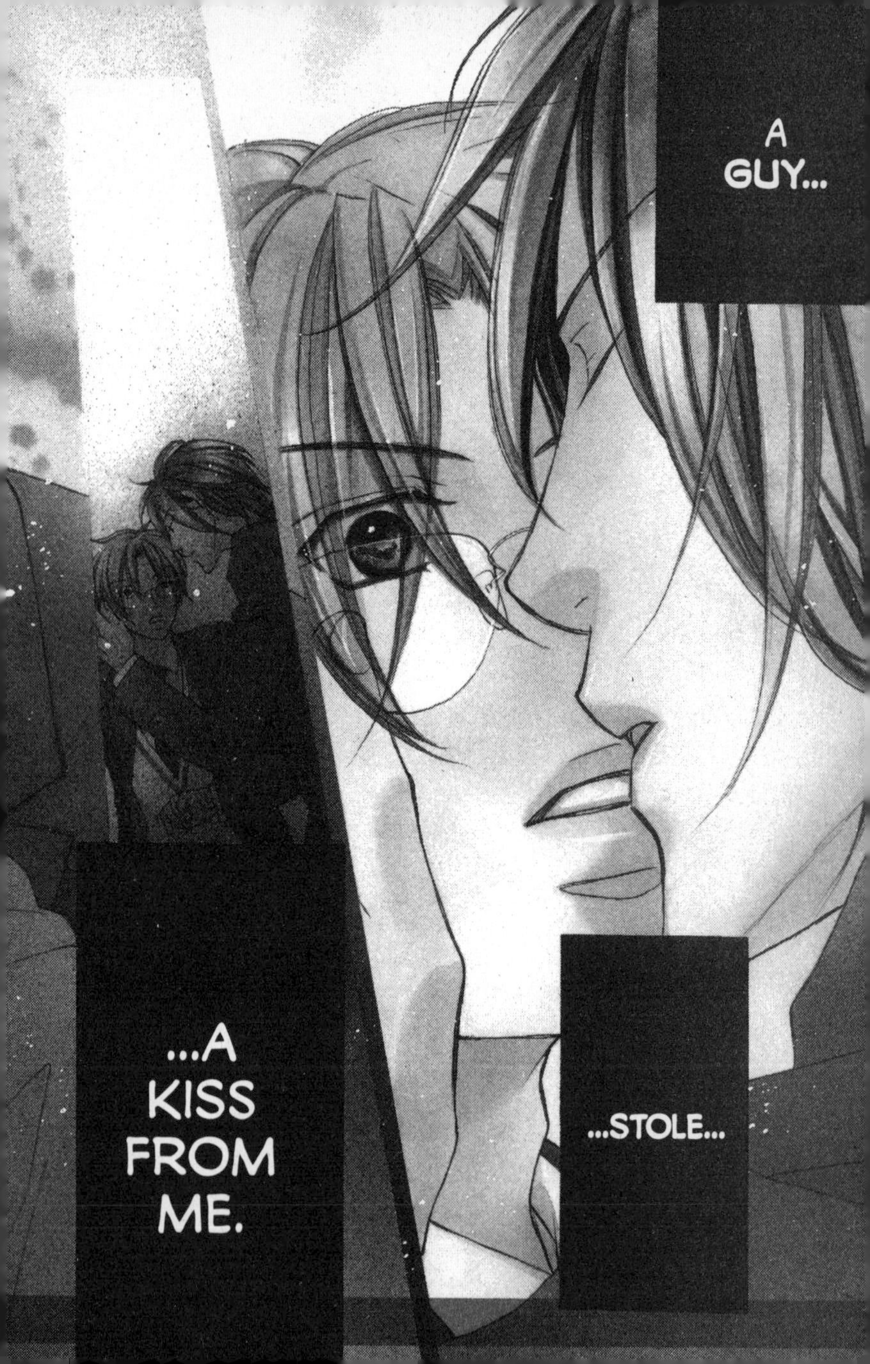
A GUY...
...STOLE...
...A KISS FROM ME.

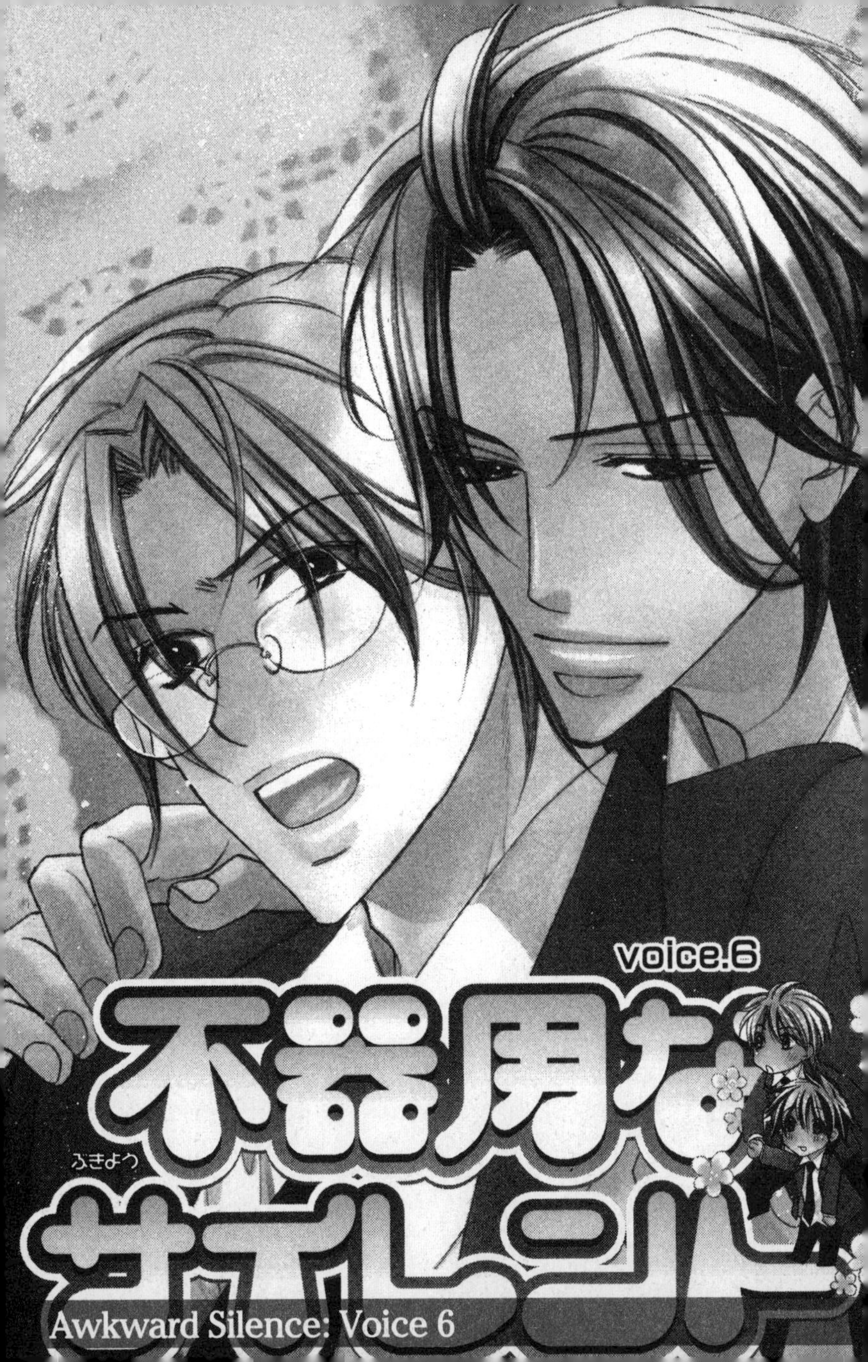
voice.6
不器用な
ぶきよう
サイレント
Awkward Silence: Voice 6

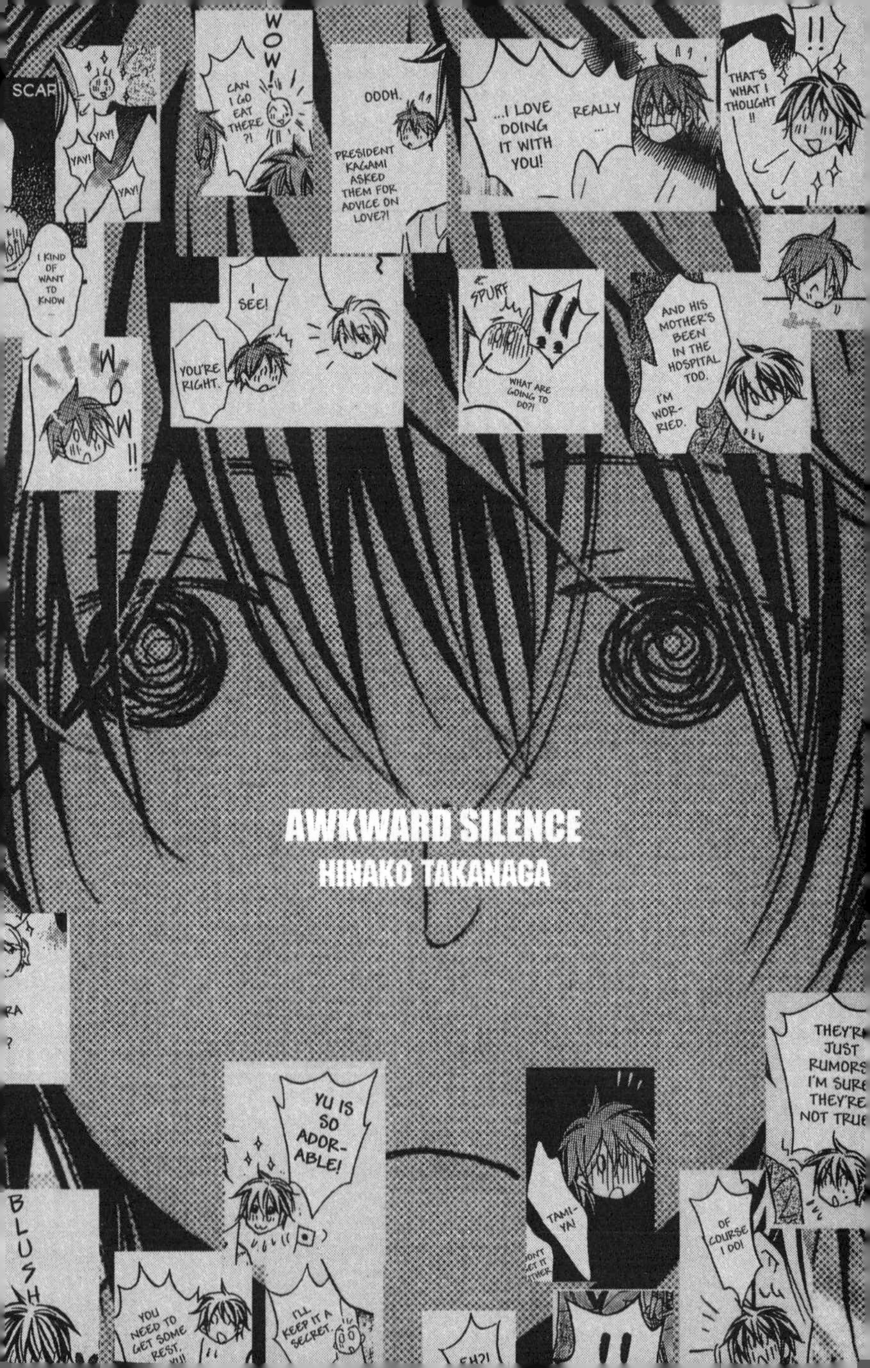
!!
THAT'S WHAT I THOUGHT!!
...I LOVE DOING IT WITH YOU!
REALLY...
OOOH.
PRESIDENT KAGAMI ASKED THEM FOR ADVICE ON LOVE?!
WOW!
CAN I GO EAT THERE?!
YAY!
YAY!
YAY!
AND HIS MOTHER'S BEEN IN THE HOSPITAL TOO.
I'M WOR-RIED.
SPURT
!!
WHAT ARE GOING TO DO?!
I SEE!
YOU'RE RIGHT.
I KIND OF WANT TO KNOW...
WOW!!
AWKWARD SILENCE
HINAKO TAKANAGA
OF COURSE I DO!
TAMI-YA!
YU IS SO ADORABLE!
BLUSH
I'LL KEEP IT A SECRET.
YOU NEED TO GET SOME REST.

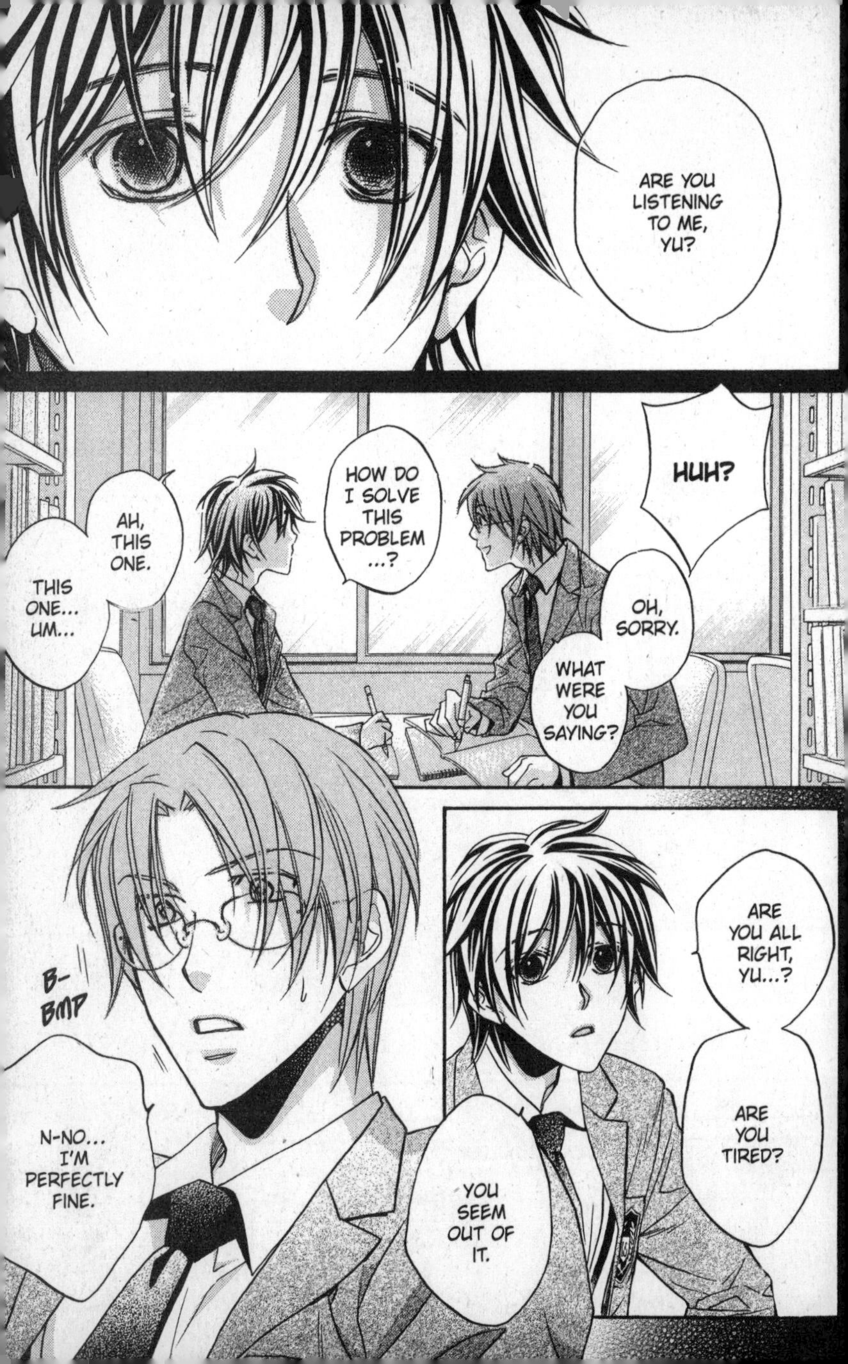
ARE YOU LISTENING TO ME, YU?
HUH?
OH, SORRY.
WHAT WERE YOU SAYING?
HOW DO I SOLVE THIS PROBLEM ...?
AH, THIS ONE.
THIS ONE... UM...
ARE YOU ALL RIGHT, YU...?
ARE YOU TIRED?
YOU SEEM OUT OF IT.
B-BMP
N-NO... I'M PERFECTLY FINE.

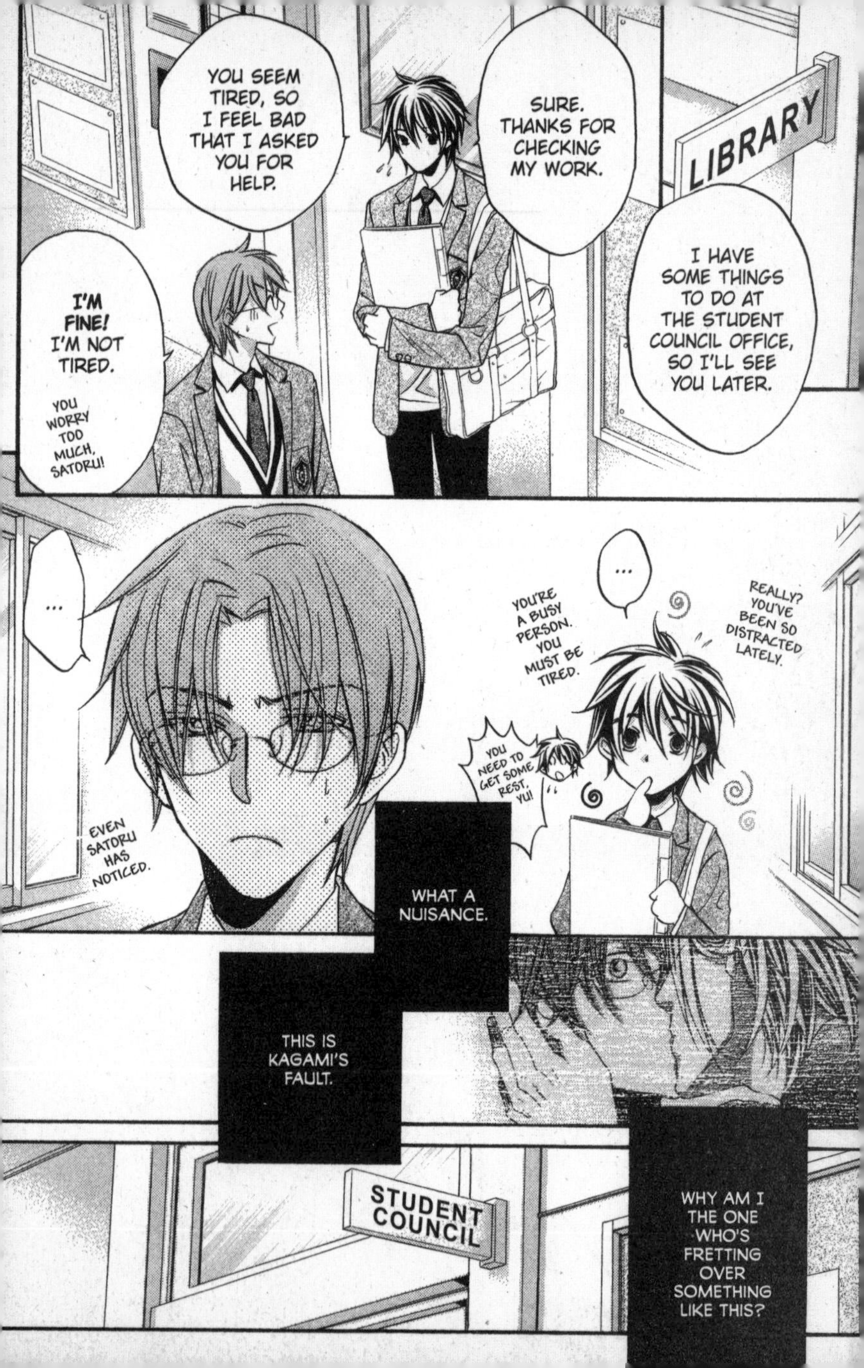
LIBRARY
SURE. THANKS FOR CHECKING MY WORK.
I HAVE SOME THINGS TO DO AT THE STUDENT COUNCIL OFFICE, SO I'LL SEE YOU LATER.
YOU SEEM TIRED, SO I FEEL BAD THAT I ASKED YOU FOR HELP.
I'M FINE! I'M NOT TIRED.
YOU WORRY TOO MUCH, SATORU!
REALLY? YOU'VE BEEN SO DISTRACTED LATELY.
...
YOU'RE A BUSY PERSON. YOU MUST BE TIRED.
YOU NEED TO GET SOME REST, YU!
...
EVEN SATORU HAS NOTICED.
WHAT A NUISANCE.
THIS IS KAGAMI'S FAULT.
STUDENT COUNCIL
WHY AM I THE ONE WHO'S FRETTING OVER SOMETHING LIKE THIS?

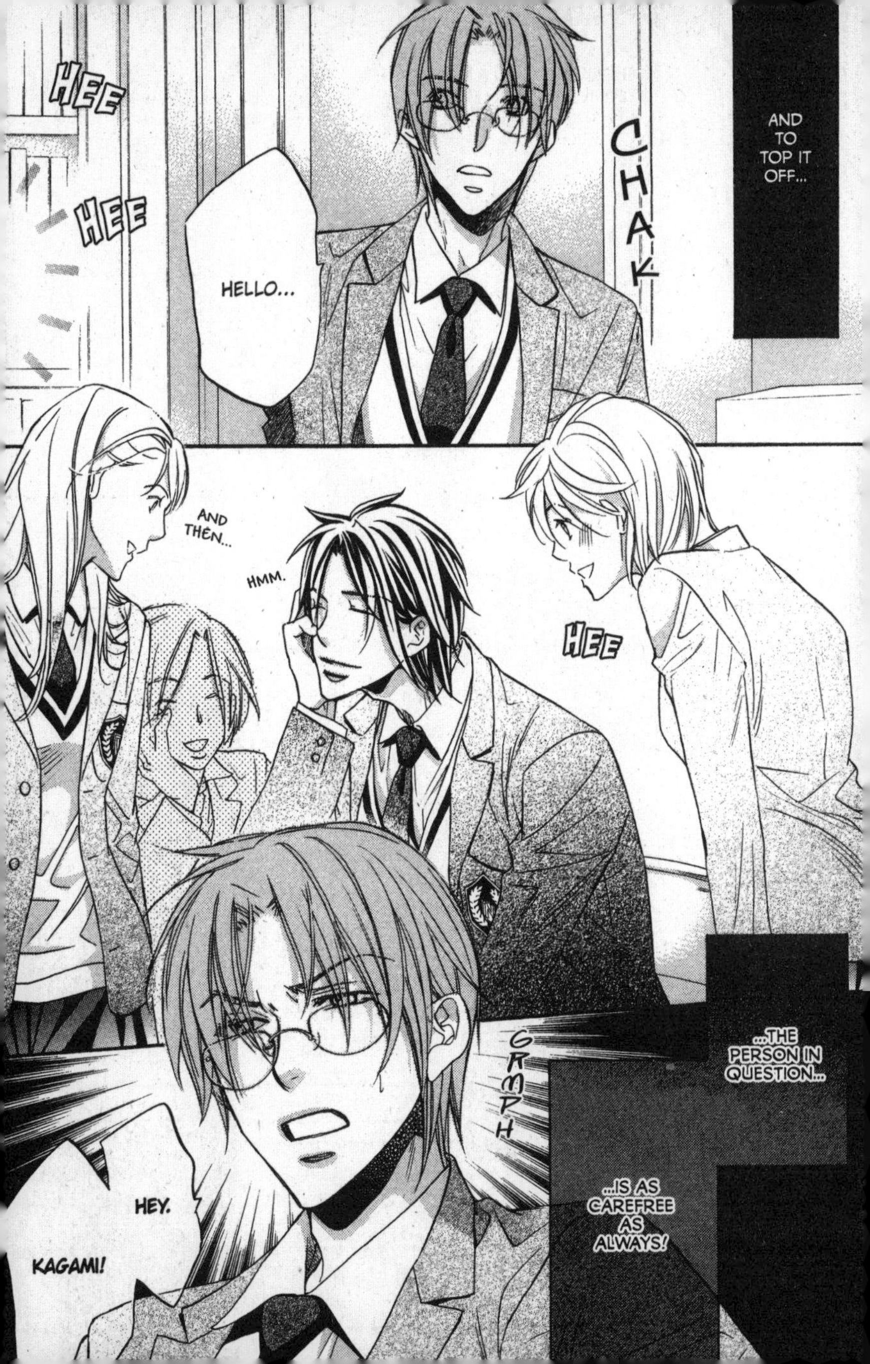
AND TO TOP IT OFF...
CHAK
HELLO...
HEE
HEE
HEE
HMM.
AND THEN...
...THE PERSON IN QUESTION...
GRMPH
...IS AS CAREFREE AS ALWAYS!
HEY.
KAGAMI!

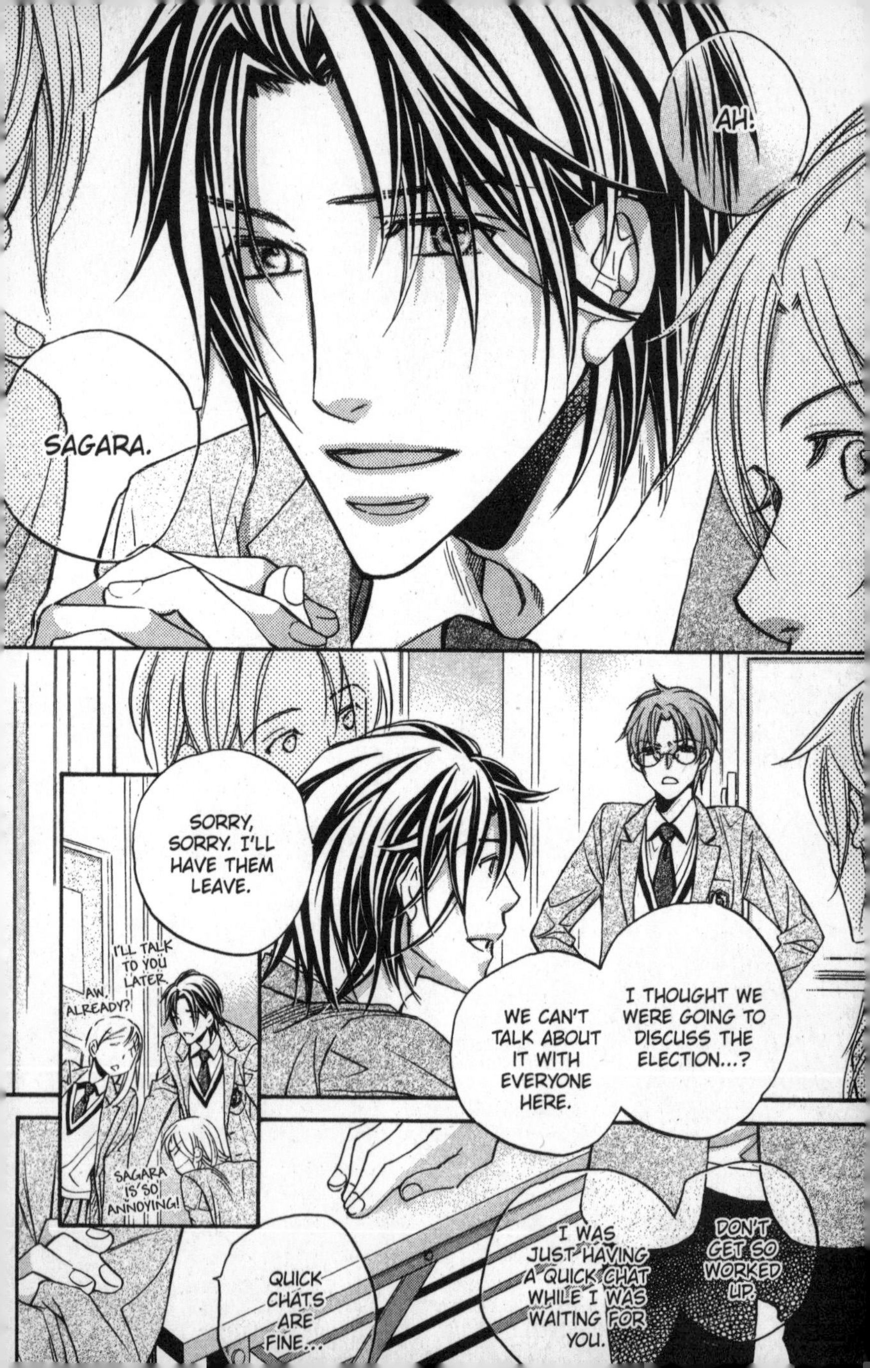
AH.
SAGARA.
I THOUGHT WE WERE GOING TO DISCUSS THE ELECTION...?
WE CAN'T TALK ABOUT IT WITH EVERYONE HERE.
SORRY, SORRY. I'LL HAVE THEM LEAVE.
I'LL TALK TO YOU LATER.
AW, ALREADY?
SAGARA IS SO ANNOYING!
DON'T GET SO WORKED UP.
I WAS JUST HAVING A QUICK CHAT WHILE I WAS WAITING FOR YOU.
QUICK CHATS ARE FINE...

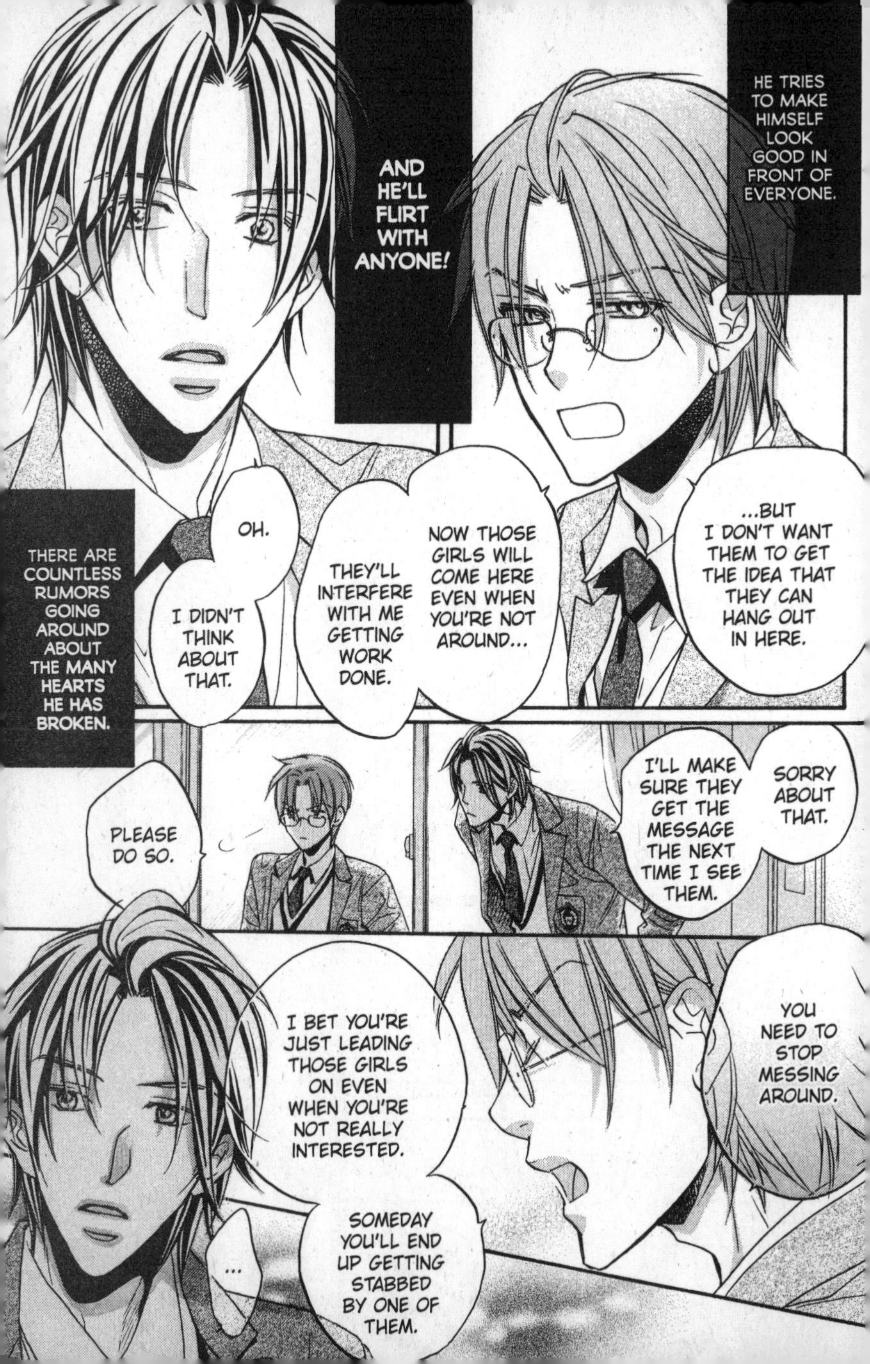
HE TRIES TO MAKE HIMSELF LOOK GOOD IN FRONT OF EVERYONE.
AND HE'LL FLIRT WITH ANYONE!
...BUT I DON'T WANT THEM TO GET THE IDEA THAT THEY CAN HANG OUT IN HERE.
NOW THOSE GIRLS WILL COME HERE EVEN WHEN YOU'RE NOT AROUND...
THEY'LL INTERFERE WITH ME GETTING WORK DONE.
OH.
I DIDN'T THINK ABOUT THAT.
THERE ARE COUNTLESS RUMORS GOING AROUND ABOUT THE MANY HEARTS HE HAS BROKEN.
SORRY ABOUT THAT.
I'LL MAKE SURE THEY GET THE MESSAGE THE NEXT TIME I SEE THEM.
PLEASE DO SO.
YOU NEED TO STOP MESSING AROUND.
I BET YOU'RE JUST LEADING THOSE GIRLS ON EVEN WHEN YOU'RE NOT REALLY INTERESTED.
SOMEDAY YOU'LL END UP GETTING STABBED BY ONE OF THEM.
...

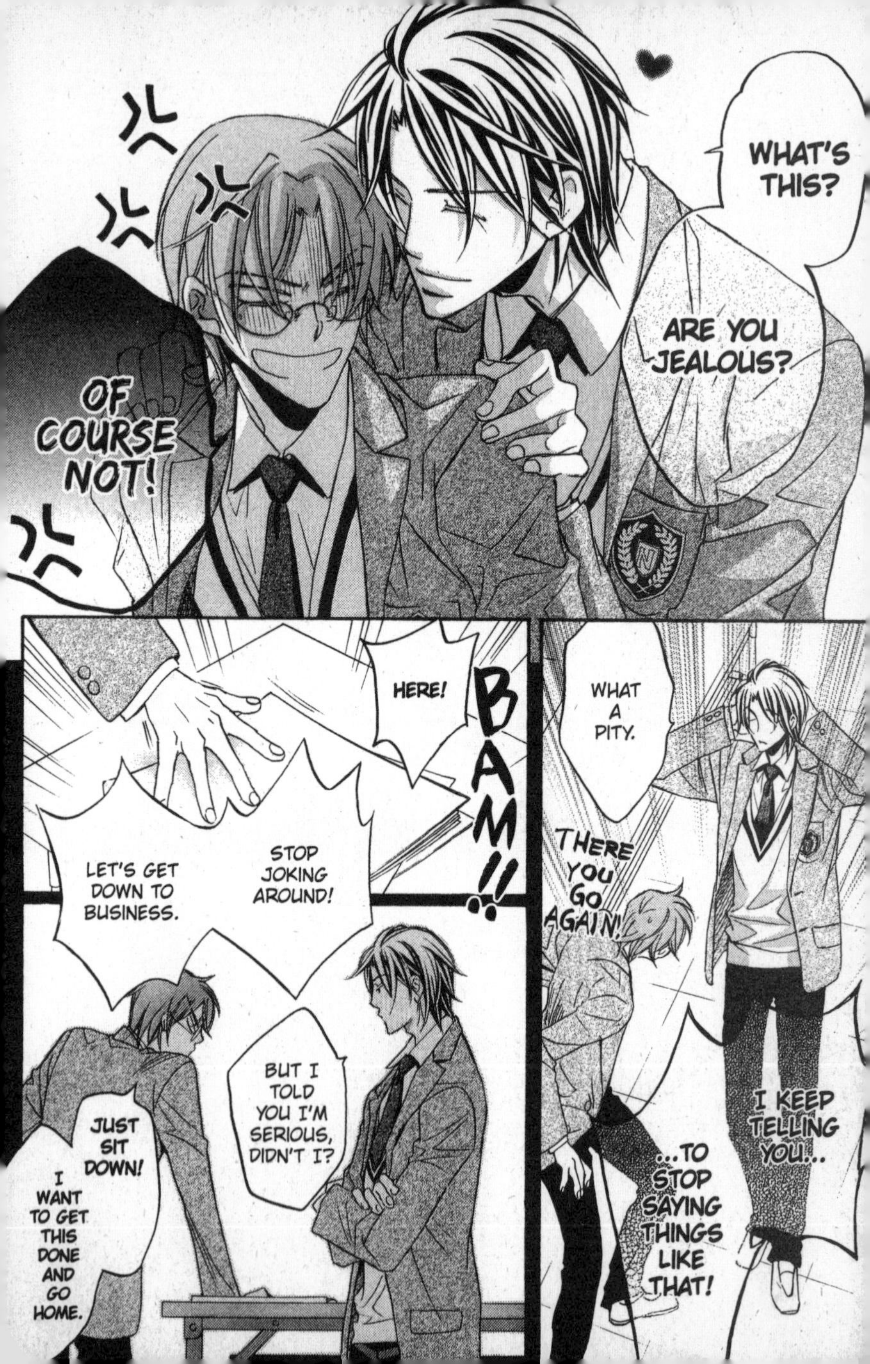
WHAT'S THIS?
ARE YOU JEALOUS?
OF COURSE NOT!
WHAT A PITY.
THERE YOU GO AGAIN!
I KEEP TELLING YOU...
...TO STOP SAYING THINGS LIKE THAT!
HERE!
BAM!!
STOP JOKING AROUND!
LET'S GET DOWN TO BUSINESS.
BUT I TOLD YOU I'M SERIOUS, DIDN'T I?
JUST SIT DOWN!
I WANT TO GET THIS DONE AND GO HOME.

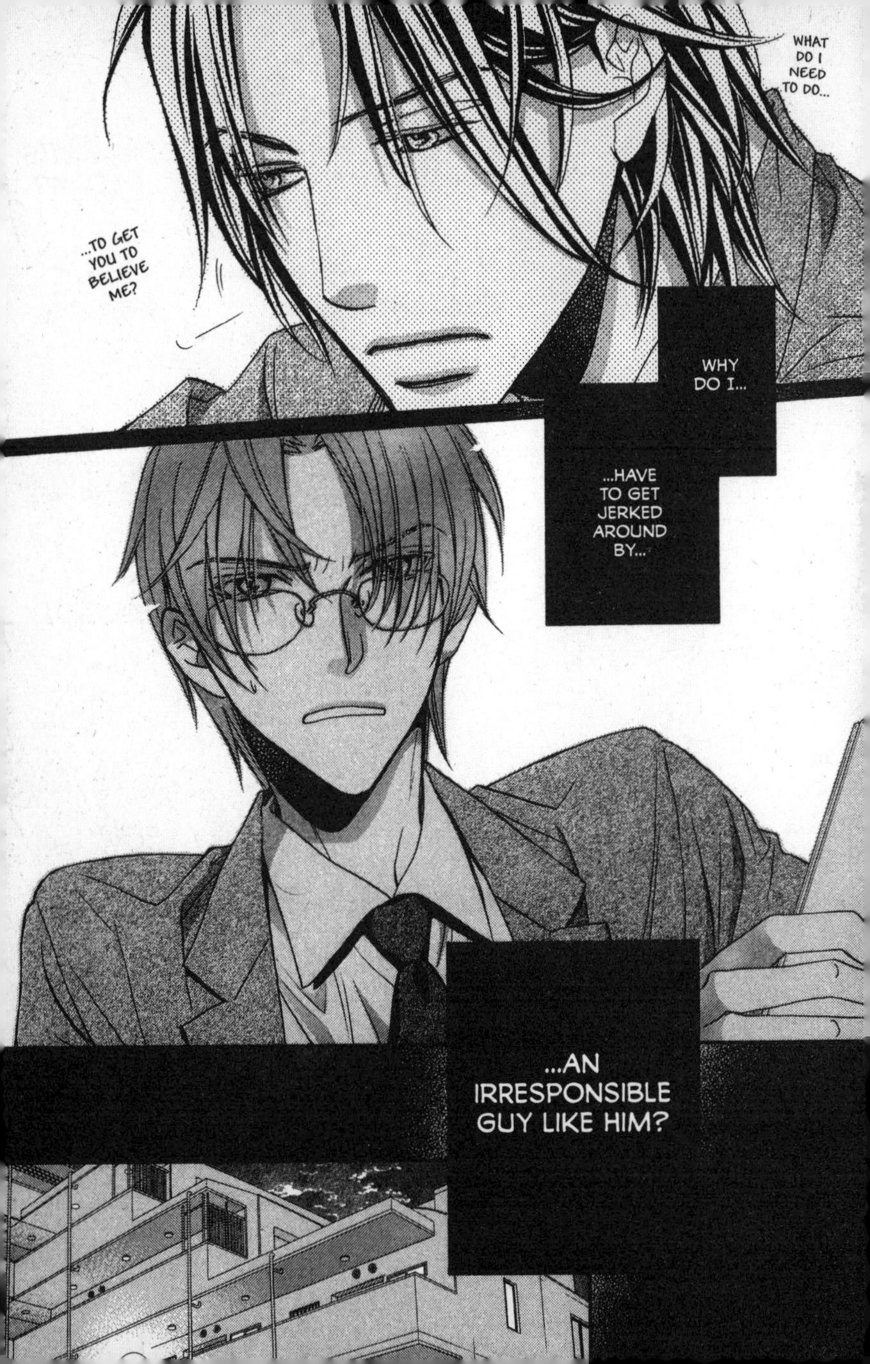
WHAT DO I NEED TO DO...
...TO GET YOU TO BELIEVE ME?
WHY DO I...
...HAVE TO GET JERKED AROUND BY...
...AN IRRESPONSIBLE GUY LIKE HIM?

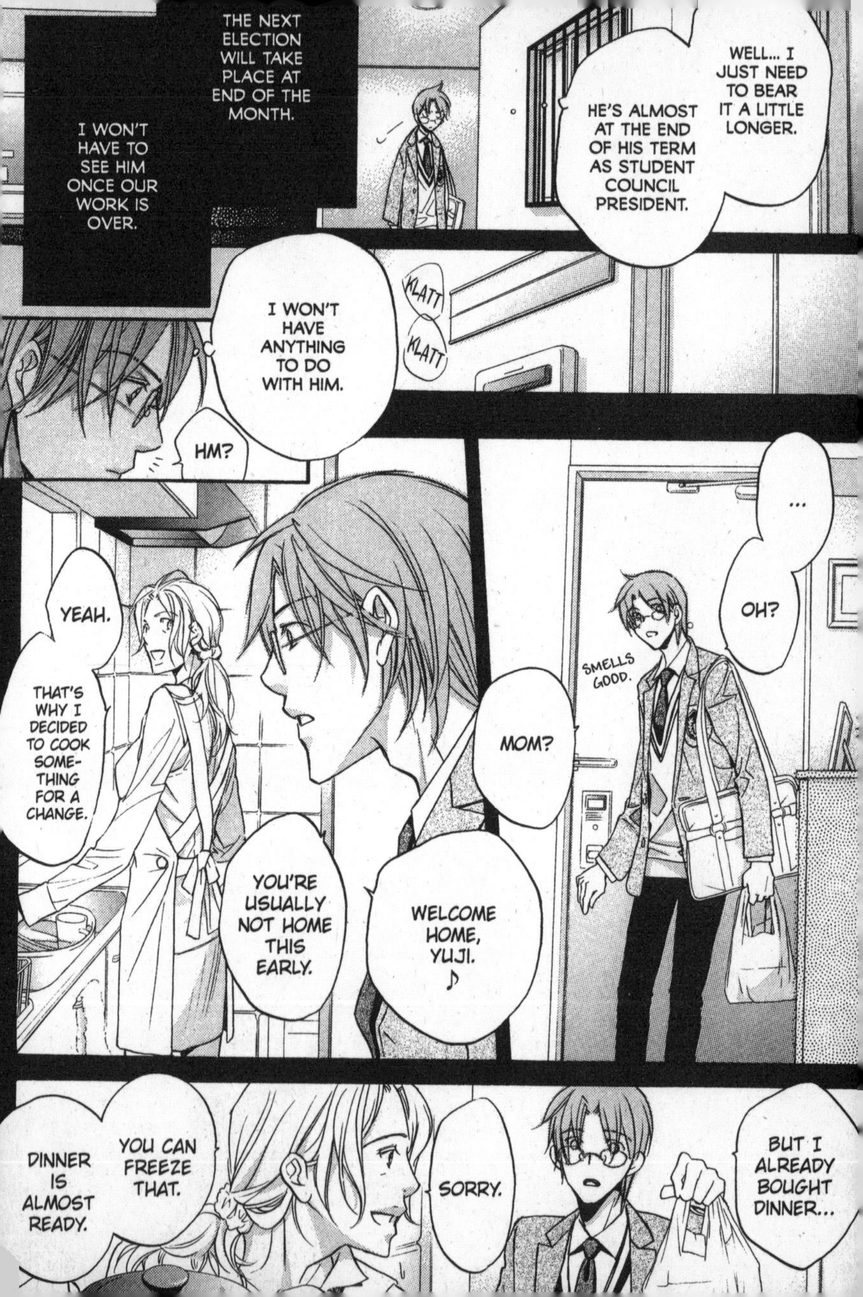
WELL... I JUST NEED TO BEAR IT A LITTLE LONGER.
HE'S ALMOST AT THE END OF HIS TERM AS STUDENT COUNCIL PRESIDENT.
THE NEXT ELECTION WILL TAKE PLACE AT END OF THE MONTH.
I WON'T HAVE TO SEE HIM ONCE OUR WORK IS OVER.
KLATT
KLATT
I WON'T HAVE ANYTHING TO DO WITH HIM.
HM?
...
OH?
SMELLS GOOD.
MOM?
WELCOME HOME, YUJI. ♪
YOU'RE USUALLY NOT HOME THIS EARLY.
YEAH.
THAT'S WHY I DECIDED TO COOK SOME-THING FOR A CHANGE.
BUT I ALREADY BOUGHT DINNER...
SORRY.
YOU CAN FREEZE THAT.
DINNER IS ALMOST READY.

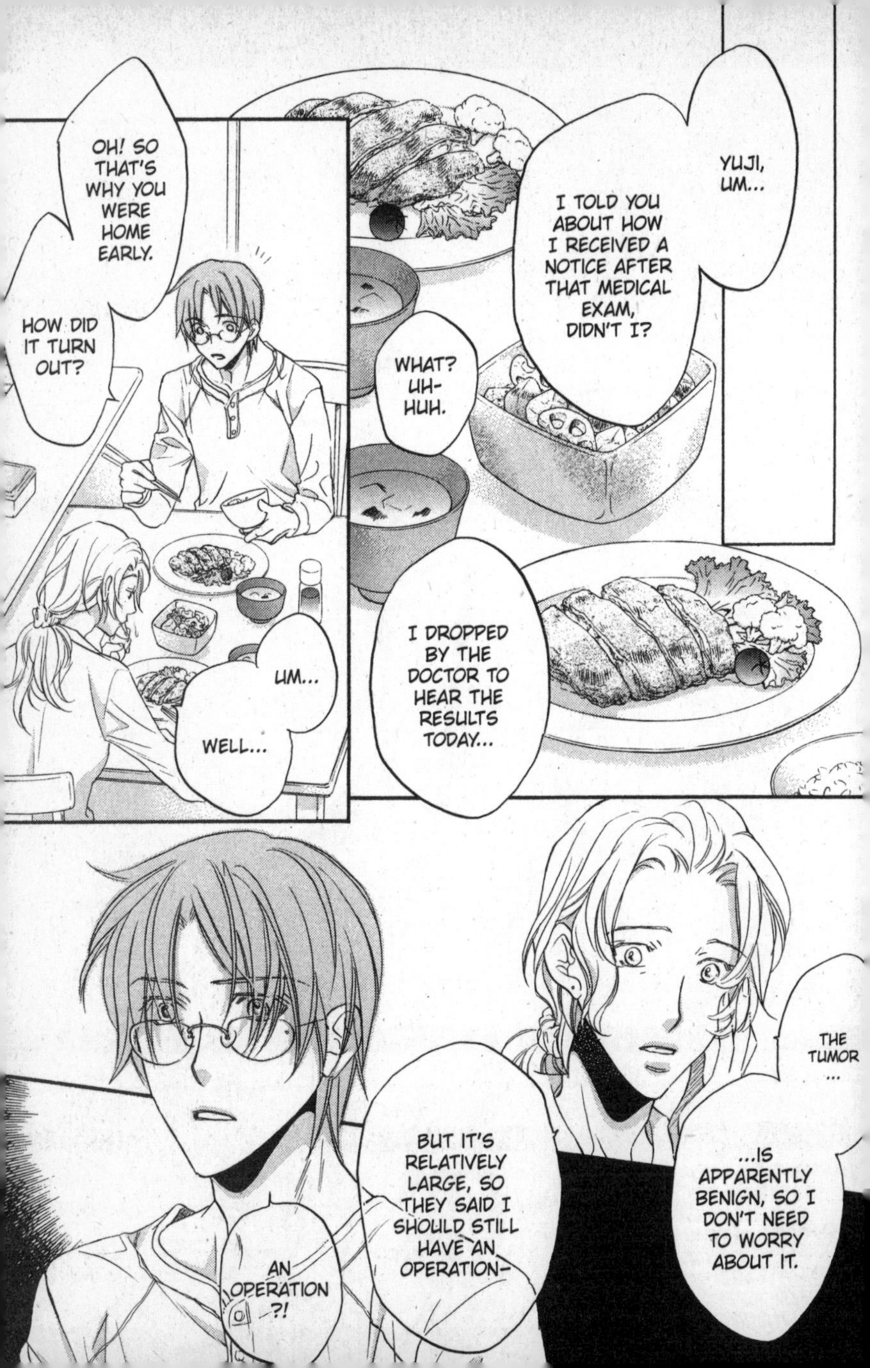
YUJI, UM...
I TOLD YOU ABOUT HOW I RECEIVED A NOTICE AFTER THAT MEDICAL EXAM, DIDN'T I?
WHAT? UH-HUH.
I DROPPED BY THE DOCTOR TO HEAR THE RESULTS TODAY...
OH! SO THAT'S WHY YOU WERE HOME EARLY.
HOW DID IT TURN OUT?
UM...
WELL...
THE TUMOR ...
...IS APPARENTLY BENIGN, SO I DON'T NEED TO WORRY ABOUT IT.
BUT IT'S RELATIVELY LARGE, SO THEY SAID I SHOULD STILL HAVE AN OPERATION-
AN OPERATION ?!

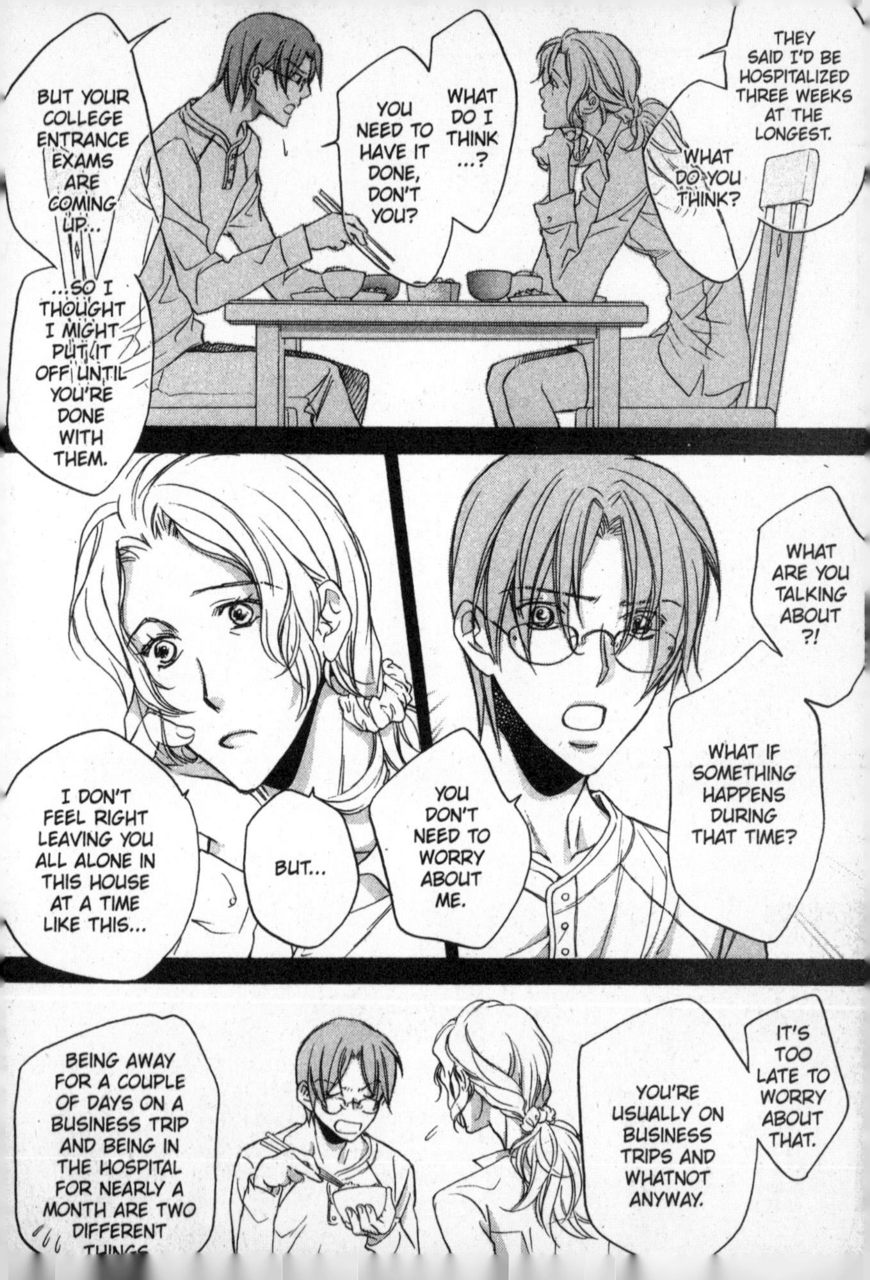
THEY SAID I'D BE HOSPITALIZED THREE WEEKS AT THE LONGEST.
WHAT DO YOU THINK?
WHAT DO I THINK ...?
YOU NEED TO HAVE IT DONE, DON'T YOU?
BUT YOUR COLLEGE ENTRANCE EXAMS ARE COMING UP...
...SO I THOUGHT I MIGHT PUT IT OFF UNTIL YOU'RE DONE WITH THEM.
WHAT ARE YOU TALKING ABOUT ?!
WHAT IF SOMETHING HAPPENS DURING THAT TIME?
YOU DON'T NEED TO WORRY ABOUT ME.
BUT...
I DON'T FEEL RIGHT LEAVING YOU ALL ALONE IN THIS HOUSE AT A TIME LIKE THIS...
IT'S TOO LATE TO WORRY ABOUT THAT.
YOU'RE USUALLY ON BUSINESS TRIPS AND WHATNOT ANYWAY.
BEING AWAY FOR A COUPLE OF DAYS ON A BUSINESS TRIP AND BEING IN THE HOSPITAL FOR NEARLY A MONTH ARE TWO DIFFERENT

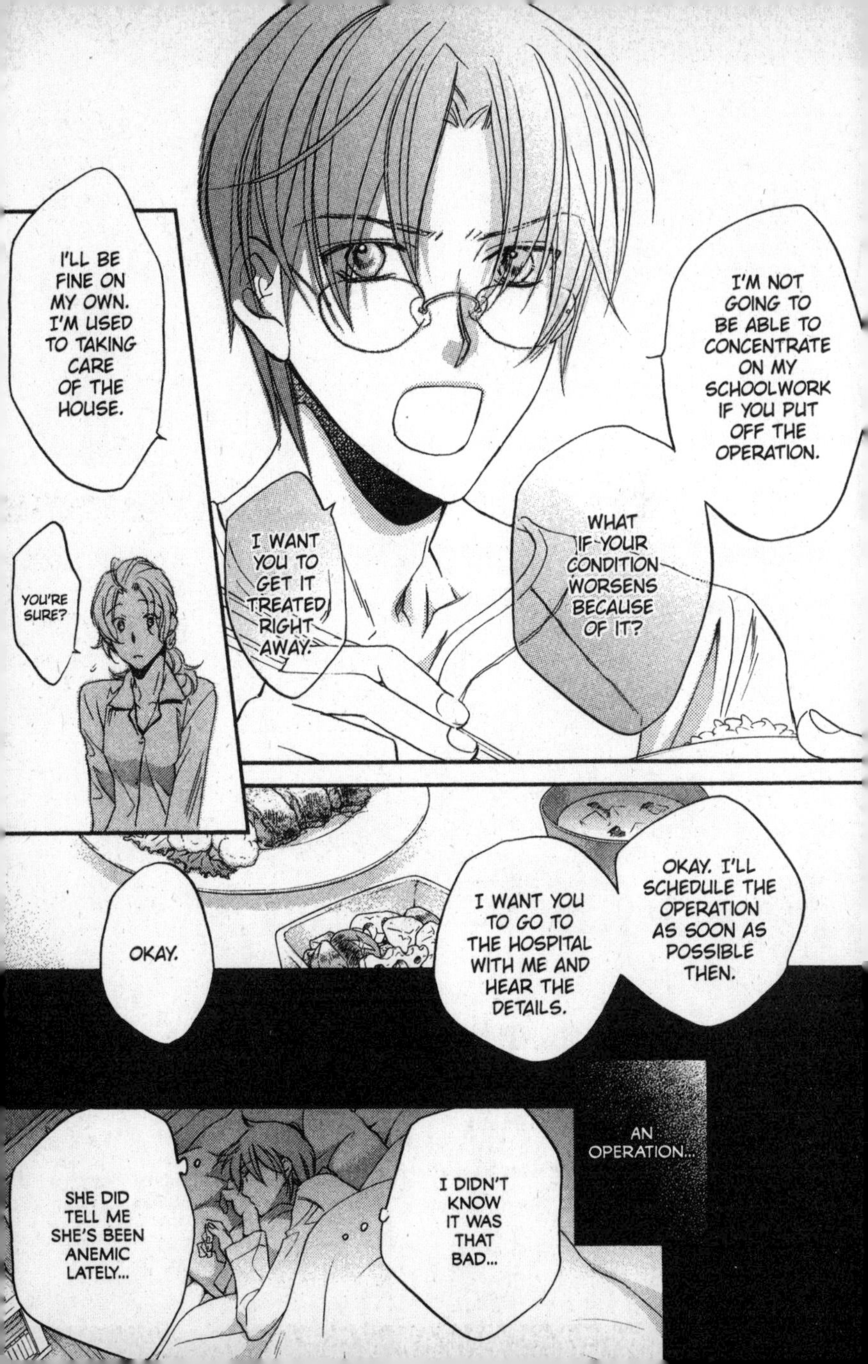
I'M NOT GOING TO BE ABLE TO CONCENTRATE ON MY SCHOOLWORK IF YOU PUT OFF THE OPERATION.
WHAT IF YOUR CONDITION WORSENS BECAUSE OF IT?
I WANT YOU TO GET IT TREATED RIGHT AWAY.
I'LL BE FINE ON MY OWN. I'M USED TO TAKING CARE OF THE HOUSE.
YOU'RE SURE?
OKAY. I'LL SCHEDULE THE OPERATION AS SOON AS POSSIBLE THEN.
I WANT YOU TO GO TO THE HOSPITAL WITH ME AND HEAR THE DETAILS.
OKAY.
AN OPERATION...
I DIDN'T KNOW IT WAS THAT BAD...
SHE DID TELL ME SHE'S BEEN ANEMIC LATELY...

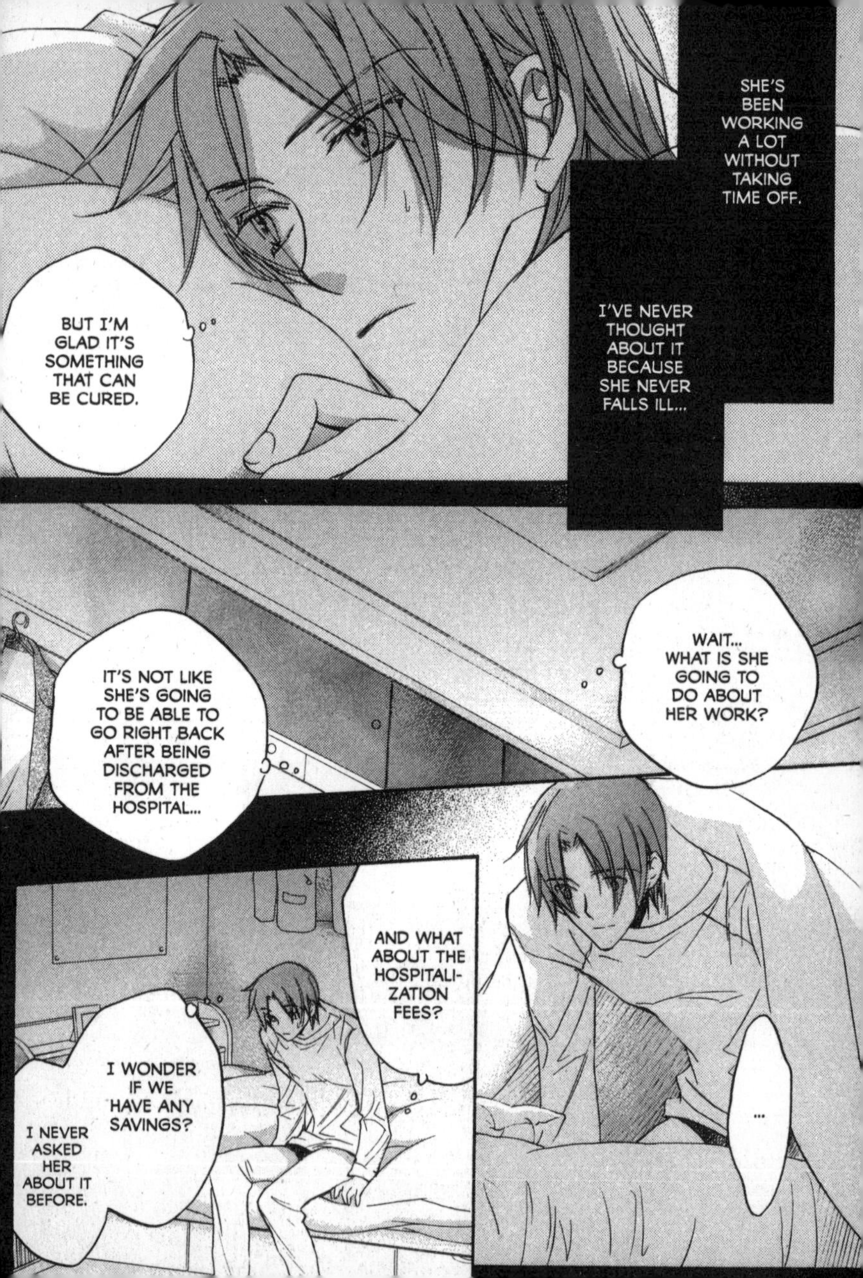
SHE'S BEEN WORKING A LOT WITHOUT TAKING TIME OFF.
I'VE NEVER THOUGHT ABOUT IT BECAUSE SHE NEVER FALLS ILL...
BUT I'M GLAD IT'S SOMETHING THAT CAN BE CURED.
WAIT... WHAT IS SHE GOING TO DO ABOUT HER WORK?
IT'S NOT LIKE SHE'S GOING TO BE ABLE TO GO RIGHT BACK AFTER BEING DISCHARGED FROM THE HOSPITAL...
...
AND WHAT ABOUT THE HOSPITALI-ZATION FEES?
I WONDER IF WE HAVE ANY SAVINGS?
I NEVER ASKED HER ABOUT IT BEFORE.

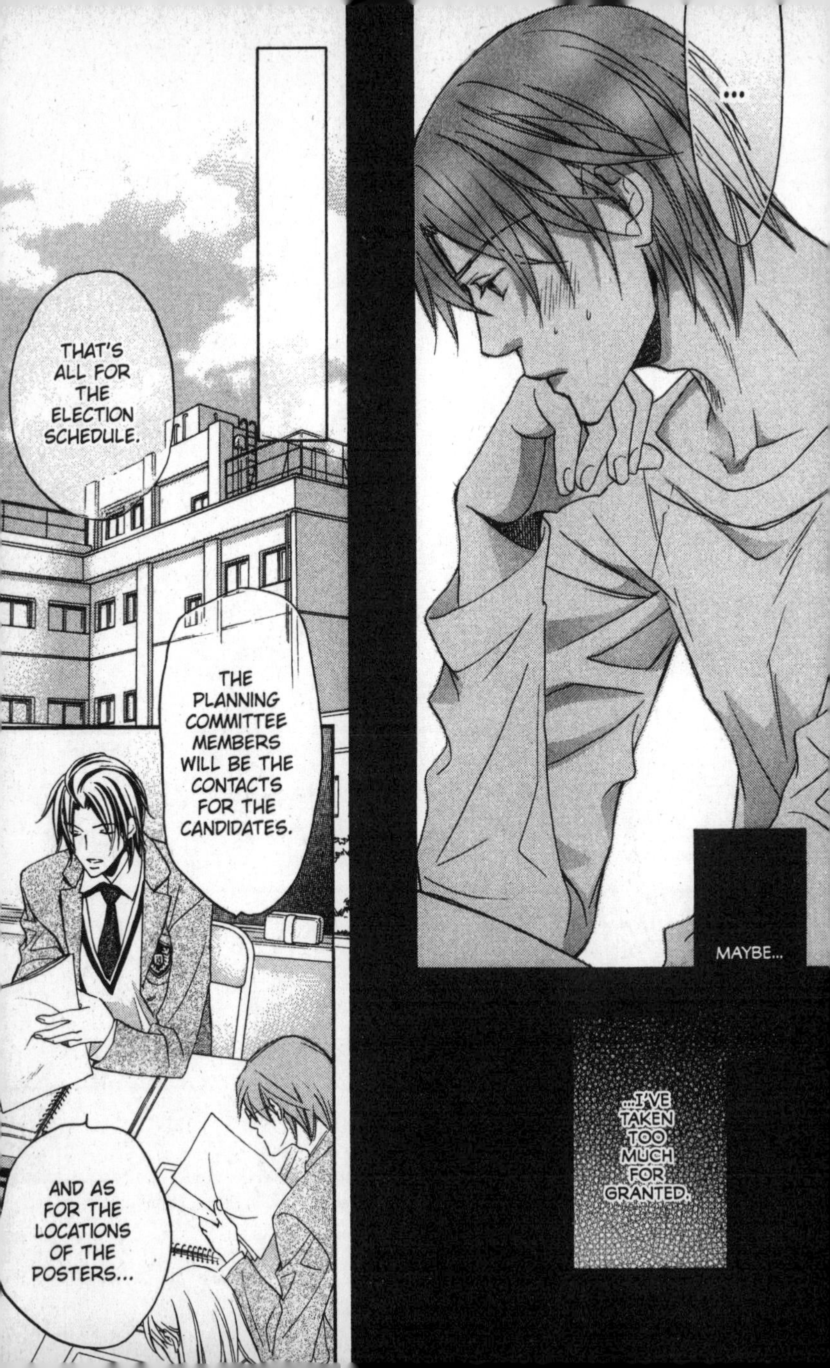
...
MAYBE...
...I'VE TAKEN TOO MUCH FOR GRANTED.
THAT'S ALL FOR THE ELECTION SCHEDULE.
THE PLANNING COMMITTEE MEMBERS WILL BE THE CONTACTS FOR THE CANDIDATES.
AND AS FOR THE LOCATIONS OF THE POSTERS...

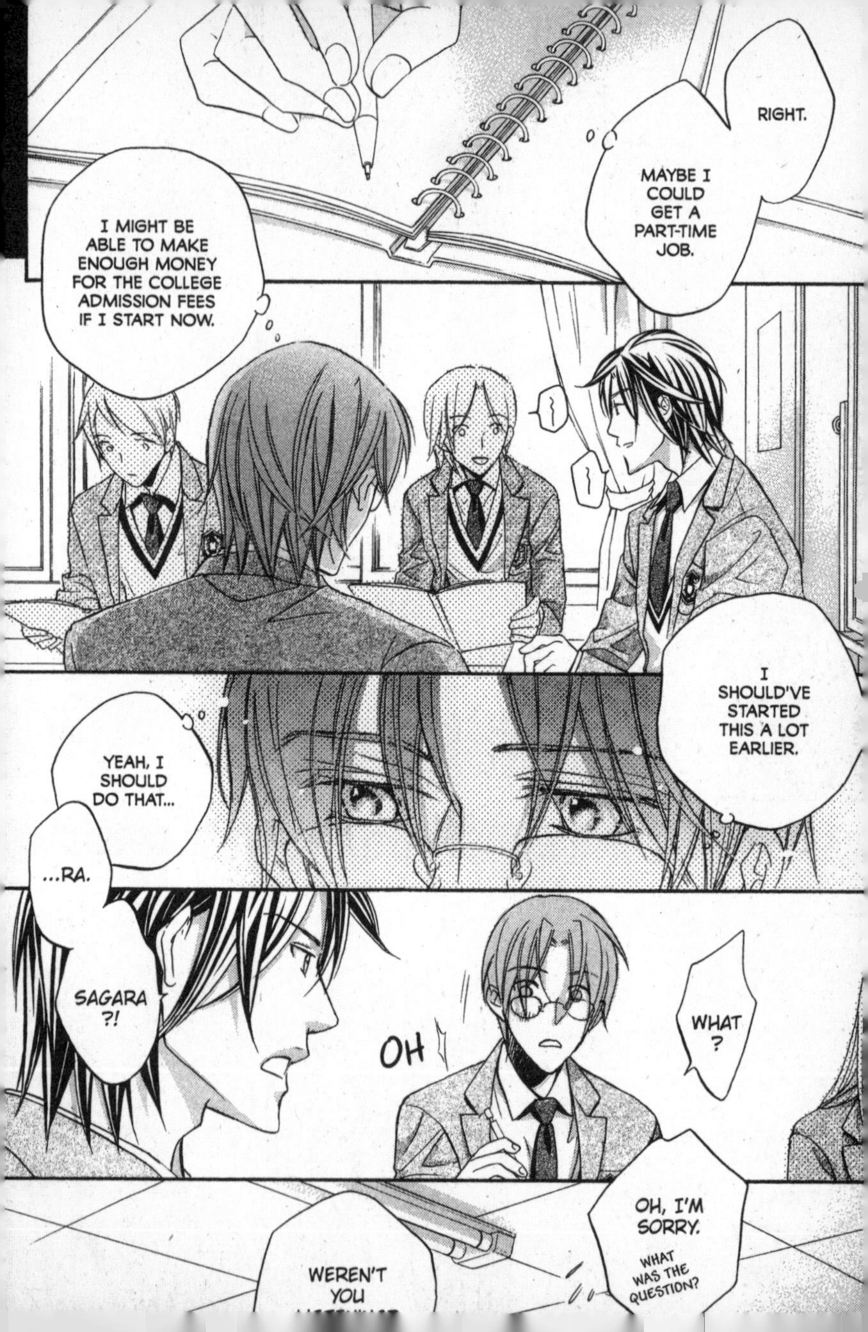
RIGHT.
MAYBE I COULD GET A PART-TIME JOB.
I MIGHT BE ABLE TO MAKE ENOUGH MONEY FOR THE COLLEGE ADMISSION FEES IF I START NOW.
I SHOULD'VE STARTED THIS A LOT EARLIER.
YEAH, I SHOULD DO THAT...
WHAT?
OH
...RA.
SAGARA?!
OH, I'M SORRY.
WHAT WAS THE QUESTION?
WEREN'T YOU

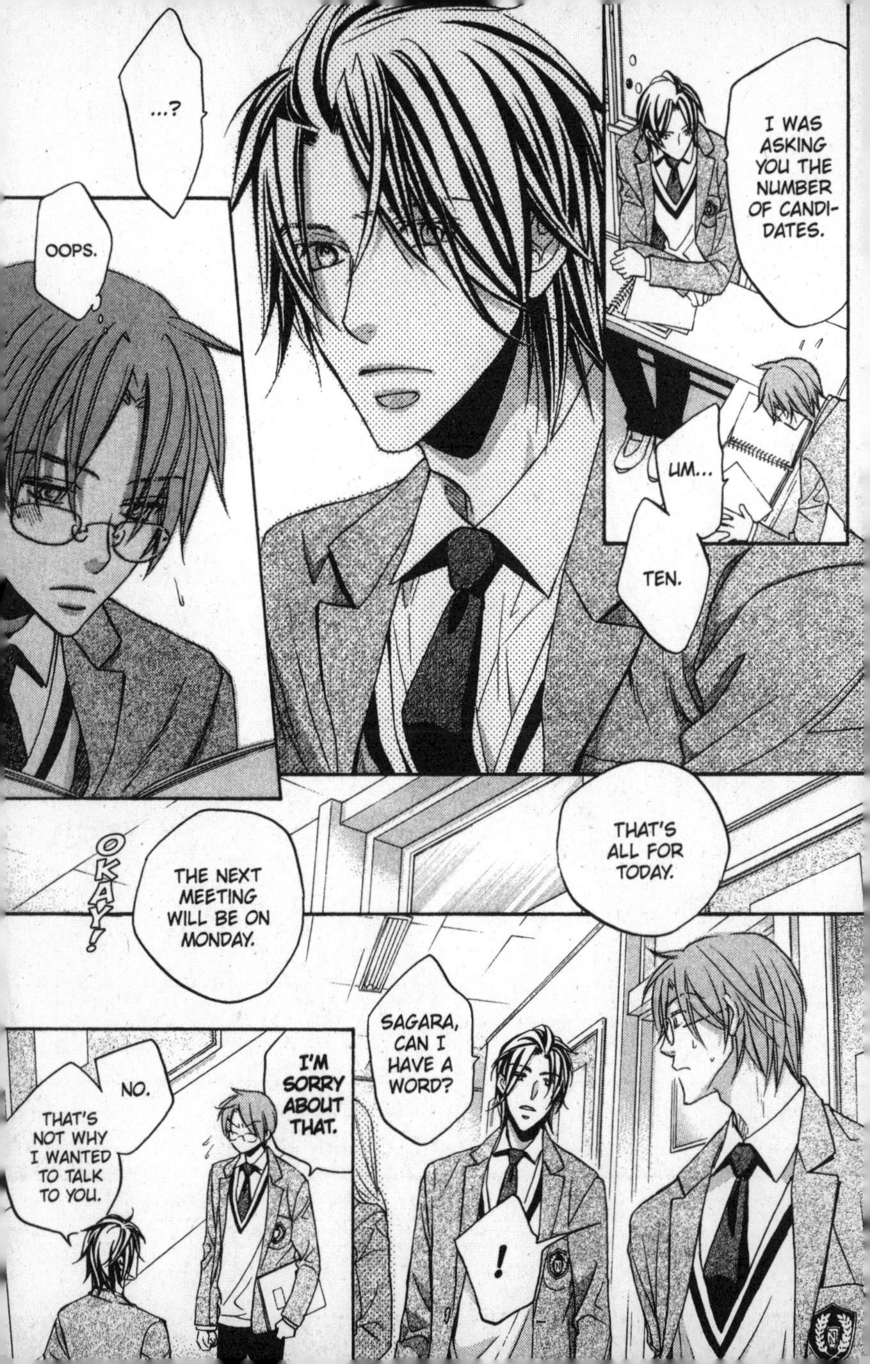
I WAS ASKING YOU THE NUMBER OF CANDIDATES.
UM...
TEN.
...?
OOPS.
THAT'S ALL FOR TODAY.
THE NEXT MEETING WILL BE ON MONDAY.
OKAY!
SAGARA, CAN I HAVE A WORD?
!
I'M SORRY ABOUT THAT.
NO.
THAT'S NOT WHY I WANTED TO TALK TO YOU.

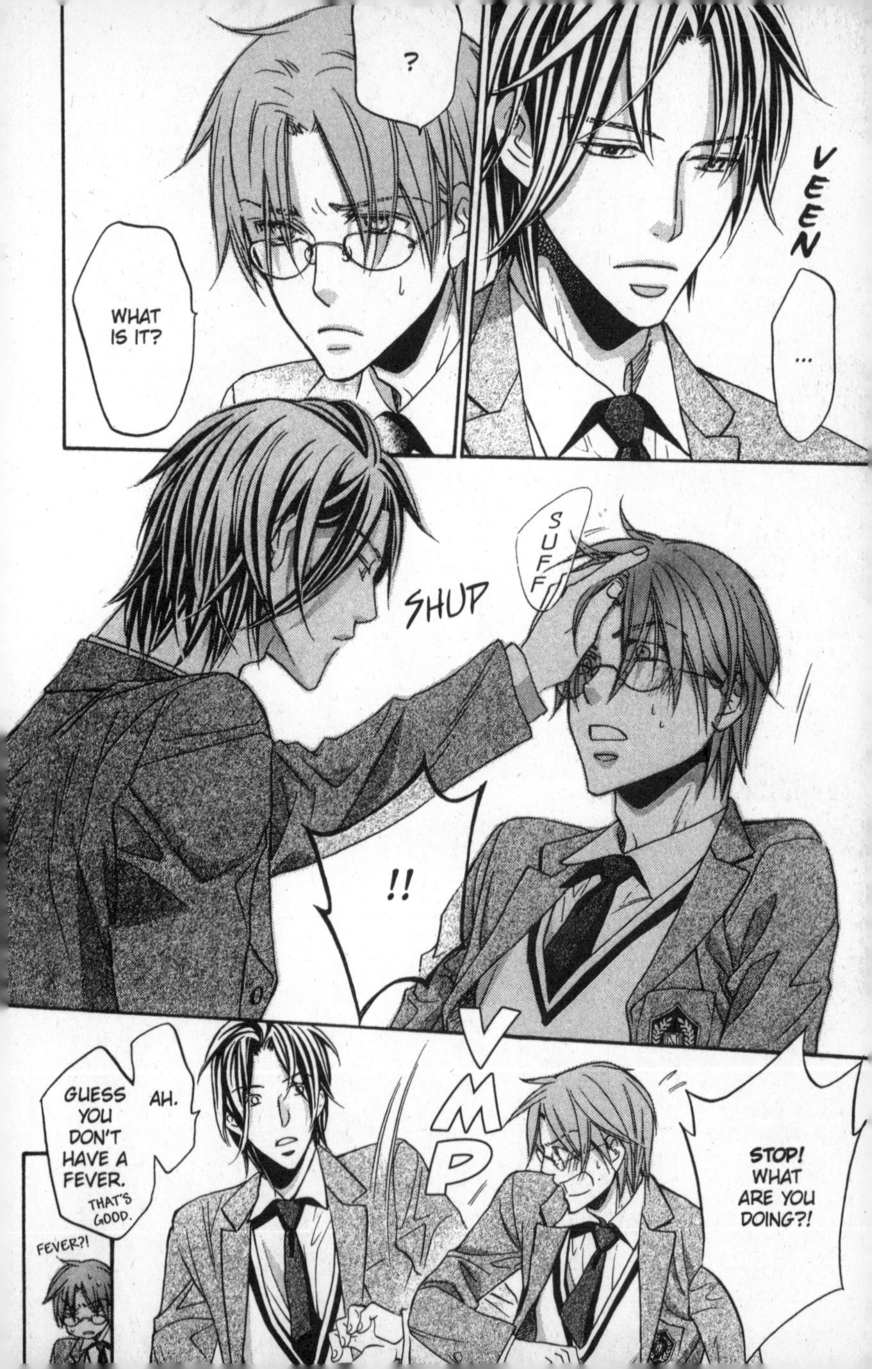
VEEN
...
?
WHAT IS IT?
SUFF
SHUP
!!
STOP! WHAT ARE YOU DOING?!
VMP
AH.
GUESS YOU DON'T HAVE A FEVER.
THAT'S GOOD.
FEVER?!

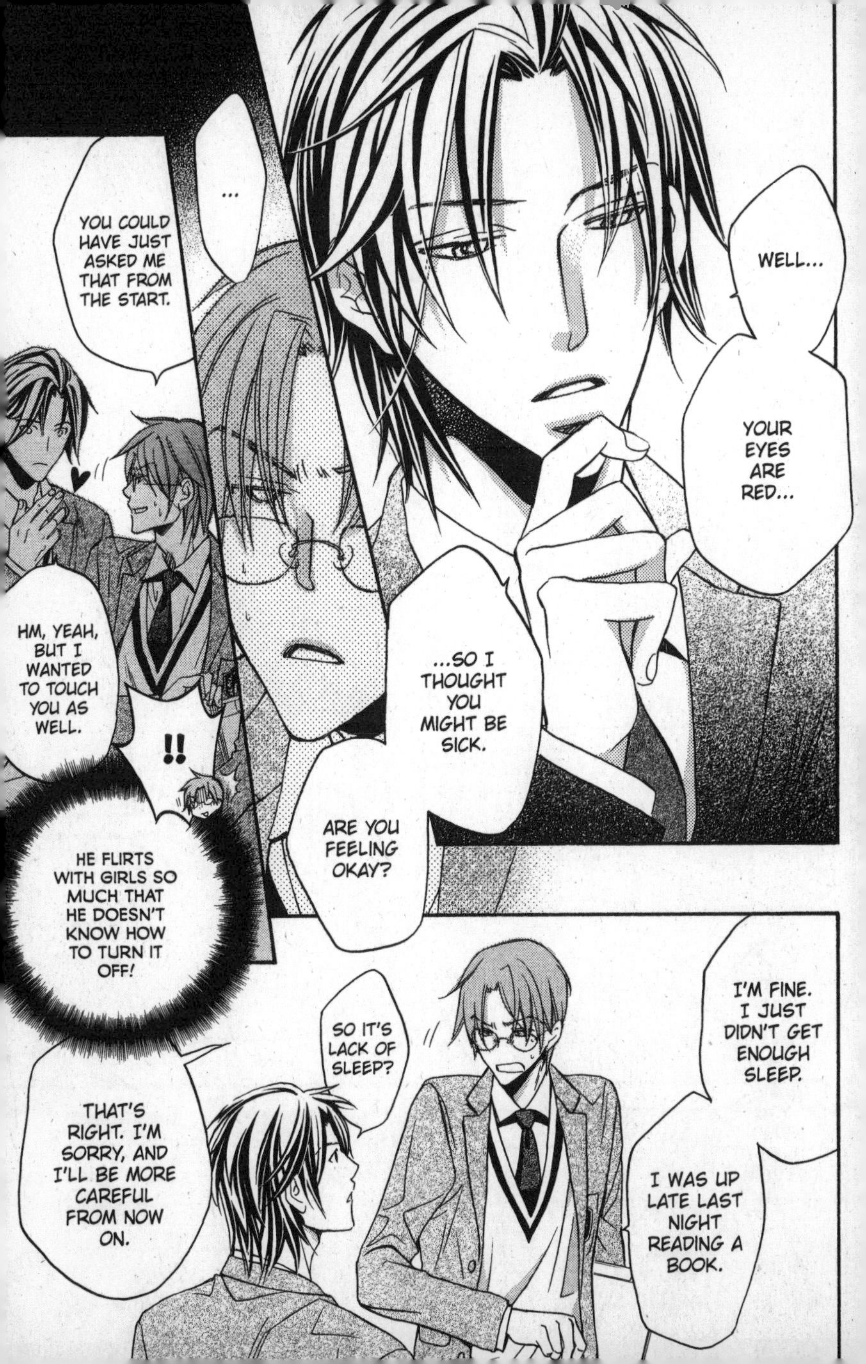
WELL...
YOUR EYES ARE RED...
...SO I THOUGHT YOU MIGHT BE SICK.
ARE YOU FEELING OKAY?
...
YOU COULD HAVE JUST ASKED ME THAT FROM THE START.
HM, YEAH, BUT I WANTED TO TOUCH YOU AS WELL.
!!
HE FLIRTS WITH GIRLS SO MUCH THAT HE DOESN'T KNOW HOW TO TURN IT OFF!
I'M FINE. I JUST DIDN'T GET ENOUGH SLEEP.
I WAS UP LATE LAST NIGHT READING A BOOK.
SO IT'S LACK OF SLEEP?
THAT'S RIGHT. I'M SORRY, AND I'LL BE MORE CAREFUL FROM NOW ON.

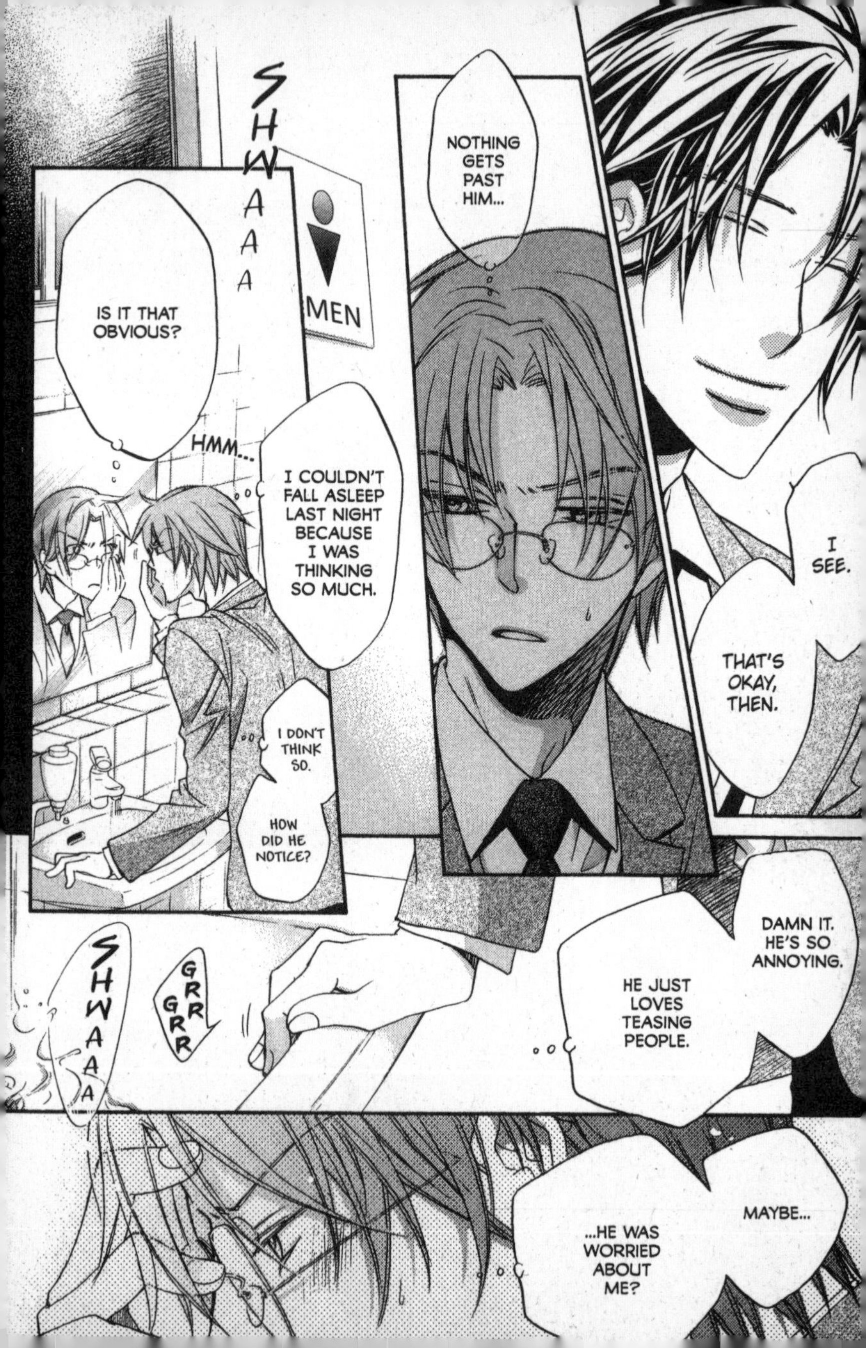
I SEE.
THAT'S OKAY, THEN.
NOTHING GETS PAST HIM...
SHWAAAA
MEN
IS IT THAT OBVIOUS?
HMM...
I COULDN'T FALL ASLEEP LAST NIGHT BECAUSE I WAS THINKING SO MUCH.
I DON'T THINK SO.
HOW DID HE NOTICE?
DAMN IT. HE'S SO ANNOYING.
HE JUST LOVES TEASING PEOPLE.
GRR GRR
SHWAAAA
MAYBE...
...HE WAS WORRIED ABOUT ME?

NO. WHENEVER HE HAS THE OPPORTUNITY ...
...HE PLAYS AROUND WITH ME AS IF I WERE A TOY.
AAAAH, I HATE THIS.
I SHOULD JUST IGNORE IT, BUT I HATE HOW HE HAS ME TWISTED AROUND HIS LITTLE FINGER.
I HAVE TO BE CAREFUL.
IT CAN'T COME SOON ENOUGH...
I CAN'T LET MY GUARD DOWN.
I CAN'T WAIT FOR THE STUDENT COUNCIL TERM TO END.

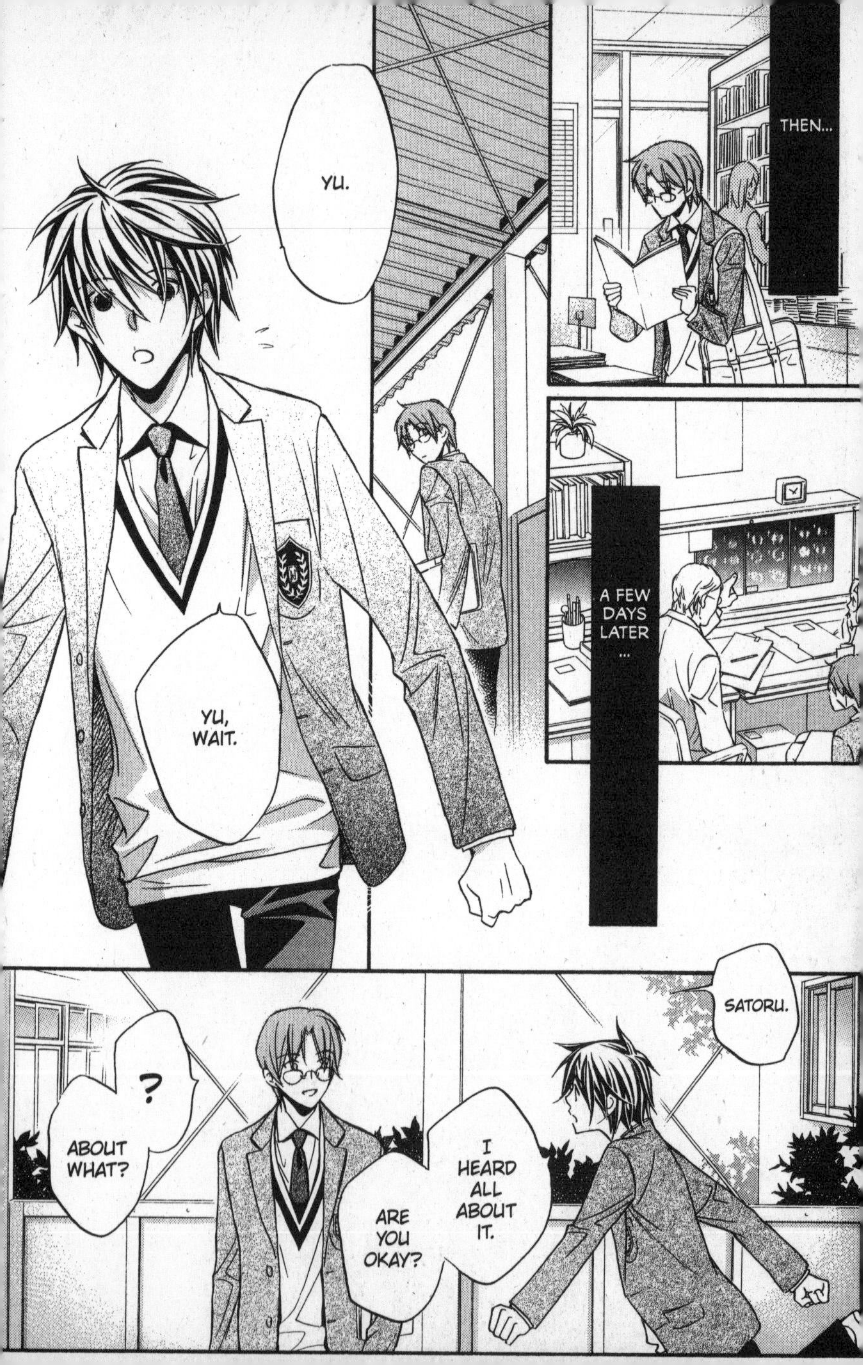
THEN...
A FEW DAYS LATER ...
YU.
YU, WAIT.
SATORU.
I HEARD ALL ABOUT IT.
ARE YOU OKAY?
?
ABOUT WHAT?

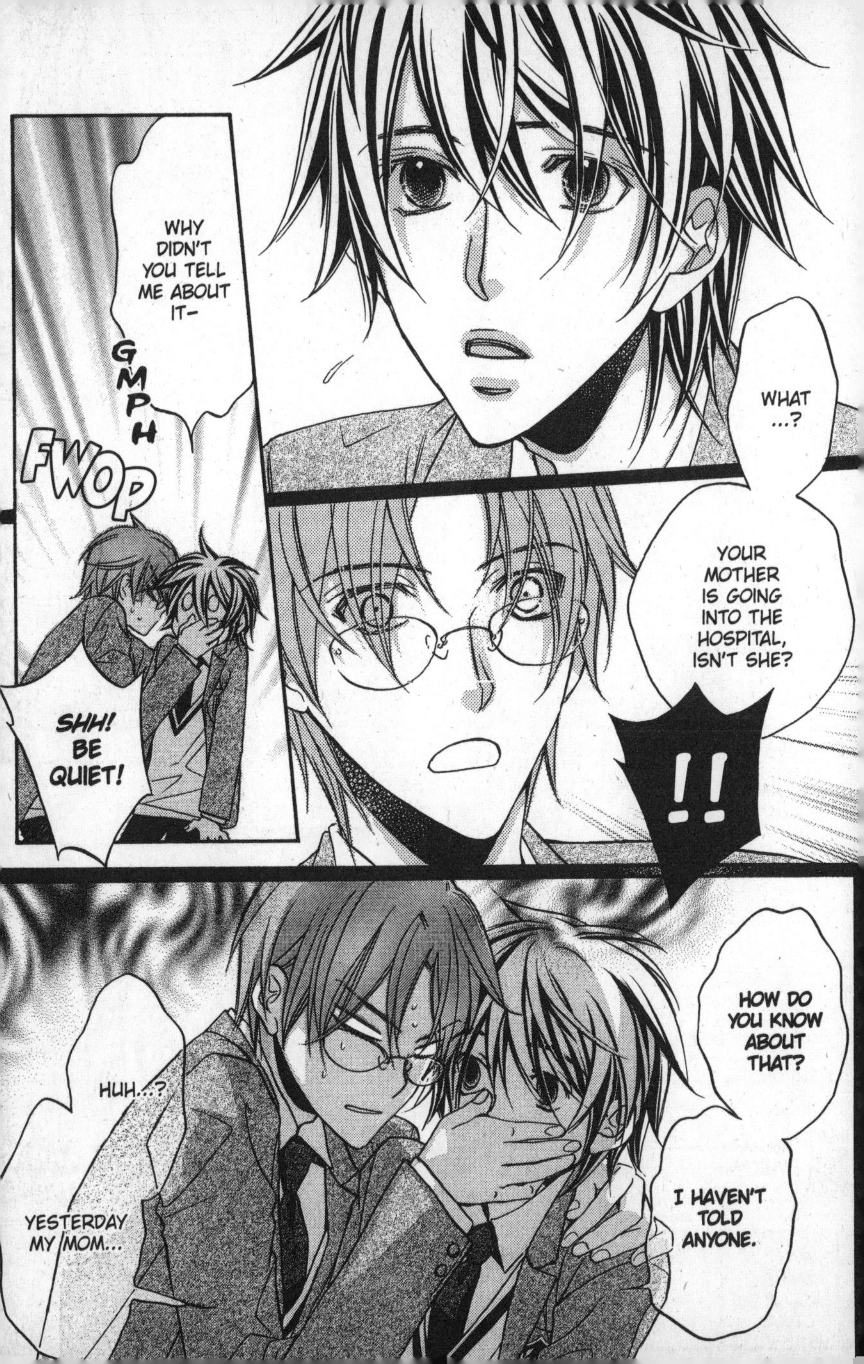
WHAT ...?
YOUR MOTHER IS GOING INTO THE HOSPITAL, ISN'T SHE?
!!
WHY DIDN'T YOU TELL ME ABOUT IT-
GMPH
FWOP
SHH! BE QUIET!
HOW DO YOU KNOW ABOUT THAT?
I HAVEN'T TOLD ANYONE.
HUH...?
YESTERDAY MY MOM...

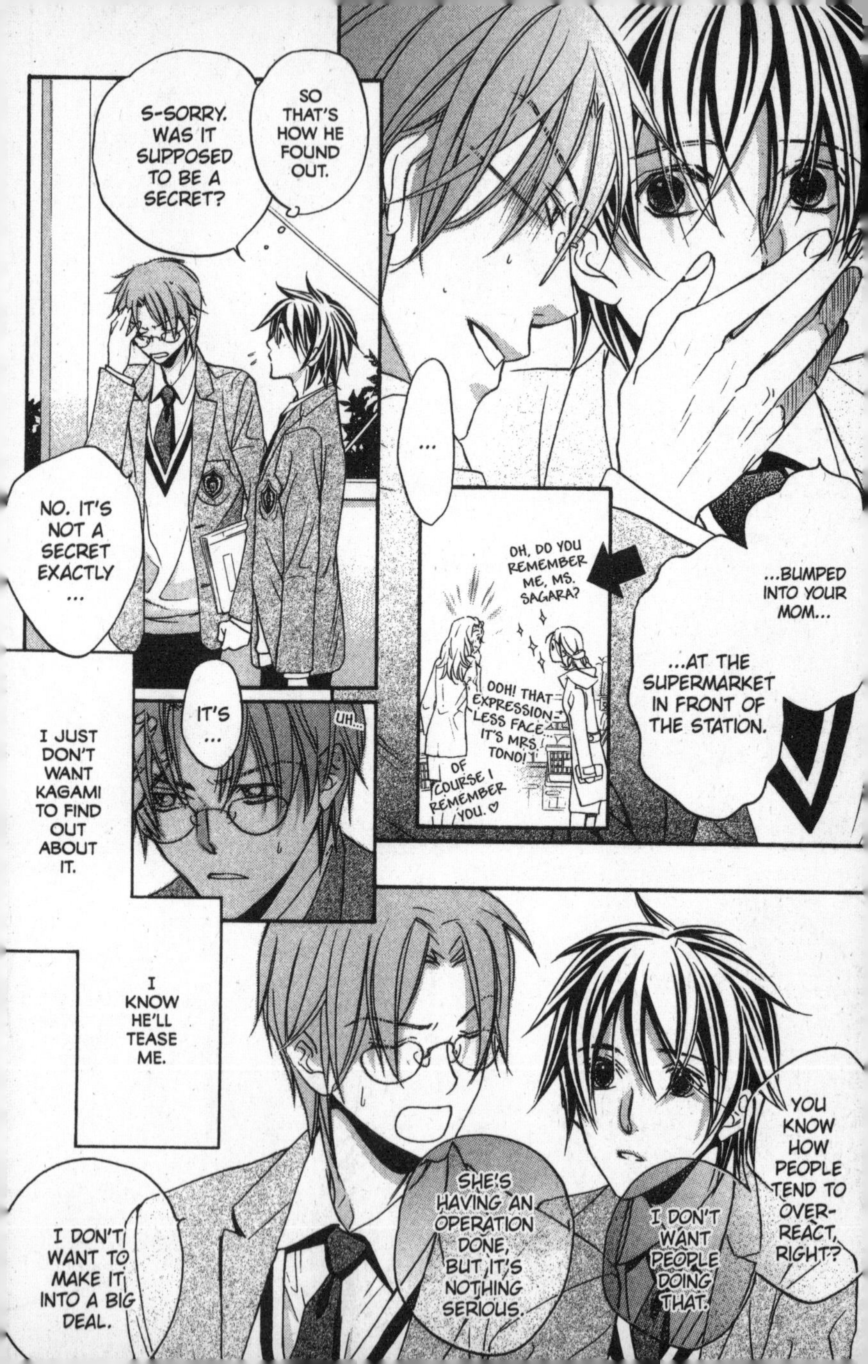
...BUMPED INTO YOUR MOM...
...AT THE SUPERMARKET IN FRONT OF THE STATION.
...
OH, DO YOU REMEMBER ME, MS. SAGARA?
OOH! THAT EXPRESSIONLESS FACE... IT'S MRS. TONO!
OF COURSE I REMEMBER YOU.♡
SO THAT'S HOW HE FOUND OUT.
S-SORRY. WAS IT SUPPOSED TO BE A SECRET?
NO. IT'S NOT A SECRET EXACTLY ...
UH...
IT'S ...
I JUST DON'T WANT KAGAMI TO FIND OUT ABOUT IT.
I KNOW HE'LL TEASE ME.
YOU KNOW HOW PEOPLE TEND TO OVER-REACT, RIGHT?
I DON'T WANT PEOPLE DOING THAT.
SHE'S HAVING AN OPERATION DONE, BUT IT'S NOTHING SERIOUS.
I DON'T WANT TO MAKE IT INTO A BIG DEAL.

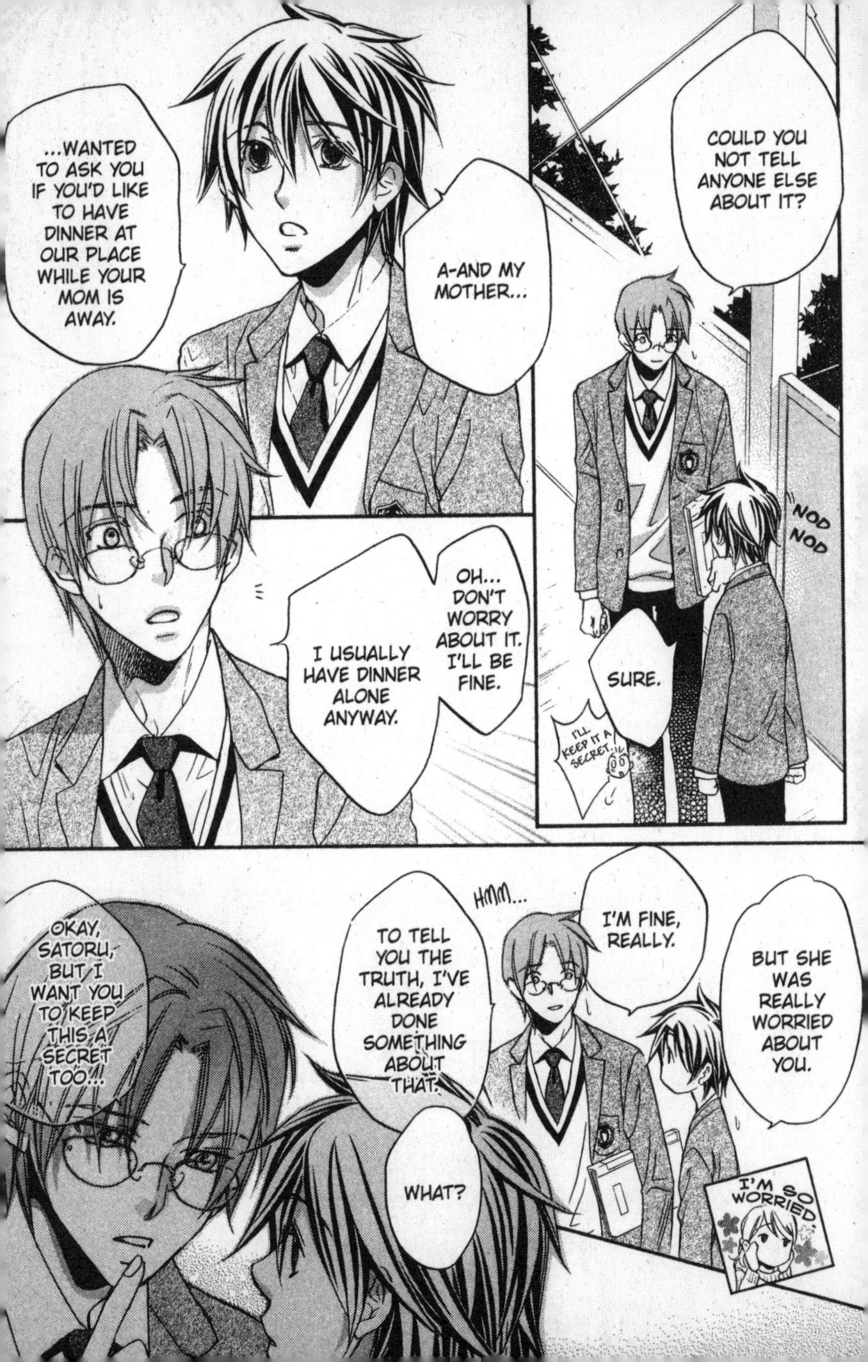
COULD YOU NOT TELL ANYONE ELSE ABOUT IT?
NOD NOD
SURE.
I'LL KEEP IT A SECRET.
A-AND MY MOTHER...
...WANTED TO ASK YOU IF YOU'D LIKE TO HAVE DINNER AT OUR PLACE WHILE YOUR MOM IS AWAY.
OH... DON'T WORRY ABOUT IT. I'LL BE FINE.
I USUALLY HAVE DINNER ALONE ANYWAY.
BUT SHE WAS REALLY WORRIED ABOUT YOU.
I'M FINE, REALLY.
HMM...
TO TELL YOU THE TRUTH, I'VE ALREADY DONE SOMETHING ABOUT THAT.
OKAY, SATORU, BUT I WANT YOU TO KEEP THIS A SECRET TOO...!
I'M SO WORRIED.
WHAT?

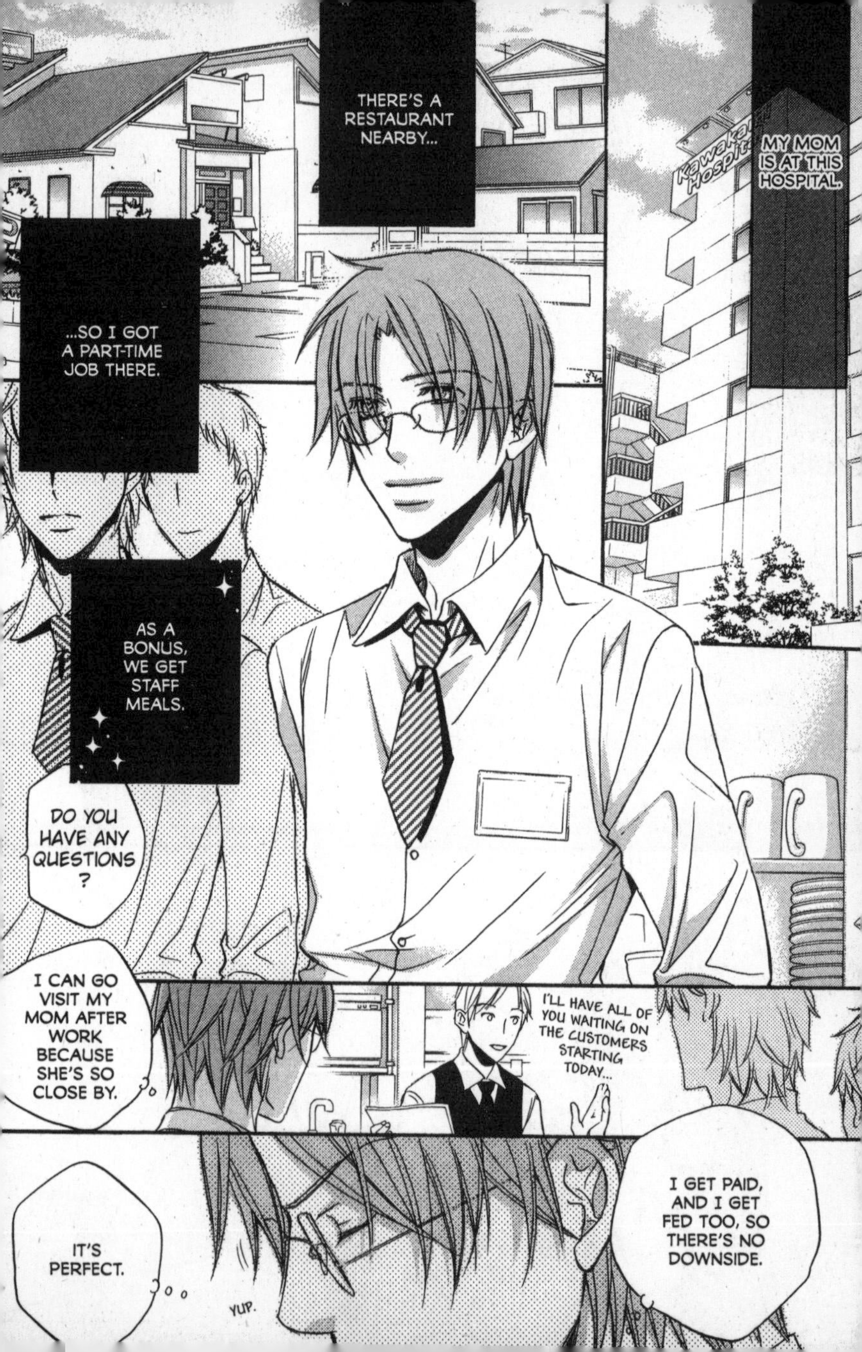
MY MOM IS AT THIS HOSPITAL.
THERE'S A RESTAURANT NEARBY...
...SO I GOT A PART-TIME JOB THERE.
AS A BONUS, WE GET STAFF MEALS.
DO YOU HAVE ANY QUESTIONS?
I'LL HAVE ALL OF YOU WAITING ON THE CUSTOMERS STARTING TODAY...
I CAN GO VISIT MY MOM AFTER WORK BECAUSE SHE'S SO CLOSE BY.
I GET PAID, AND I GET FED TOO, SO THERE'S NO DOWNSIDE.
IT'S PERFECT.
YUP.

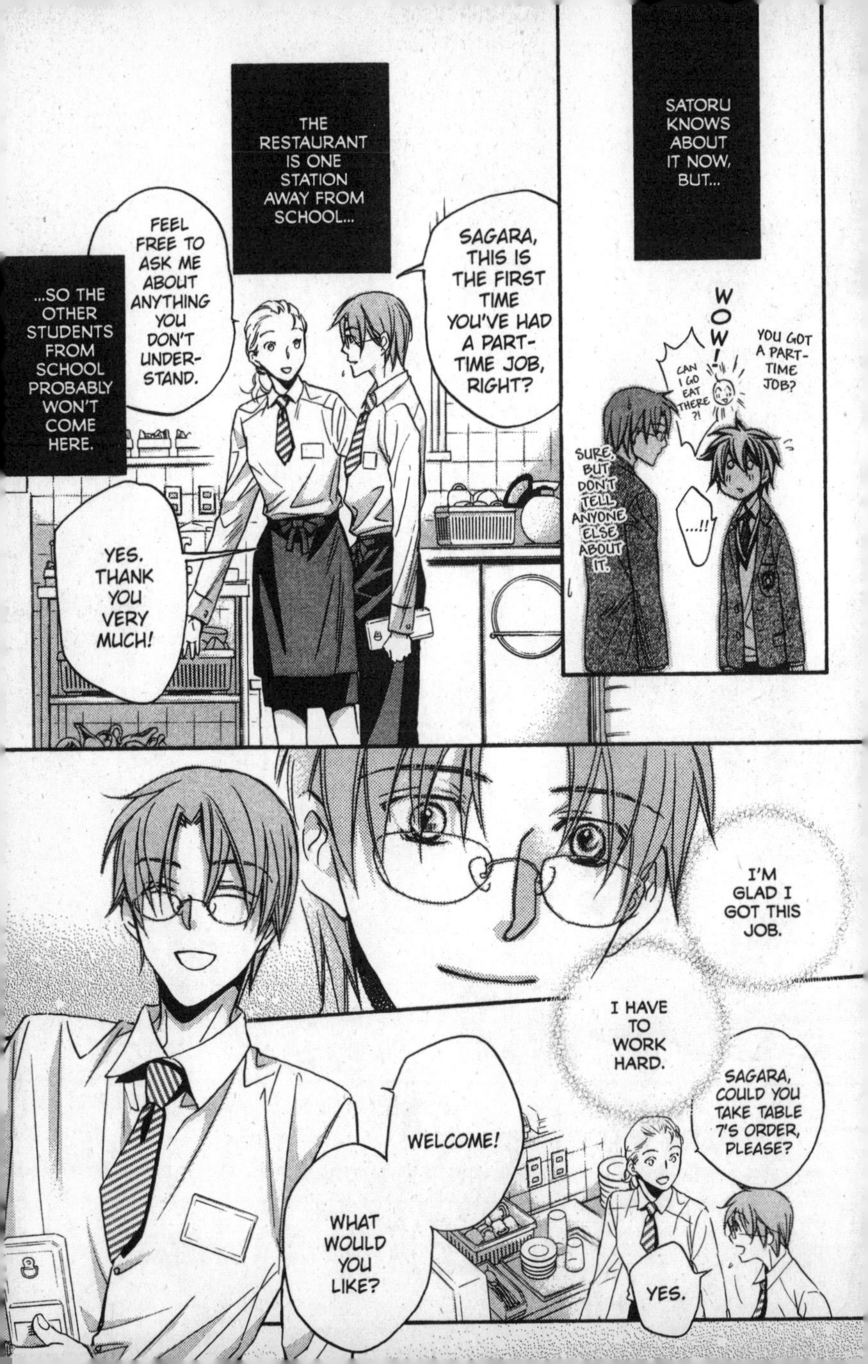
SATORU KNOWS ABOUT IT NOW, BUT...
YOU GOT A PART-TIME JOB?
WOW!
CAN I GO EAT THERE?!
SURE, BUT DON'T TELL ANYONE ELSE ABOUT IT.
...!!
THE RESTAURANT IS ONE STATION AWAY FROM SCHOOL...
...SO THE OTHER STUDENTS FROM SCHOOL PROBABLY WON'T COME HERE.
SAGARA, THIS IS THE FIRST TIME YOU'VE HAD A PART-TIME JOB, RIGHT?
FEEL FREE TO ASK ME ABOUT ANYTHING YOU DON'T UNDER-STAND.
YES. THANK YOU VERY MUCH!
I'M GLAD I GOT THIS JOB.
I HAVE TO WORK HARD.
SAGARA, COULD YOU TAKE TABLE 7'S ORDER, PLEASE?
YES.
WELCOME!
WHAT WOULD YOU LIKE?

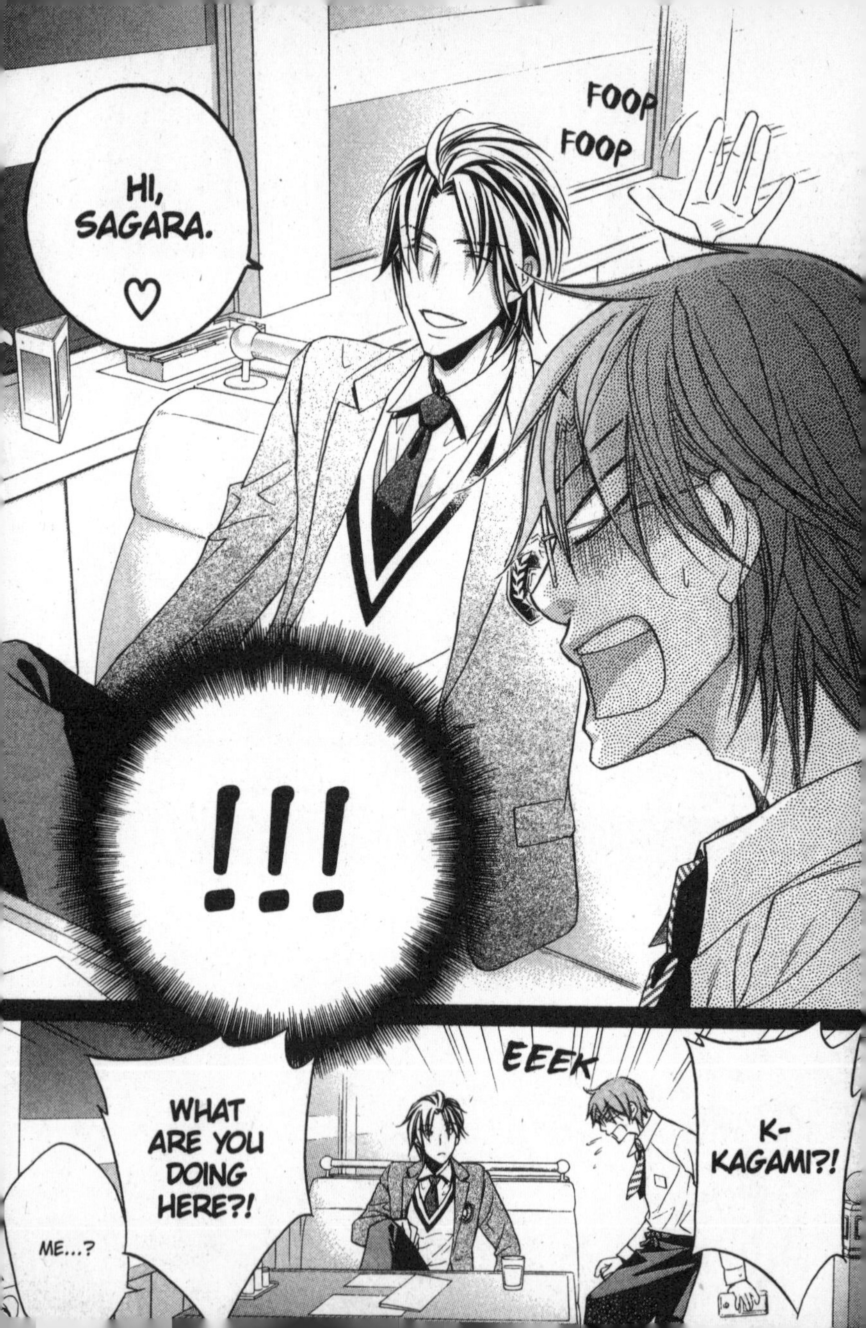
FOOP
FOOP
HI, SAGARA. ♡
!!!
K-KAGAMI?!
EEEK
WHAT ARE YOU DOING HERE?!
ME...?

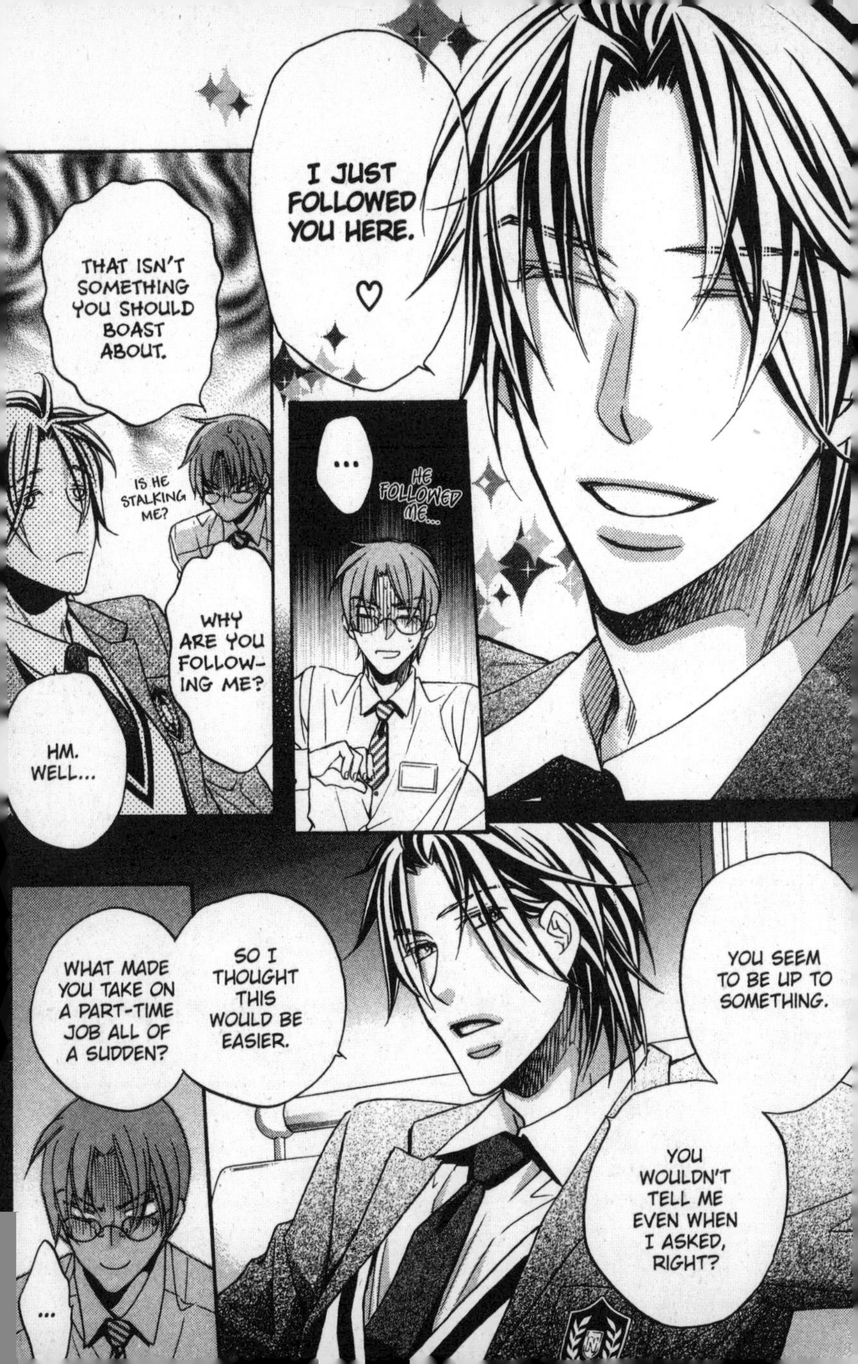

I JUST FOLLOWED YOU HERE. ♡
...
HE FOLLOWED ME...
THAT ISN'T SOMETHING YOU SHOULD BOAST ABOUT.
IS HE STALKING ME?
WHY ARE YOU FOLLOW-ING ME?
HM. WELL...
YOU SEEM TO BE UP TO SOMETHING.
YOU WOULDN'T TELL ME EVEN WHEN I ASKED, RIGHT?
SO I THOUGHT THIS WOULD BE EASIER.
WHAT MADE YOU TAKE ON A PART-TIME JOB ALL OF A SUDDEN?
...

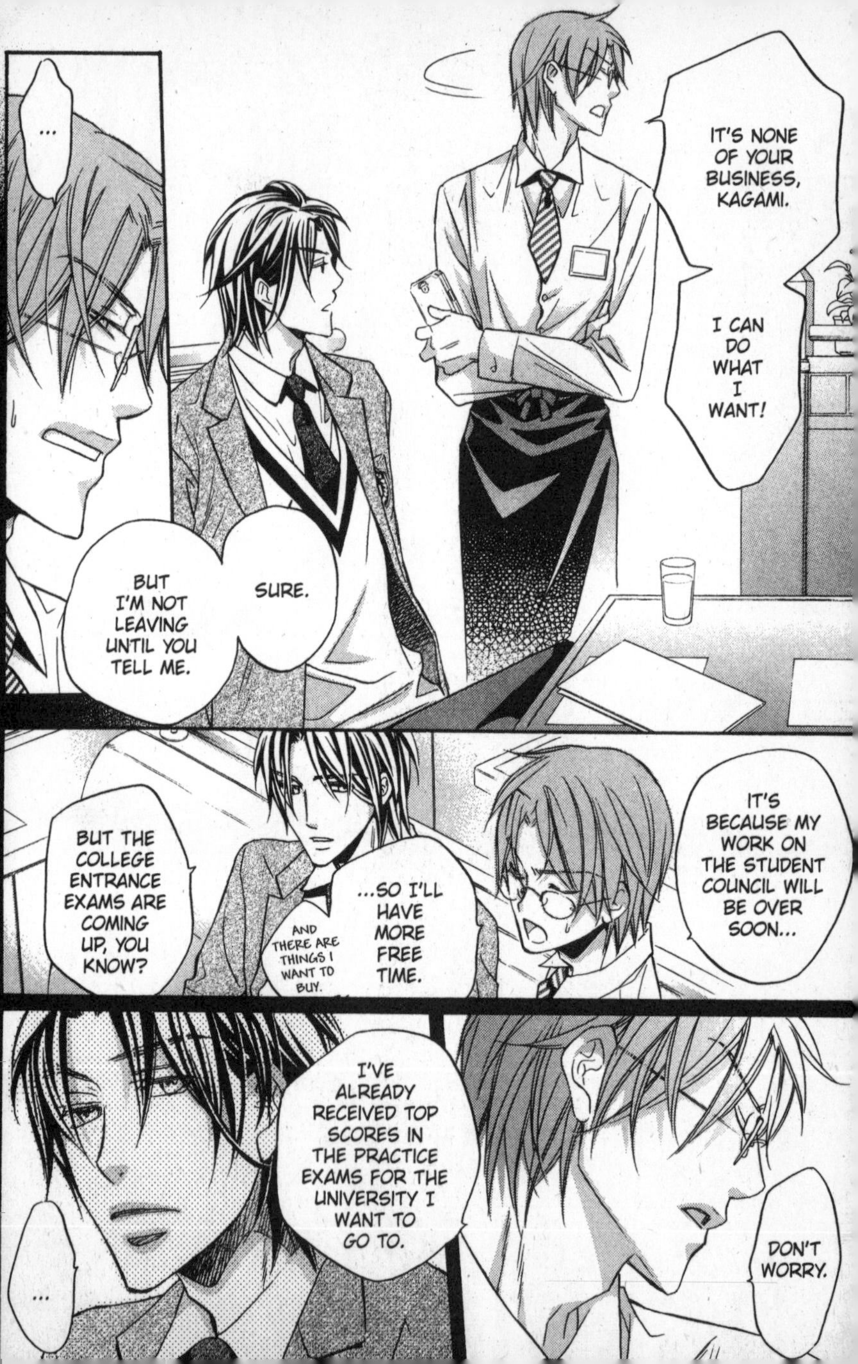
IT'S NONE OF YOUR BUSINESS, KAGAMI.
I CAN DO WHAT I WANT!
SURE.
BUT I'M NOT LEAVING UNTIL YOU TELL ME.
...
IT'S BECAUSE MY WORK ON THE STUDENT COUNCIL WILL BE OVER SOON...
...SO I'LL HAVE MORE FREE TIME.
AND THERE ARE THINGS I WANT TO BUY.
BUT THE COLLEGE ENTRANCE EXAMS ARE COMING UP, YOU KNOW?
DON'T WORRY.
I'VE ALREADY RECEIVED TOP SCORES IN THE PRACTICE EXAMS FOR THE UNIVERSITY I WANT TO GO TO.
...

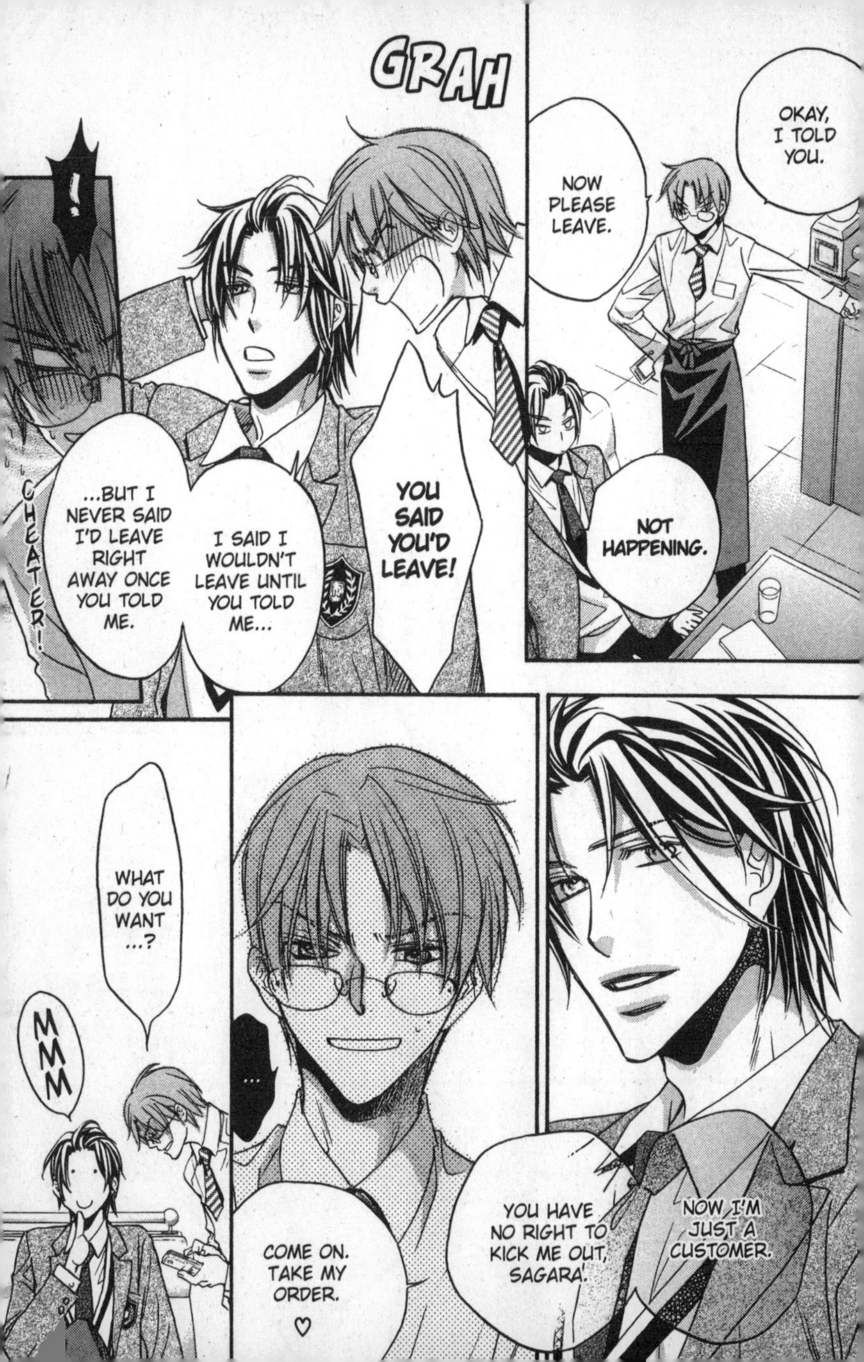
OKAY, I TOLD YOU.
NOW PLEASE LEAVE.
NOT HAPPENING.
GRAH
!
YOU SAID YOU'D LEAVE!
I SAID I WOULDN'T LEAVE UNTIL YOU TOLD ME...
...BUT I NEVER SAID I'D LEAVE RIGHT AWAY ONCE YOU TOLD ME.
CHEATER!
NOW I'M JUST A CUSTOMER.
YOU HAVE NO RIGHT TO KICK ME OUT, SAGARA.
...
COME ON. TAKE MY ORDER. ♡
WHAT DO YOU WANT ...?
MMM

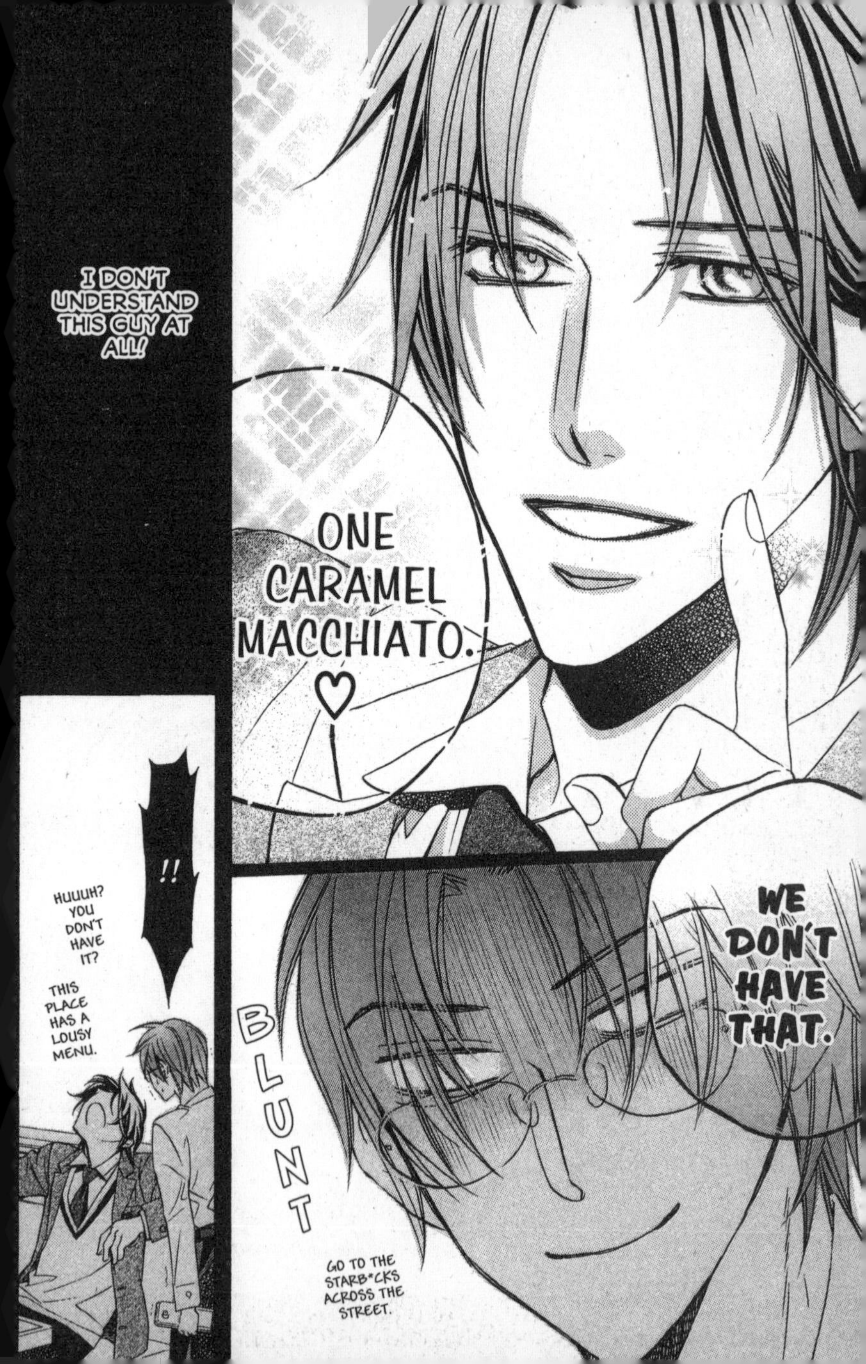
ONE CARAMEL MACCHIATO. ♡
WE DON'T HAVE THAT.
BLUNT
GO TO THE STARB*CKS ACROSS THE STREET.
!!
HUUUH? YOU DON'T HAVE IT?
THIS PLACE HAS A LOUSY MENU.
I DON'T UNDERSTAND THIS GUY AT ALL!

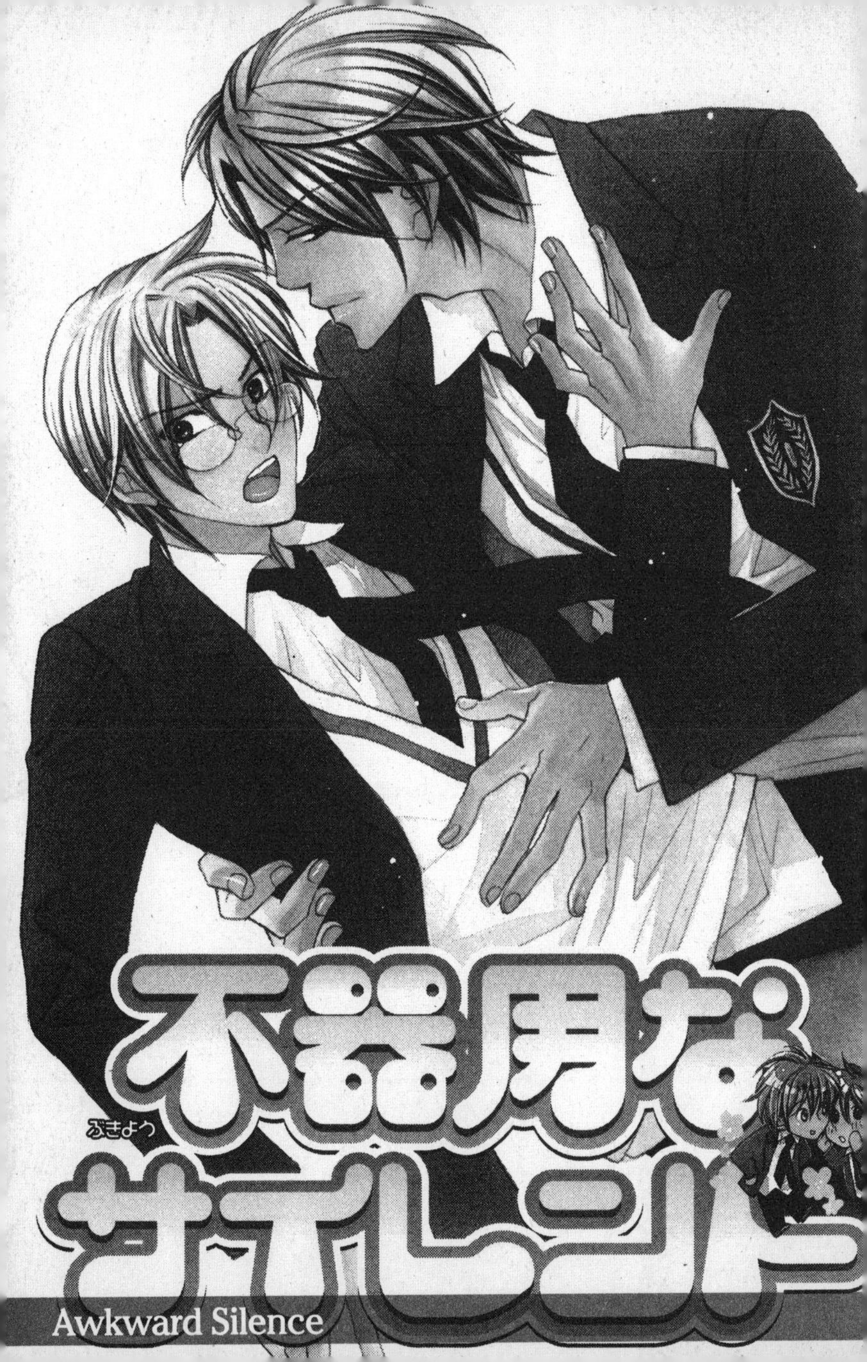
不器用なサイレント
ぶきよう
Awkward Silence

AWKWARD SILENCE

HINAKO TAKANAGA

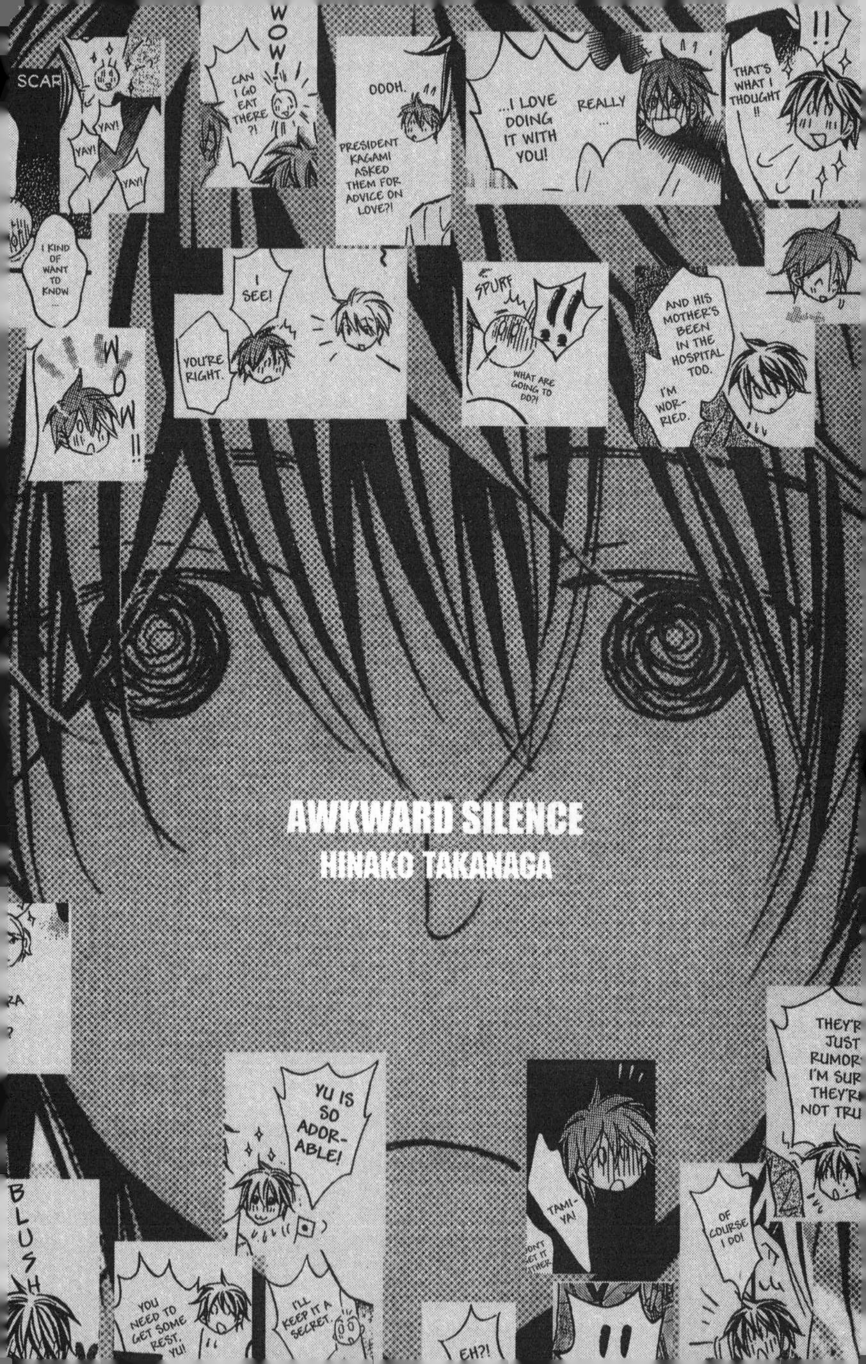
!!
THAT'S WHAT I THOUGHT !!
REALLY ...
...I LOVE DOING IT WITH YOU!
OOOH.
PRESIDENT KAGAMI ASKED THEM FOR ADVICE ON LOVE?!
WOW!
CAN I GO EAT THERE ?!
YAY!
YAY!
YAY!
SCAR
AND HIS MOTHER'S BEEN IN THE HOSPITAL TOO.
I'M WOR-RIED.
SPURT
!!
WHAT ARE GOING TO DO?!
I SEE!
YOU'RE RIGHT.
I KIND OF WANT TO KNOW ...
WOW !!
THEY'R JUST RUMOR I'M SUR THEY'R NOT TRU
OF COURSE I DO!
TAMI-YA!
YU IS SO ADOR-ABLE!
BLUSH
EH?!
I'LL KEEP IT A SECRET.
YOU NEED TO GET SOME REST, YU!

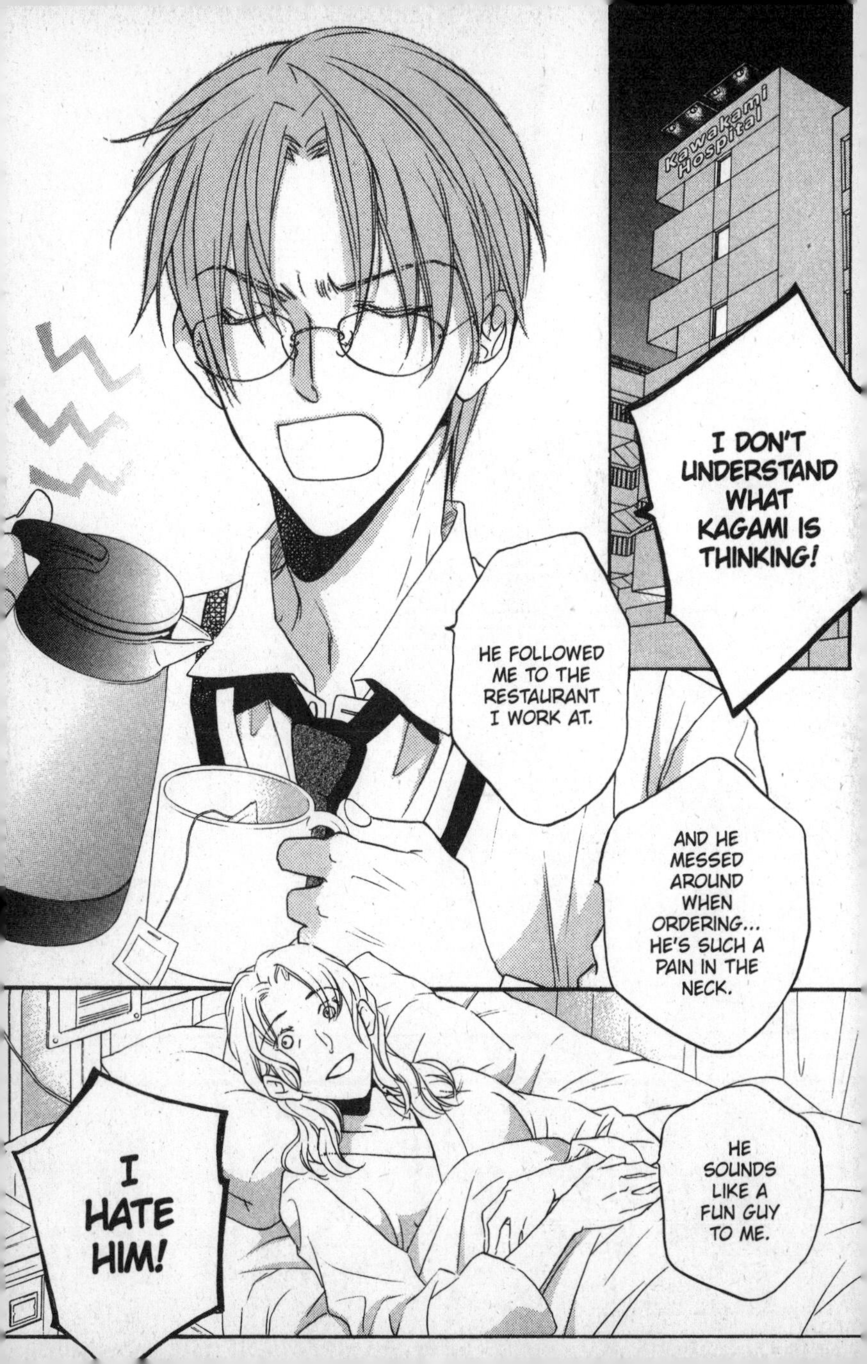
Kawakami Hospital
I DON'T UNDERSTAND WHAT KAGAMI IS THINKING!
HE FOLLOWED ME TO THE RESTAURANT I WORK AT.
AND HE MESSED AROUND WHEN ORDERING... HE'S SUCH A PAIN IN THE NECK.
HE SOUNDS LIKE A FUN GUY TO ME.
I HATE HIM!

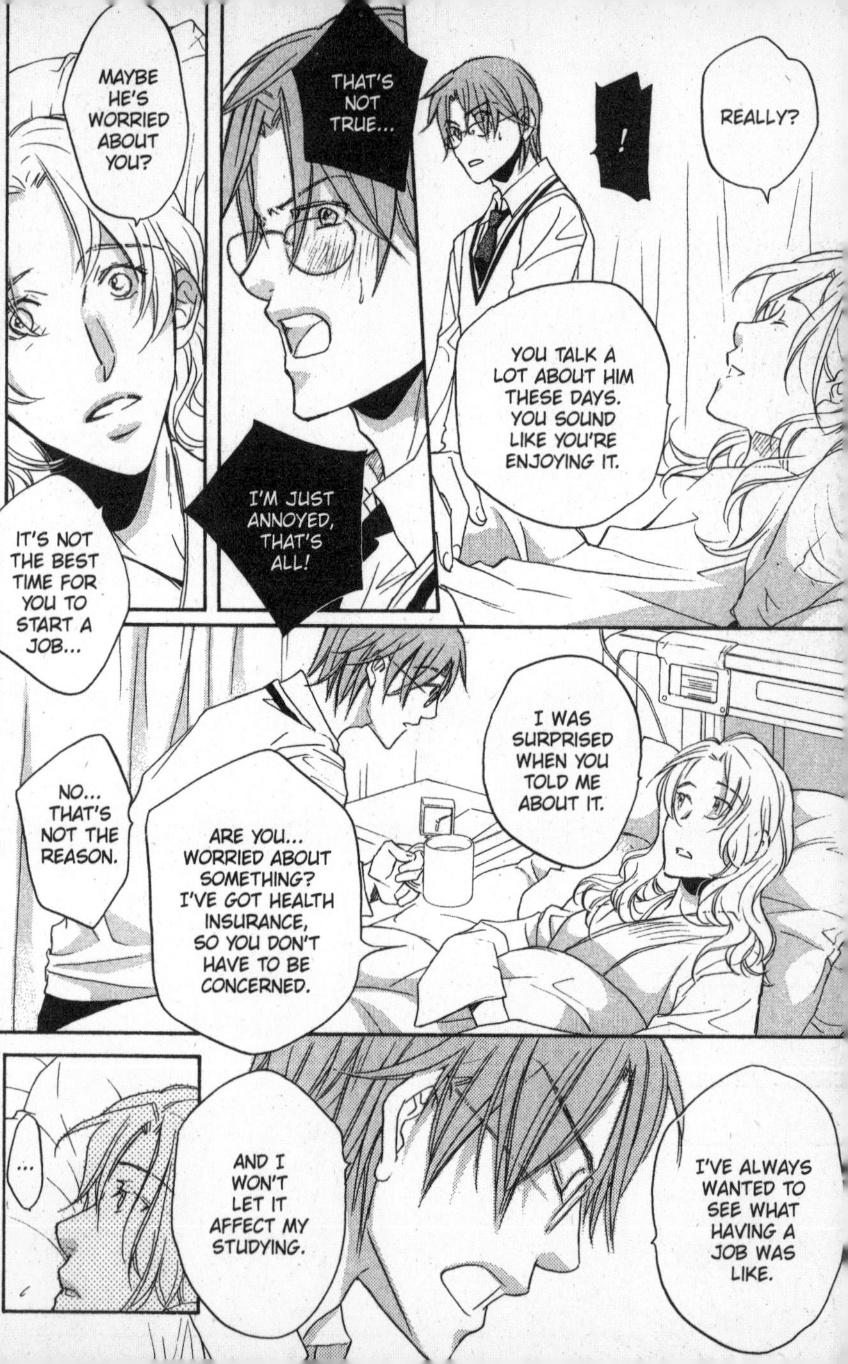
REALLY?
!
YOU TALK A LOT ABOUT HIM THESE DAYS. YOU SOUND LIKE YOU'RE ENJOYING IT.
THAT'S NOT TRUE...
I'M JUST ANNOYED, THAT'S ALL!
MAYBE HE'S WORRIED ABOUT YOU?
IT'S NOT THE BEST TIME FOR YOU TO START A JOB...
I WAS SURPRISED WHEN YOU TOLD ME ABOUT IT.
ARE YOU... WORRIED ABOUT SOMETHING? I'VE GOT HEALTH INSURANCE, SO YOU DON'T HAVE TO BE CONCERNED.
NO... THAT'S NOT THE REASON.
I'VE ALWAYS WANTED TO SEE WHAT HAVING A JOB WAS LIKE.
AND I WON'T LET IT AFFECT MY STUDYING.
...

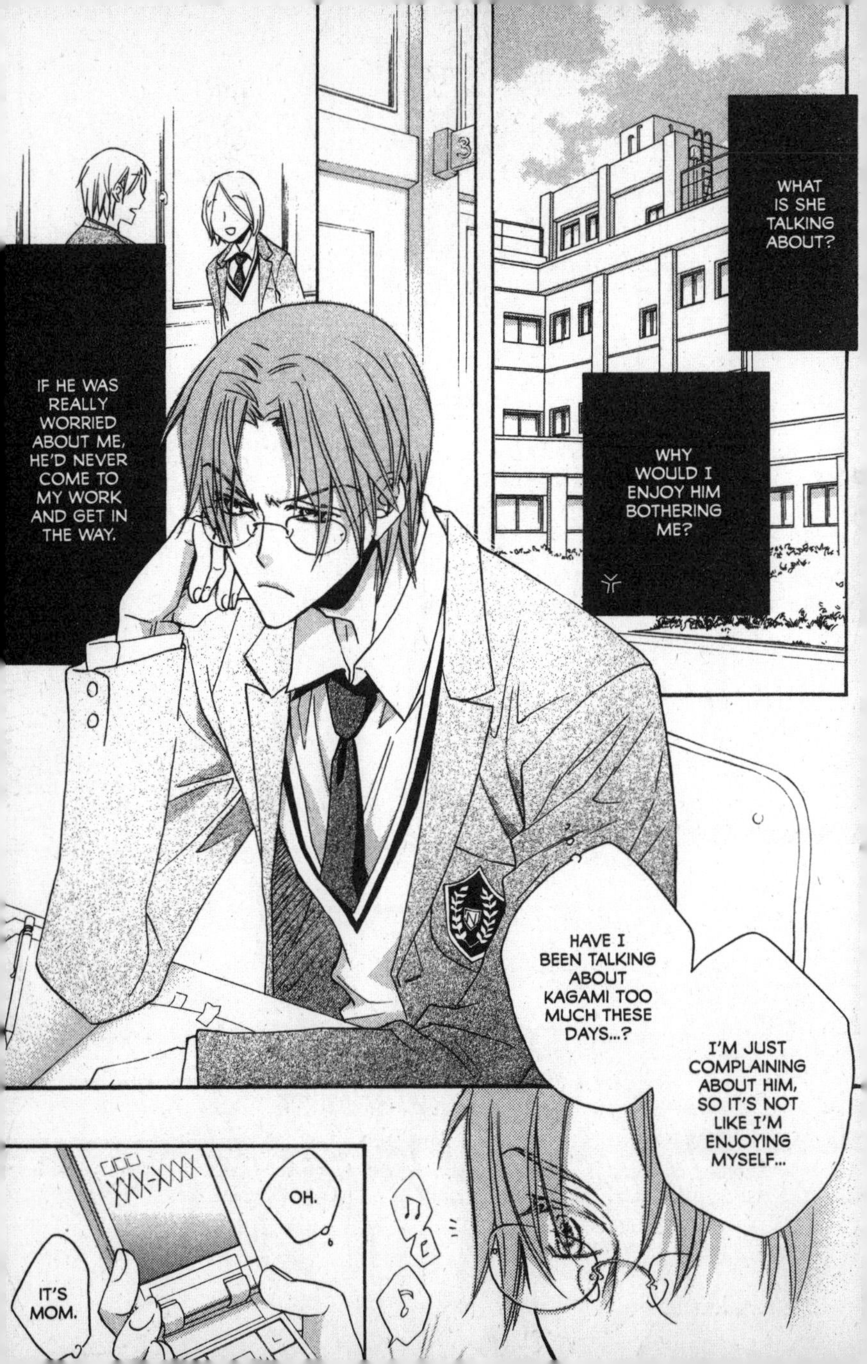
WHAT IS SHE TALKING ABOUT?
WHY WOULD I ENJOY HIM BOTHERING ME?
IF HE WAS REALLY WORRIED ABOUT ME, HE'D NEVER COME TO MY WORK AND GET IN THE WAY.
HAVE I BEEN TALKING ABOUT KAGAMI TOO MUCH THESE DAYS...?
I'M JUST COMPLAINING ABOUT HIM, SO IT'S NOT LIKE I'M ENJOYING MYSELF...
OH.
XXX-XXXX
IT'S MOM.

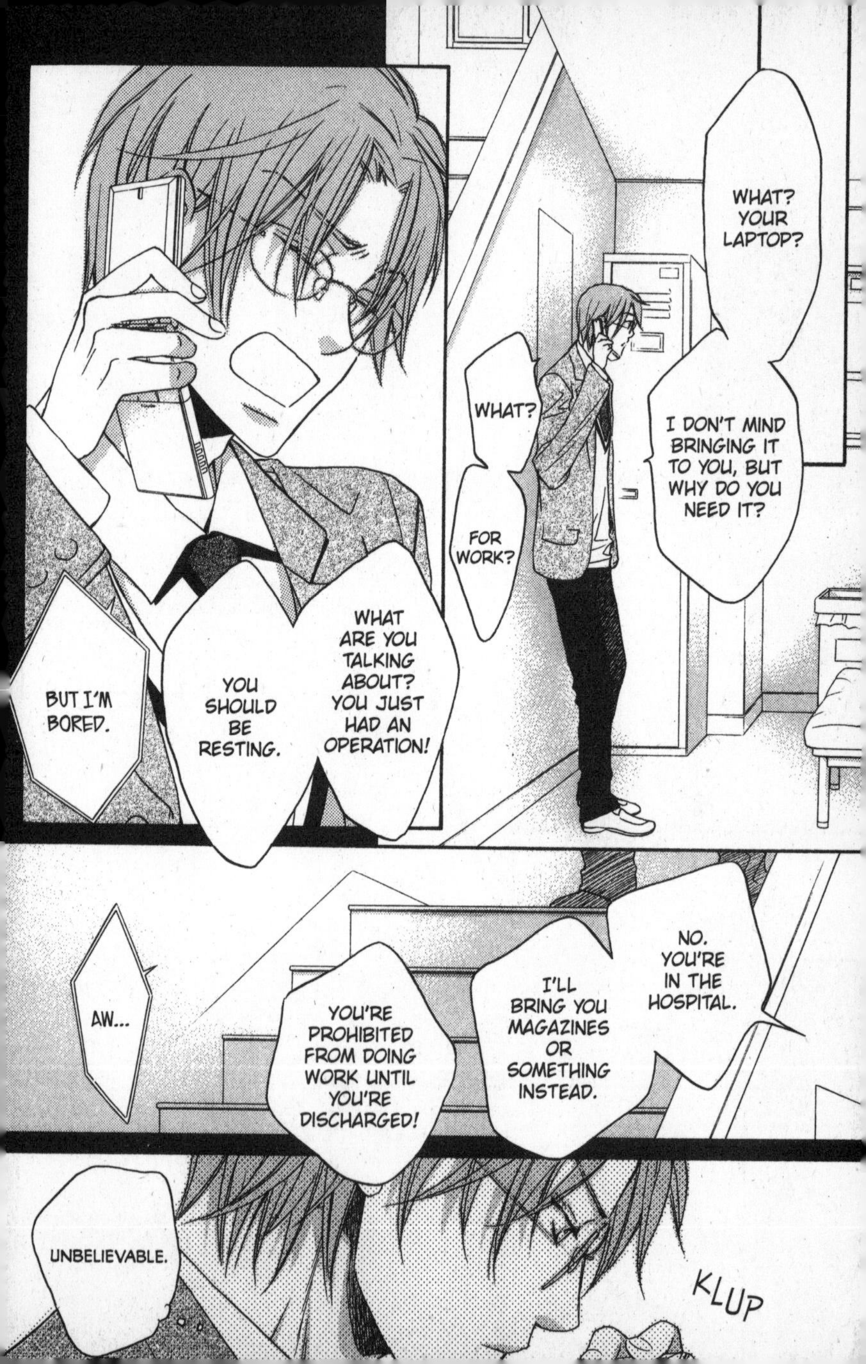
WHAT? YOUR LAPTOP?
I DON'T MIND BRINGING IT TO YOU, BUT WHY DO YOU NEED IT?
WHAT?
FOR WORK?
WHAT ARE YOU TALKING ABOUT? YOU JUST HAD AN OPERATION!
YOU SHOULD BE RESTING.
BUT I'M BORED.
NO. YOU'RE IN THE HOSPITAL.
I'LL BRING YOU MAGAZINES OR SOMETHING INSTEAD.
YOU'RE PROHIBITED FROM DOING WORK UNTIL YOU'RE DISCHARGED!
AW...
KLUP
UNBELIEVABLE.

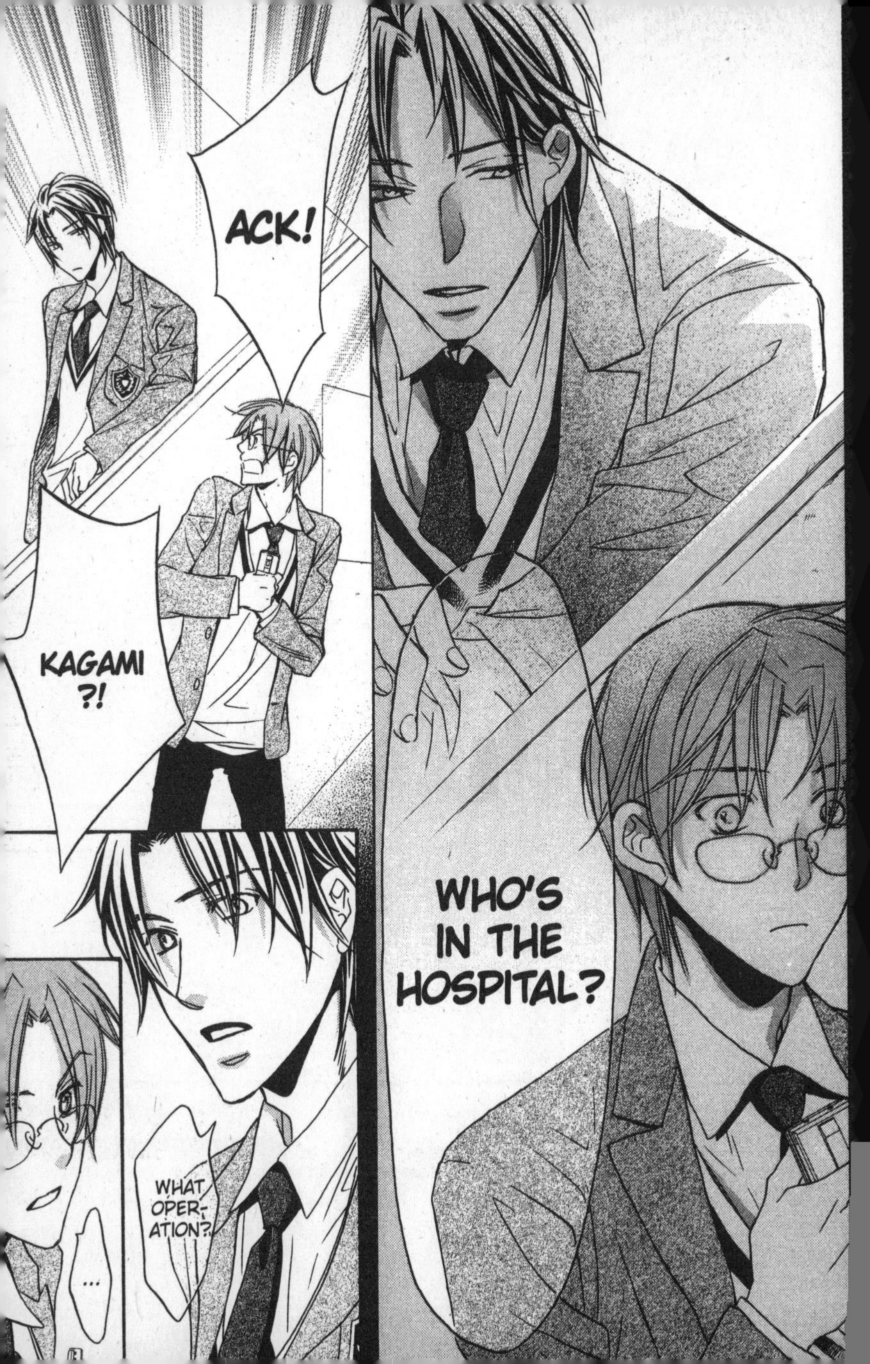
WHO'S IN THE HOSPITAL?
ACK!
KAGAMI ?!
WHAT OPER-ATION?
...

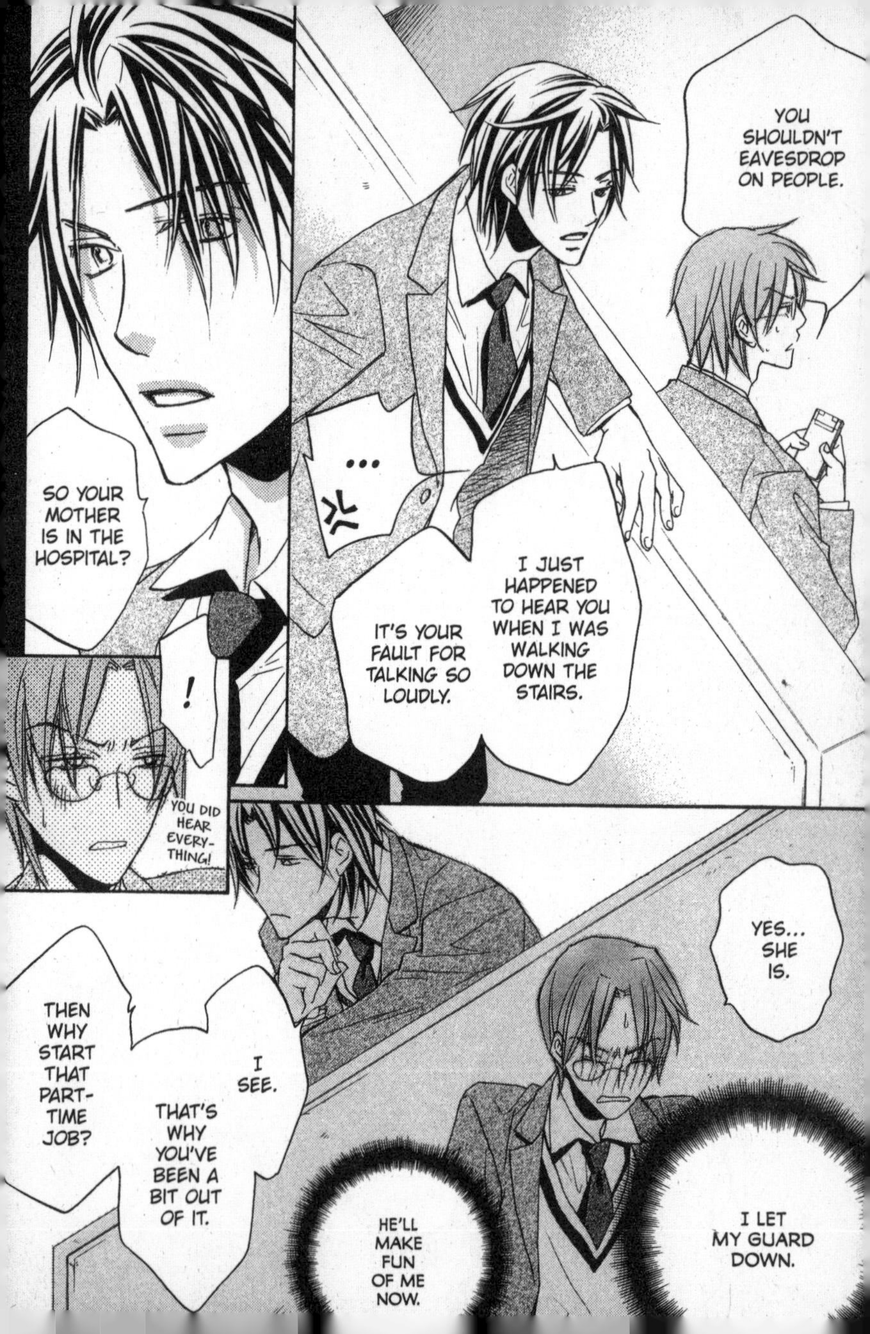
YOU SHOULDN'T EAVESDROP ON PEOPLE.
...
I JUST HAPPENED TO HEAR YOU WHEN I WAS WALKING DOWN THE STAIRS.
IT'S YOUR FAULT FOR TALKING SO LOUDLY.
SO YOUR MOTHER IS IN THE HOSPITAL?
!
YOU DID HEAR EVERY-THING!
YES... SHE IS.
I SEE.
THAT'S WHY YOU'VE BEEN A BIT OUT OF IT.
THEN WHY START THAT PART-TIME JOB?
I LET MY GUARD DOWN.
HE'LL MAKE FUN OF ME NOW.

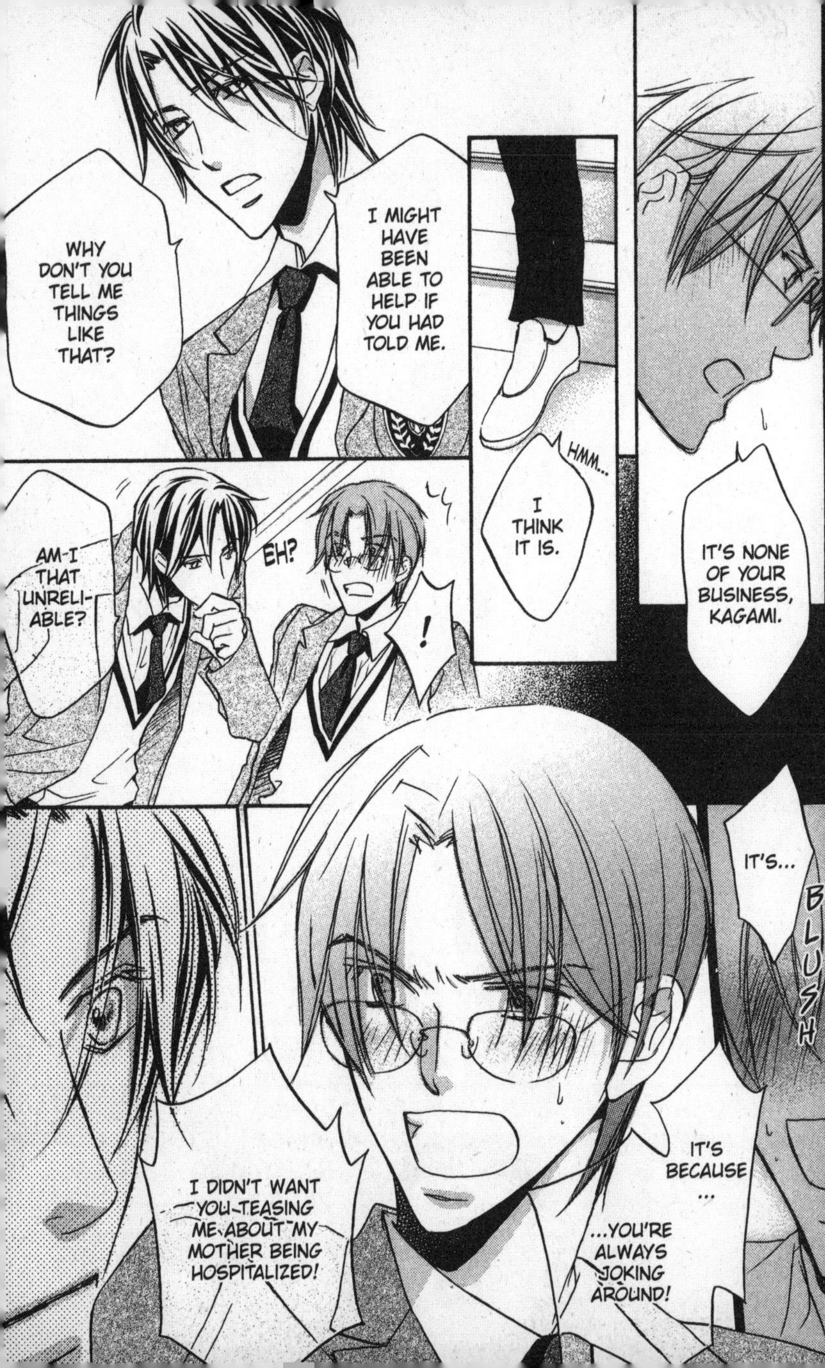
WHY DON'T YOU TELL ME THINGS LIKE THAT?
I MIGHT HAVE BEEN ABLE TO HELP IF YOU HAD TOLD ME.
IT'S NONE OF YOUR BUSINESS, KAGAMI.
HMM...
I THINK IT IS.
AM I THAT UNRELIABLE?
EH?
!
IT'S...
BLUSH
IT'S BECAUSE...
...YOU'RE ALWAYS JOKING AROUND!
I DIDN'T WANT YOU TEASING ME ABOUT MY MOTHER BEING HOSPITALIZED!

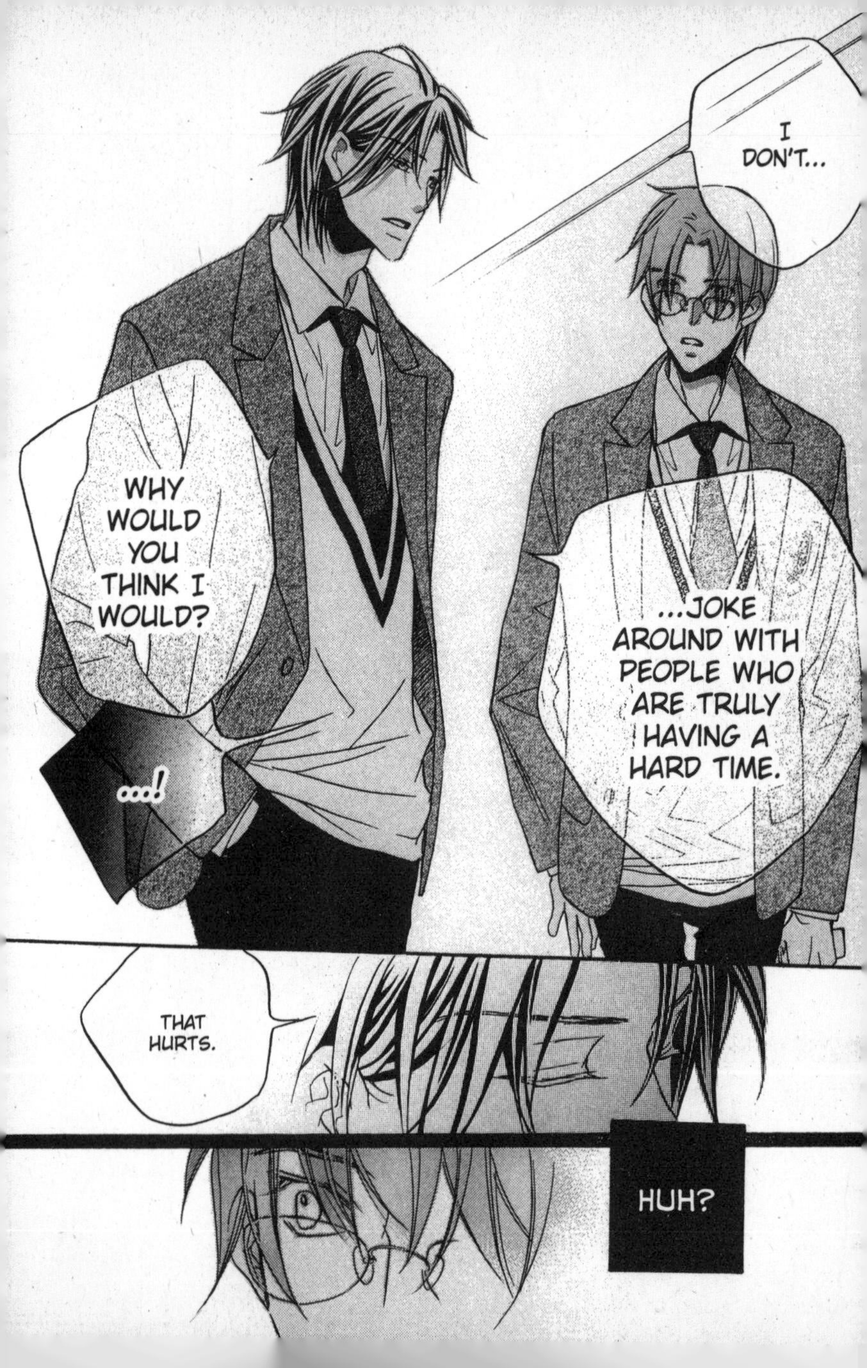
I DON'T...
...JOKE AROUND WITH PEOPLE WHO ARE TRULY HAVING A HARD TIME.
WHY WOULD YOU THINK I WOULD?
...!
THAT HURTS.
HUH?

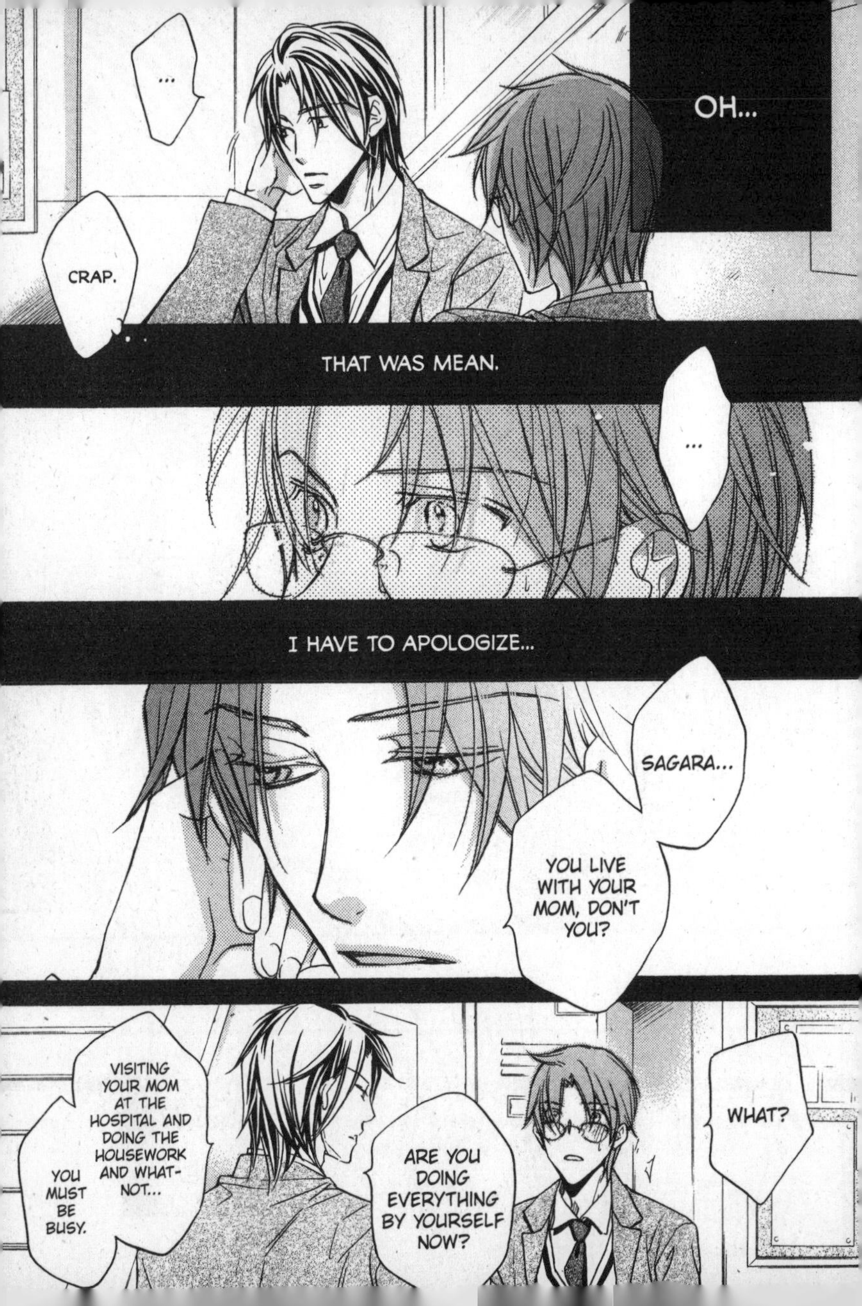
OH...
...
CRAP.
THAT WAS MEAN.
...
I HAVE TO APOLOGIZE...
SAGARA...
YOU LIVE WITH YOUR MOM, DON'T YOU?
WHAT?
ARE YOU DOING EVERYTHING BY YOURSELF NOW?
VISITING YOUR MOM AT THE HOSPITAL AND DOING THE HOUSEWORK AND WHAT-NOT...
YOU MUST BE BUSY.

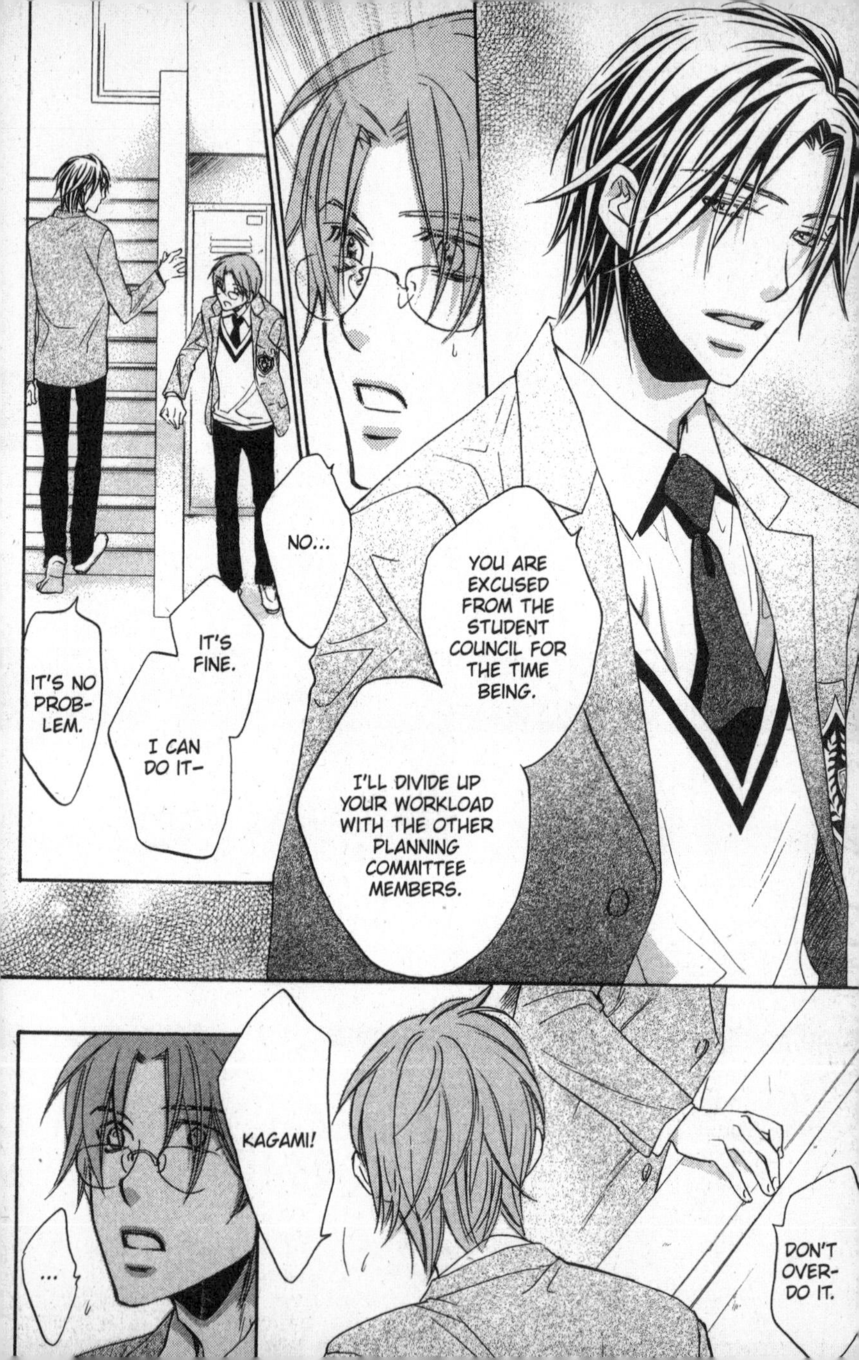
YOU ARE EXCUSED FROM THE STUDENT COUNCIL FOR THE TIME BEING.
I'LL DIVIDE UP YOUR WORKLOAD WITH THE OTHER PLANNING COMMITTEE MEMBERS.
NO...
IT'S FINE.
I CAN DO IT-
IT'S NO PROB-LEM.
DON'T OVER-DO IT.
KAGAMI!
...

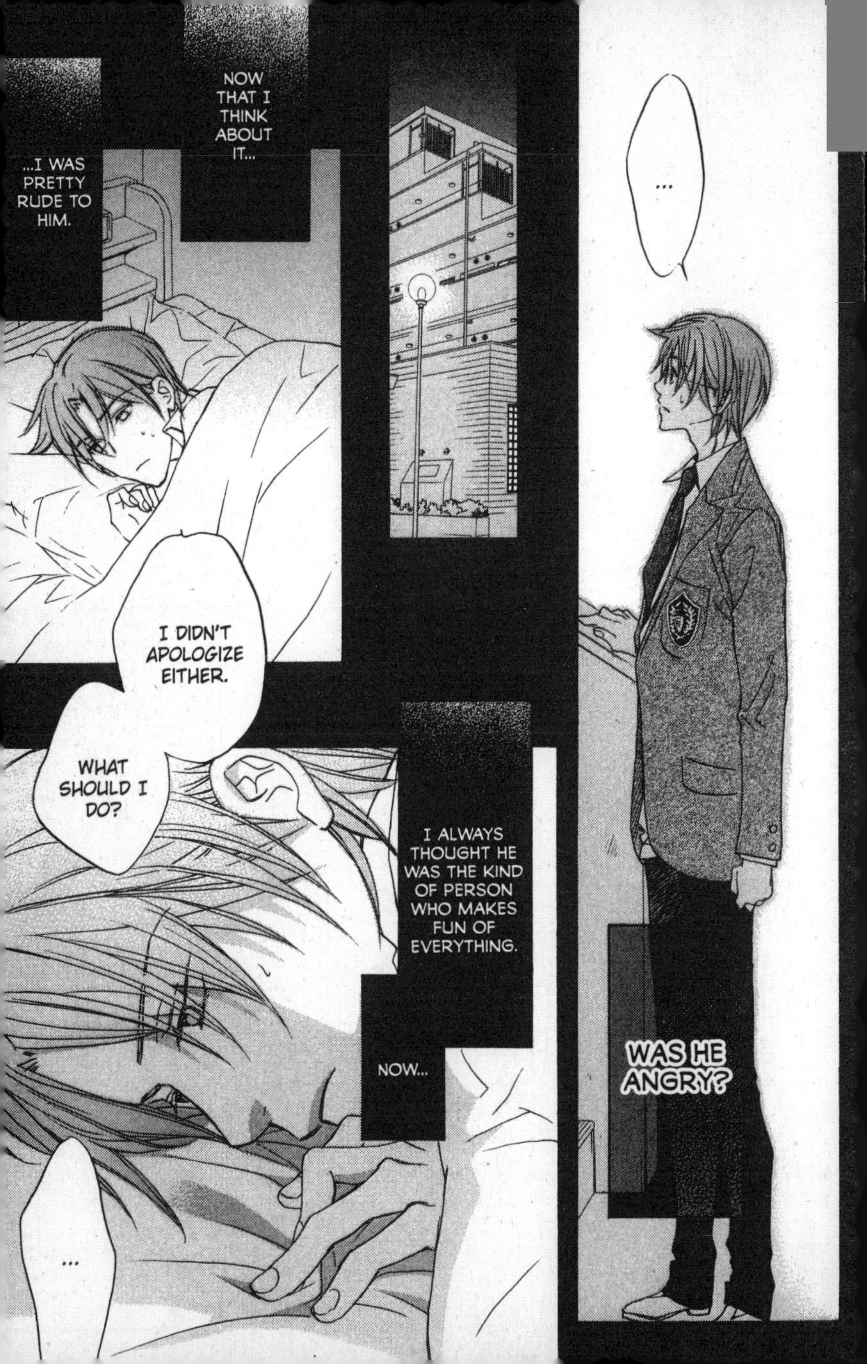
...
WAS HE ANGRY?
NOW THAT I THINK ABOUT IT...
...I WAS PRETTY RUDE TO HIM.
I DIDN'T APOLOGIZE EITHER.
WHAT SHOULD I DO?
I ALWAYS THOUGHT HE WAS THE KIND OF PERSON WHO MAKES FUN OF EVERYTHING.
NOW...
...

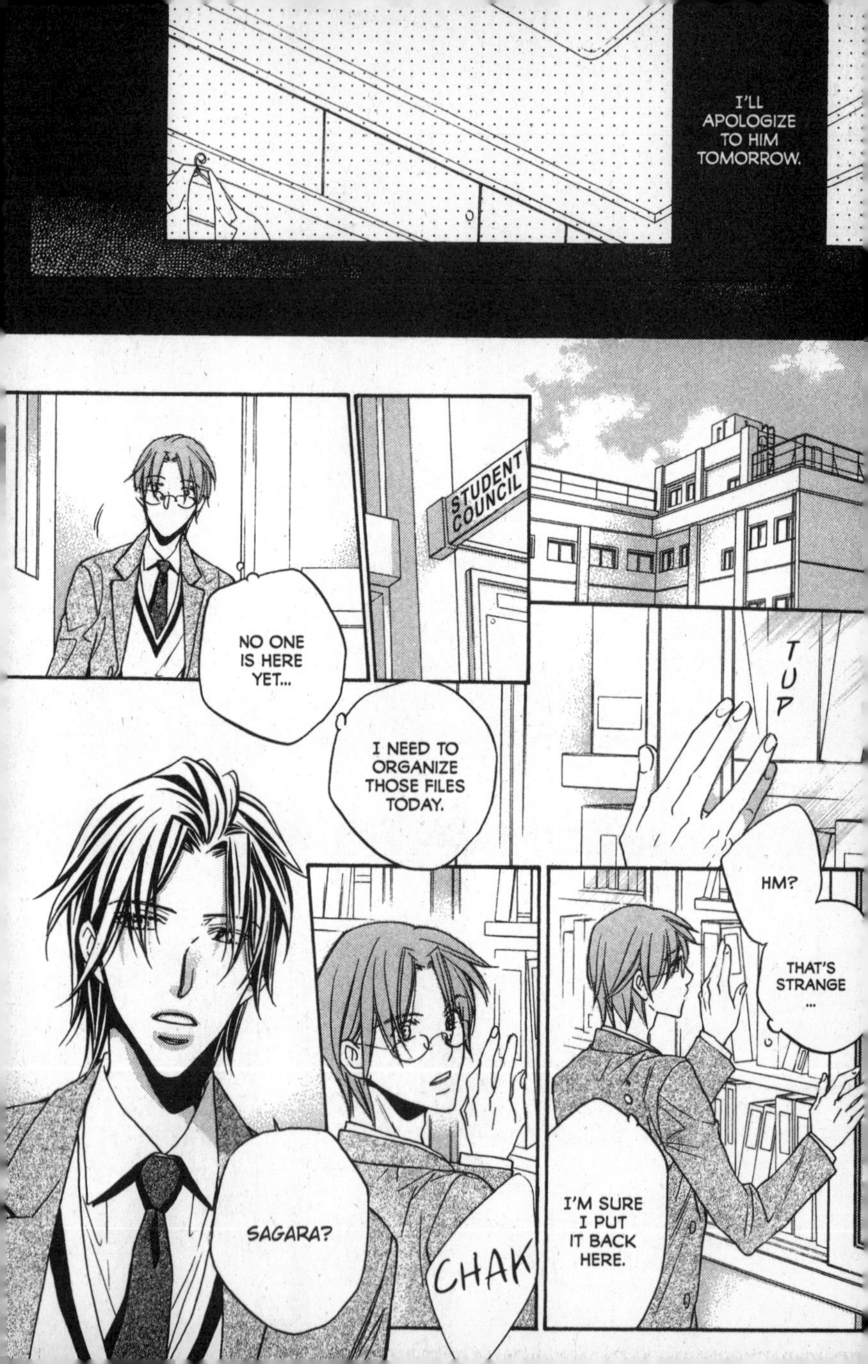
I'LL APOLOGIZE TO HIM TOMORROW.
STUDENT COUNCIL
NO ONE IS HERE YET...
I NEED TO ORGANIZE THOSE FILES TODAY.
TUP
HM?
THAT'S STRANGE ...
I'M SURE I PUT IT BACK HERE.
CHAK
SAGARA?

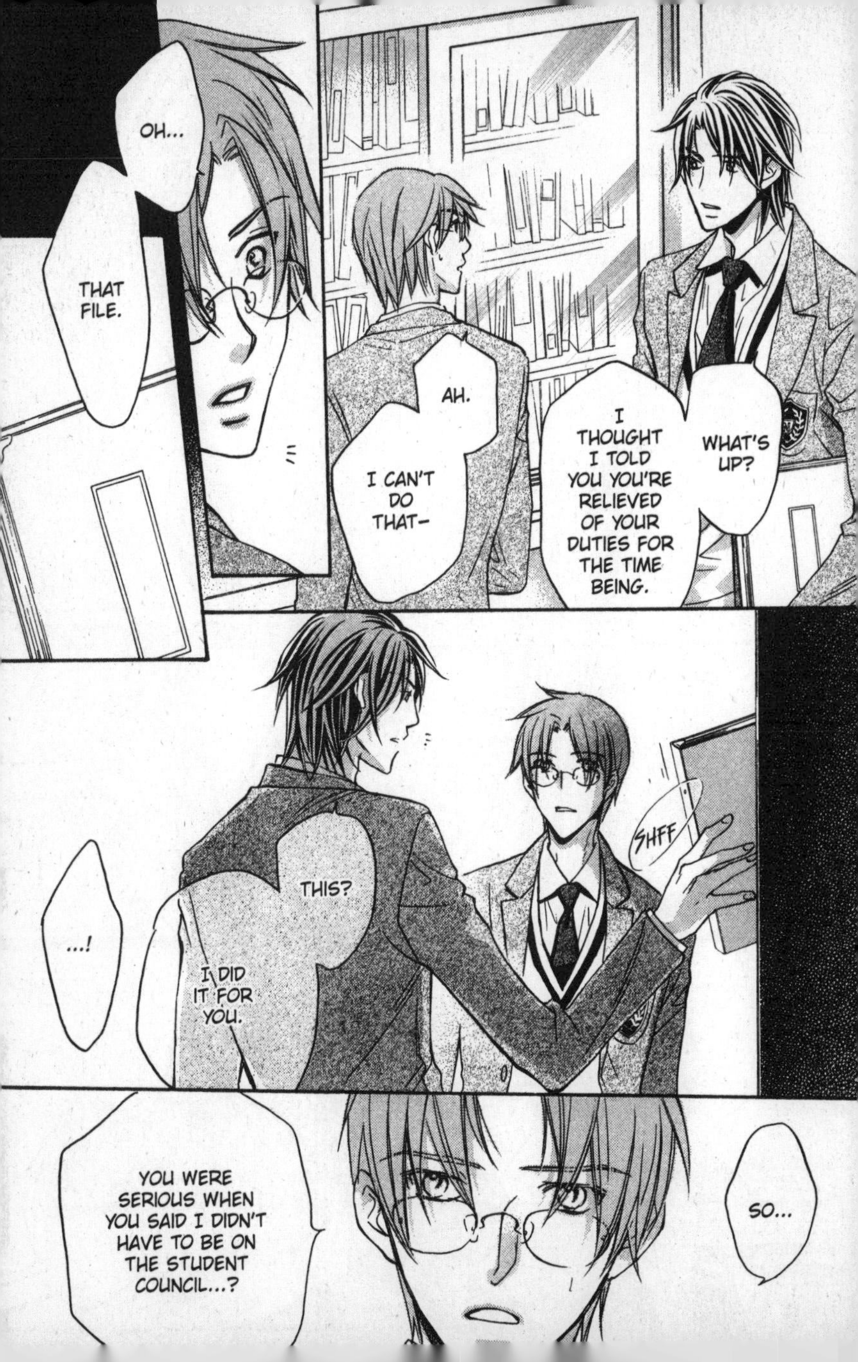
WHAT'S UP?
I THOUGHT I TOLD YOU YOU'RE RELIEVED OF YOUR DUTIES FOR THE TIME BEING.
AH.
I CAN'T DO THAT–
OH...
THAT FILE.
SHFF
THIS?
I DID IT FOR YOU.
...!
SO...
YOU WERE SERIOUS WHEN YOU SAID I DIDN'T HAVE TO BE ON THE STUDENT COUNCIL...?

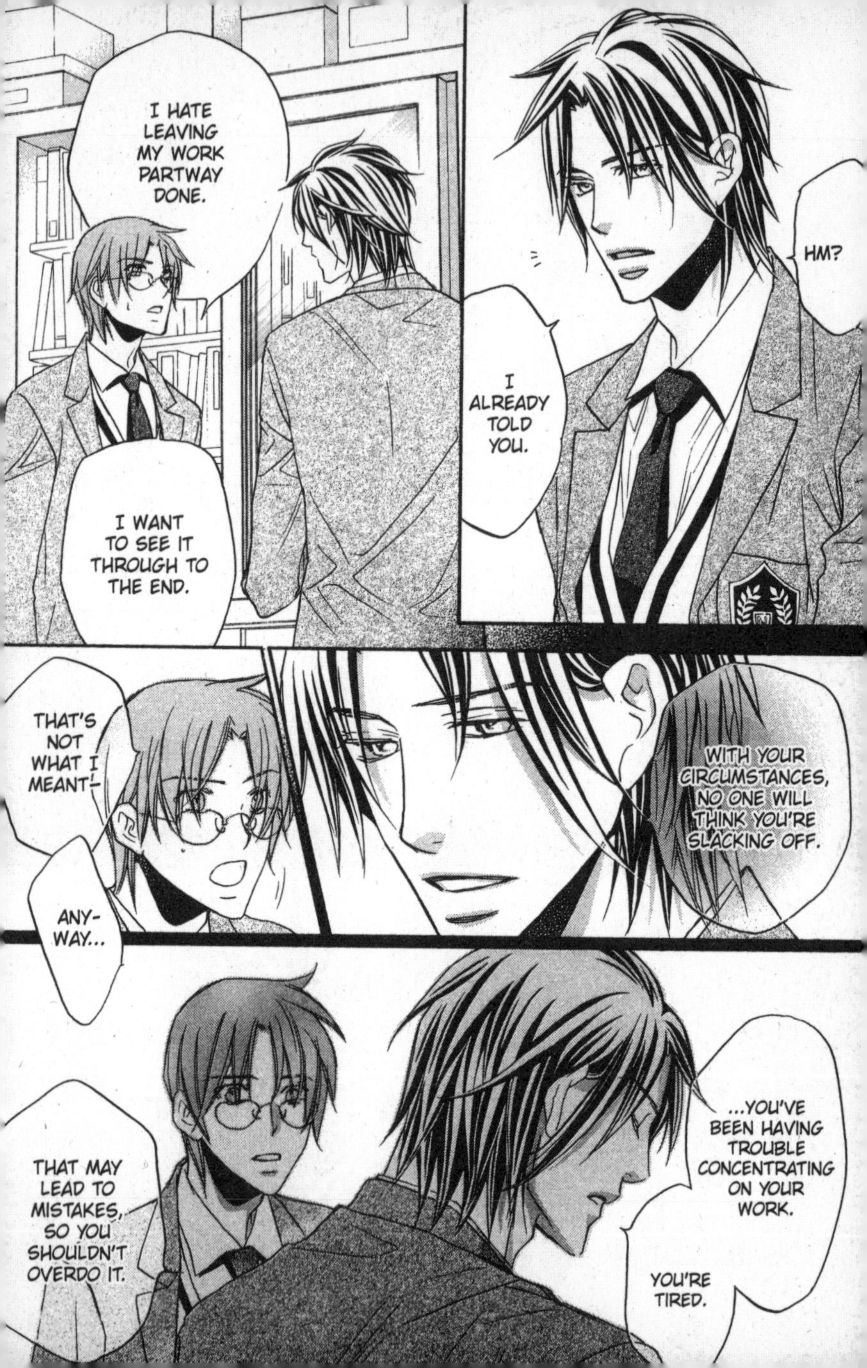
HM?
I ALREADY TOLD YOU.
I HATE LEAVING MY WORK PARTWAY DONE.
I WANT TO SEE IT THROUGH TO THE END.
WITH YOUR CIRCUMSTANCES, NO ONE WILL THINK YOU'RE SLACKING OFF.
THAT'S NOT WHAT I MEANT—
ANY-WAY...
...YOU'VE BEEN HAVING TROUBLE CONCENTRATING ON YOUR WORK.
YOU'RE TIRED.
THAT MAY LEAD TO MISTAKES, SO YOU SHOULDN'T OVERDO IT.

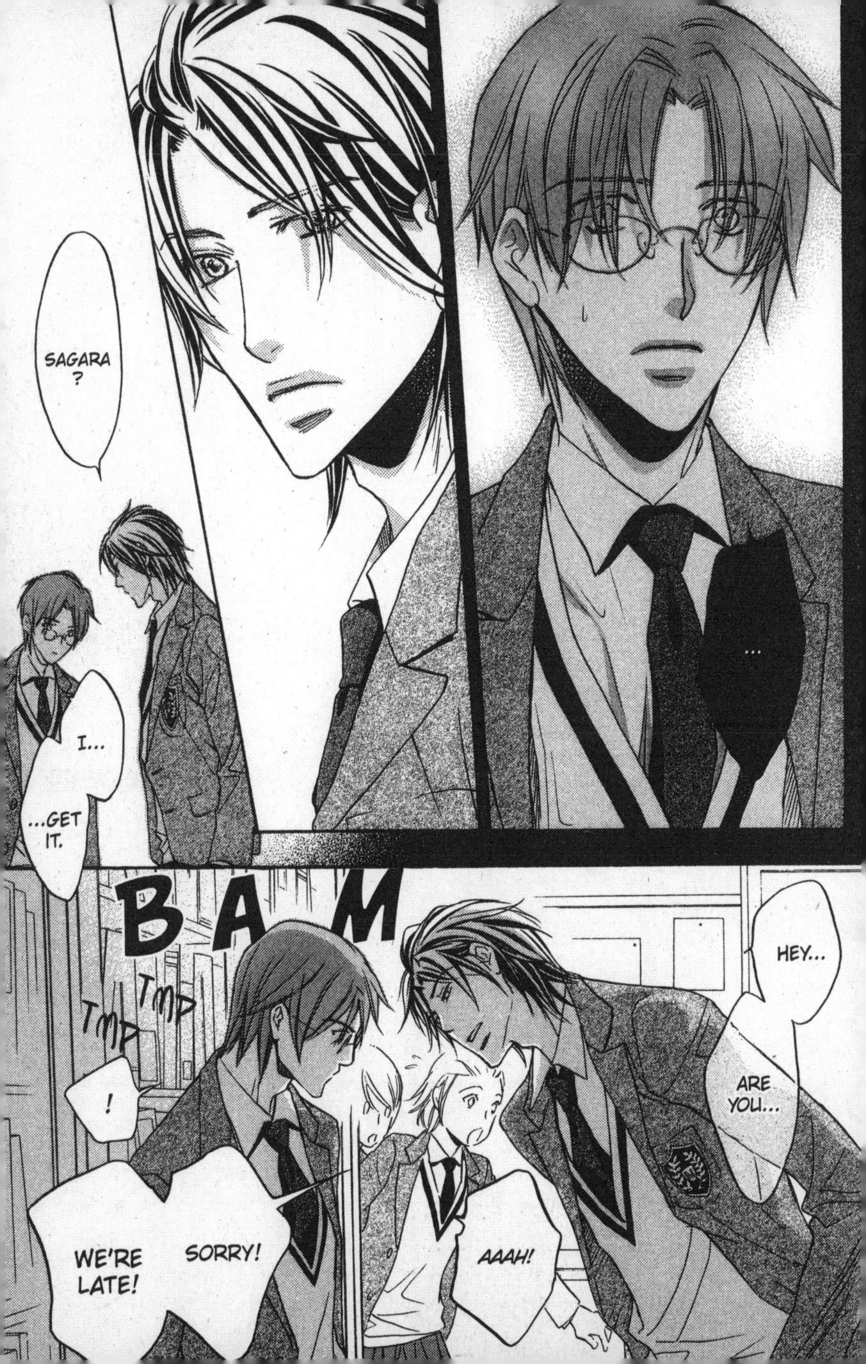
...
SAGARA ?
I...
...GET IT.
HEY...
ARE YOU...
BAM
TMP
TMP
!
AAAH!
SORRY!
WE'RE LATE!

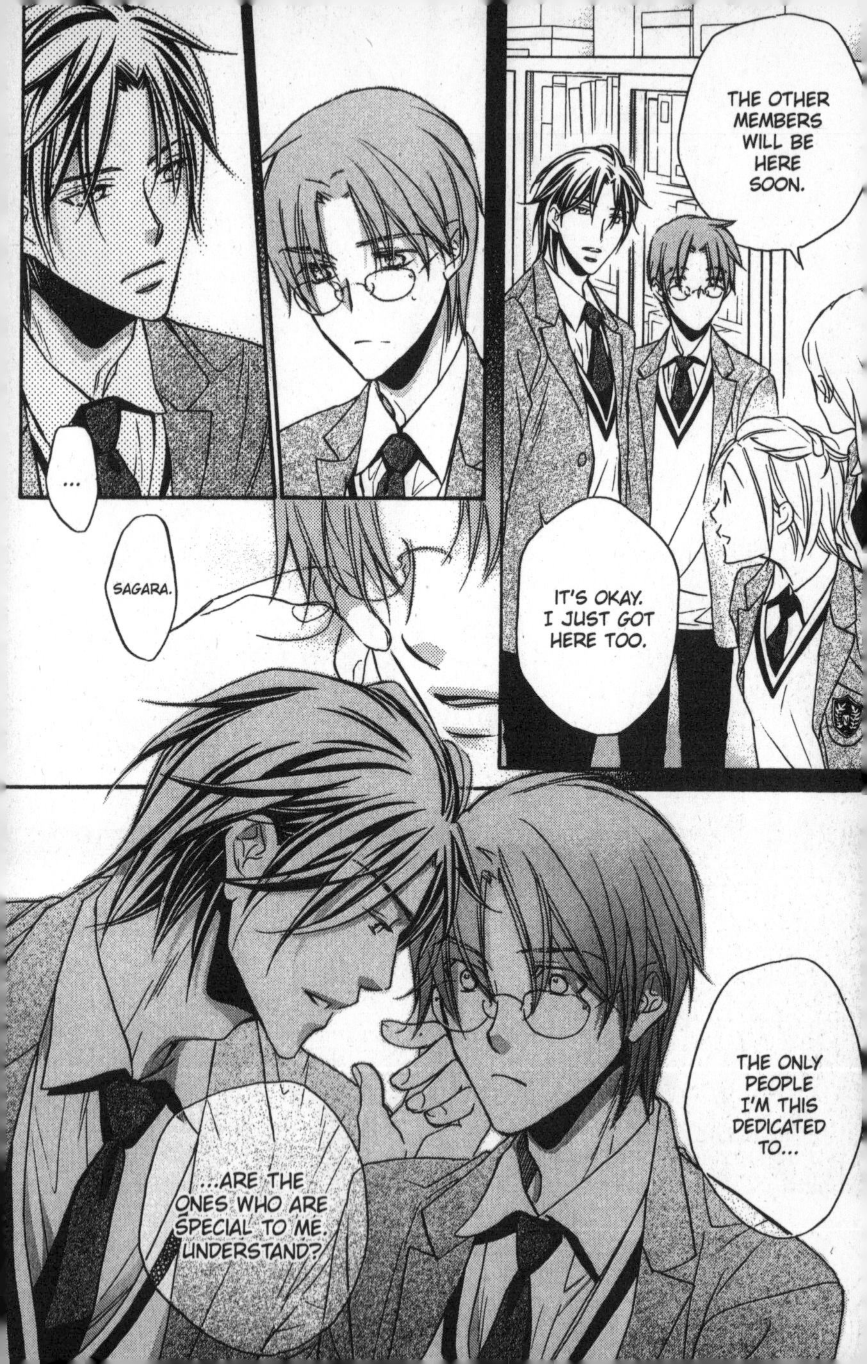
THE OTHER MEMBERS WILL BE HERE SOON.
IT'S OKAY. I JUST GOT HERE TOO.
...
SAGARA.
THE ONLY PEOPLE I'M THIS DEDICATED TO...
...ARE THE ONES WHO ARE SPECIAL TO ME. UNDERSTAND?

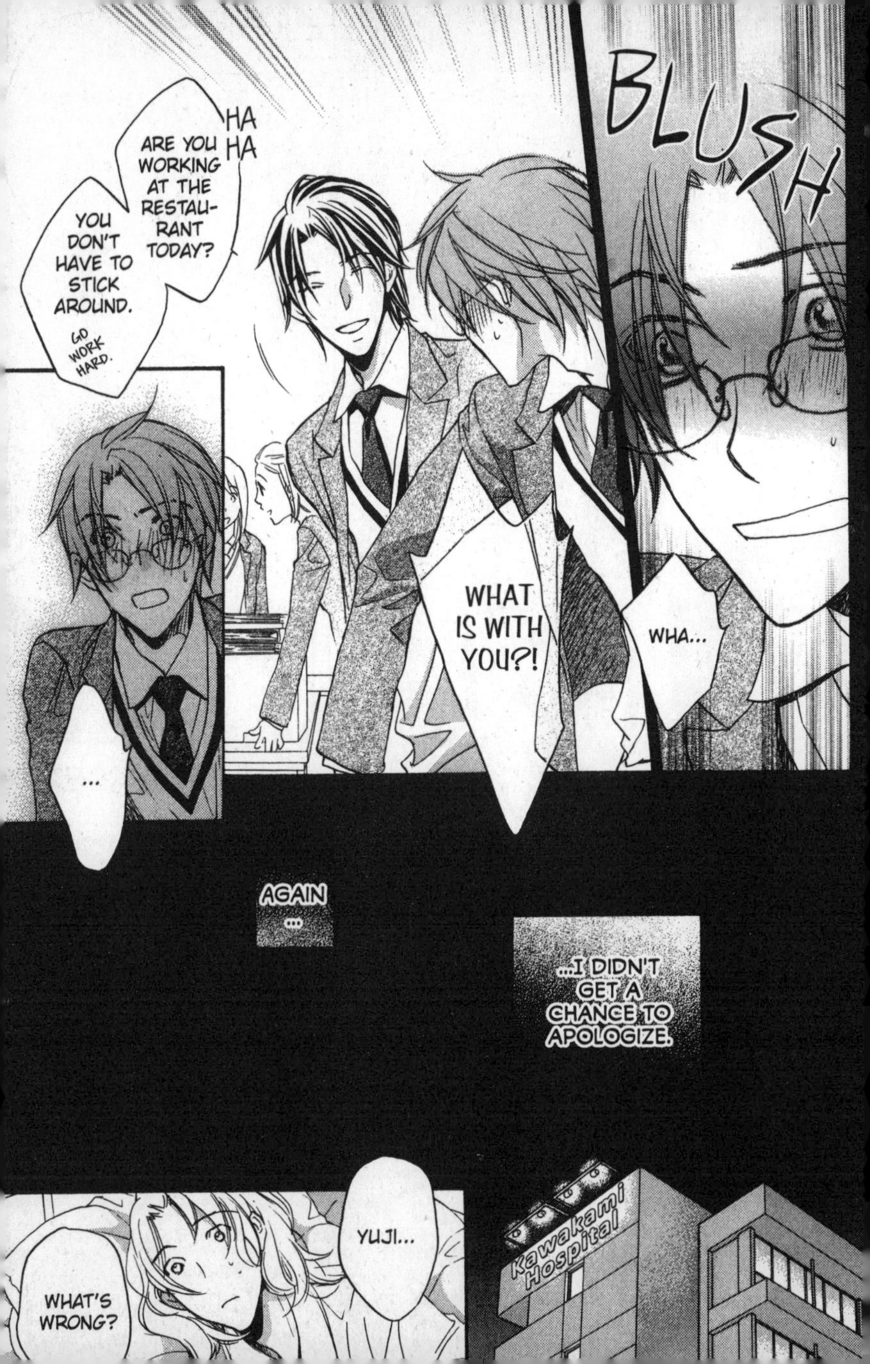
BLUSH
WHA...
HA HA
ARE YOU WORKING AT THE RESTAU-RANT TODAY?
YOU DON'T HAVE TO STICK AROUND.
GO WORK HARD.
WHAT IS WITH YOU?!
...
AGAIN ...
...I DIDN'T GET A CHANCE TO APOLOGIZE.
Kawakami Hospital
YUJI...
WHAT'S WRONG?

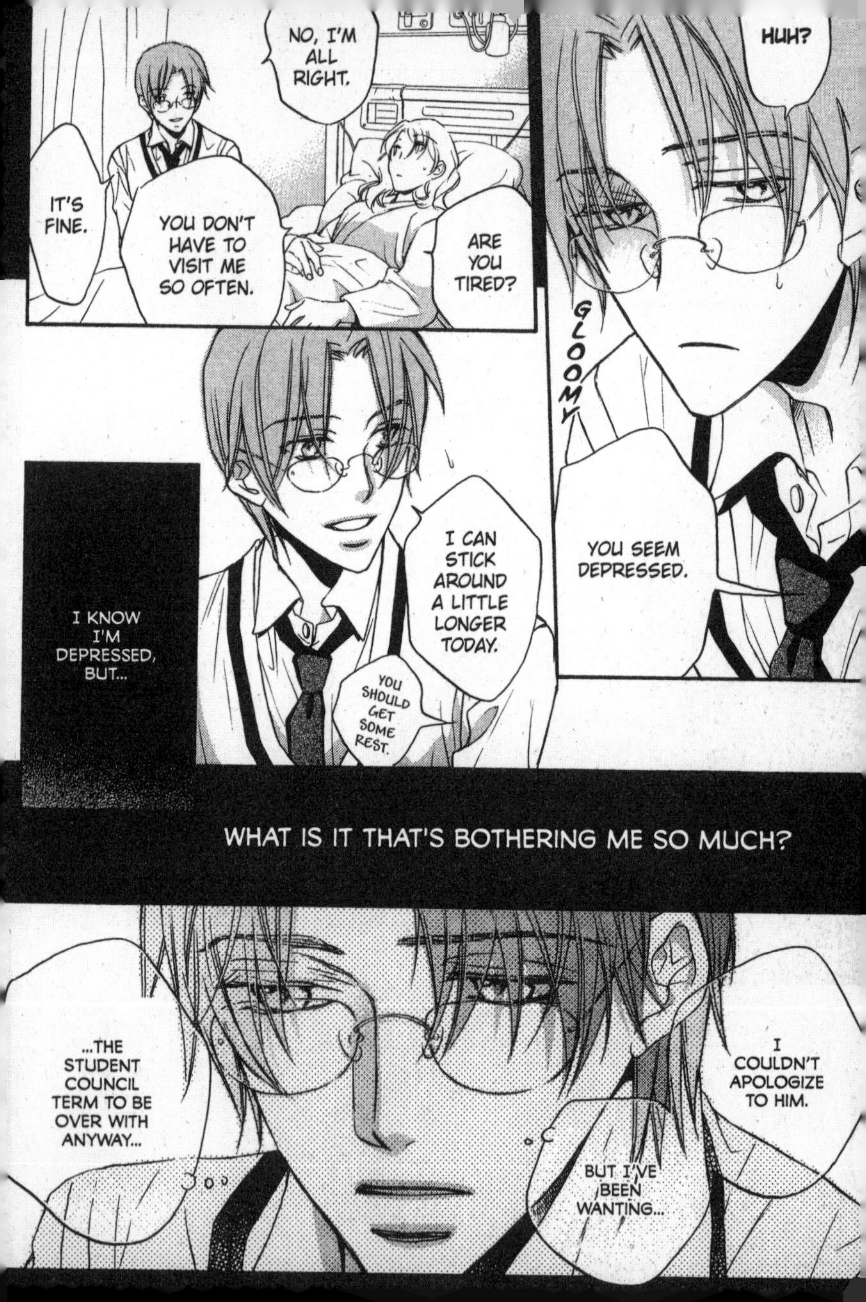
HUH?
GLOOMY
YOU SEEM DEPRESSED.
NO, I'M ALL RIGHT.
ARE YOU TIRED?
YOU DON'T HAVE TO VISIT ME SO OFTEN.
IT'S FINE.
I CAN STICK AROUND A LITTLE LONGER TODAY.
YOU SHOULD GET SOME REST.
I KNOW I'M DEPRESSED, BUT...
WHAT IS IT THAT'S BOTHERING ME SO MUCH?
I COULDN'T APOLOGIZE TO HIM.
BUT I'VE BEEN WANTING...
...THE STUDENT COUNCIL TERM TO BE OVER WITH ANYWAY...

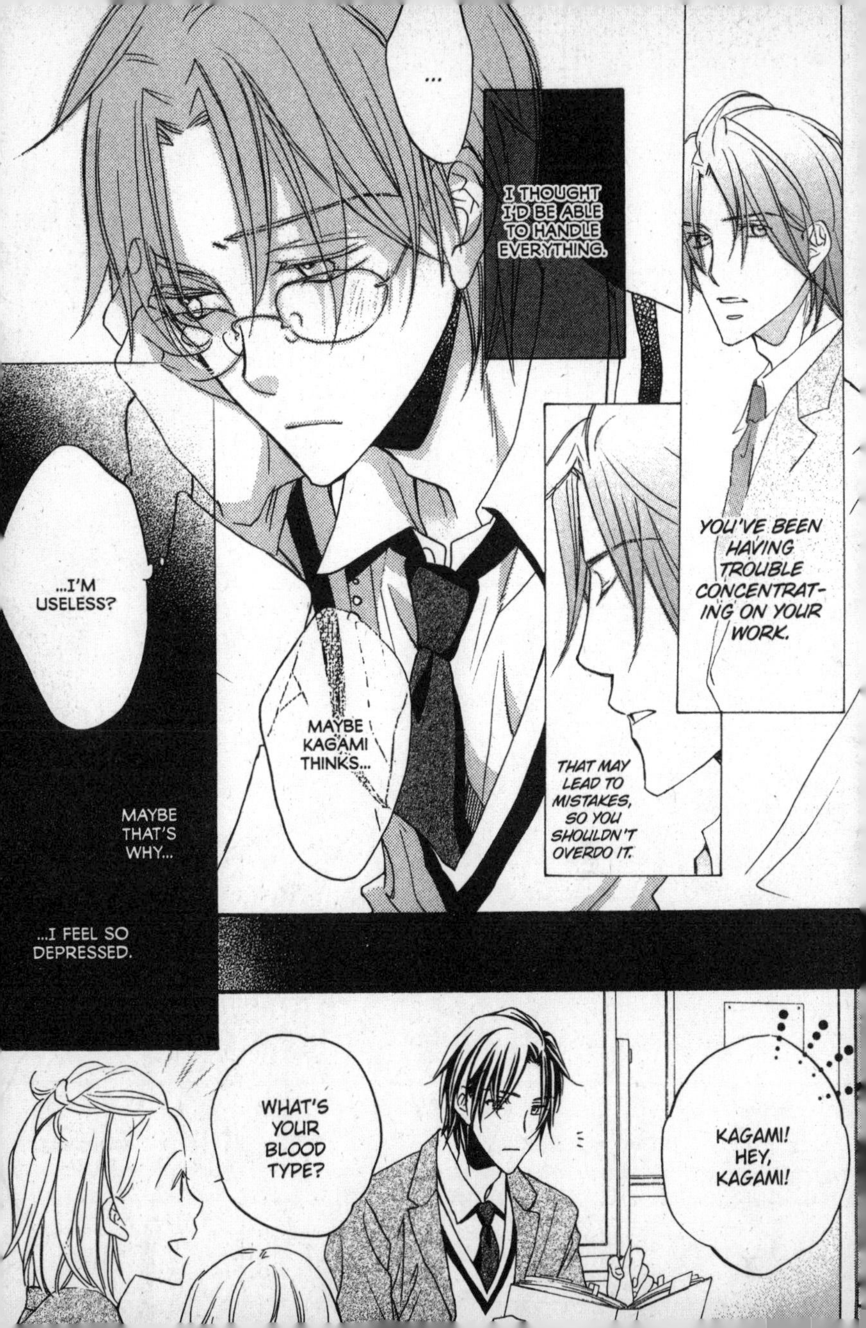
YOU'VE BEEN HAVING TROUBLE CONCENTRAT-ING ON YOUR WORK.
THAT MAY LEAD TO MISTAKES, SO YOU SHOULDN'T OVERDO IT.
...
I THOUGHT I'D BE ABLE TO HANDLE EVERYTHING.
MAYBE KAGAMI THINKS...
...I'M USELESS?
MAYBE THAT'S WHY...
...I FEEL SO DEPRESSED.
KAGAMI! HEY, KAGAMI!
WHAT'S YOUR BLOOD TYPE?

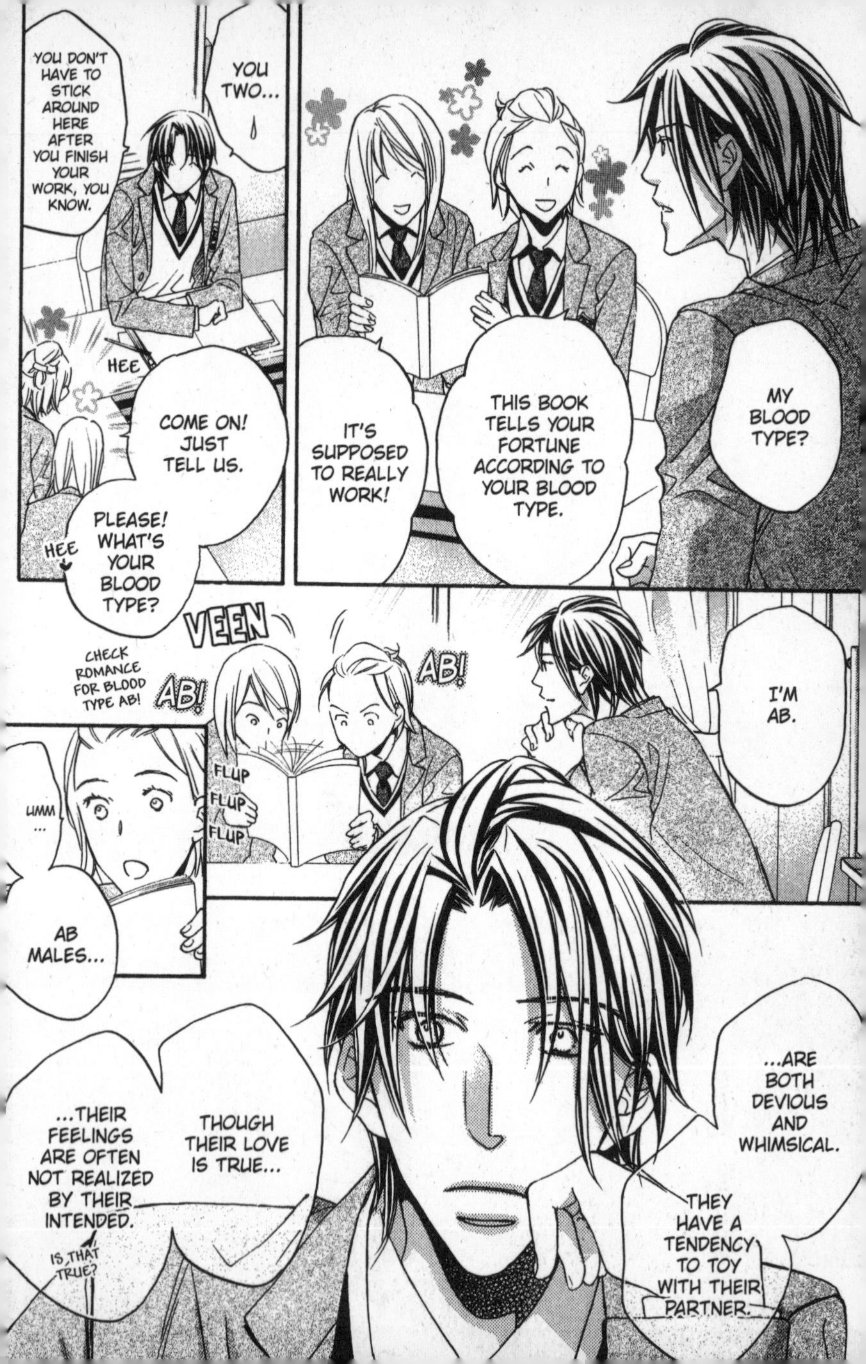
MY BLOOD TYPE?
THIS BOOK TELLS YOUR FORTUNE ACCORDING TO YOUR BLOOD TYPE.
IT'S SUPPOSED TO REALLY WORK!
YOU TWO...
YOU DON'T HAVE TO STICK AROUND HERE AFTER YOU FINISH YOUR WORK, YOU KNOW.
HEE
COME ON! JUST TELL US.
HEE
PLEASE! WHAT'S YOUR BLOOD TYPE?
I'M AB.
AB!
VEEN
AB!
CHECK ROMANCE FOR BLOOD TYPE AB!
FLUP
FLUP
FLUP
UMM ...
AB MALES...
...ARE BOTH DEVIOUS AND WHIMSICAL.
THEY HAVE A TENDENCY TO TOY WITH THEIR PARTNER.
THOUGH THEIR LOVE IS TRUE...
...THEIR FEELINGS ARE OFTEN NOT REALIZED BY THEIR INTENDED.
IS THAT TRUE?

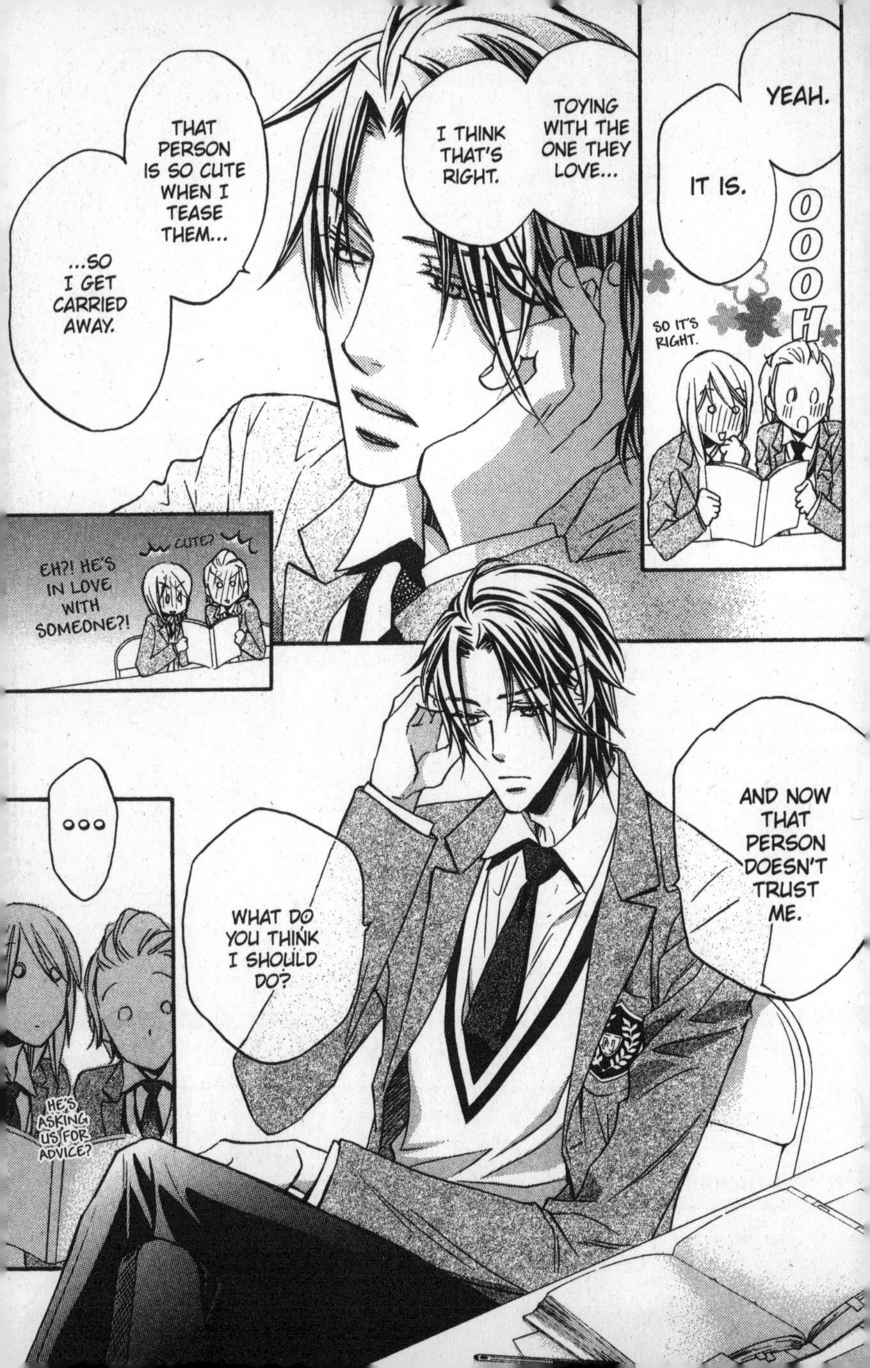
YEAH.
IT IS.
OOOOH
SO IT'S RIGHT.
TOYING WITH THE ONE THEY LOVE...
I THINK THAT'S RIGHT.
THAT PERSON IS SO CUTE WHEN I TEASE THEM...
...SO I GET CARRIED AWAY.
CUTE?
EH?! HE'S IN LOVE WITH SOMEONE?!
AND NOW THAT PERSON DOESN'T TRUST ME.
WHAT DO YOU THINK I SHOULD DO?
...
HE'S ASKING US FOR ADVICE?

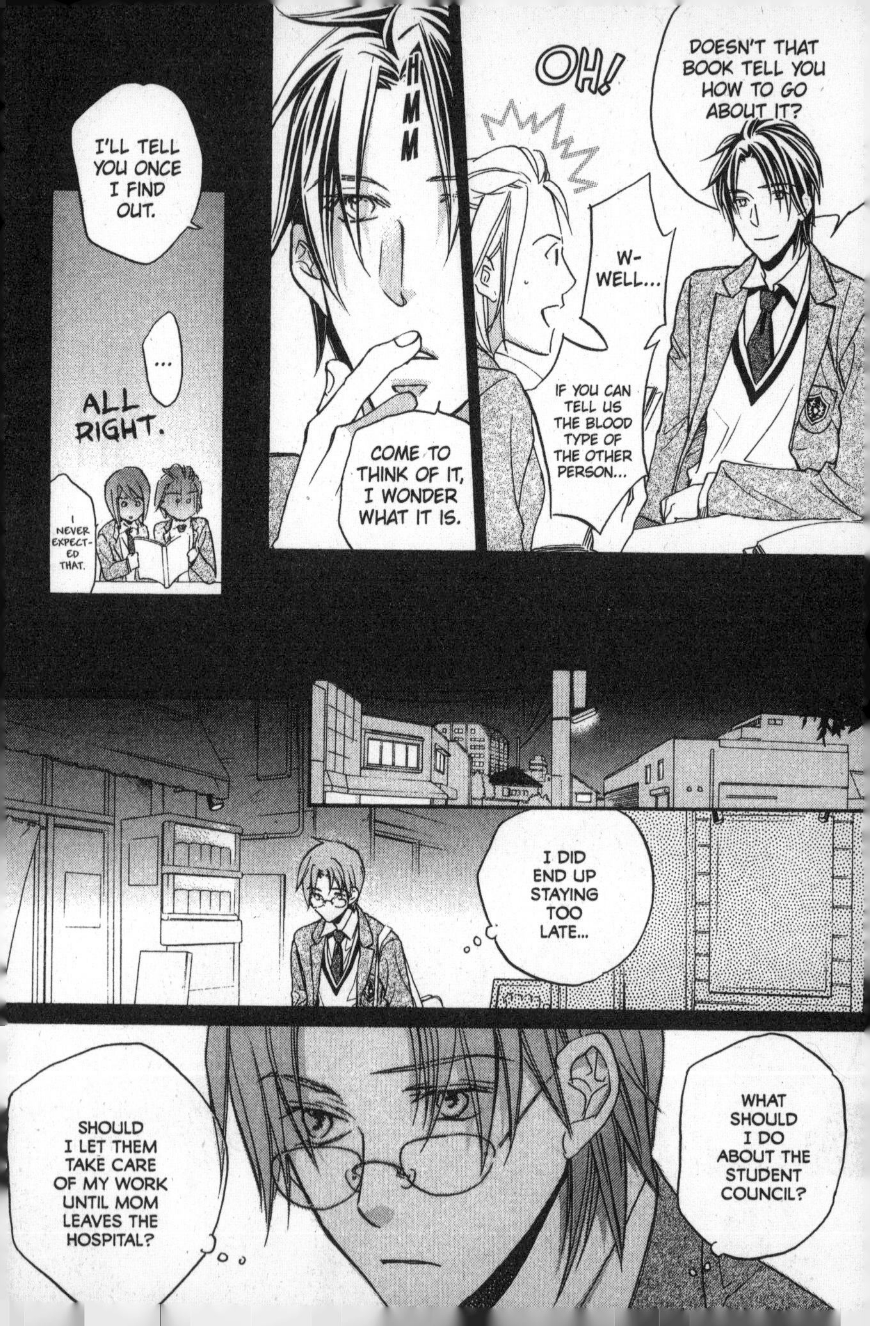
DOESN'T THAT BOOK TELL YOU HOW TO GO ABOUT IT?
OH!
W-WELL...
IF YOU CAN TELL US THE BLOOD TYPE OF THE OTHER PERSON...
HMM
COME TO THINK OF IT, I WONDER WHAT IT IS.
I'LL TELL YOU ONCE I FIND OUT.
...
ALL RIGHT.
I NEVER EXPECT-ED THAT.
I DID END UP STAYING TOO LATE...
WHAT SHOULD I DO ABOUT THE STUDENT COUNCIL?
SHOULD I LET THEM TAKE CARE OF MY WORK UNTIL MOM LEAVES THE HOSPITAL?

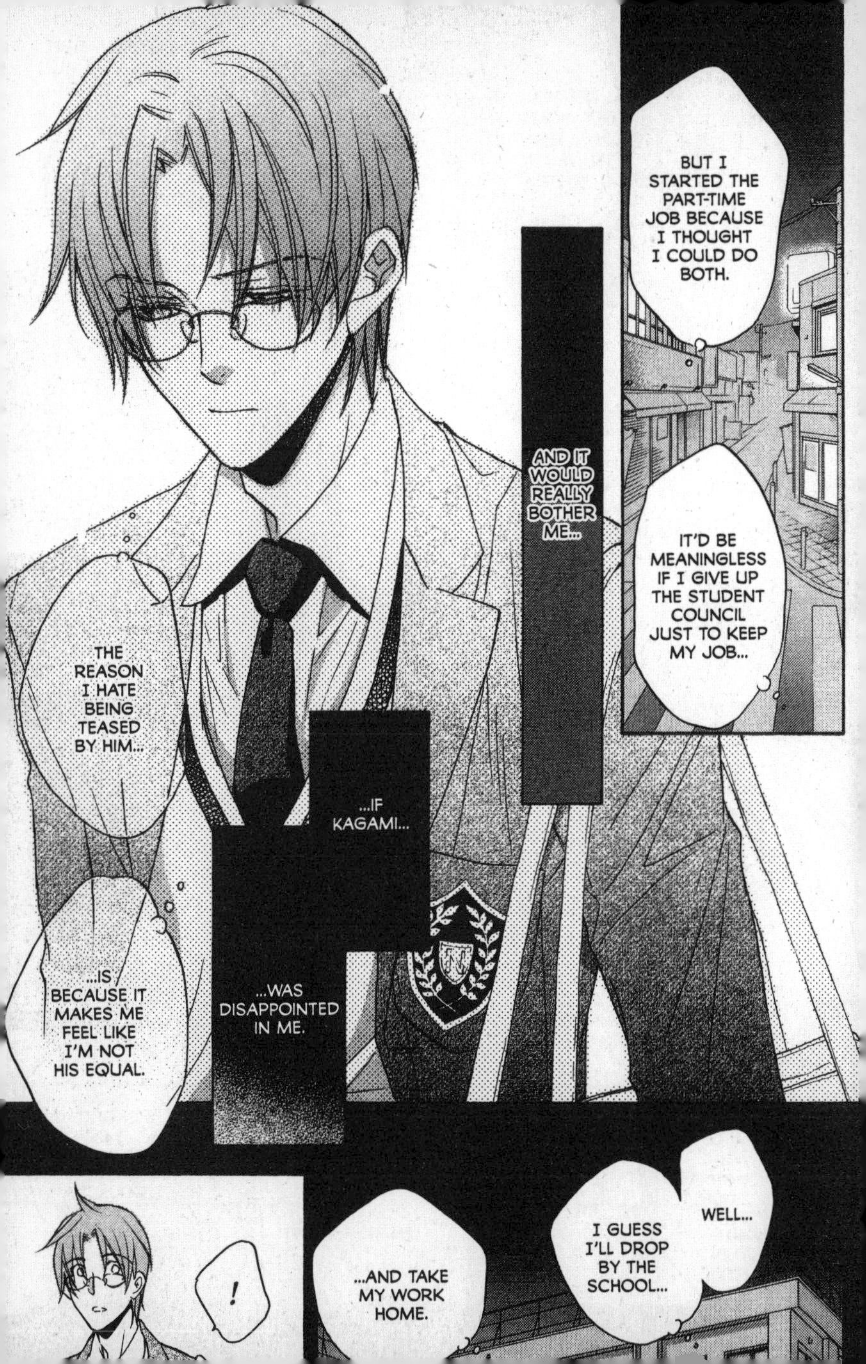
BUT I STARTED THE PART-TIME JOB BECAUSE I THOUGHT I COULD DO BOTH.
IT'D BE MEANINGLESS IF I GIVE UP THE STUDENT COUNCIL JUST TO KEEP MY JOB...
AND IT WOULD REALLY BOTHER ME...
...IF KAGAMI...
...WAS DISAPPOINTED IN ME.
THE REASON I HATE BEING TEASED BY HIM...
...IS BECAUSE IT MAKES ME FEEL LIKE I'M NOT HIS EQUAL.
WELL...
I GUESS I'LL DROP BY THE SCHOOL...
...AND TAKE MY WORK HOME.
!

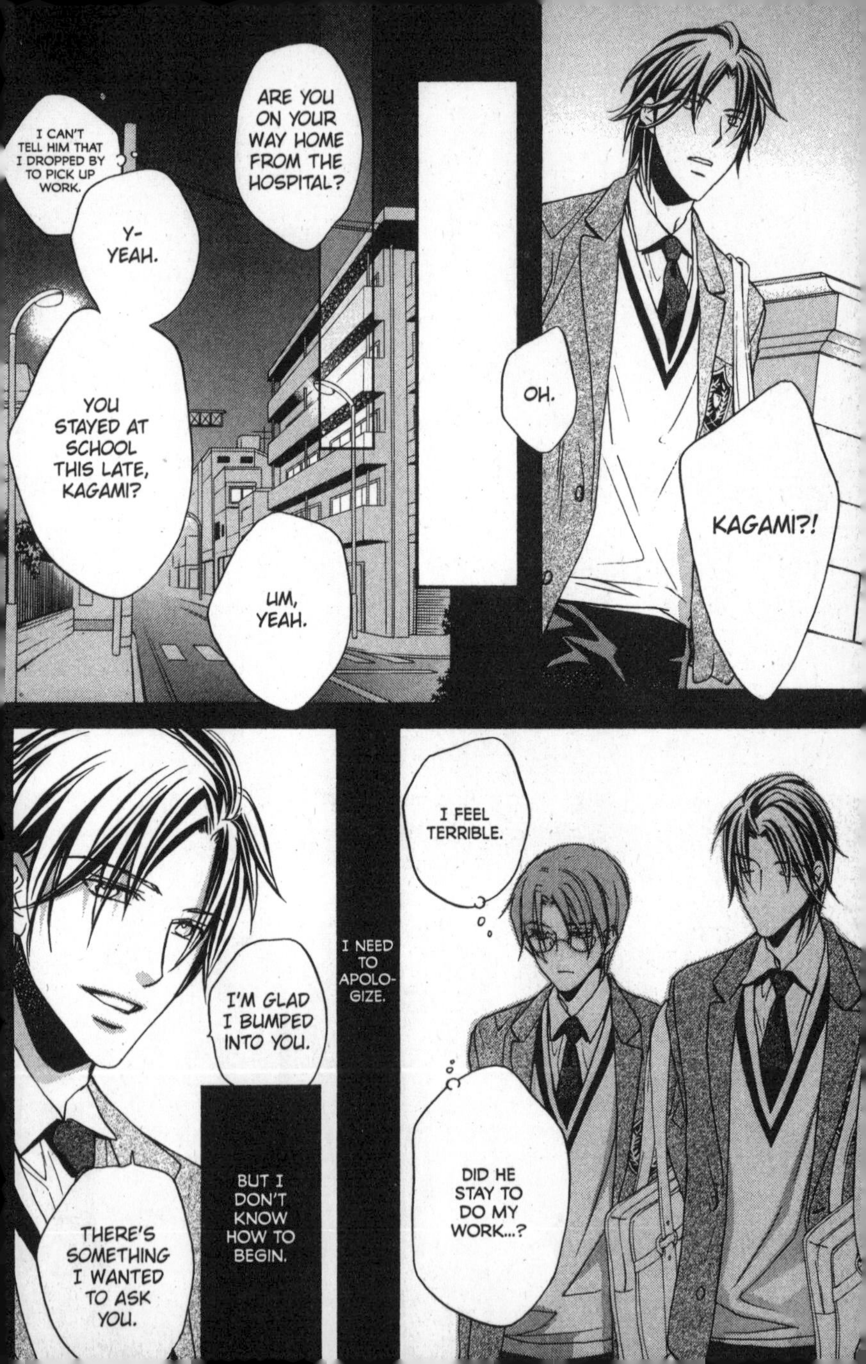
OH.
KAGAMI?!
ARE YOU ON YOUR WAY HOME FROM THE HOSPITAL?
I CAN'T TELL HIM THAT I DROPPED BY TO PICK UP WORK.
Y-YEAH.
YOU STAYED AT SCHOOL THIS LATE, KAGAMI?
UM, YEAH.
I FEEL TERRIBLE.
DID HE STAY TO DO MY WORK...?
I NEED TO APOLO-GIZE.
BUT I DON'T KNOW HOW TO BEGIN.
I'M GLAD I BUMPED INTO YOU.
THERE'S SOMETHING I WANTED TO ASK YOU.

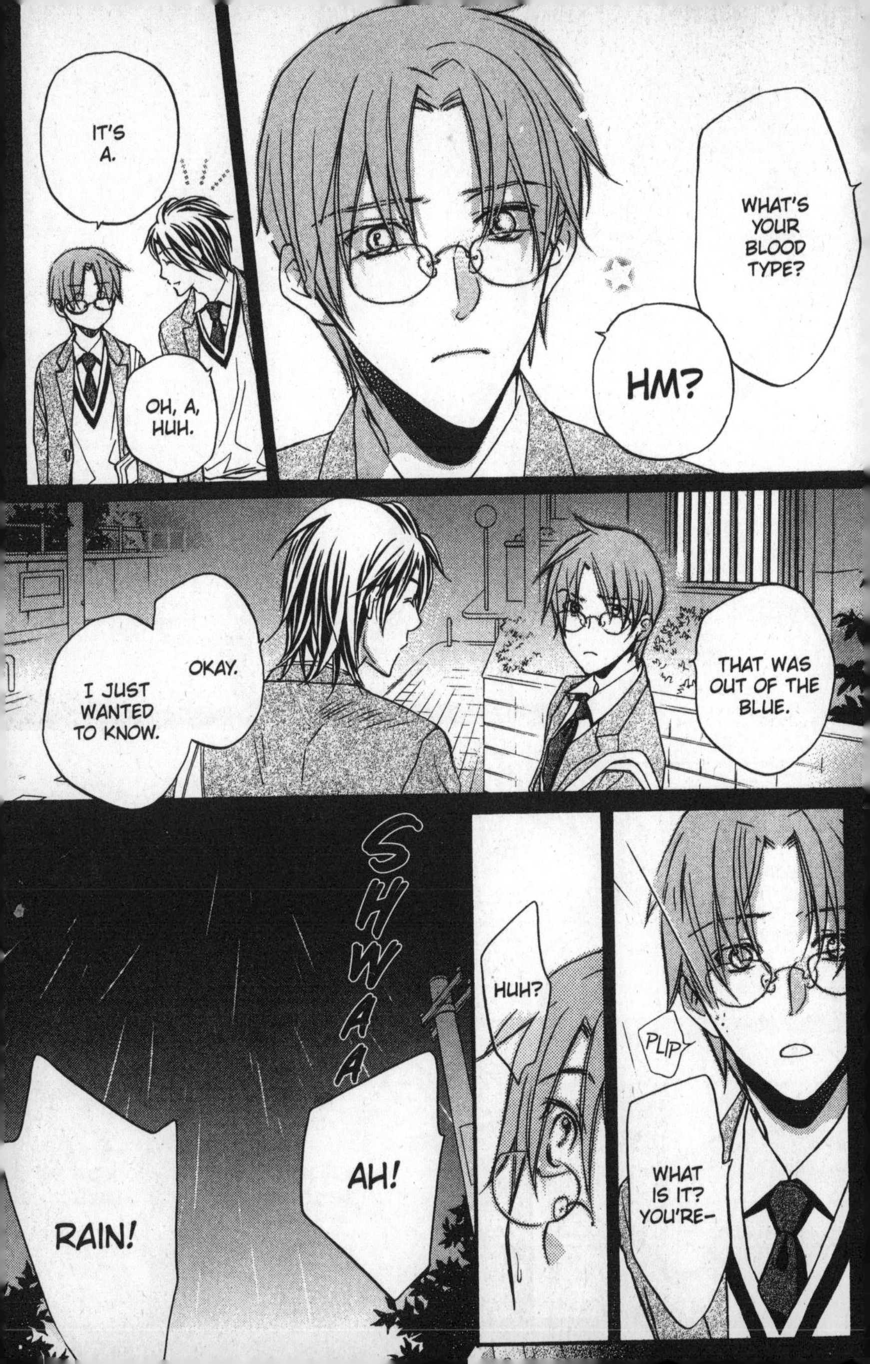
WHAT'S YOUR BLOOD TYPE?
HM?
IT'S A.
OH, A, HUH.
THAT WAS OUT OF THE BLUE.
OKAY.
I JUST WANTED TO KNOW.
PLIP
WHAT IS IT? YOU'RE-
HUH?
SHWAAA
AH!
RAIN!

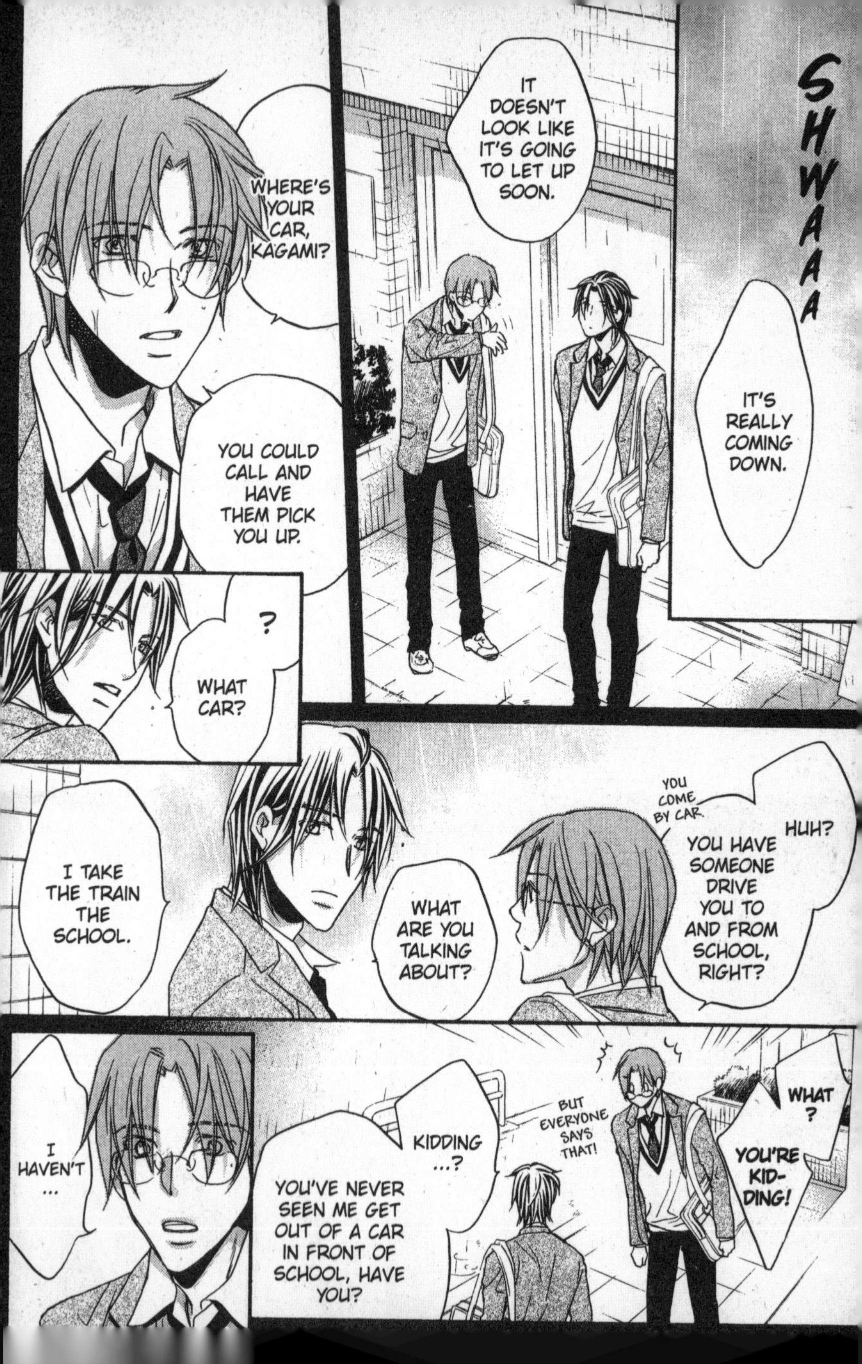
SHWAAAA
IT'S REALLY COMING DOWN.
IT DOESN'T LOOK LIKE IT'S GOING TO LET UP SOON.
WHERE'S YOUR CAR, KAGAMI?
YOU COULD CALL AND HAVE THEM PICK YOU UP.
?
WHAT CAR?
HUH?
YOU HAVE SOMEONE DRIVE YOU TO AND FROM SCHOOL, RIGHT?
YOU COME BY CAR.
WHAT ARE YOU TALKING ABOUT?
I TAKE THE TRAIN THE SCHOOL.
WHAT?
YOU'RE KID-DING!
BUT EVERYONE SAYS THAT!
KIDDING ...?
YOU'VE NEVER SEEN ME GET OUT OF A CAR IN FRONT OF SCHOOL, HAVE YOU?
I HAVEN'T ...

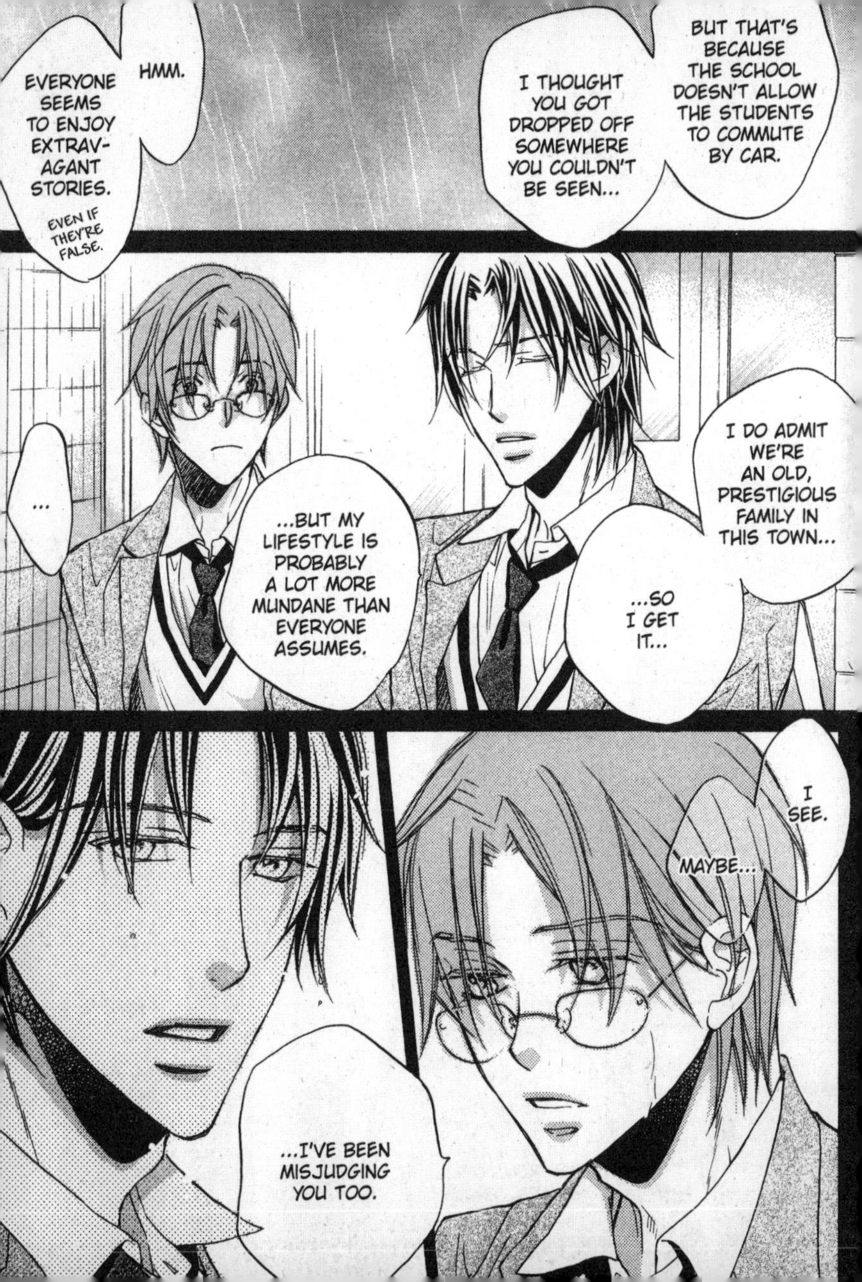
BUT THAT'S BECAUSE THE SCHOOL DOESN'T ALLOW THE STUDENTS TO COMMUTE BY CAR.
I THOUGHT YOU GOT DROPPED OFF SOMEWHERE YOU COULDN'T BE SEEN...
HMM.
EVERYONE SEEMS TO ENJOY EXTRAV-AGANT STORIES.
EVEN IF THEY'RE FALSE.
I DO ADMIT WE'RE AN OLD, PRESTIGIOUS FAMILY IN THIS TOWN...
...SO I GET IT...
...BUT MY LIFESTYLE IS PROBABLY A LOT MORE MUNDANE THAN EVERYONE ASSUMES.
...
I SEE.
MAYBE...
...I'VE BEEN MISJUDGING YOU TOO.

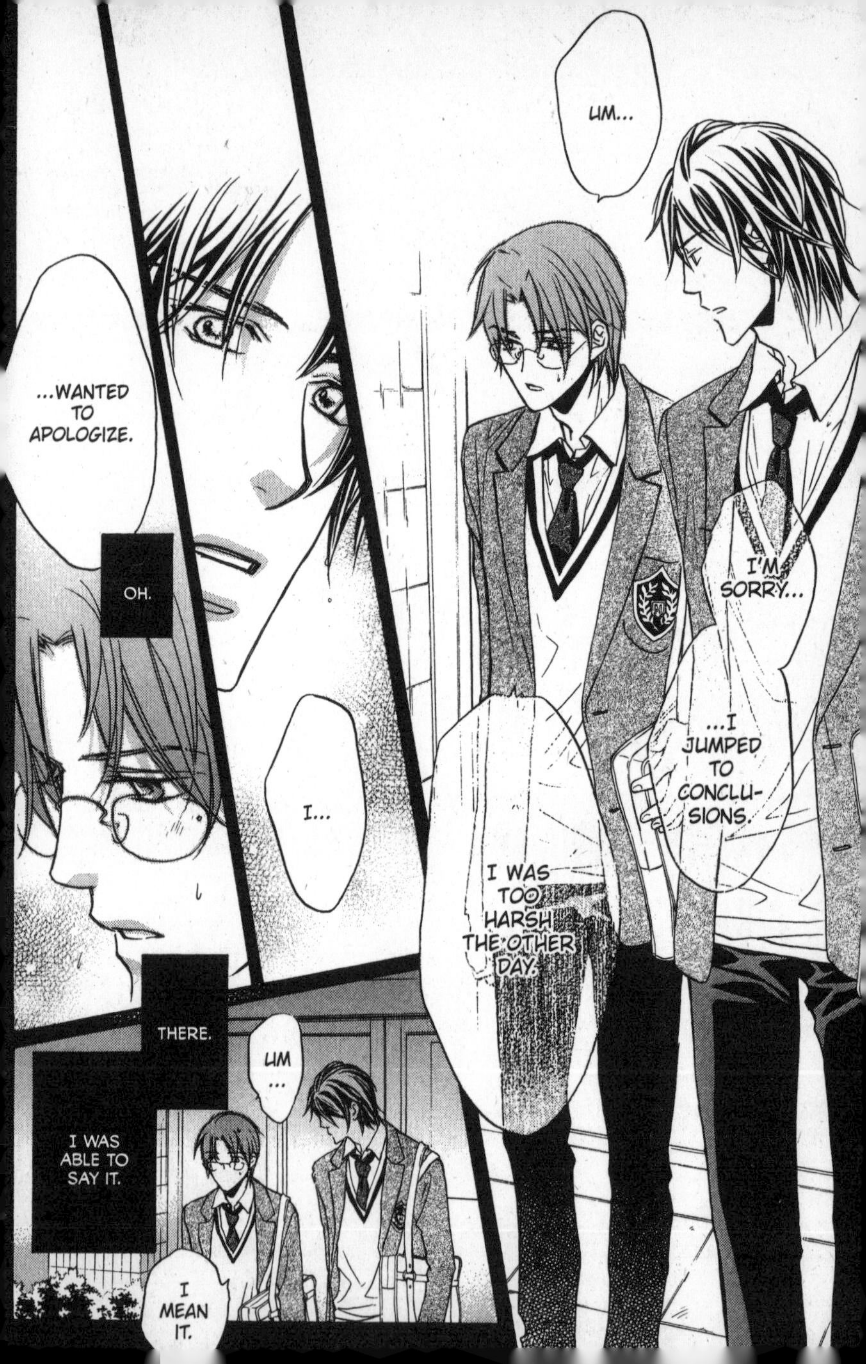
UM...
I'M SORRY...
...I JUMPED TO CONCLUSIONS.
I WAS TOO HARSH THE OTHER DAY.
I...
...WANTED TO APOLOGIZE.
OH.
THERE.
UM ...
I WAS ABLE TO SAY IT.
I MEAN IT.

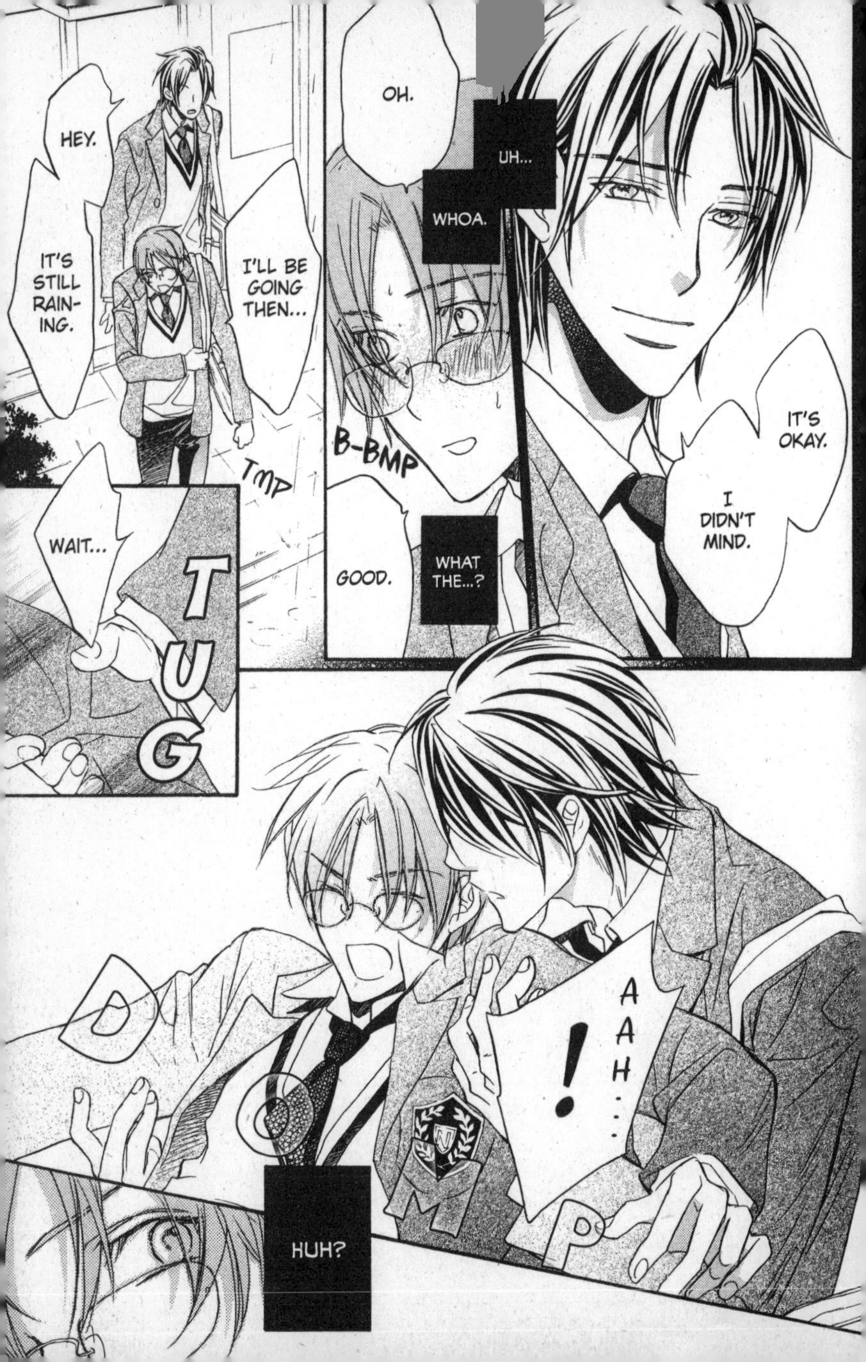
OH.
UH...
WHOA.
IT'S OKAY.
I DIDN'T MIND.
B-BMP
WHAT THE...?
GOOD.
I'LL BE GOING THEN...
TMP
HEY.
IT'S STILL RAIN-ING.
WAIT...
TUG
AAH...
!
DOMP
HUH?

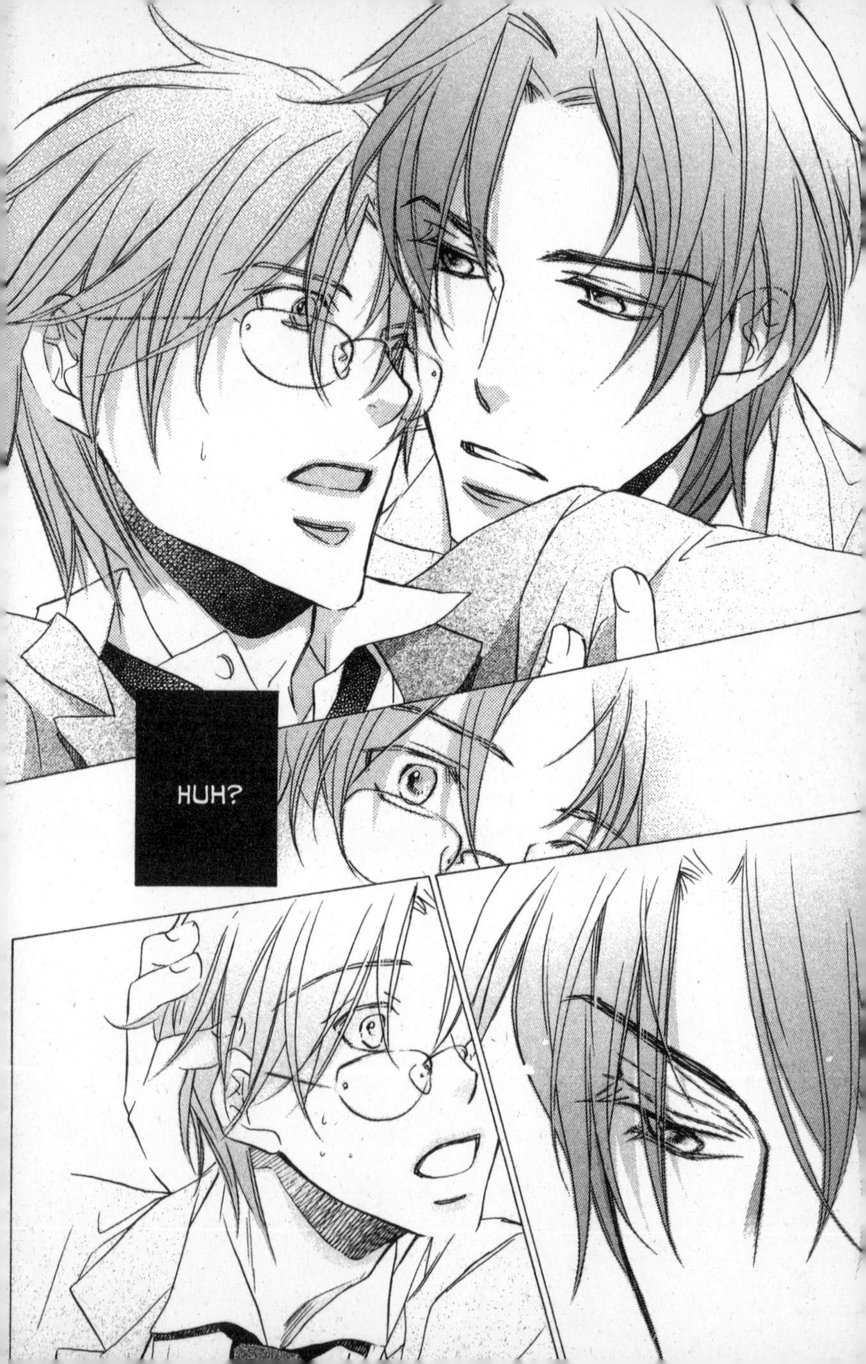
HUH?

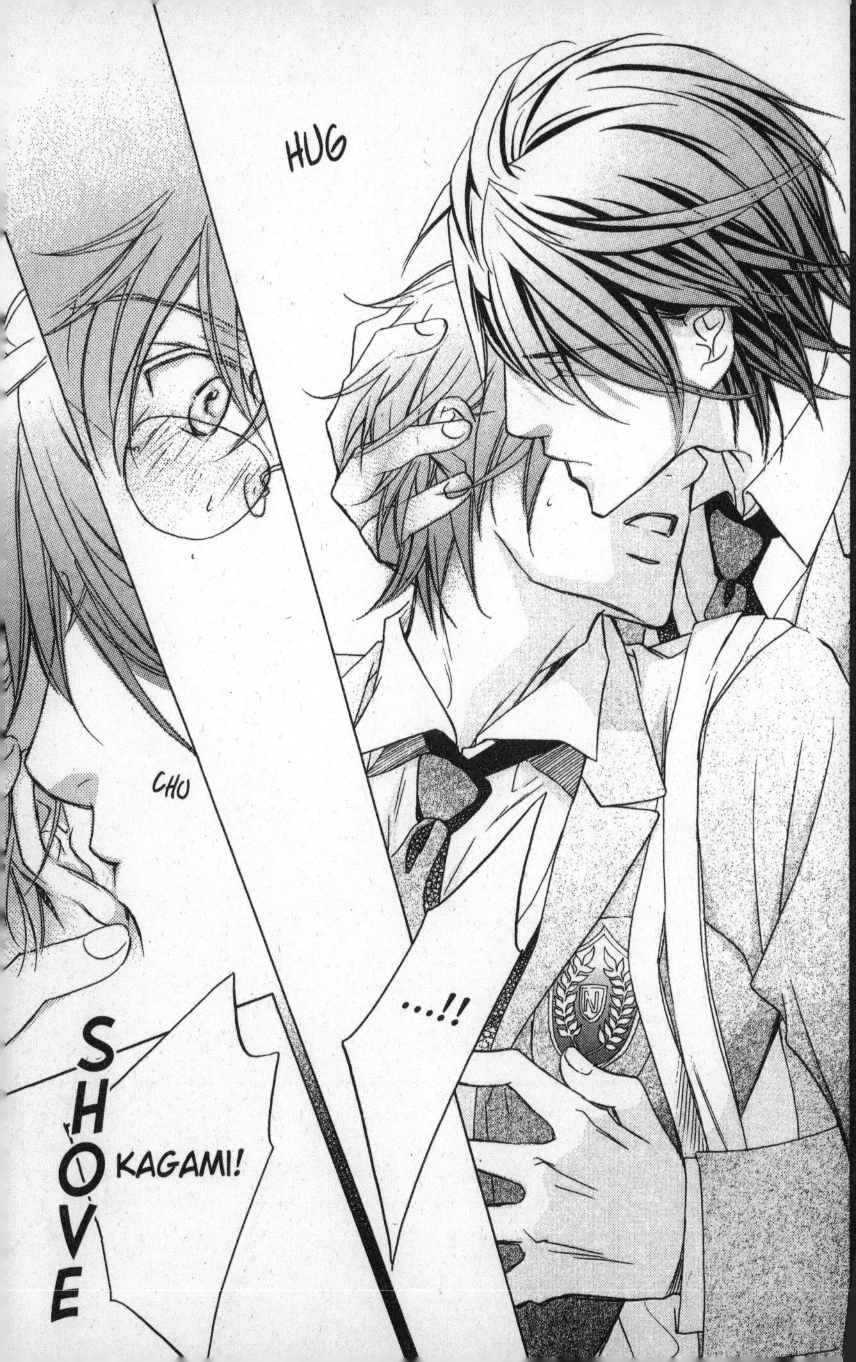
HUG
...!!
CHU
SHOVE
KAGAMI!

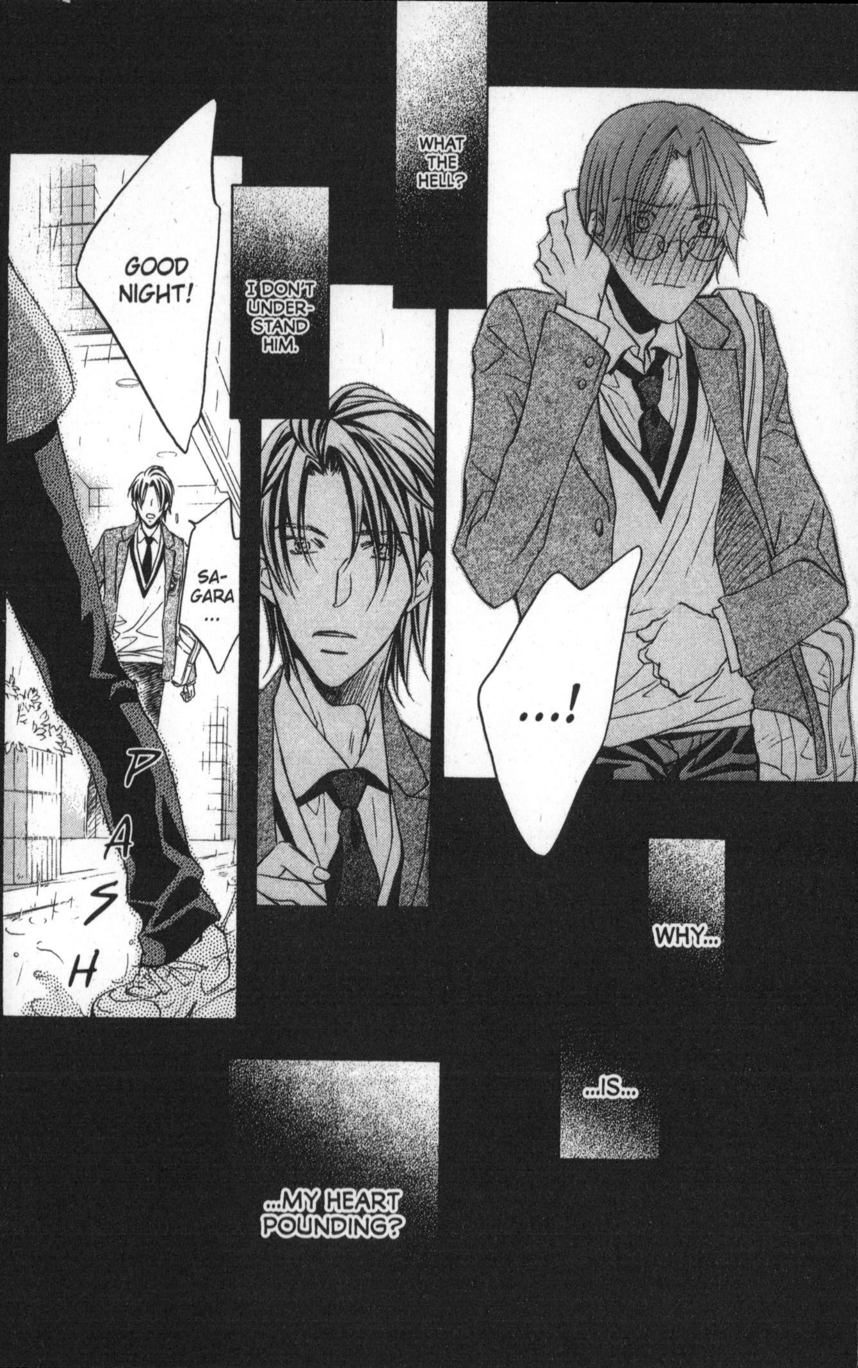
...!
WHAT THE HELL?
I DON'T UNDERSTAND HIM.
GOOD NIGHT!
SA-GARA ...
PASH
WHY...
...IS...
...MY HEART POUNDING?

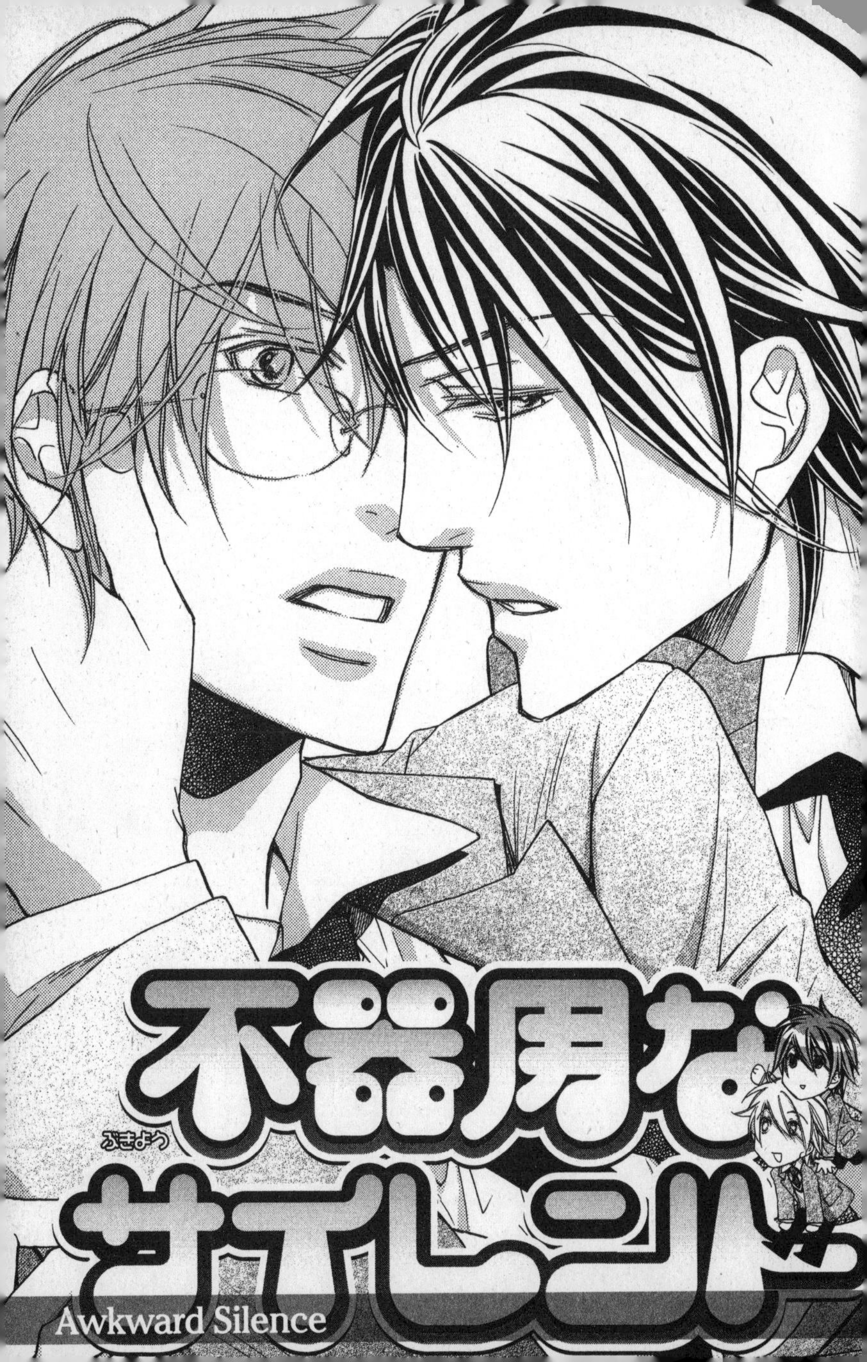
ぶきよう
不器用なサイレント
Awkward Silence

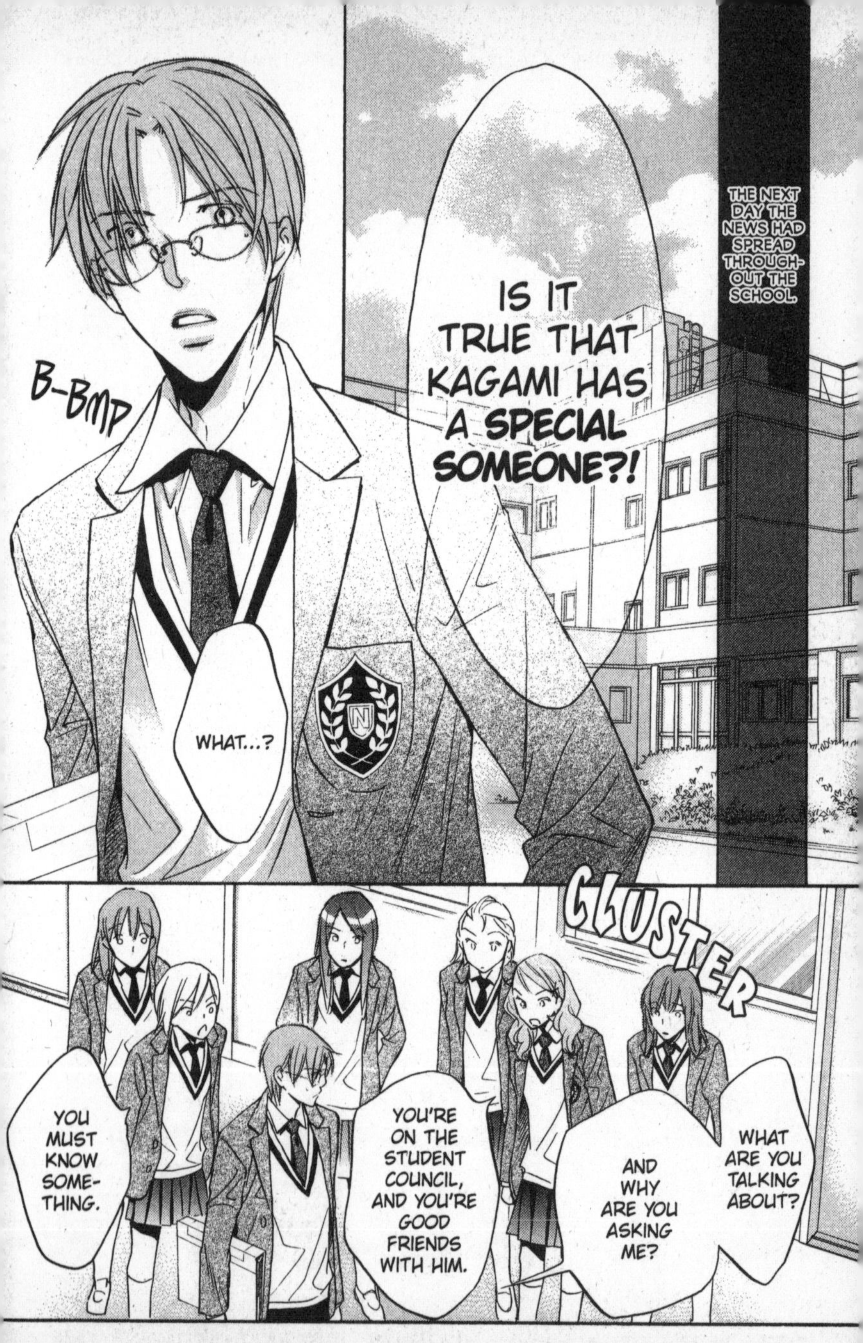
THE NEXT DAY THE NEWS HAD SPREAD THROUGH-OUT THE SCHOOL.
IS IT TRUE THAT KAGAMI HAS A SPECIAL SOMEONE?!
B-BMP
WHAT...?
CLUSTER
WHAT ARE YOU TALKING ABOUT?
AND WHY ARE YOU ASKING ME?
YOU'RE ON THE STUDENT COUNCIL, AND YOU'RE GOOD FRIENDS WITH HIM.
YOU MUST KNOW SOME-THING.

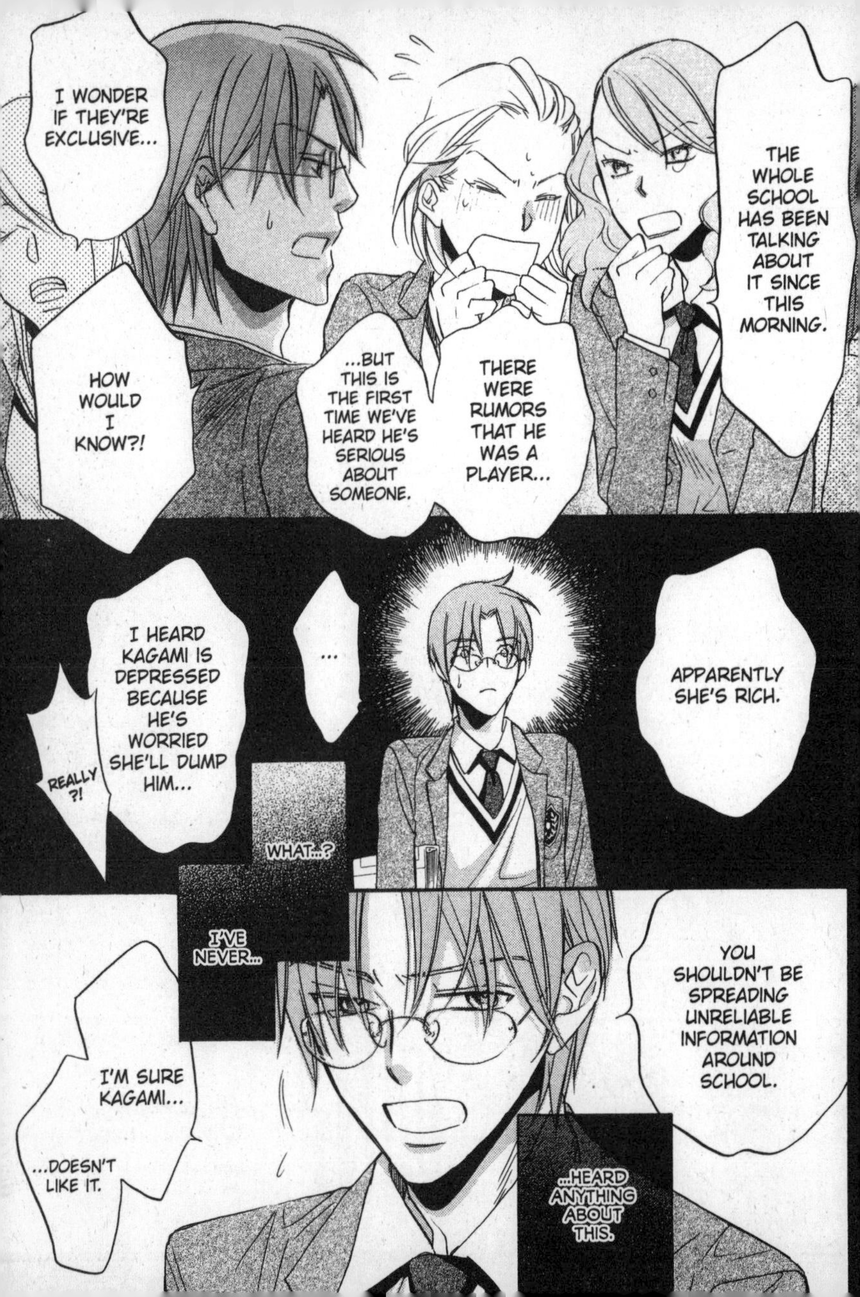
THE WHOLE SCHOOL HAS BEEN TALKING ABOUT IT SINCE THIS MORNING.
THERE WERE RUMORS THAT HE WAS A PLAYER...
...BUT THIS IS THE FIRST TIME WE'VE HEARD HE'S SERIOUS ABOUT SOMEONE.
I WONDER IF THEY'RE EXCLUSIVE...
HOW WOULD I KNOW?!
APPARENTLY SHE'S RICH.
...
I HEARD KAGAMI IS DEPRESSED BECAUSE HE'S WORRIED SHE'LL DUMP HIM...
REALLY ?!
WHAT...?
I'VE NEVER...
YOU SHOULDN'T BE SPREADING UNRELIABLE INFORMATION AROUND SCHOOL.
...HEARD ANYTHING ABOUT THIS.
I'M SURE KAGAMI...
...DOESN'T LIKE IT.

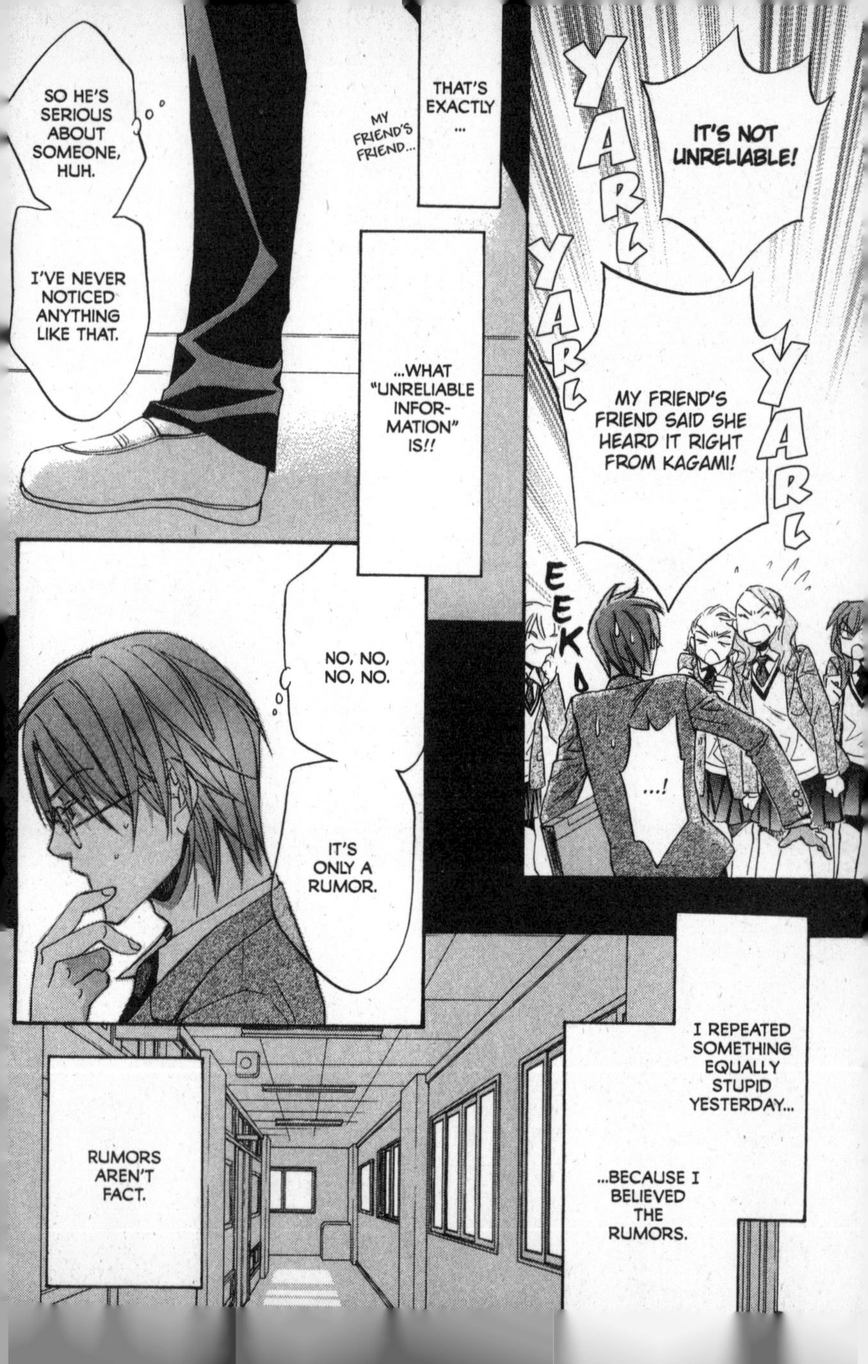
YARL YARL
IT'S NOT UNRELIABLE!
YARL YARL
YARL YARL
MY FRIEND'S FRIEND SAID SHE HEARD IT RIGHT FROM KAGAMI!
EEK
...!
THAT'S EXACTLY ...
MY FRIEND'S FRIEND...
...WHAT "UNRELIABLE INFORMATION" IS!!
SO HE'S SERIOUS ABOUT SOMEONE, HUH.
I'VE NEVER NOTICED ANYTHING LIKE THAT.
NO, NO, NO, NO.
IT'S ONLY A RUMOR.
I REPEATED SOMETHING EQUALLY STUPID YESTERDAY...
...BECAUSE I BELIEVED THE RUMORS.
RUMORS AREN'T FACT.

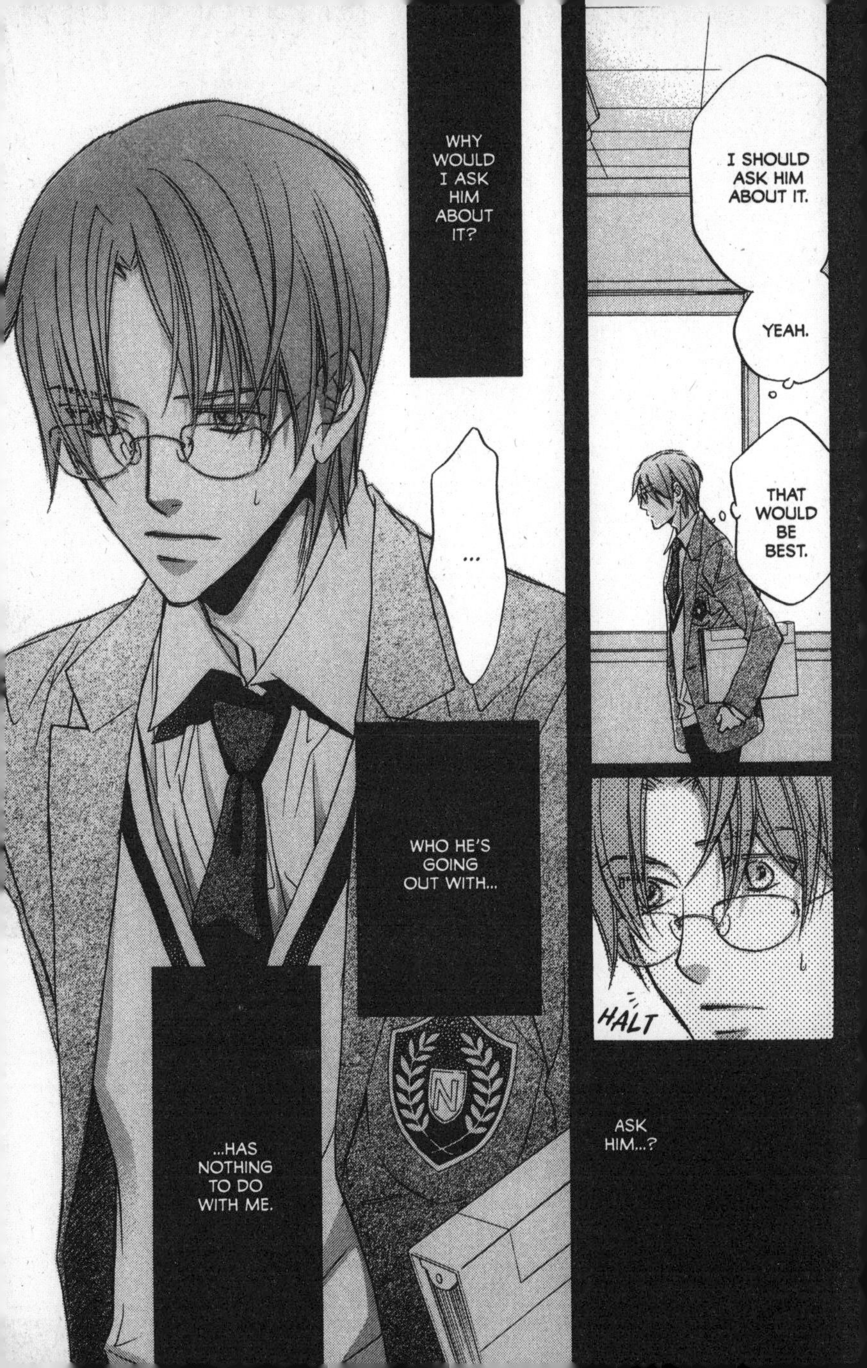
I SHOULD ASK HIM ABOUT IT.
YEAH.
THAT WOULD BE BEST.
HALT
ASK HIM...?
WHY WOULD I ASK HIM ABOUT IT?
...
WHO HE'S GOING OUT WITH...
...HAS NOTHING TO DO WITH ME.

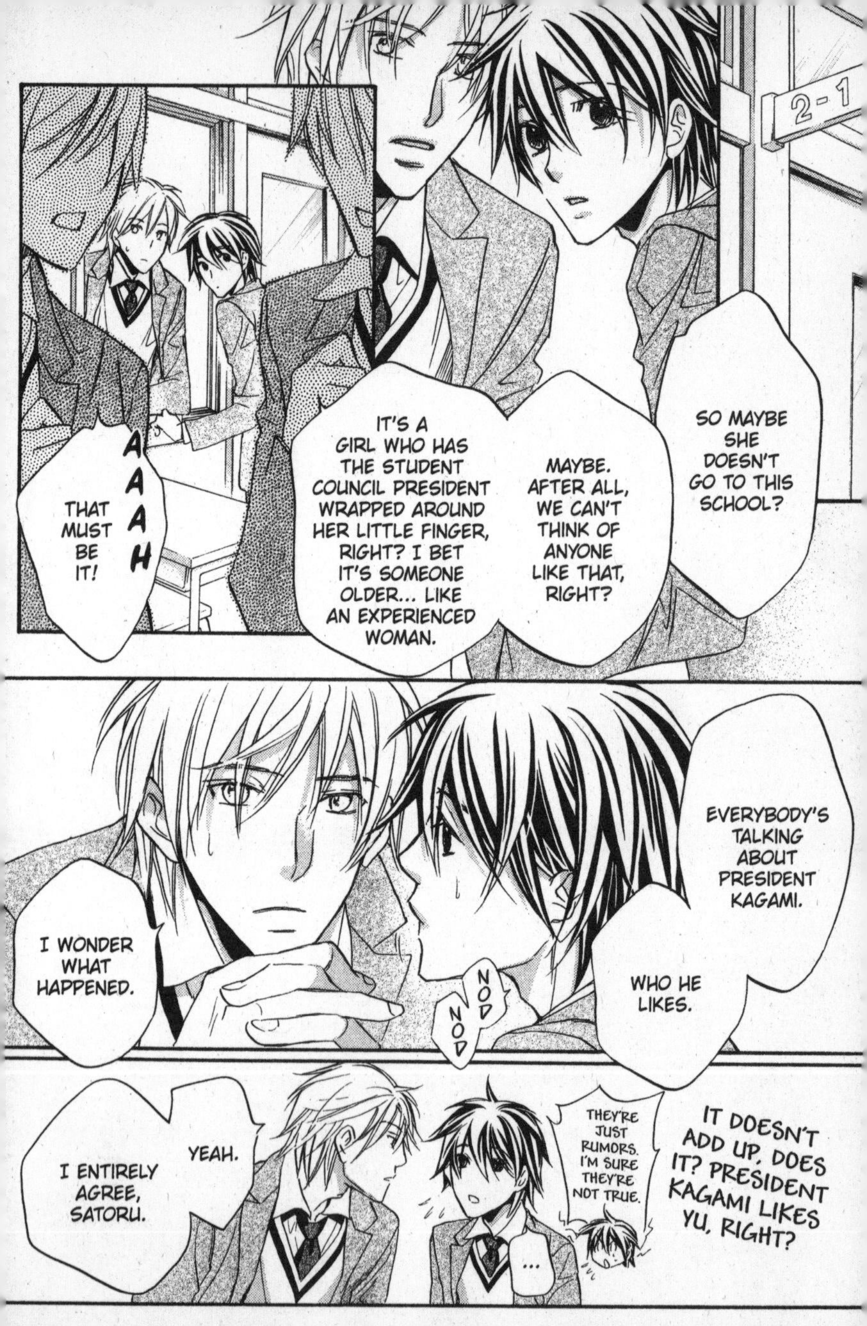
2-1
SO MAYBE SHE DOESN'T GO TO THIS SCHOOL?
MAYBE. AFTER ALL, WE CAN'T THINK OF ANYONE LIKE THAT, RIGHT?
IT'S A GIRL WHO HAS THE STUDENT COUNCIL PRESIDENT WRAPPED AROUND HER LITTLE FINGER, RIGHT? I BET IT'S SOMEONE OLDER... LIKE AN EXPERIENCED WOMAN.
AAAH
THAT MUST BE IT!
EVERYBODY'S TALKING ABOUT PRESIDENT KAGAMI.
WHO HE LIKES.
NOD NOD
I WONDER WHAT HAPPENED.
IT DOESN'T ADD UP, DOES IT? PRESIDENT KAGAMI LIKES YU, RIGHT?
THEY'RE JUST RUMORS. I'M SURE THEY'RE NOT TRUE.
...
YEAH.
I ENTIRELY AGREE, SATORU.

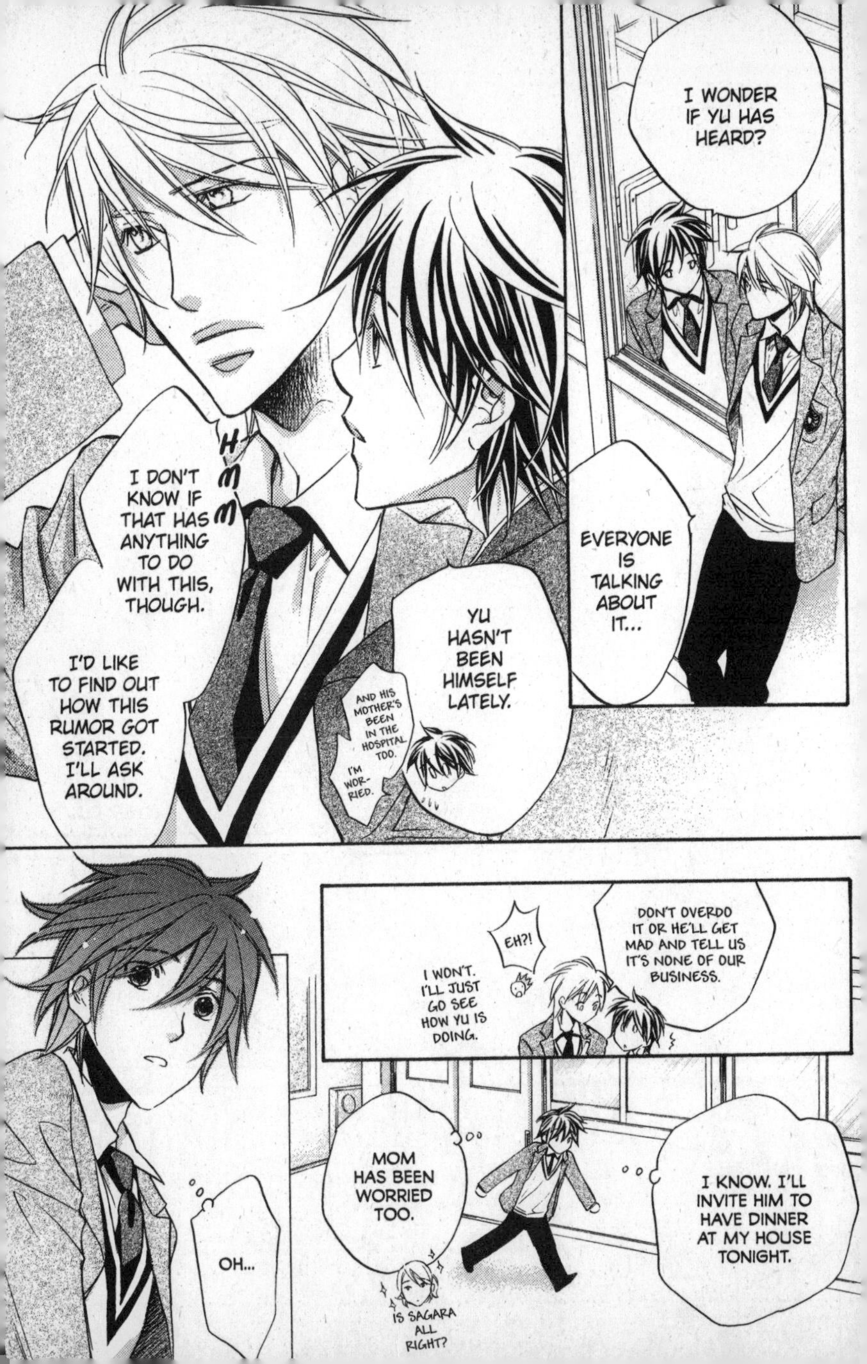
I WONDER IF YU HAS HEARD?
EVERYONE IS TALKING ABOUT IT...
YU HASN'T BEEN HIMSELF LATELY.
AND HIS MOTHER'S BEEN IN THE HOSPITAL TOO.
I'M WORRIED.
HMM
I DON'T KNOW IF THAT HAS ANYTHING TO DO WITH THIS, THOUGH.
I'D LIKE TO FIND OUT HOW THIS RUMOR GOT STARTED. I'LL ASK AROUND.
DON'T OVERDO IT OR HE'LL GET MAD AND TELL US IT'S NONE OF OUR BUSINESS.
EH?!
I WON'T. I'LL JUST GO SEE HOW YU IS DOING.
I KNOW. I'LL INVITE HIM TO HAVE DINNER AT MY HOUSE TONIGHT.
MOM HAS BEEN WORRIED TOO.
IS SAGARA ALL RIGHT?
OH...

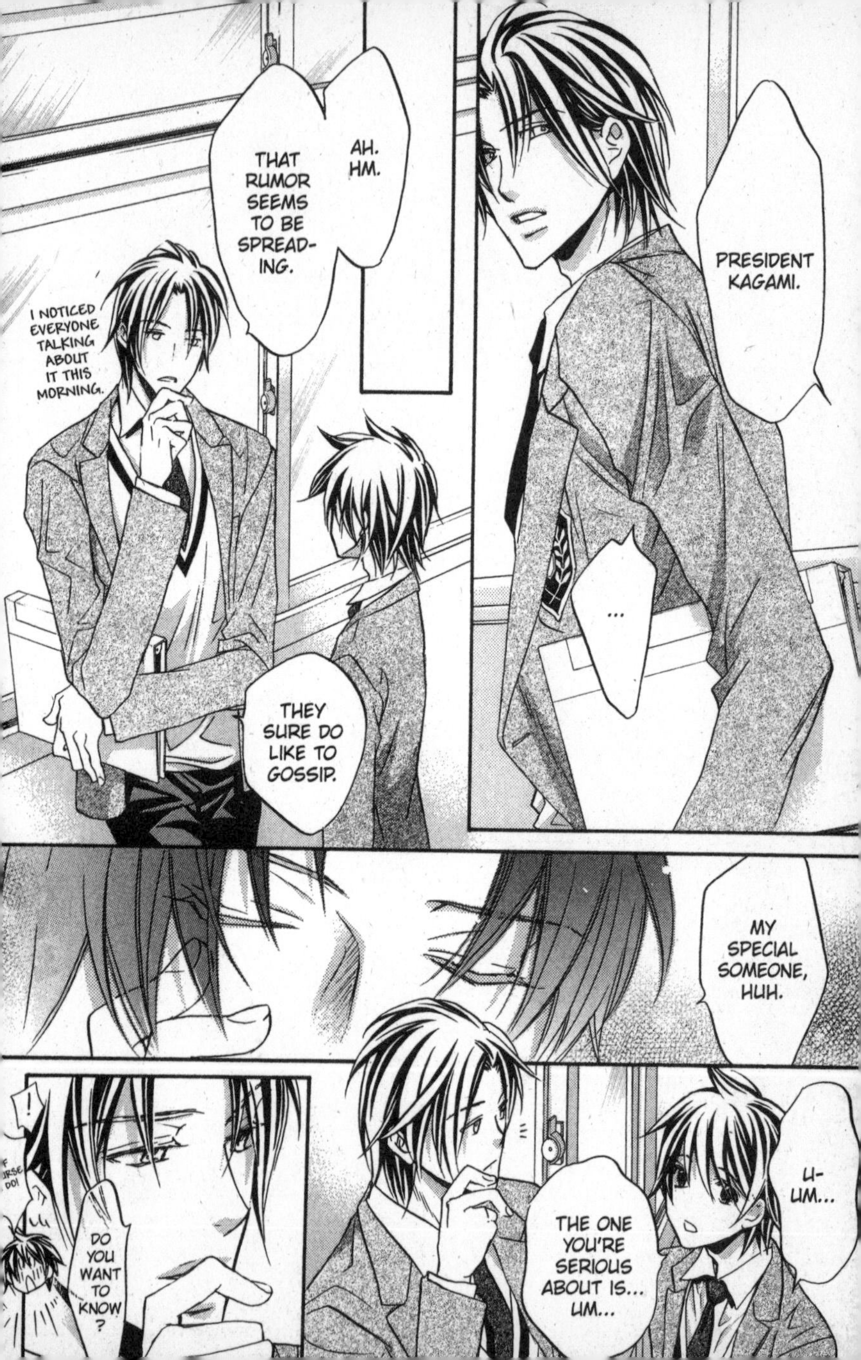
PRESIDENT KAGAMI.
...
AH. HM.
THAT RUMOR SEEMS TO BE SPREAD-ING.
I NOTICED EVERYONE TALKING ABOUT IT THIS MORNING.
THEY SURE DO LIKE TO GOSSIP.
MY SPECIAL SOMEONE, HUH.
U-UM...
THE ONE YOU'RE SERIOUS ABOUT IS... UM...
!
DO YOU WANT TO KNOW?

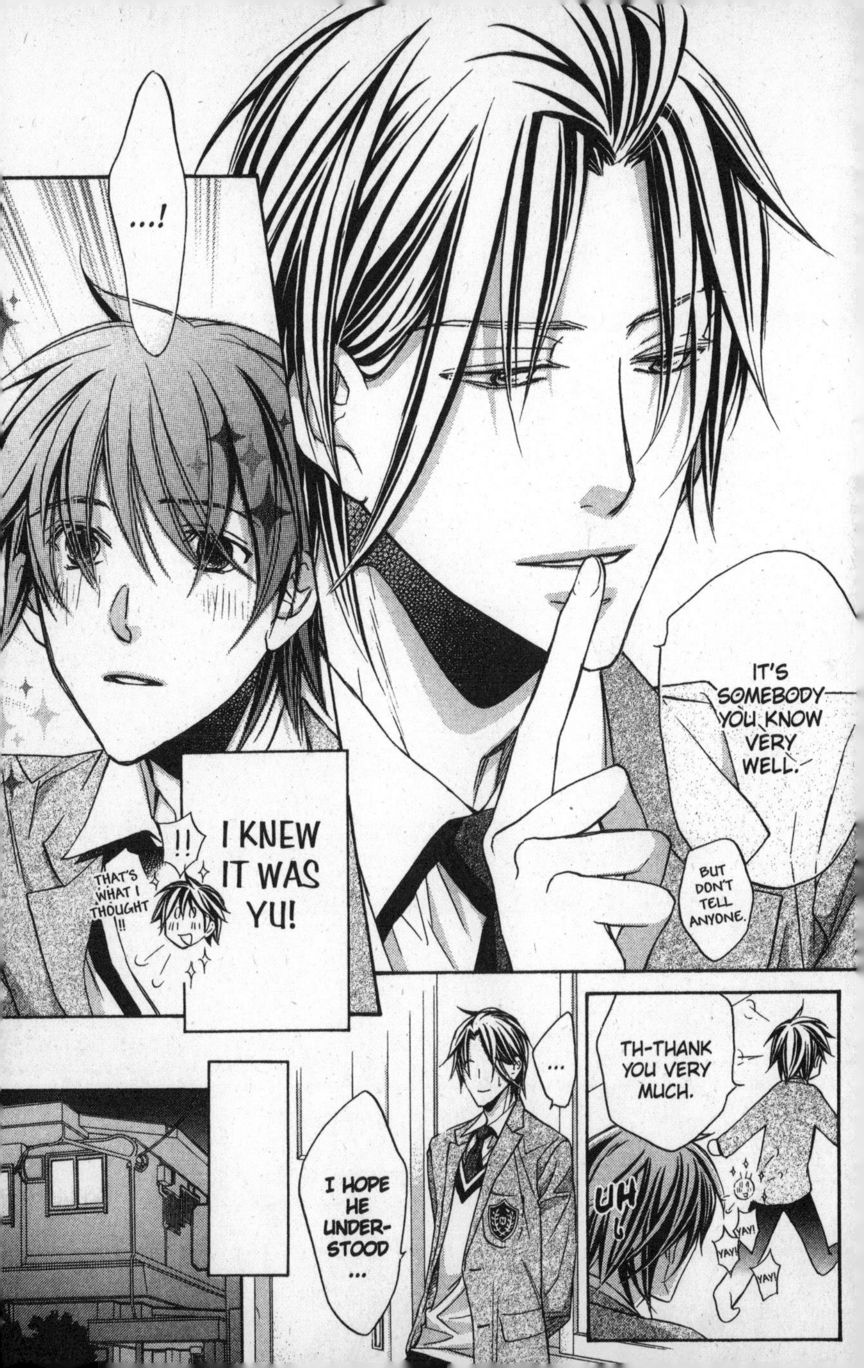
IT'S SOMEBODY YOU KNOW VERY WELL.
BUT DON'T TELL ANYONE.
...!
!!
I KNEW IT WAS YU!
THAT'S WHAT I THOUGHT !!
TH-THANK YOU VERY MUCH.
UH
YAY!
YAY!
YAY!
YAY!
...
I HOPE HE UNDER-STOOD ...

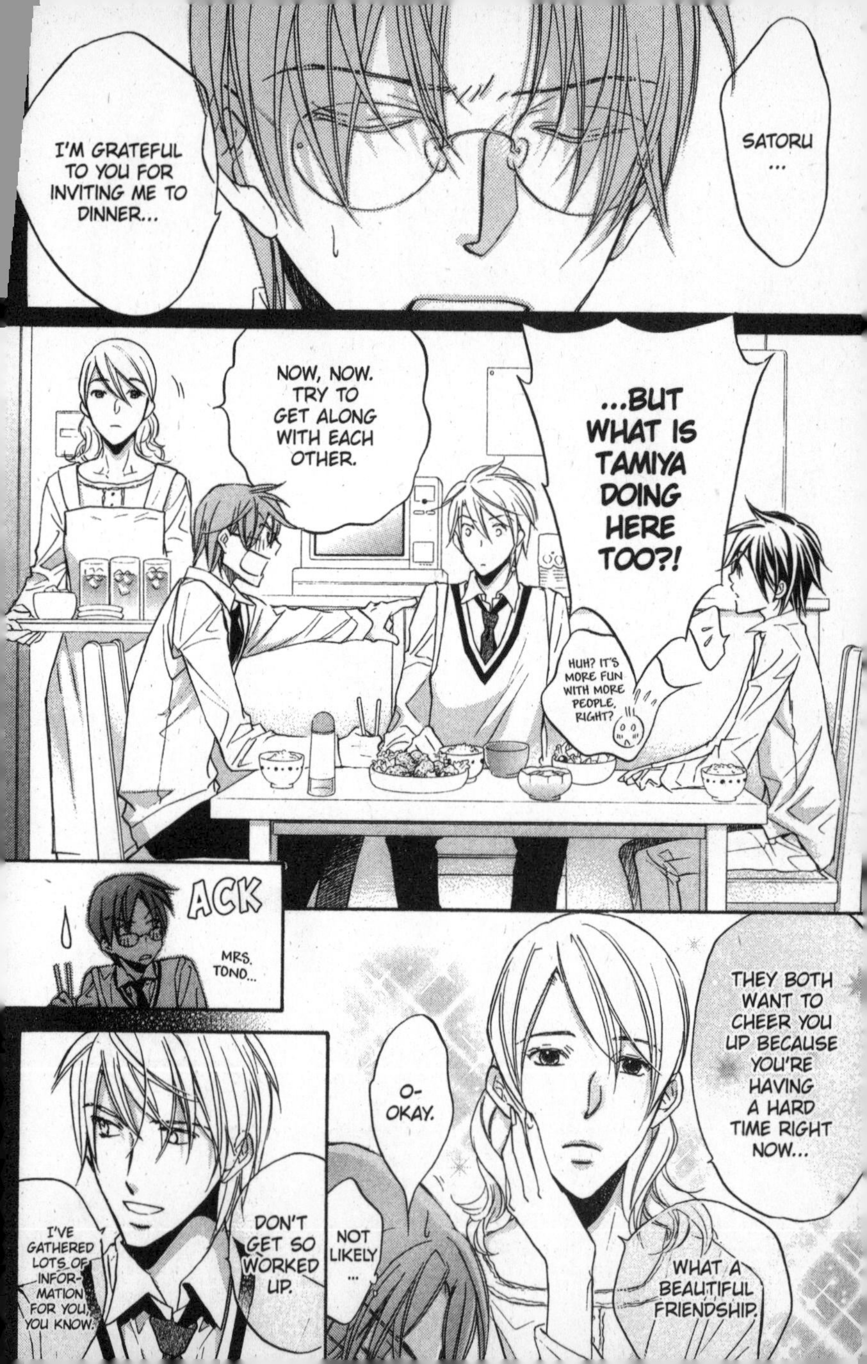
SATORU ...
I'M GRATEFUL TO YOU FOR INVITING ME TO DINNER...
...BUT WHAT IS TAMIYA DOING HERE TOO?!
HUH? IT'S MORE FUN WITH MORE PEOPLE, RIGHT?
NOW, NOW. TRY TO GET ALONG WITH EACH OTHER.
THEY BOTH WANT TO CHEER YOU UP BECAUSE YOU'RE HAVING A HARD TIME RIGHT NOW...
O-OKAY.
WHAT A BEAUTIFUL FRIENDSHIP.
NOT LIKELY ...
ACK
MRS. TONO...
DON'T GET SO WORKED UP.
I'VE GATHERED LOTS OF INFORMATION FOR YOU, YOU KNOW.

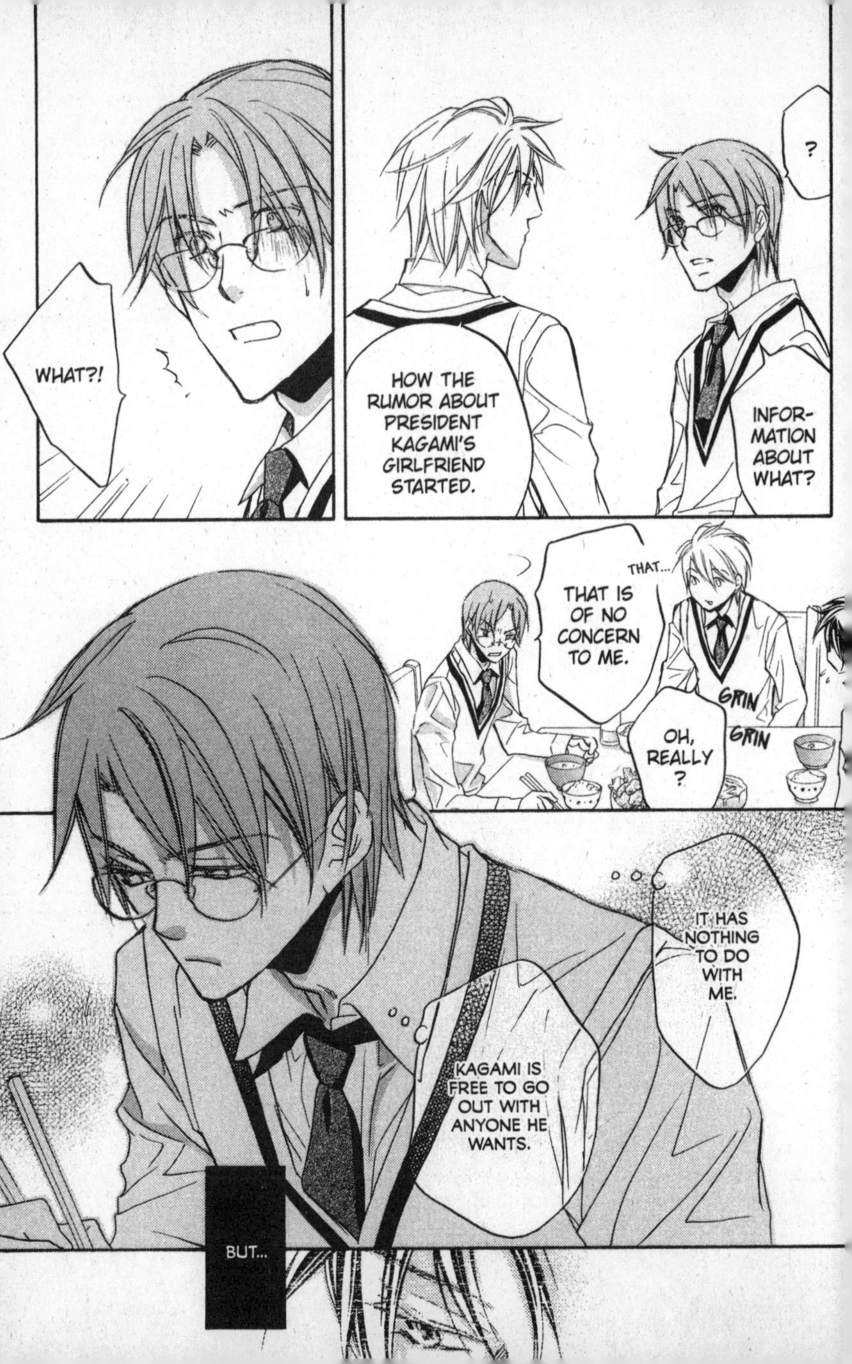
?
INFORMATION ABOUT WHAT?
HOW THE RUMOR ABOUT PRESIDENT KAGAMI'S GIRLFRIEND STARTED.
WHAT?!
THAT...
THAT IS OF NO CONCERN TO ME.
GRIN
GRIN
OH, REALLY?
IT HAS NOTHING TO DO WITH ME.
KAGAMI IS FREE TO GO OUT WITH ANYONE HE WANTS.
BUT...

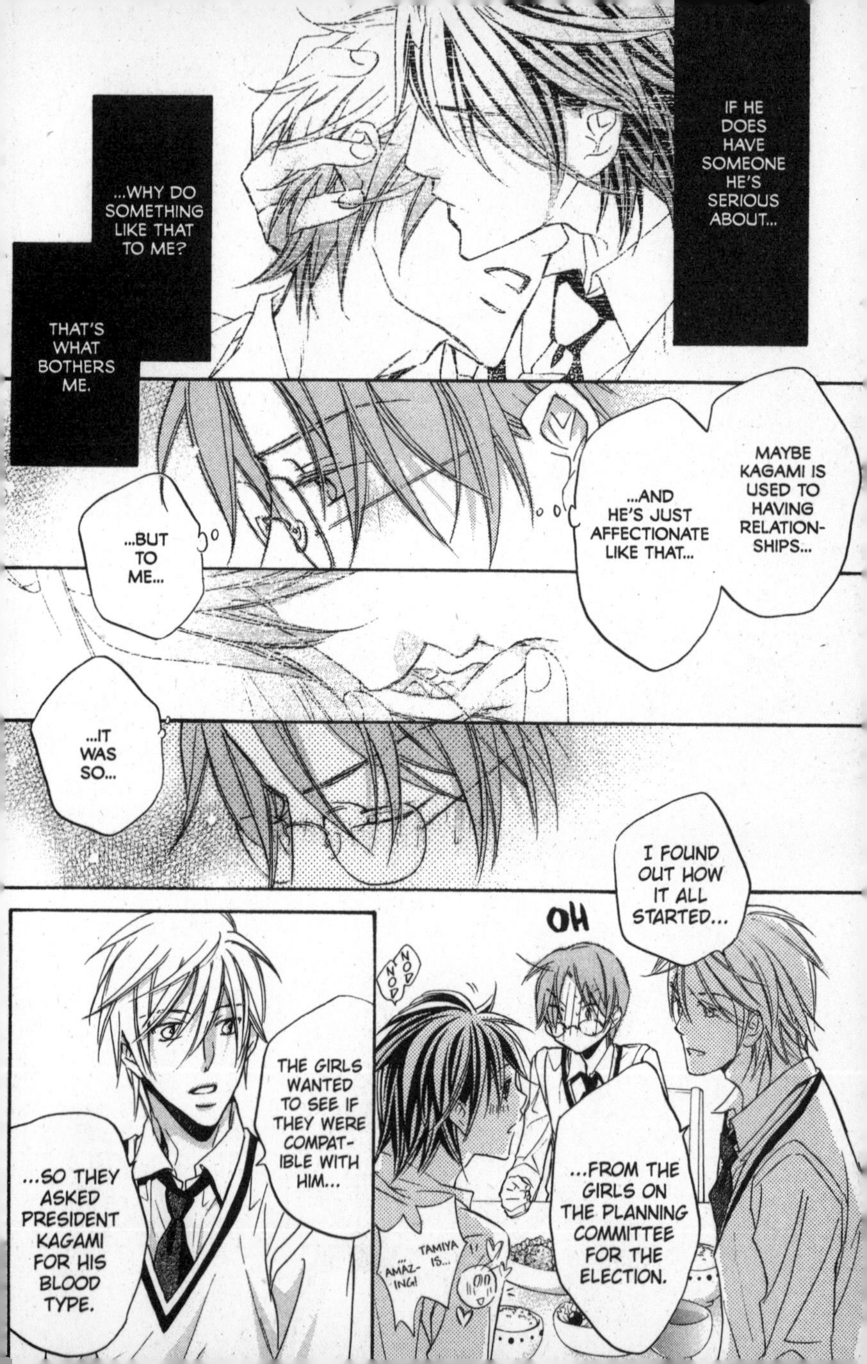
IF HE DOES HAVE SOMEONE HE'S SERIOUS ABOUT...
...WHY DO SOMETHING LIKE THAT TO ME?
THAT'S WHAT BOTHERS ME.
MAYBE KAGAMI IS USED TO HAVING RELATION-SHIPS...
...AND HE'S JUST AFFECTIONATE LIKE THAT...
...BUT TO ME...
...IT WAS SO...
I FOUND OUT HOW IT ALL STARTED...
OH
NOD NOD
...FROM THE GIRLS ON THE PLANNING COMMITTEE FOR THE ELECTION.
TAMIYA IS...
...AMAZ-ING!
THE GIRLS WANTED TO SEE IF THEY WERE COMPAT-IBLE WITH HIM...
...SO THEY ASKED PRESIDENT KAGAMI FOR HIS BLOOD TYPE.

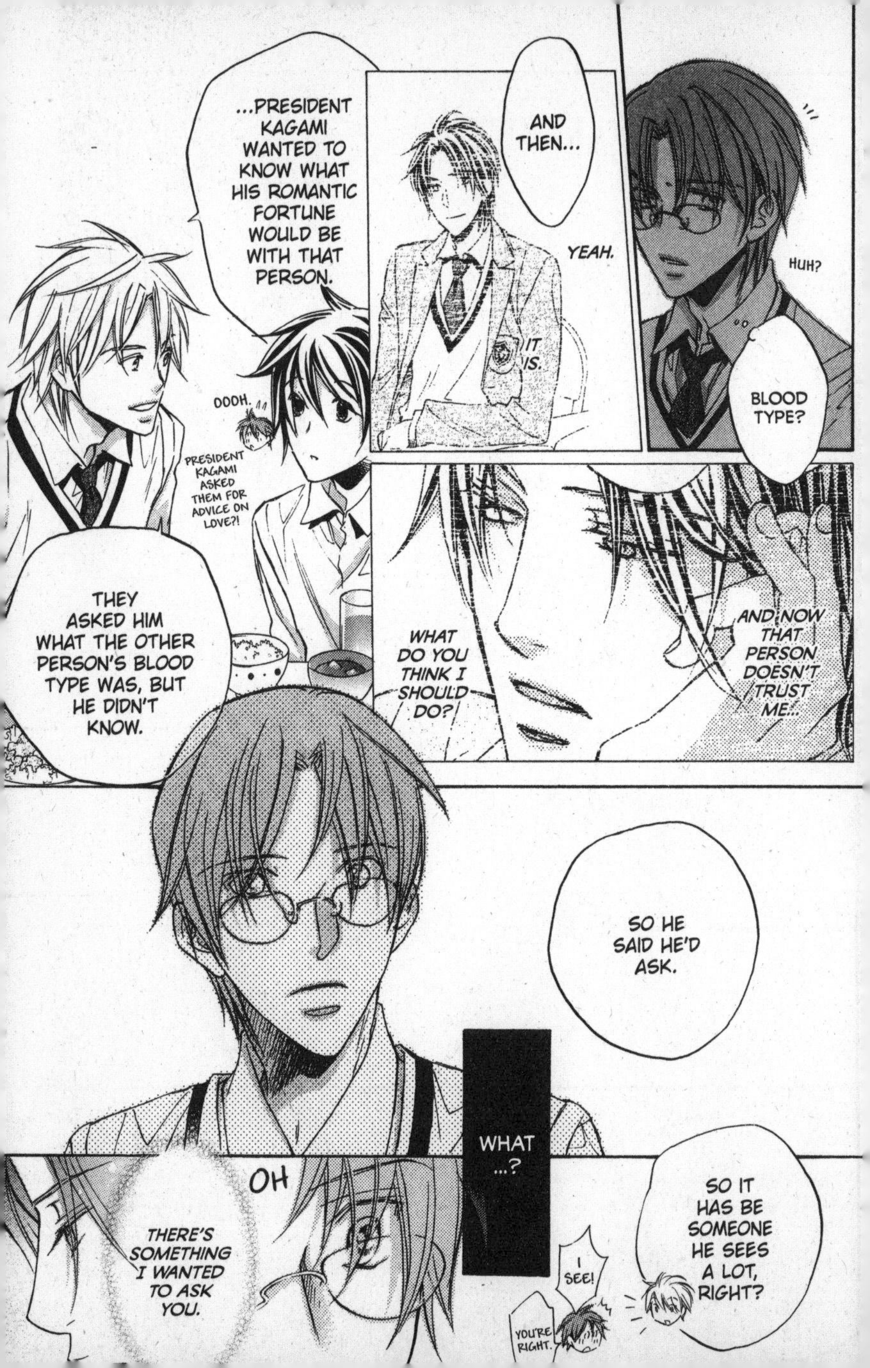
HUH?
BLOOD TYPE?
AND THEN...
YEAH.
IT IS.
AND NOW THAT PERSON DOESN'T TRUST ME...
WHAT DO YOU THINK I SHOULD DO?
...PRESIDENT KAGAMI WANTED TO KNOW WHAT HIS ROMANTIC FORTUNE WOULD BE WITH THAT PERSON.
OOOH.
PRESIDENT KAGAMI ASKED THEM FOR ADVICE ON LOVE?!
THEY ASKED HIM WHAT THE OTHER PERSON'S BLOOD TYPE WAS, BUT HE DIDN'T KNOW.
SO HE SAID HE'D ASK.
WHAT ...?
SO IT HAS BE SOMEONE HE SEES A LOT, RIGHT?
I SEE!
YOU'RE RIGHT.
OH
THERE'S SOMETHING I WANTED TO ASK YOU.

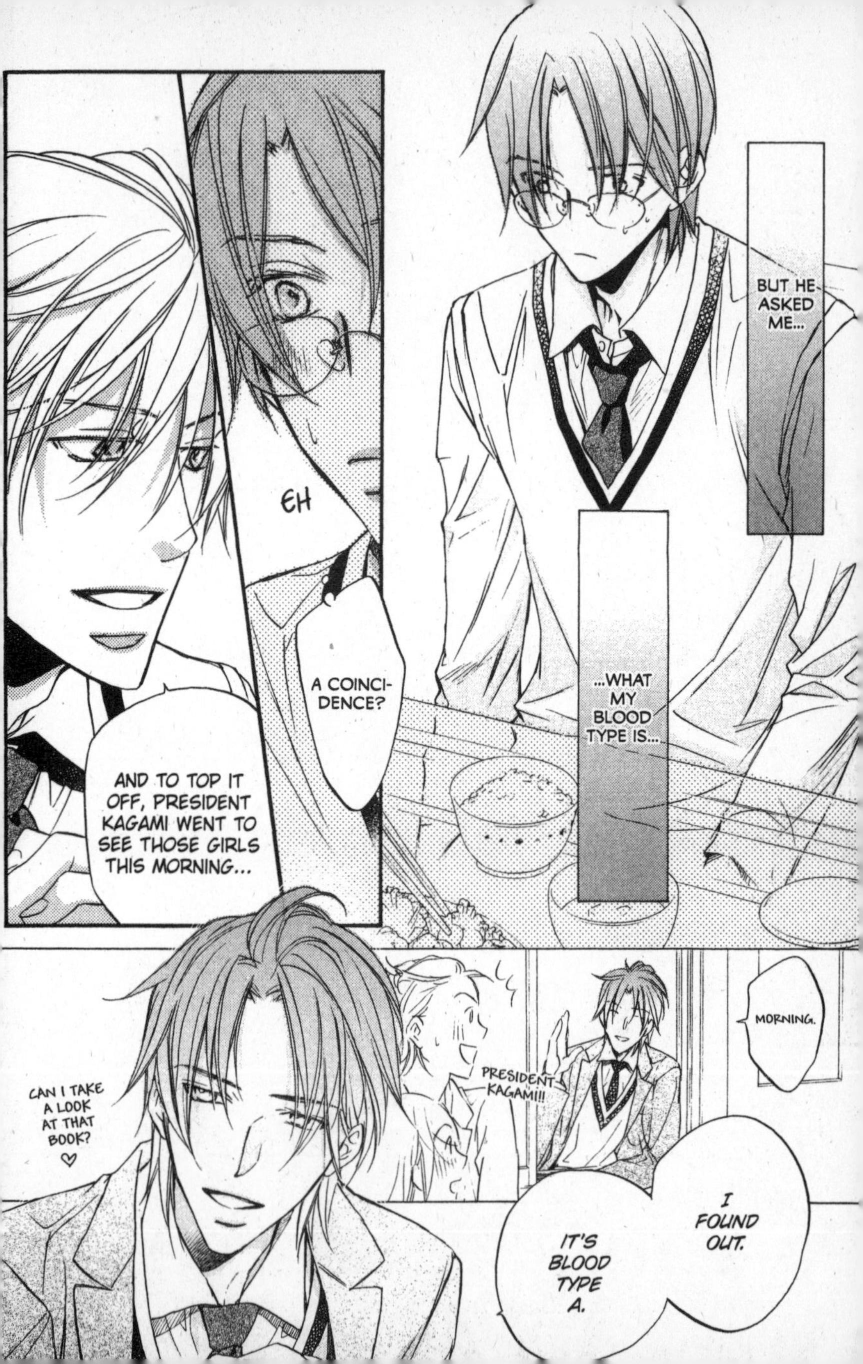
BUT HE ASKED ME...
...WHAT MY BLOOD TYPE IS...
EH
A COINCIDENCE?
AND TO TOP IT OFF, PRESIDENT KAGAMI WENT TO SEE THOSE GIRLS THIS MORNING...
MORNING.
PRESIDENT KAGAMI!!
CAN I TAKE A LOOK AT THAT BOOK? ♡
I FOUND OUT.
IT'S BLOOD TYPE A.

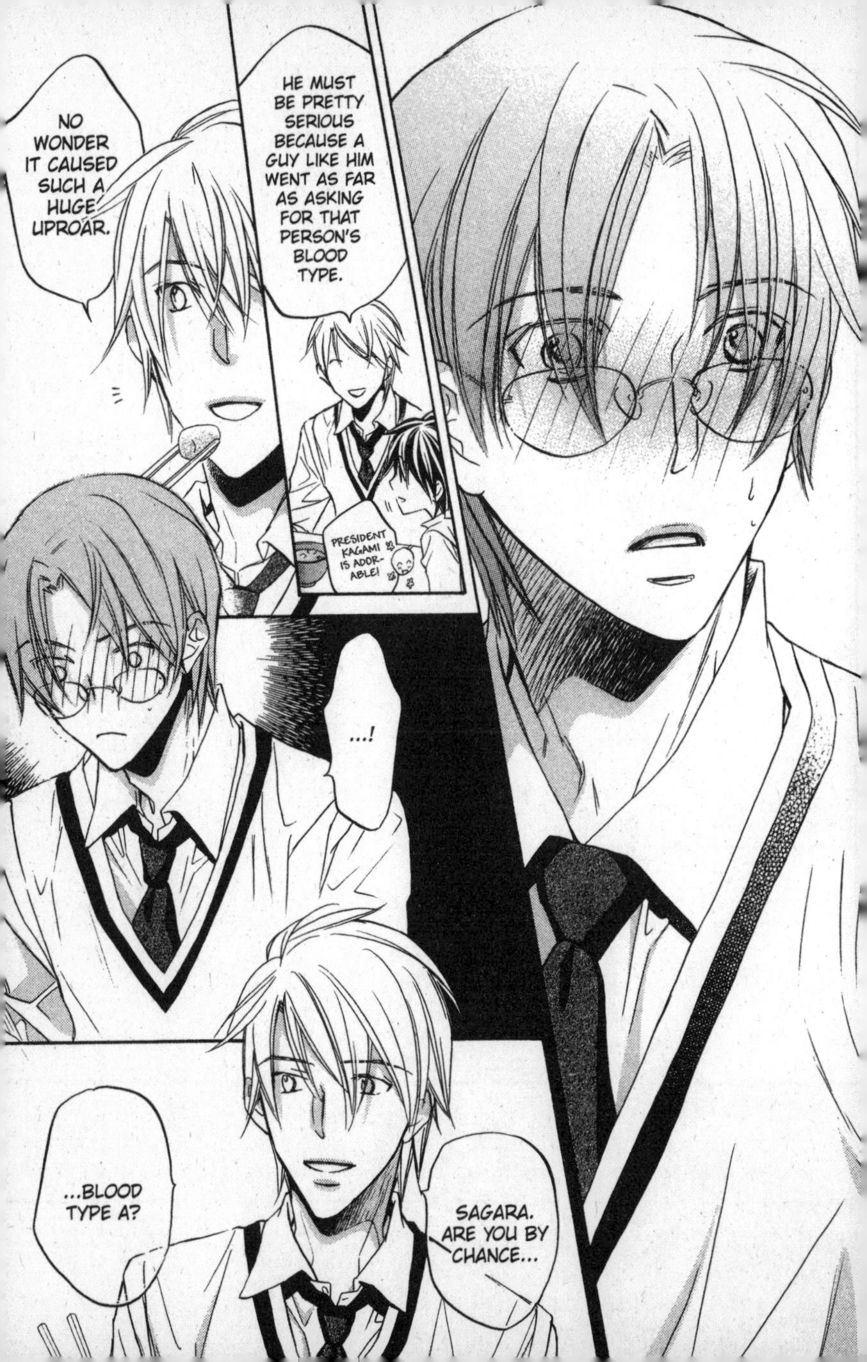
HE MUST BE PRETTY SERIOUS BECAUSE A GUY LIKE HIM WENT AS FAR AS ASKING FOR THAT PERSON'S BLOOD TYPE.
PRESIDENT KAGAMI IS ADORABLE!
NO WONDER IT CAUSED SUCH A HUGE UPROAR.
...!
SAGARA. ARE YOU BY CHANCE...
...BLOOD TYPE A?

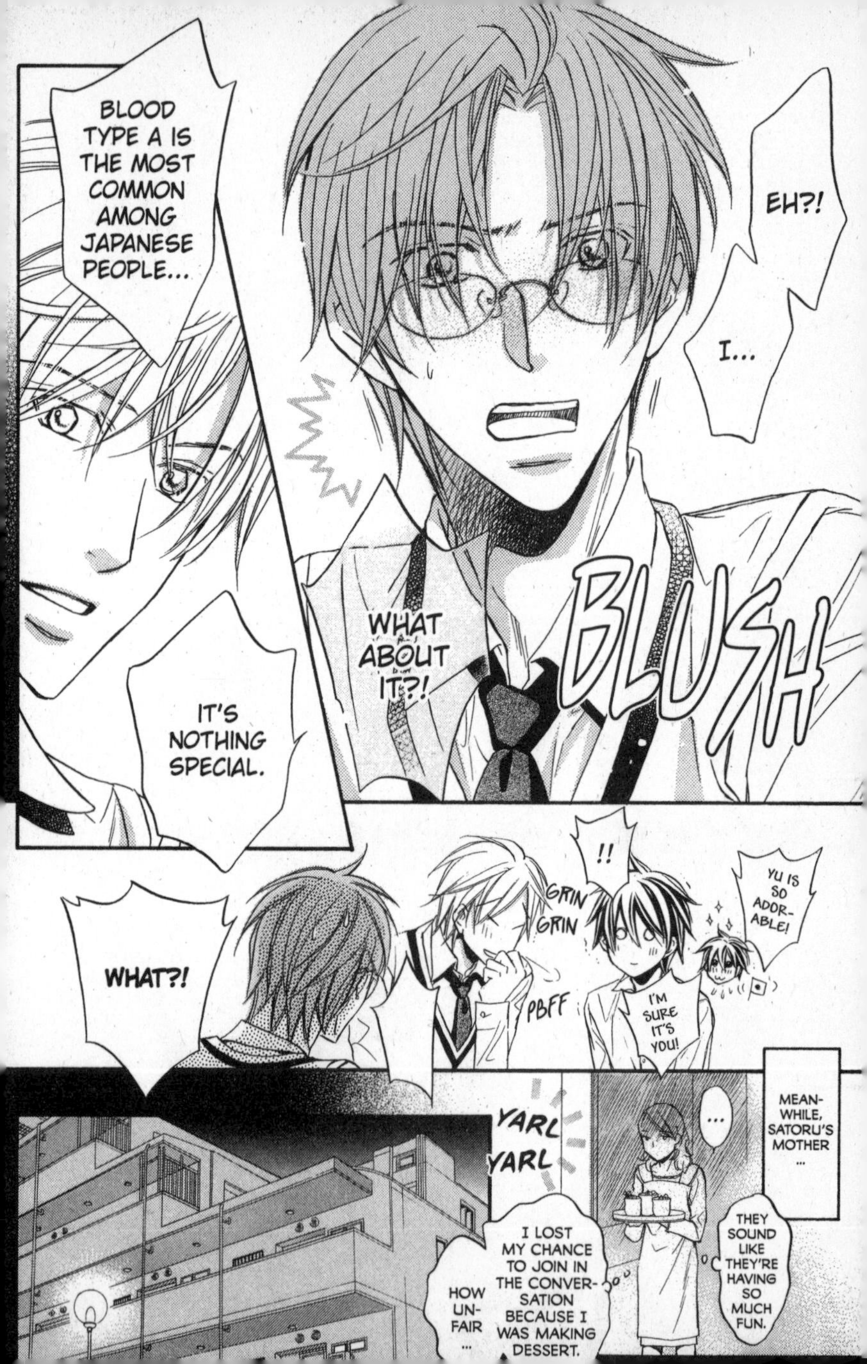
EH?!
I...
WHAT ABOUT IT?!
BLUSH
BLOOD TYPE A IS THE MOST COMMON AMONG JAPANESE PEOPLE...
IT'S NOTHING SPECIAL.
!!
YU IS SO ADORABLE!
I'M SURE IT'S YOU!
GRIN GRIN
PBFF
WHAT?!
MEANWHILE, SATORU'S MOTHER ...
...
THEY SOUND LIKE THEY'RE HAVING SO MUCH FUN.
I LOST MY CHANCE TO JOIN IN THE CONVERSATION BECAUSE I WAS MAKING DESSERT.
HOW UNFAIR ...
YARL YARL

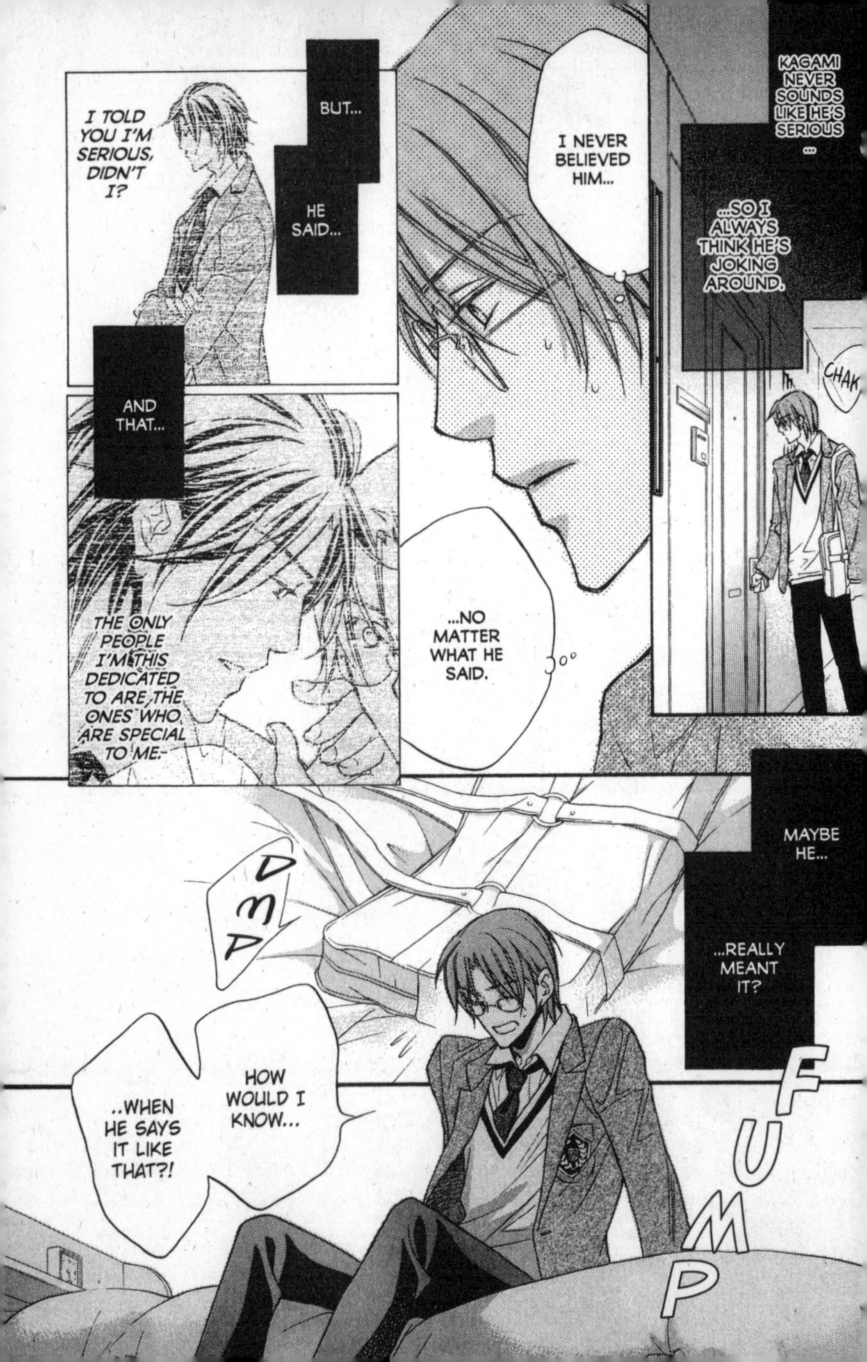
KAGAMI NEVER SOUNDS LIKE HE'S SERIOUS ...
...SO I ALWAYS THINK HE'S JOKING AROUND.
CHAK
I NEVER BELIEVED HIM...
...NO MATTER WHAT HE SAID.
BUT...
HE SAID...
I TOLD YOU I'M SERIOUS, DIDN'T I?
AND THAT...
THE ONLY PEOPLE I'M THIS DEDICATED TO ARE THE ONES WHO ARE SPECIAL TO ME.
MAYBE HE...
...REALLY MEANT IT?
DMP
FUMP
HOW WOULD I KNOW...
..WHEN HE SAYS IT LIKE THAT?!

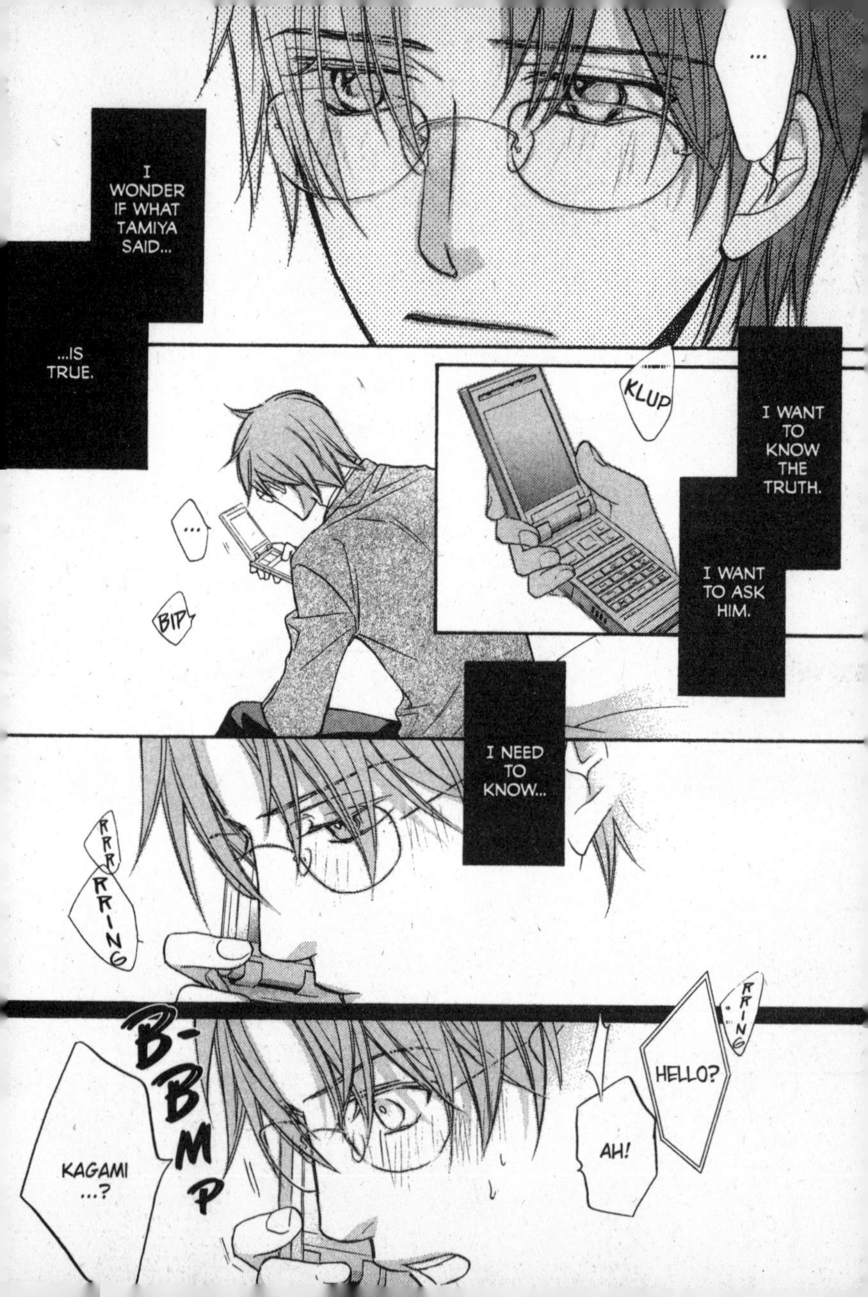
...
I WONDER IF WHAT TAMIYA SAID...
...IS TRUE.
I WANT TO KNOW THE TRUTH.
KLUP
I WANT TO ASK HIM.
...
BIP
I NEED TO KNOW...
RRRRRING
RRING
HELLO?
AH!
B-BBMP
KAGAMI ...?

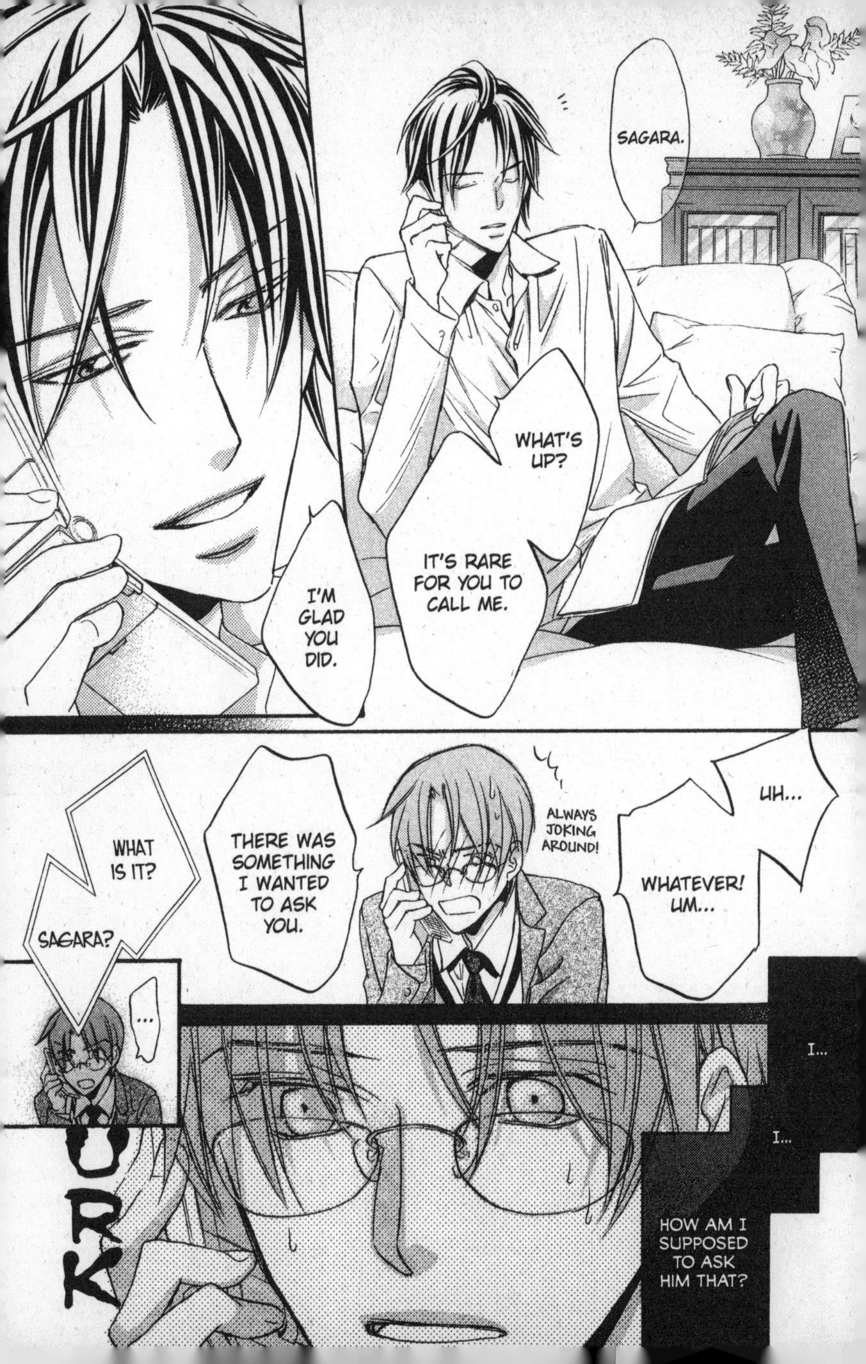
SAGARA.
WHAT'S UP?
IT'S RARE FOR YOU TO CALL ME.
I'M GLAD YOU DID.
UH...
WHATEVER! UM...
ALWAYS JOKING AROUND!
THERE WAS SOMETHING I WANTED TO ASK YOU.
WHAT IS IT?
SAGARA?
...
URK
I...
I...
HOW AM I SUPPOSED TO ASK HIM THAT?

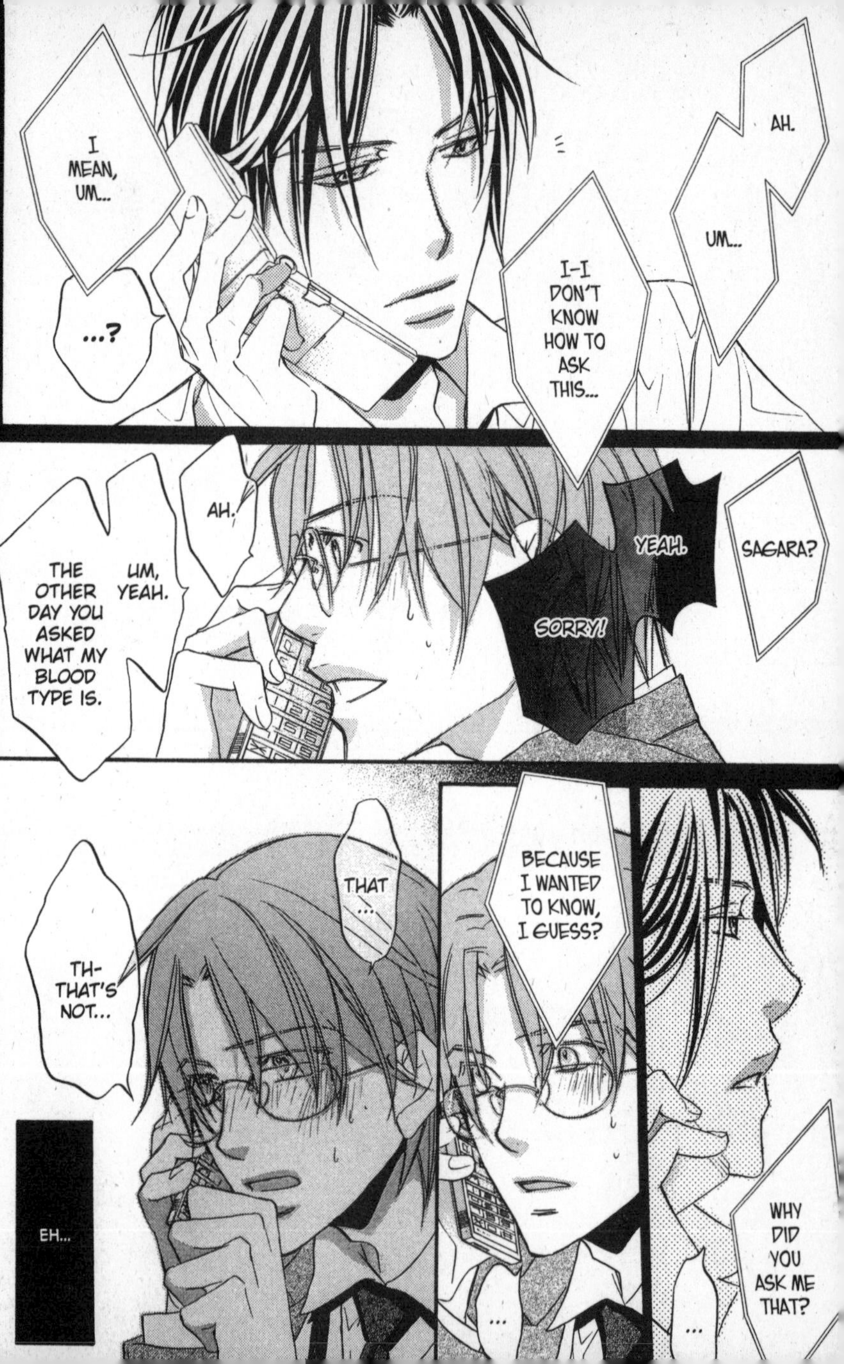
AH.
UM...
I-I DON'T KNOW HOW TO ASK THIS...
I MEAN, UM...
...?
SAGARA?
YEAH.
SORRY!
AH.
UM, YEAH.
THE OTHER DAY YOU ASKED WHAT MY BLOOD TYPE IS.
WHY DID YOU ASK ME THAT?
...
BECAUSE I WANTED TO KNOW, I GUESS?
...
THAT ...
TH-THAT'S NOT...
EH...

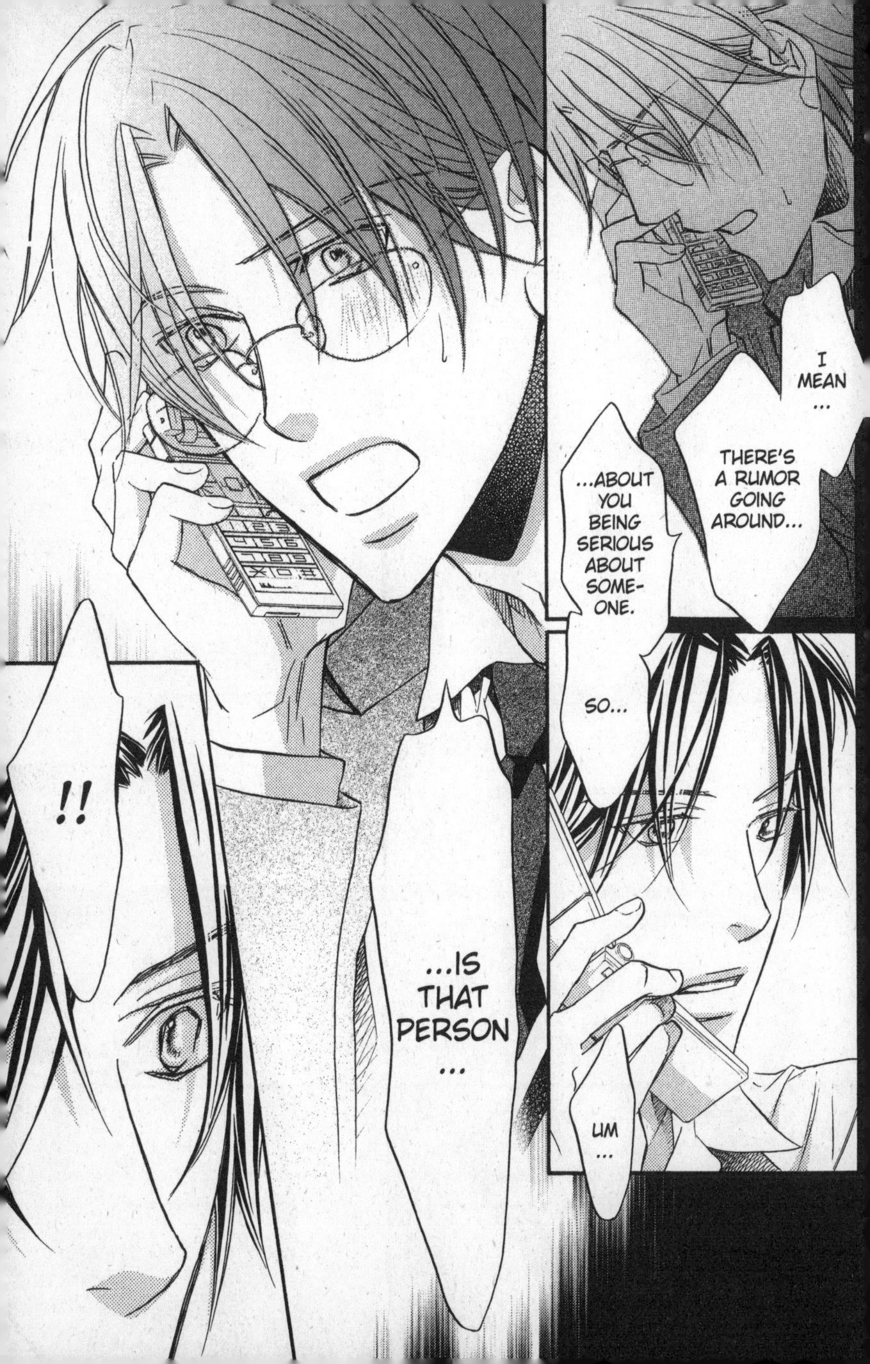
I MEAN ...
THERE'S A RUMOR GOING AROUND...
...ABOUT YOU BEING SERIOUS ABOUT SOME-ONE.
SO...
UM ...
...IS THAT PERSON ...
!!

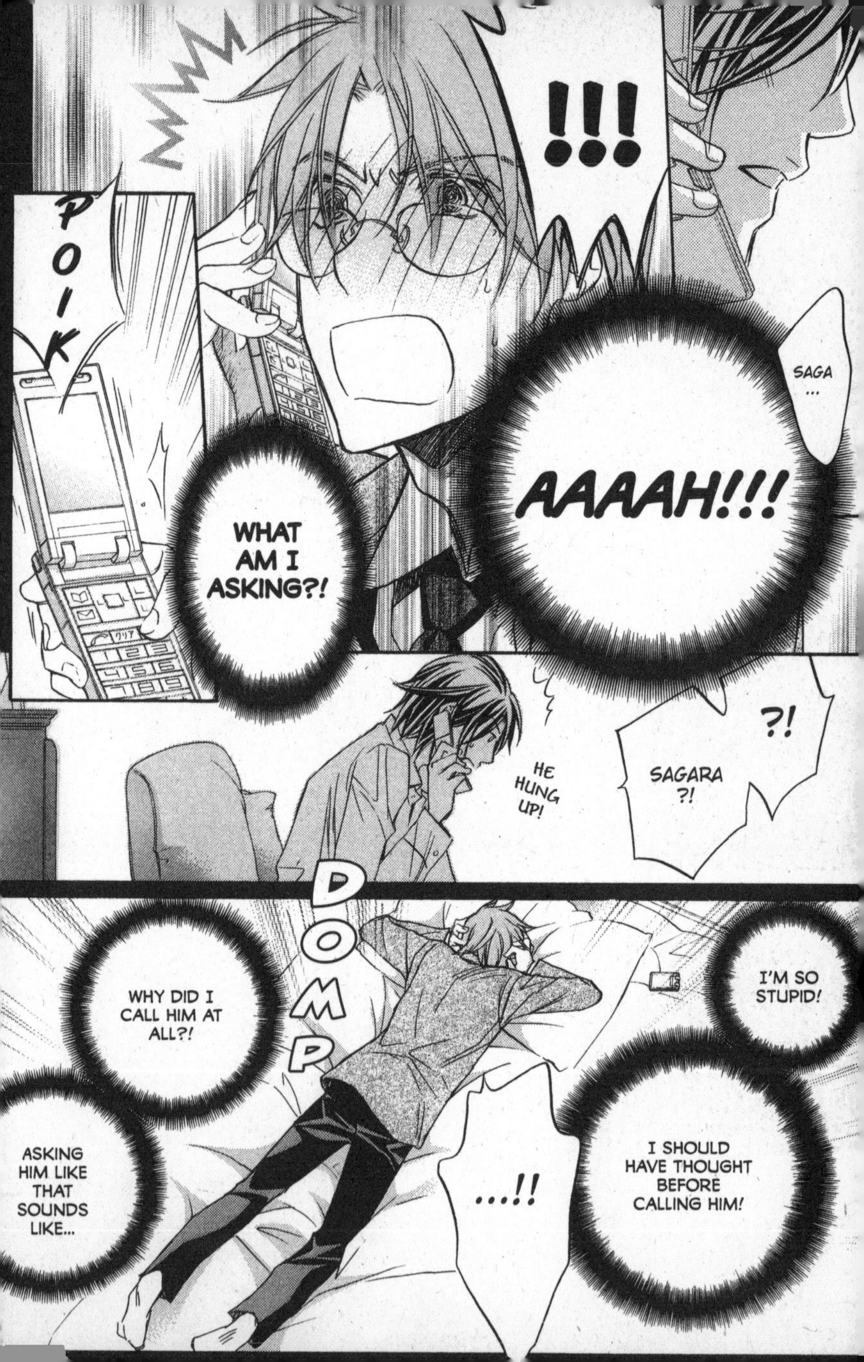
!!!
SAGA ...
AAAAH!!!
POIK
WHAT AM I ASKING?!
?!
SAGARA ?!
HE HUNG UP!
I'M SO STUPID!
DOMP
WHY DID I CALL HIM AT ALL?!
I SHOULD HAVE THOUGHT BEFORE CALLING HIM!
...!!
ASKING HIM LIKE THAT SOUNDS LIKE...

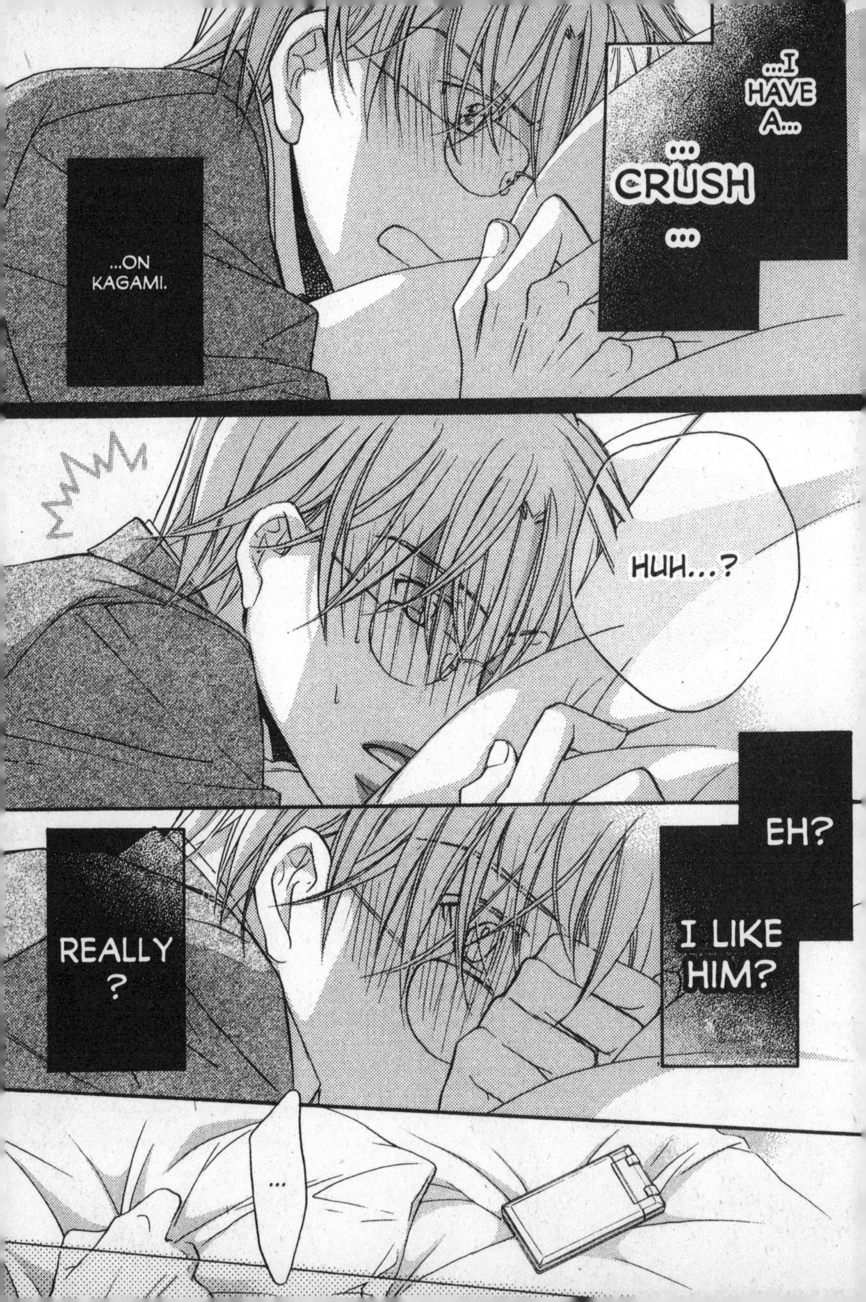
...I HAVE A...
...CRUSH...
...ON KAGAMI.
HUH...?
EH?
I LIKE HIM?
REALLY?
...

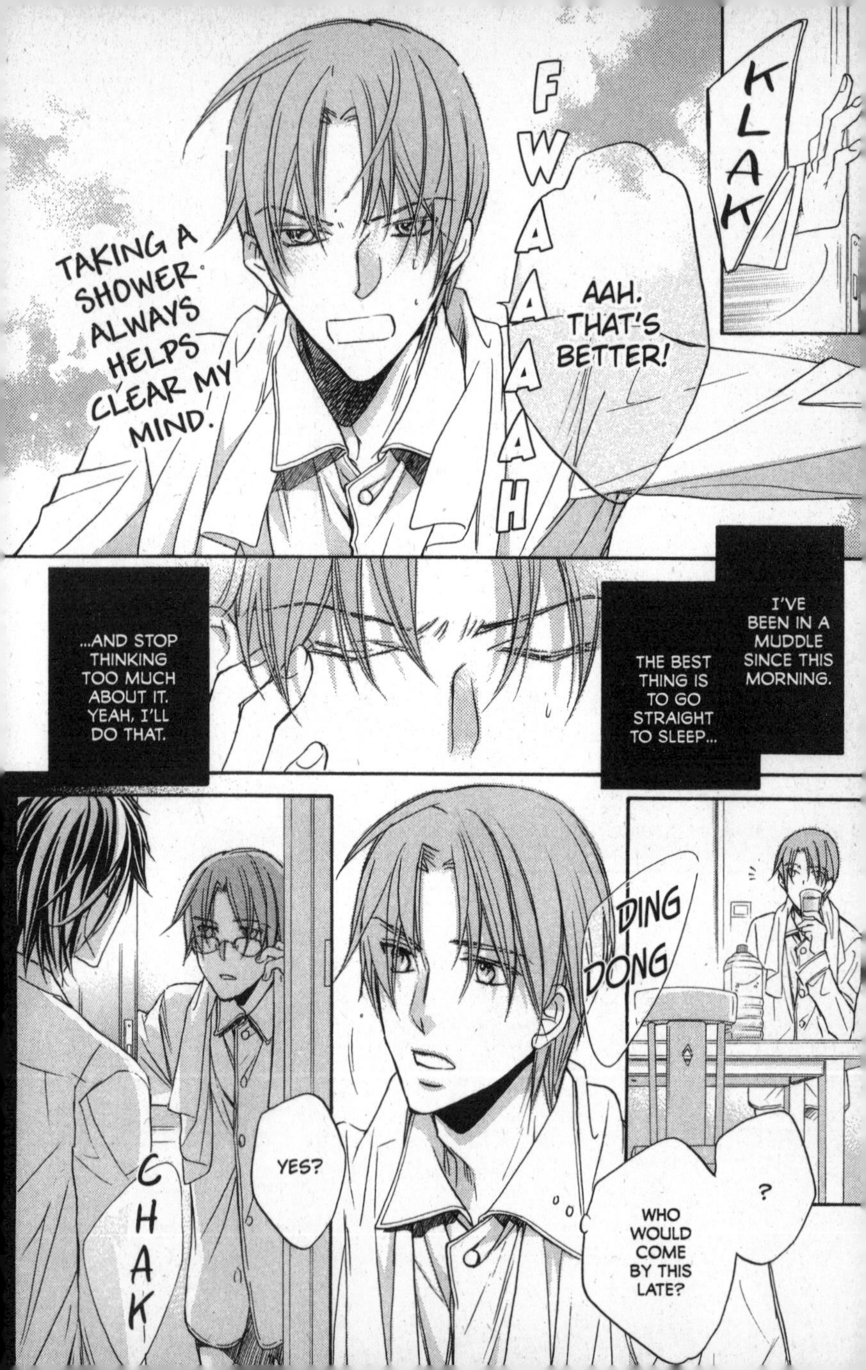
KLAK
AAH. THAT'S BETTER!
FWAAAAAH
TAKING A SHOWER ALWAYS HELPS CLEAR MY MIND.
I'VE BEEN IN A MUDDLE SINCE THIS MORNING.
THE BEST THING IS TO GO STRAIGHT TO SLEEP...
...AND STOP THINKING TOO MUCH ABOUT IT. YEAH, I'LL DO THAT.
DING DONG
?
WHO WOULD COME BY THIS LATE?
YES?
CHAK

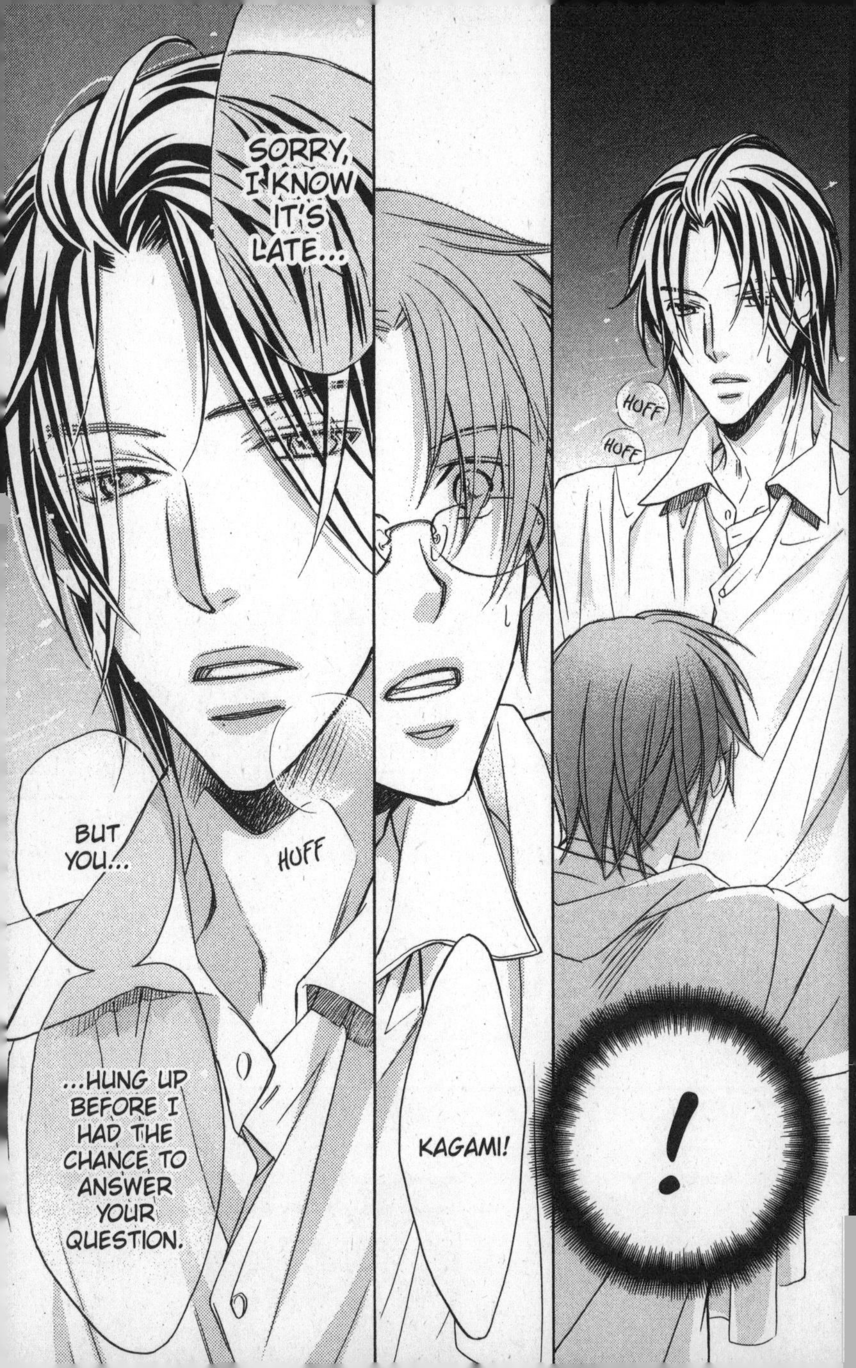
HUFF
HUFF
!
KAGAMI!
SORRY, I KNOW IT'S LATE...
BUT YOU...
HUFF
...HUNG UP BEFORE I HAD THE CHANCE TO ANSWER YOUR QUESTION.

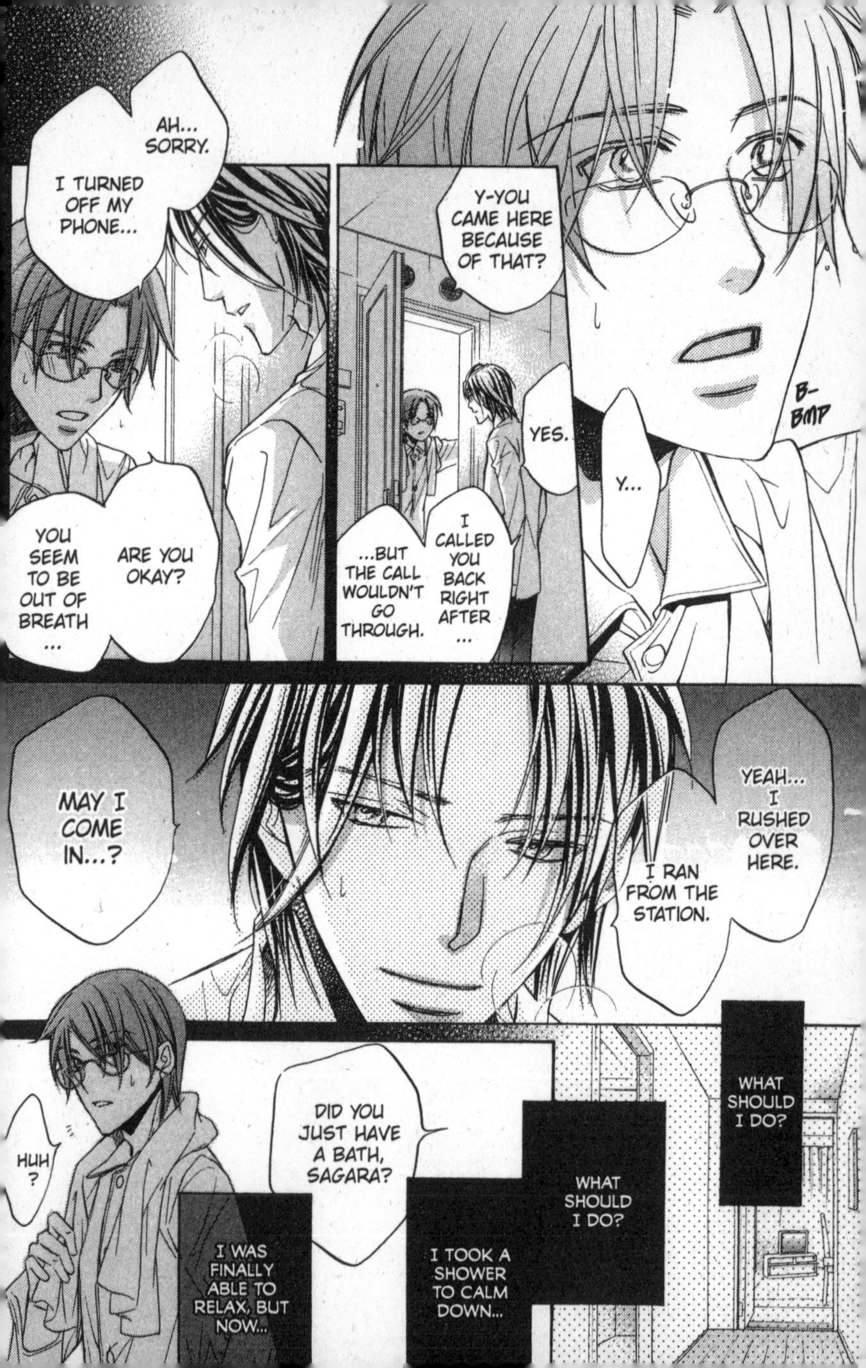
Y-YOU CAME HERE BECAUSE OF THAT?
B-BMP
Y...
YES.
I CALLED YOU BACK RIGHT AFTER...
...BUT THE CALL WOULDN'T GO THROUGH.
AH... SORRY.
I TURNED OFF MY PHONE...
ARE YOU OKAY?
YOU SEEM TO BE OUT OF BREATH...
YEAH... I RUSHED OVER HERE.
I RAN FROM THE STATION.
MAY I COME IN...?
WHAT SHOULD I DO?
WHAT SHOULD I DO?
I TOOK A SHOWER TO CALM DOWN...
DID YOU JUST HAVE A BATH, SAGARA?
I WAS FINALLY ABLE TO RELAX, BUT NOW...
HUH?

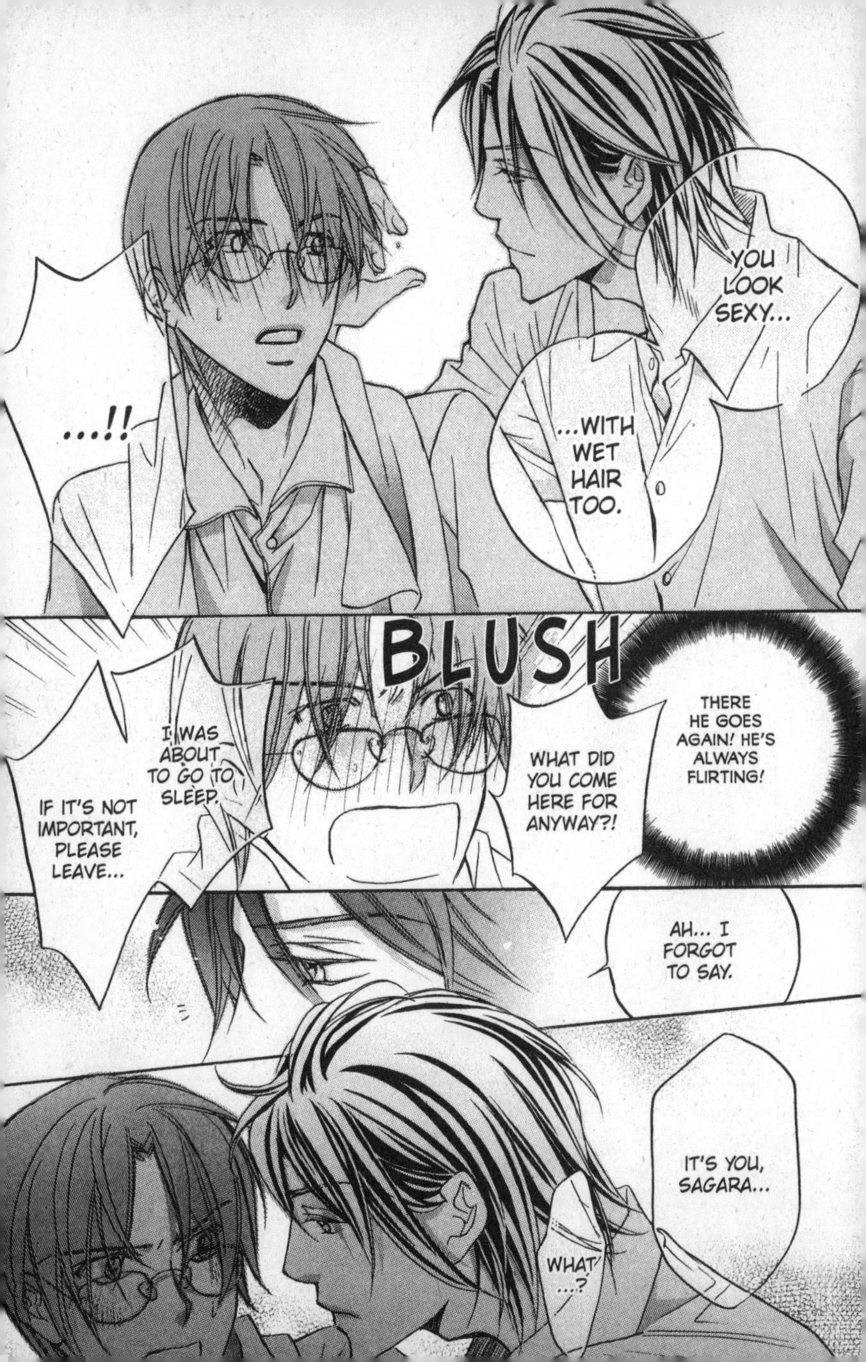
YOU LOOK SEXY...
...WITH WET HAIR TOO.
...!!
BLUSH
THERE HE GOES AGAIN! HE'S ALWAYS FLIRTING!
WHAT DID YOU COME HERE FOR ANYWAY?!
I WAS ABOUT TO GO TO SLEEP.
IF IT'S NOT IMPORTANT, PLEASE LEAVE...
AH... I FORGOT TO SAY.
IT'S YOU, SAGARA...
WHAT ...?

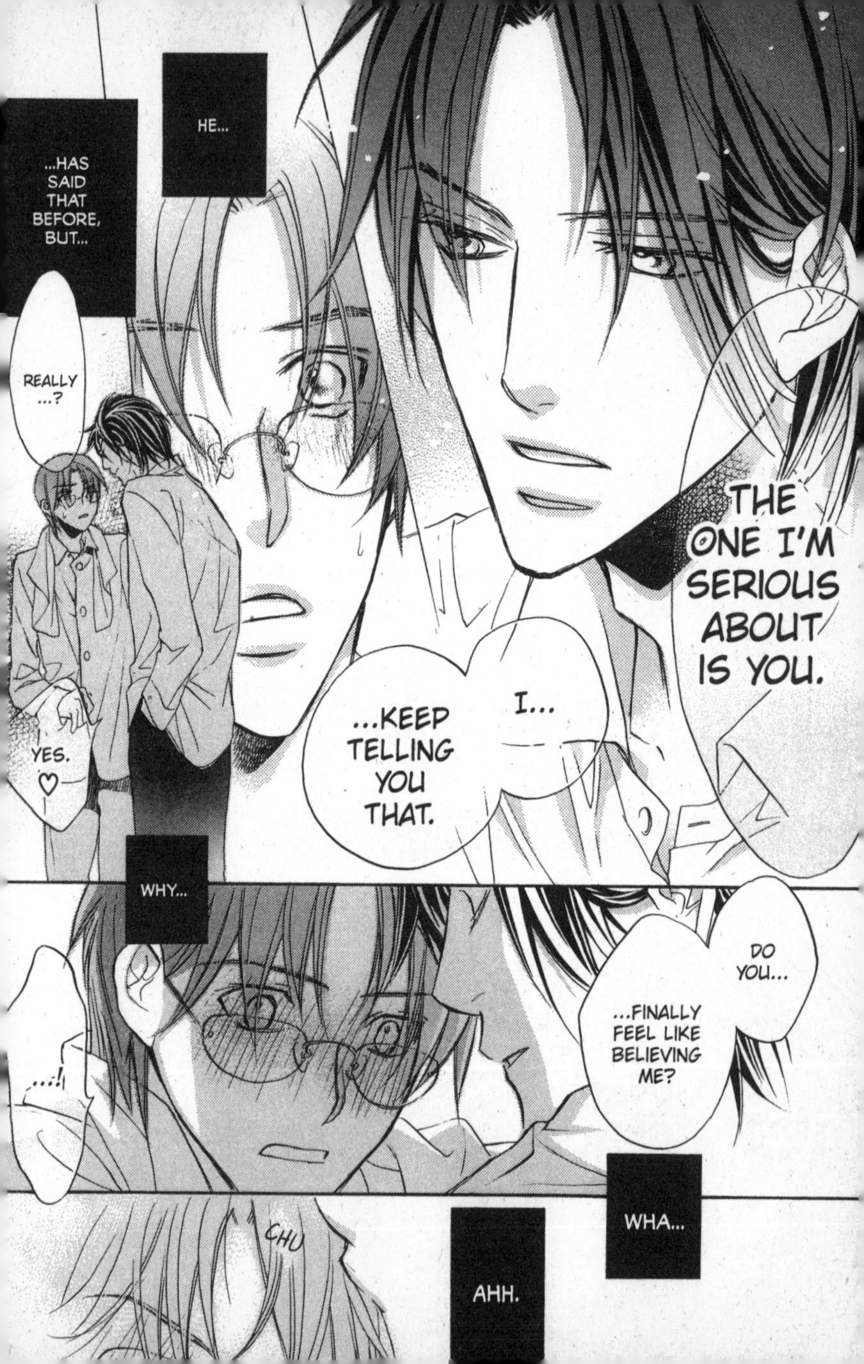
THE ONE I'M SERIOUS ABOUT IS YOU.
I... ...KEEP TELLING YOU THAT.
HE...
...HAS SAID THAT BEFORE, BUT...
REALLY ...?
YES. ♡
DO YOU... ...FINALLY FEEL LIKE BELIEVING ME?
WHY...
...!
WHA...
AHH.
CHU

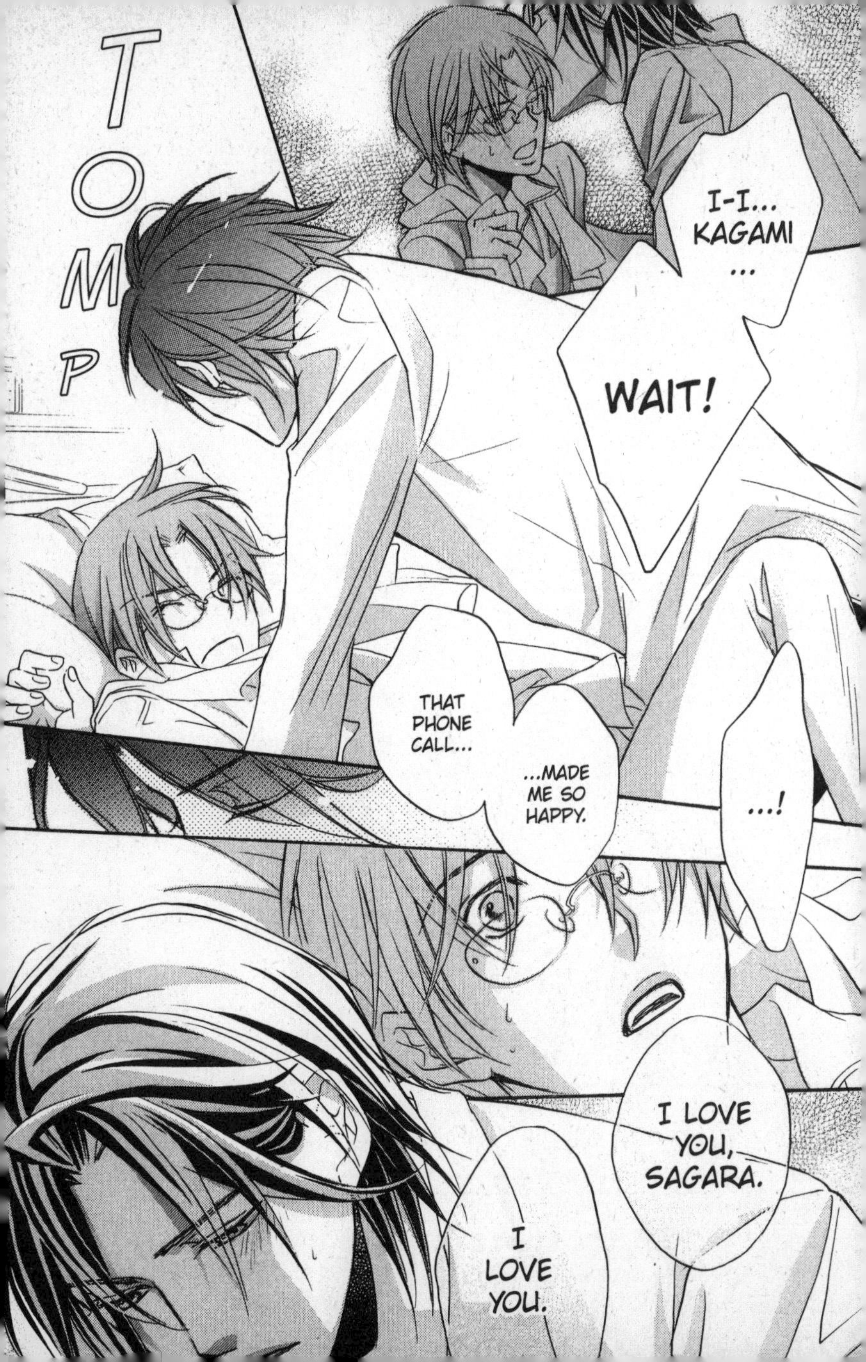
I-I... KAGAMI ...
WAIT!
TOMP
THAT PHONE CALL...
...MADE ME SO HAPPY.
...!
I LOVE YOU, SAGARA.
I LOVE YOU.

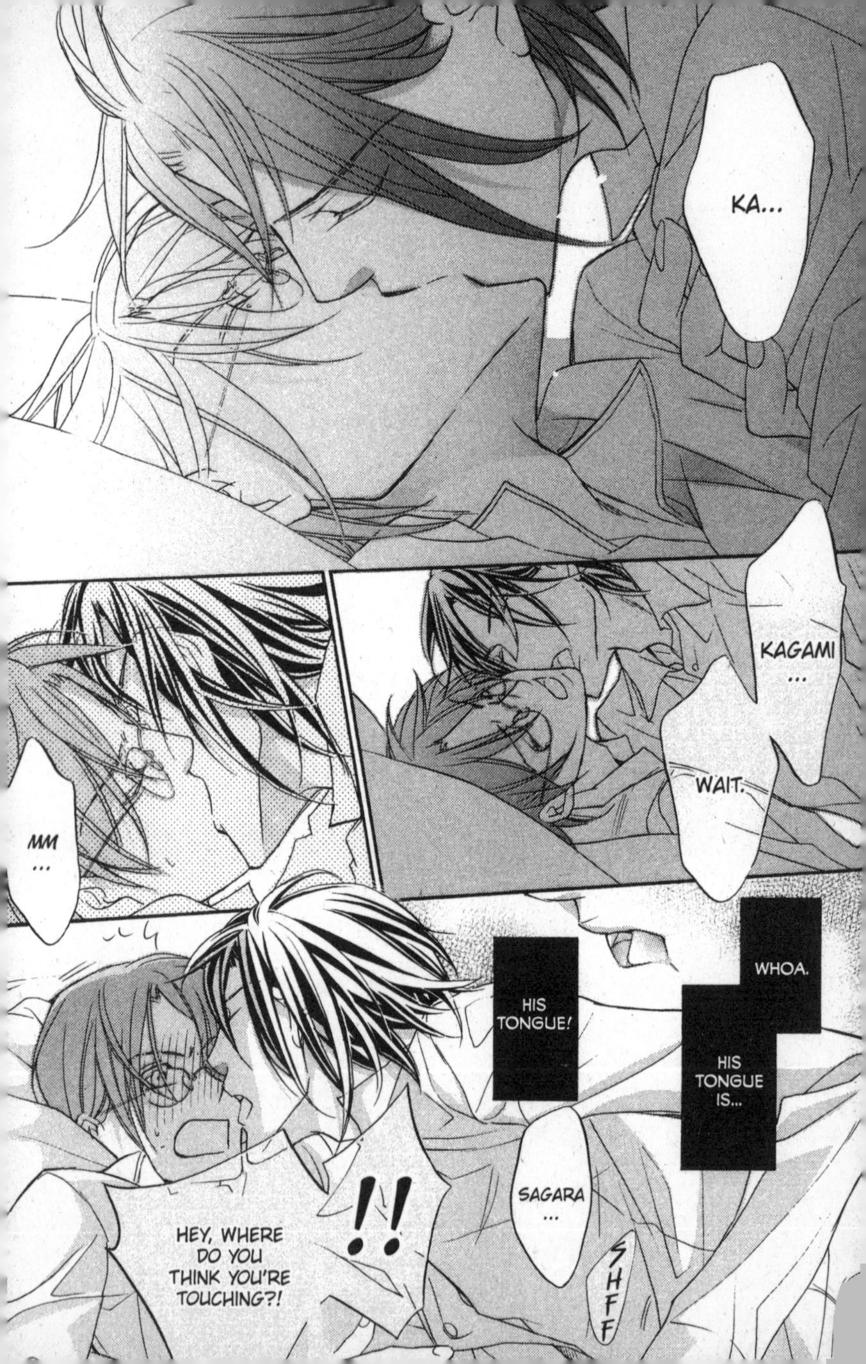
KA...
KAGAMI ...
WAIT.
MM ...
WHOA.
HIS TONGUE IS...
HIS TONGUE!
SAGARA ...
SHFF
!!
HEY, WHERE DO YOU THINK YOU'RE TOUCHING?!

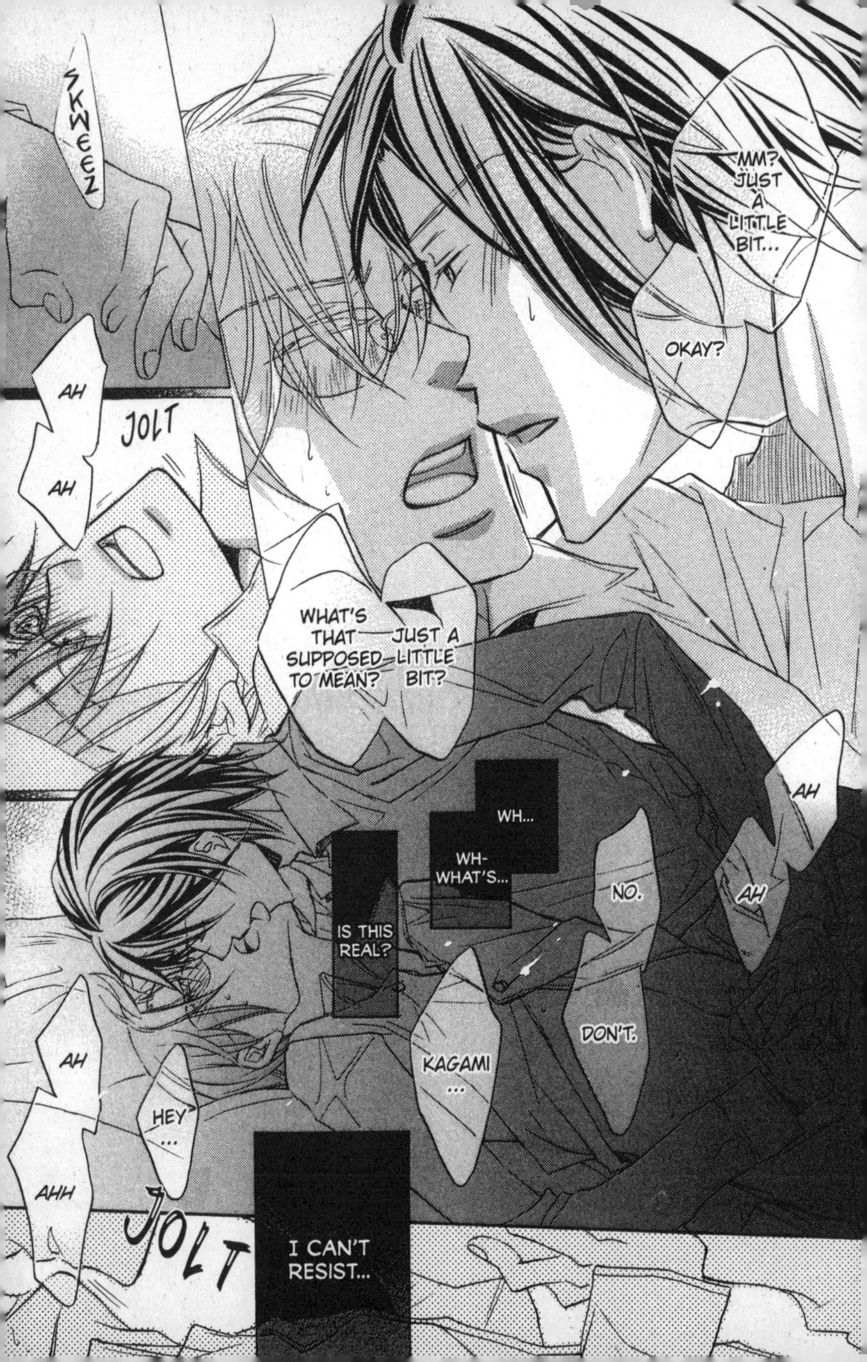
MM? JUST A LITTLE BIT...
OKAY?
SKWEEZ
AH
JOLT
AH
WHAT'S THAT SUPPOSED TO MEAN? JUST A LITTLE BIT?
AH
AH
WH...
WH- WHAT'S...
NO.
IS THIS REAL?
DON'T.
KAGAMI...
AH
HEY...
AHH
JOLT
I CAN'T RESIST...

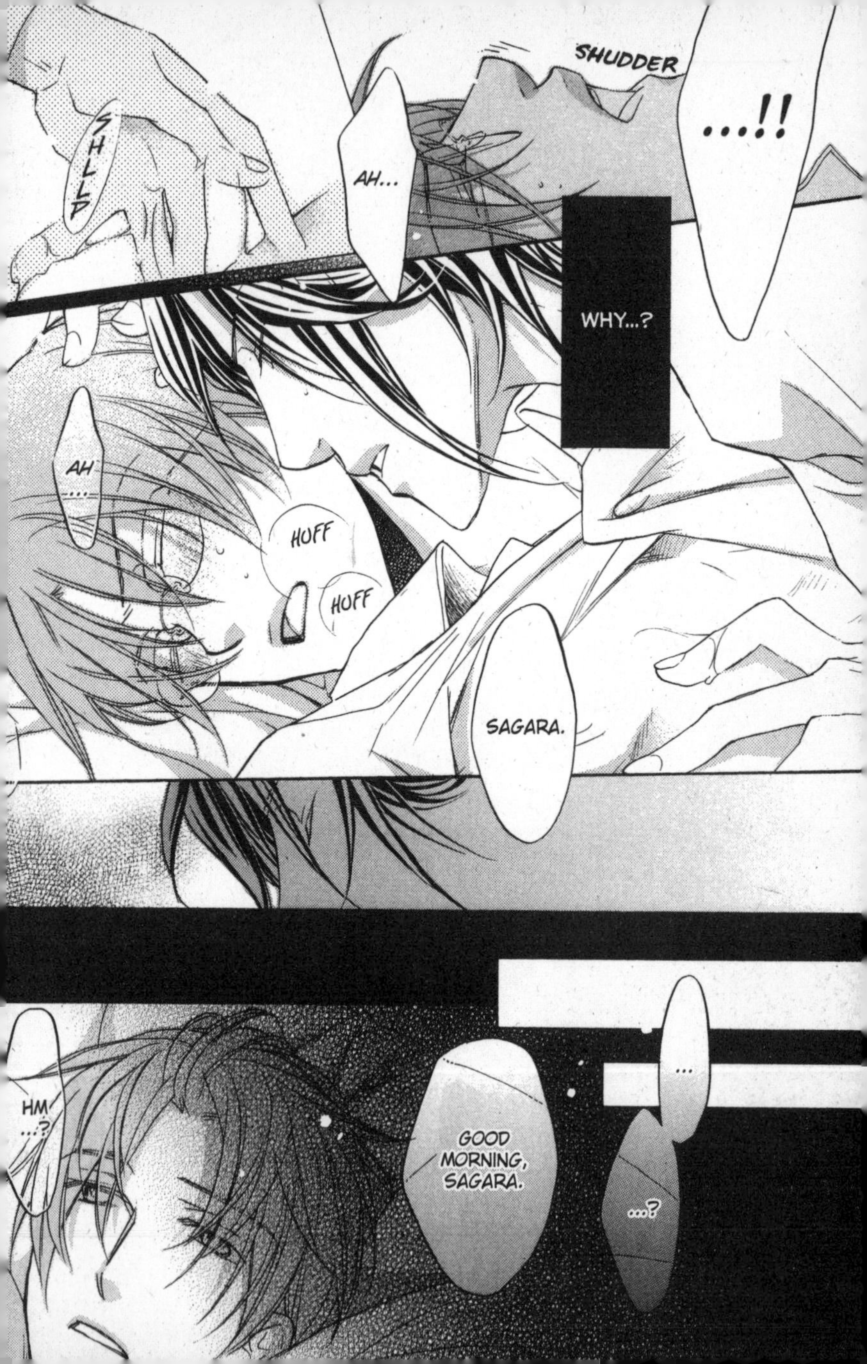
SHUDDER
...!!
AH...
SHLLP
WHY...?
SAGARA.
HUFF
HUFF
AH ...
...
...?
GOOD MORNING, SAGARA.
HM ...?

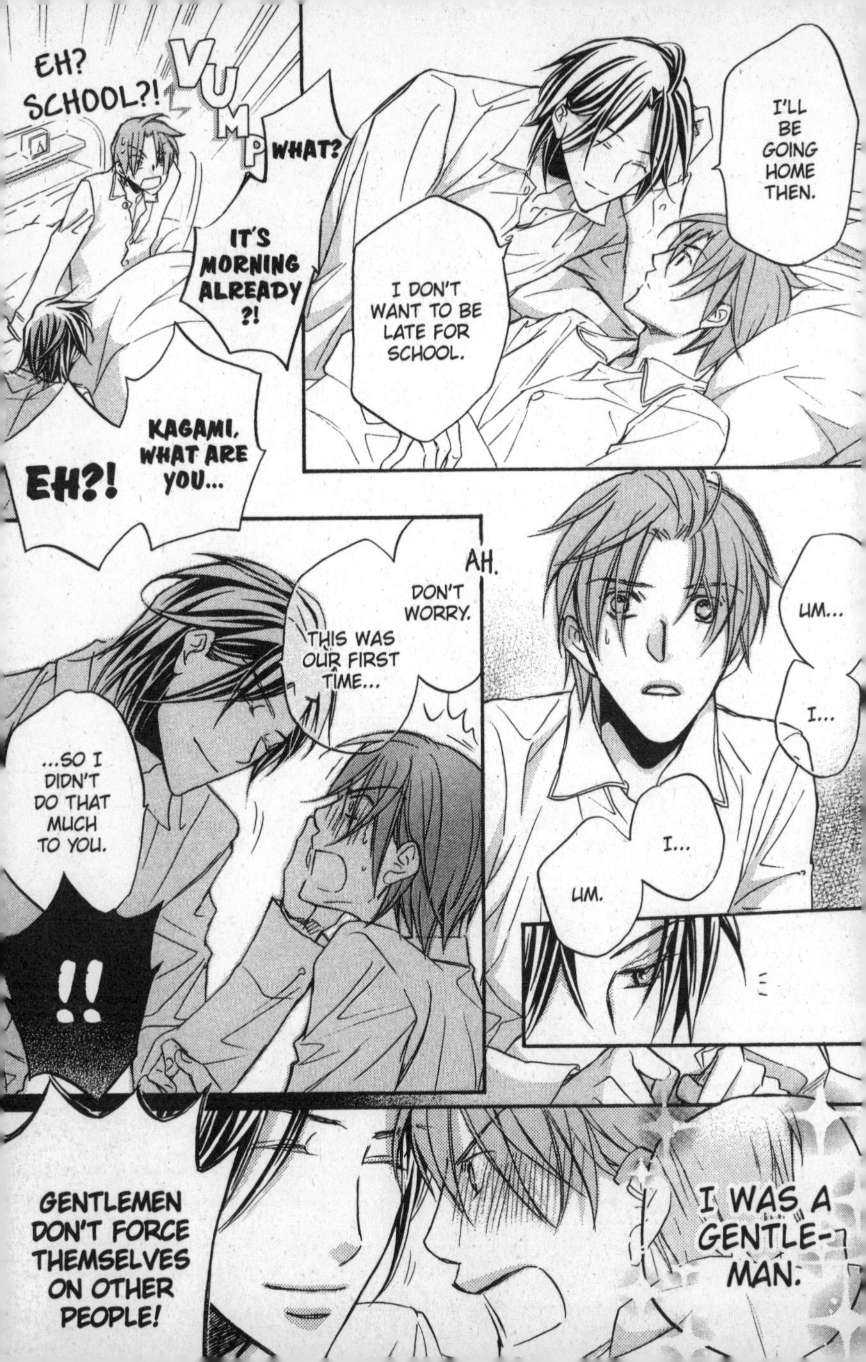
I'LL BE GOING HOME THEN.
I DON'T WANT TO BE LATE FOR SCHOOL.
VUMP
WHAT?
EH? SCHOOL?!
IT'S MORNING ALREADY?!
KAGAMI, WHAT ARE YOU...
EH?!
UM...
I...
I...
UM.
AH.
DON'T WORRY.
THIS WAS OUR FIRST TIME...
...SO I DIDN'T DO THAT MUCH TO YOU.
!!
I WAS A GENTLEMAN.
GENTLEMEN DON'T FORCE THEMSELVES ON OTHER PEOPLE!

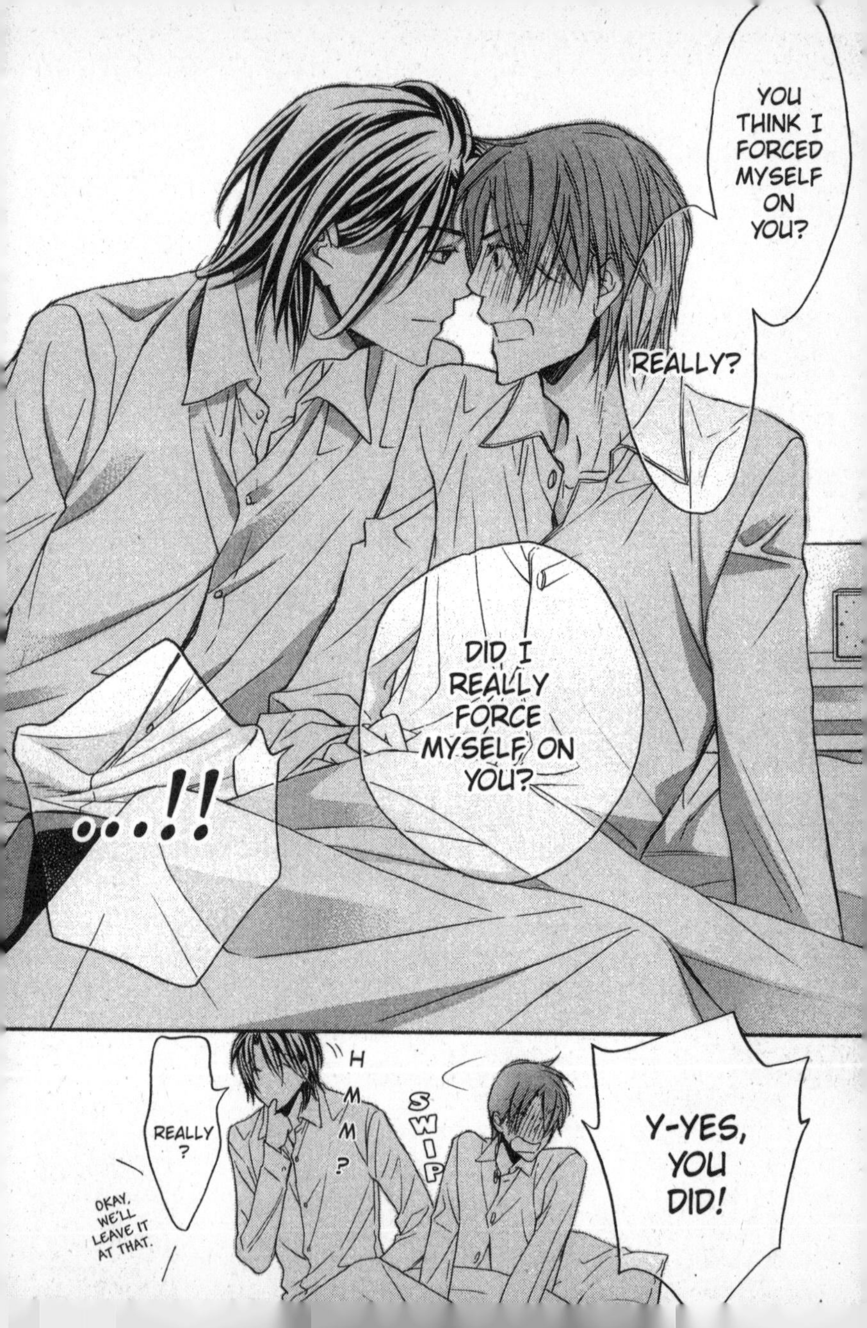
YOU THINK I FORCED MYSELF ON YOU?
REALLY?
DID I REALLY FORCE MYSELF ON YOU?
O...!!
Y-YES, YOU DID!
SWIP
HMM?
REALLY?
OKAY, WE'LL LEAVE IT AT THAT.

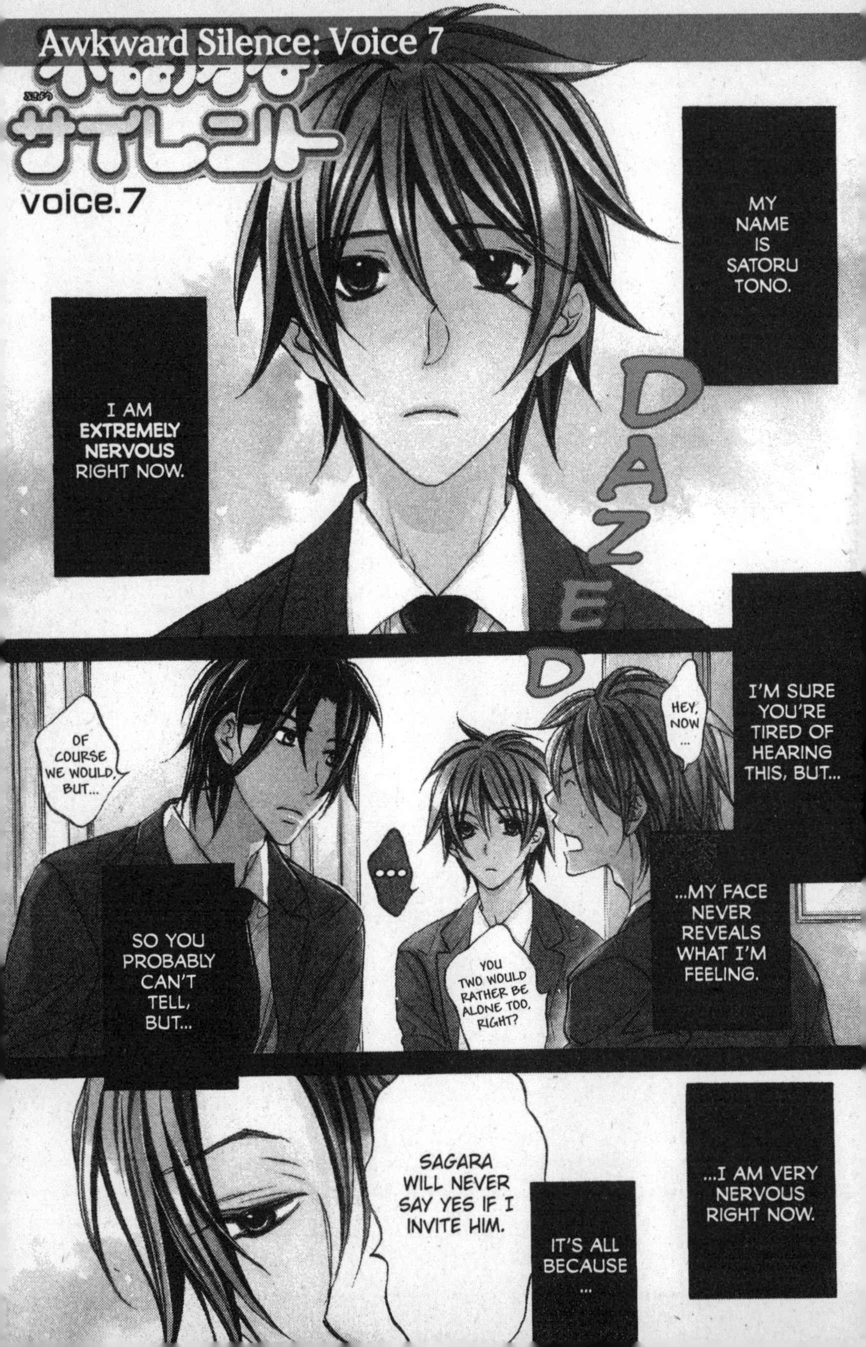
Awkward Silence: Voice 7
voice.7
MY NAME IS SATORU TONO.
DAZED
I AM EXTREMELY NERVOUS RIGHT NOW.
I'M SURE YOU'RE TIRED OF HEARING THIS, BUT...
HEY, NOW...
...MY FACE NEVER REVEALS WHAT I'M FEELING.
YOU TWO WOULD RATHER BE ALONE TOO, RIGHT?
...
OF COURSE WE WOULD, BUT...
SO YOU PROBABLY CAN'T TELL, BUT...
...I AM VERY NERVOUS RIGHT NOW.
IT'S ALL BECAUSE...
SAGARA WILL NEVER SAY YES IF I INVITE HIM.

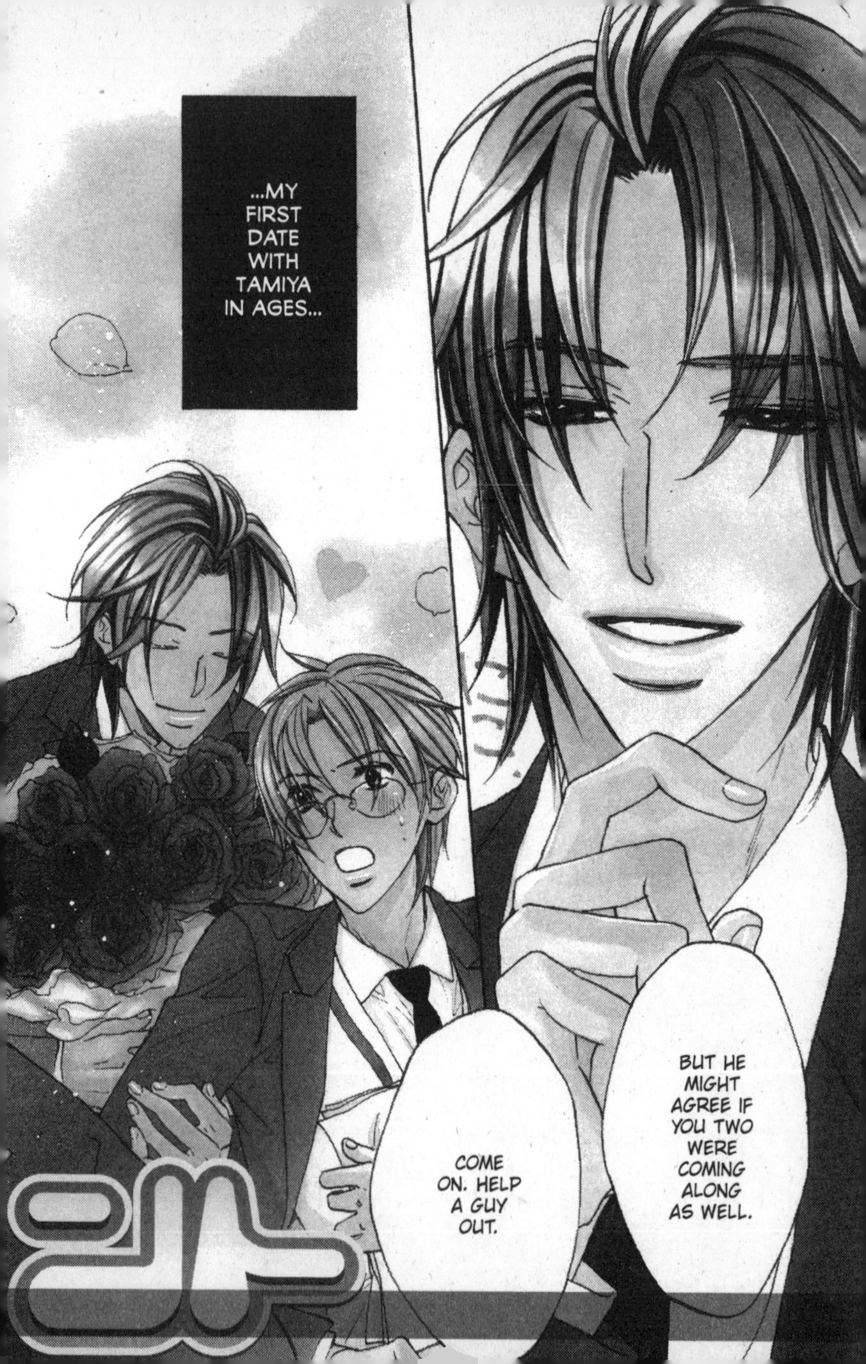
BUT HE MIGHT AGREE IF YOU TWO WERE COMING ALONG AS WELL.
COME ON. HELP A GUY OUT.
...MY FIRST DATE WITH TAMIYA IN AGES...

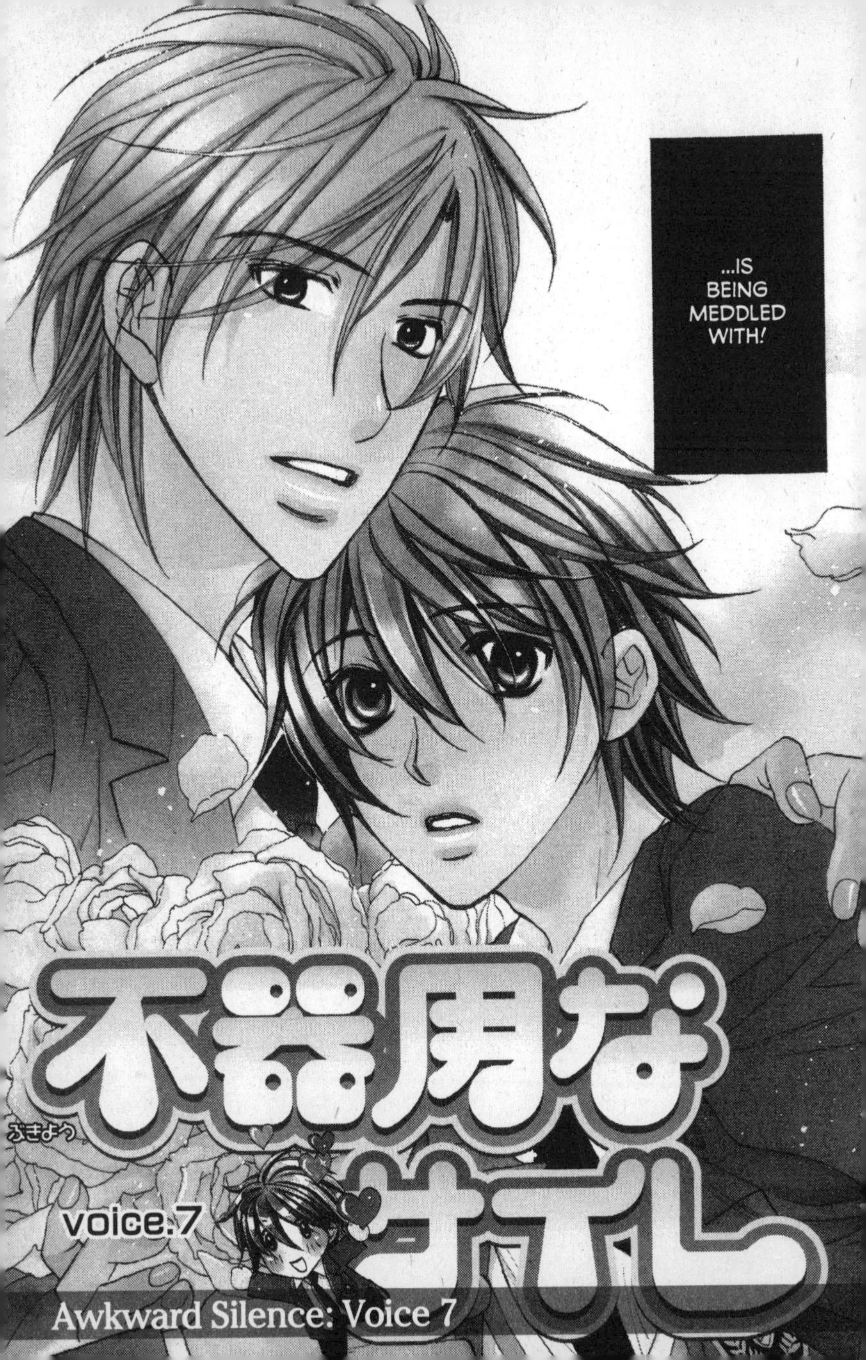
...IS
BEING
MEDDLED
WITH!
ぶきよう
不器用なオレ
voice.7
Awkward Silence: Voice 7

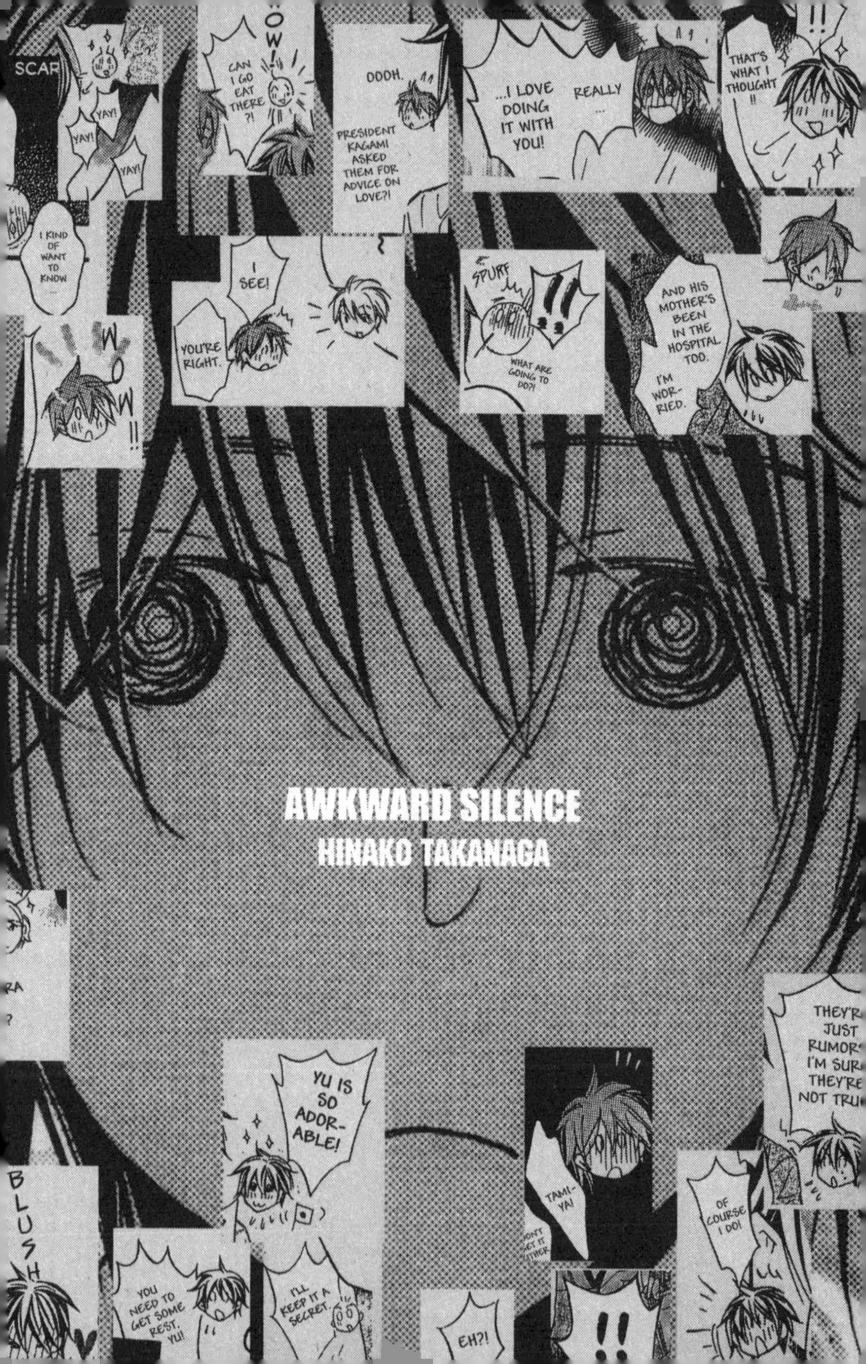

!!
THAT'S WHAT I THOUGHT !!
REALLY ...
...I LOVE DOING IT WITH YOU!
OOOH.
PRESIDENT KAGAMI ASKED THEM FOR ADVICE ON LOVE?!
WOW!
CAN I GO EAT THERE ?!
SCAR
YAY!
YAY!
YAY!
AND HIS MOTHER'S BEEN IN THE HOSPITAL TOO.
I'M WOR-RIED.
SPURF
!!
WHAT ARE GOING TO DO?!
I SEE!
YOU'RE RIGHT.
I KIND OF WANT TO KNOW ...
WOW!!
AWKWARD SILENCE
HINAKO TAKANAGA
THEY'R JUST RUMORS I'M SUR THEY'RE NOT TRU
OF COURSE I DO!
!!
TAMI-YA!
DON'T GET IT EITHER.
YU IS SO ADOR-ABLE!
BLUSH
I'LL KEEP IT A SECRET.
YOU NEED TO GET SOME REST, YU!
!!
EH?!

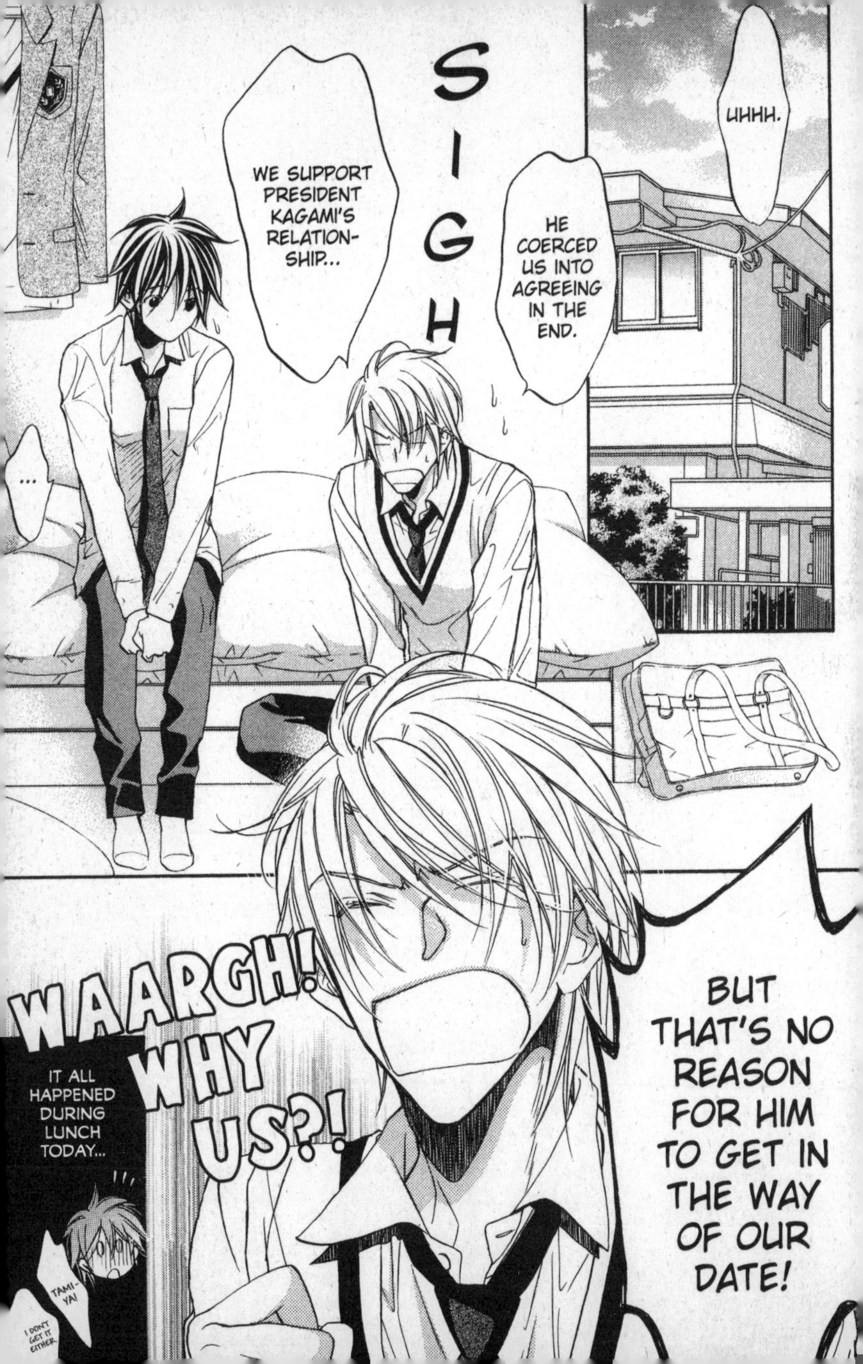
UHHH.
HE COERCED US INTO AGREEING IN THE END.
SIGH
WE SUPPORT PRESIDENT KAGAMI'S RELATION-SHIP...
...
BUT THAT'S NO REASON FOR HIM TO GET IN THE WAY OF OUR DATE!
WAARGH! WHY US?!
IT ALL HAPPENED DURING LUNCH TODAY...
!!!
TAMI-YA!
I DON'T GET IT EITHER

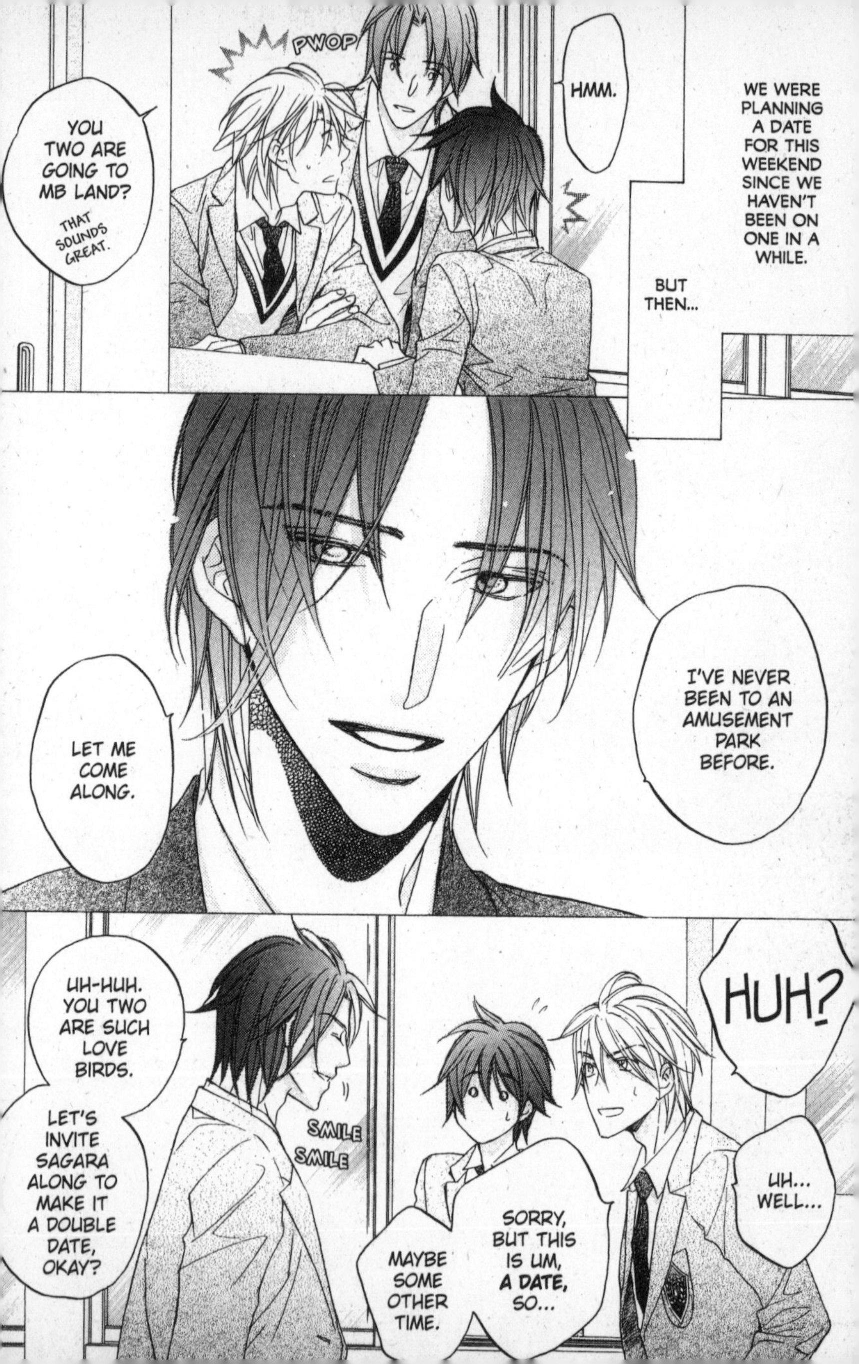
WE WERE PLANNING A DATE FOR THIS WEEKEND SINCE WE HAVEN'T BEEN ON ONE IN A WHILE.
BUT THEN...
HMM.
PWOP
YOU TWO ARE GOING TO MB LAND?
THAT SOUNDS GREAT.
I'VE NEVER BEEN TO AN AMUSEMENT PARK BEFORE.
LET ME COME ALONG.
HUH?
UH... WELL...
SORRY, BUT THIS IS UM, **A DATE,** SO...
MAYBE SOME OTHER TIME.
SMILE
SMILE
UH-HUH. YOU TWO ARE SUCH LOVE BIRDS.
LET'S INVITE SAGARA ALONG TO MAKE IT A DOUBLE DATE, OKAY?

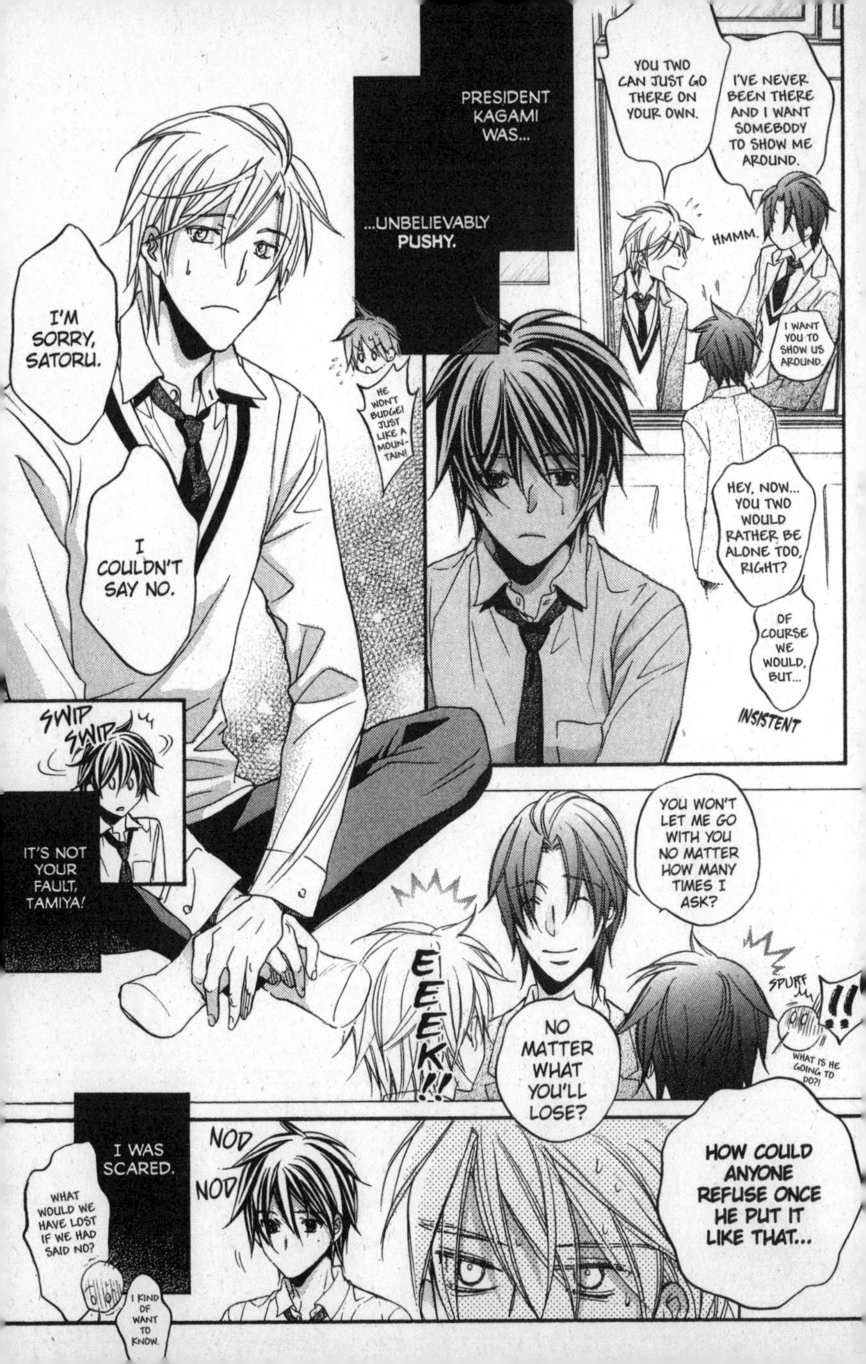
I'VE NEVER BEEN THERE AND I WANT SOMEBODY TO SHOW ME AROUND.
YOU TWO CAN JUST GO THERE ON YOUR OWN.
HMMM.
I WANT YOU TO SHOW US AROUND.
PRESIDENT KAGAMI WAS...
...UNBELIEVABLY PUSHY.
HEY, NOW... YOU TWO WOULD RATHER BE ALONE TOO, RIGHT?
OF COURSE WE WOULD, BUT...
INSISTENT
HE WON'T BUDGE! JUST LIKE A MOUN-TAIN!
I'M SORRY, SATORU.
I COULDN'T SAY NO.
SWIP SWIP
IT'S NOT YOUR FAULT, TAMIYA!
YOU WON'T LET ME GO WITH YOU NO MATTER HOW MANY TIMES I ASK?
SPURF
!!
WHAT IS HE GOING TO DO?!
NO MATTER WHAT YOU'LL LOSE?
EEEK!!
HOW COULD ANYONE REFUSE ONCE HE PUT IT LIKE THAT...
NOD NOD
I WAS SCARED.
WHAT WOULD WE HAVE LOST IF WE HAD SAID NO?
I KIND OF WANT TO KNOW.

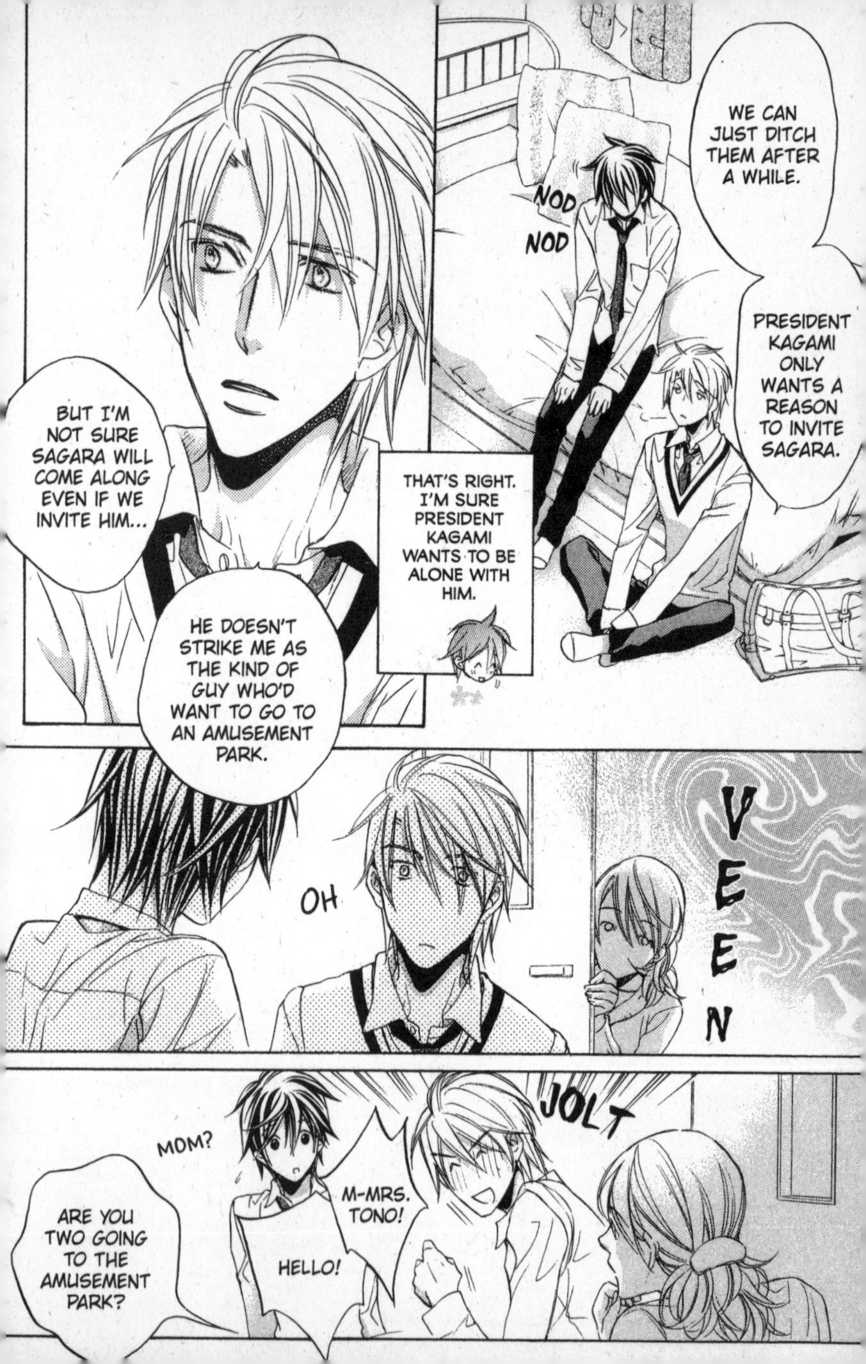
WE CAN JUST DITCH THEM AFTER A WHILE.
NOD
NOD
PRESIDENT KAGAMI ONLY WANTS A REASON TO INVITE SAGARA.
THAT'S RIGHT. I'M SURE PRESIDENT KAGAMI WANTS TO BE ALONE WITH HIM.
BUT I'M NOT SURE SAGARA WILL COME ALONG EVEN IF WE INVITE HIM...
HE DOESN'T STRIKE ME AS THE KIND OF GUY WHO'D WANT TO GO TO AN AMUSEMENT PARK.
VEEN
OH
JOLT
M-MRS. TONO!
HELLO!
MOM?
ARE YOU TWO GOING TO THE AMUSEMENT PARK?

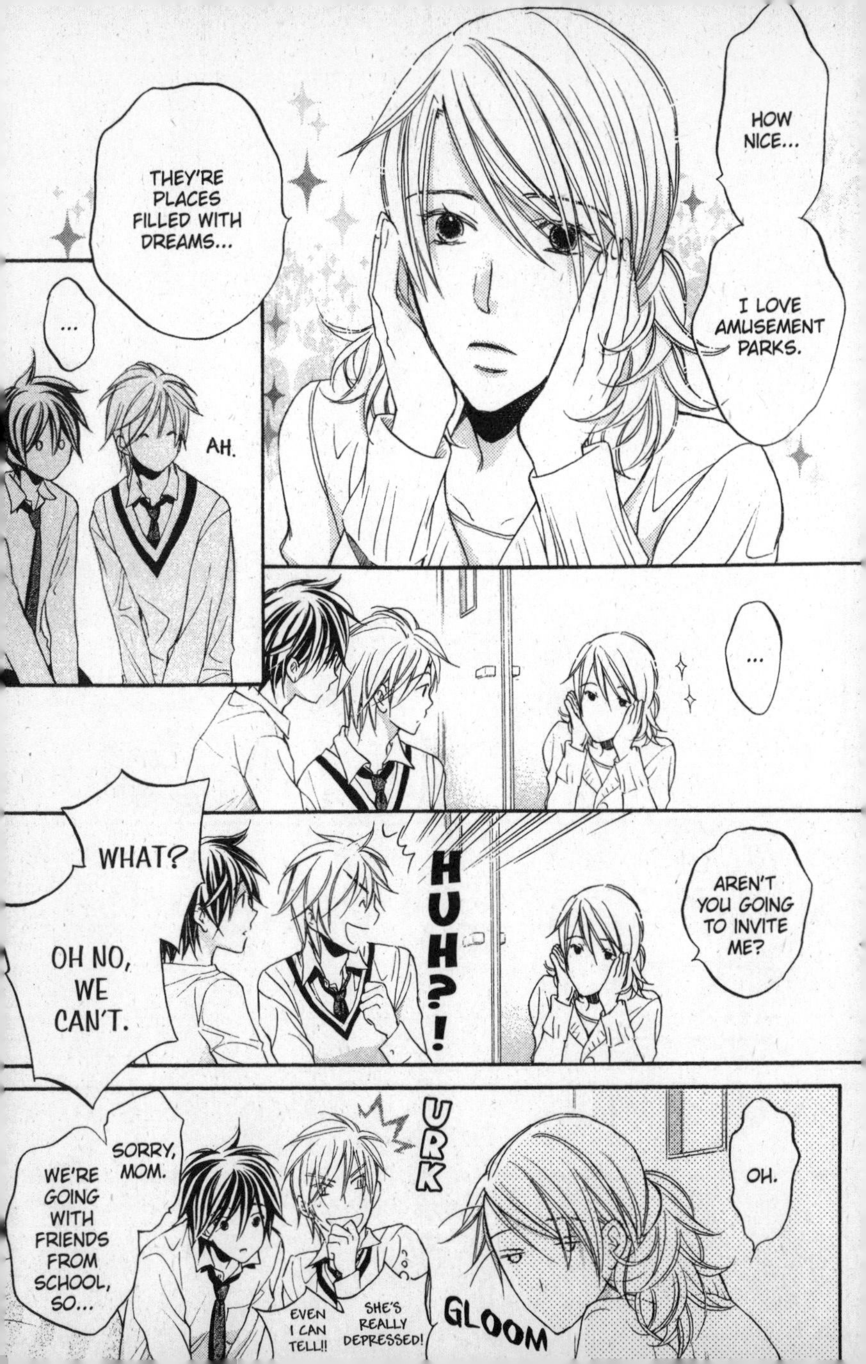
HOW NICE...
I LOVE AMUSEMENT PARKS.
THEY'RE PLACES FILLED WITH DREAMS...
...
AH.
...
AREN'T YOU GOING TO INVITE ME?
HUH?!
WHAT?
OH NO, WE CAN'T.
OH.
URK
SORRY, MOM.
WE'RE GOING WITH FRIENDS FROM SCHOOL, SO...
GLOOM
SHE'S REALLY DEPRESSED!
EVEN I CAN TELL!!

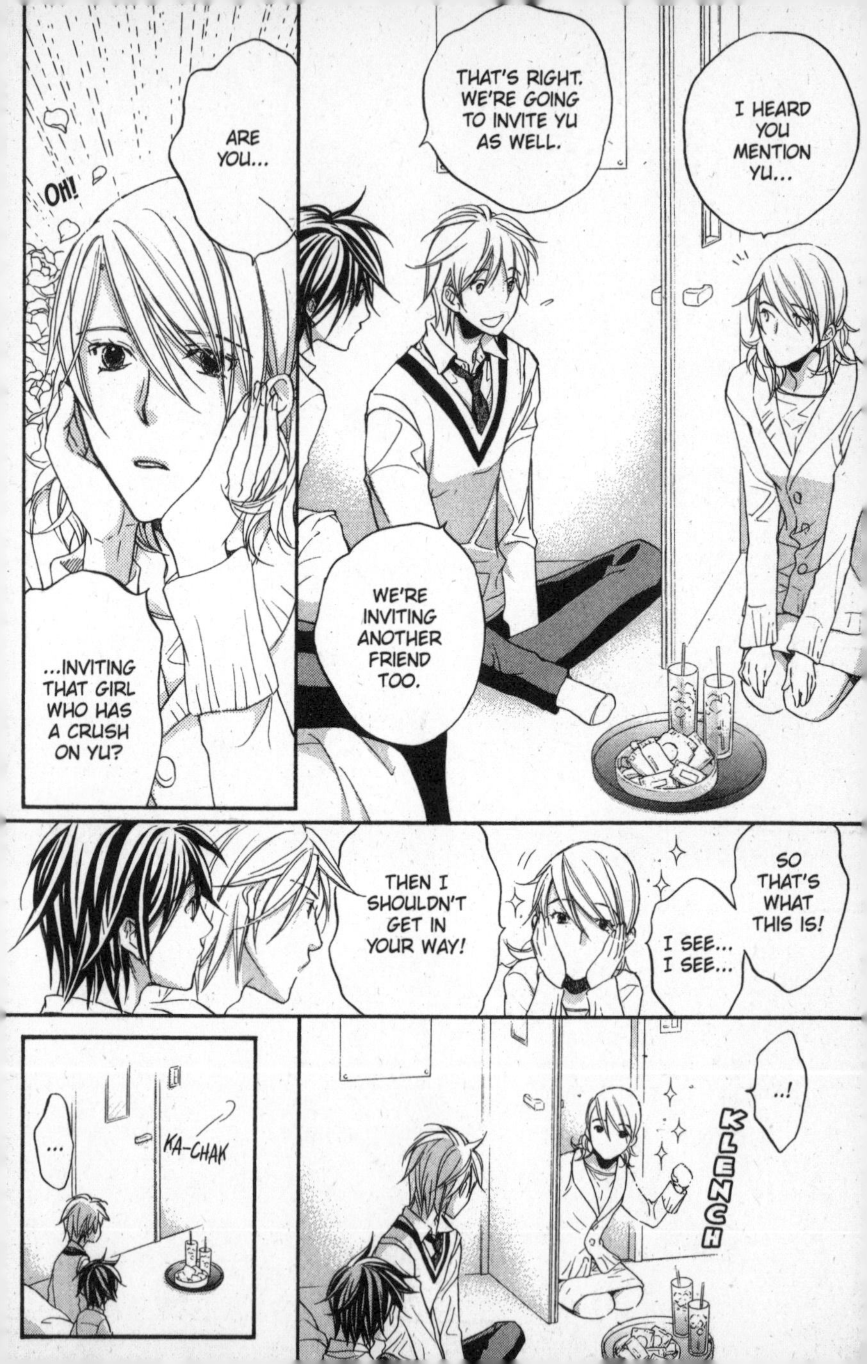
I HEARD YOU MENTION YU...
THAT'S RIGHT. WE'RE GOING TO INVITE YU AS WELL.
WE'RE INVITING ANOTHER FRIEND TOO.
ARE YOU...
OH!
...INVITING THAT GIRL WHO HAS A CRUSH ON YU?
SO THAT'S WHAT THIS IS!
I SEE... I SEE...
THEN I SHOULDN'T GET IN YOUR WAY!
...!
KLENCH
...
KA-CHAK

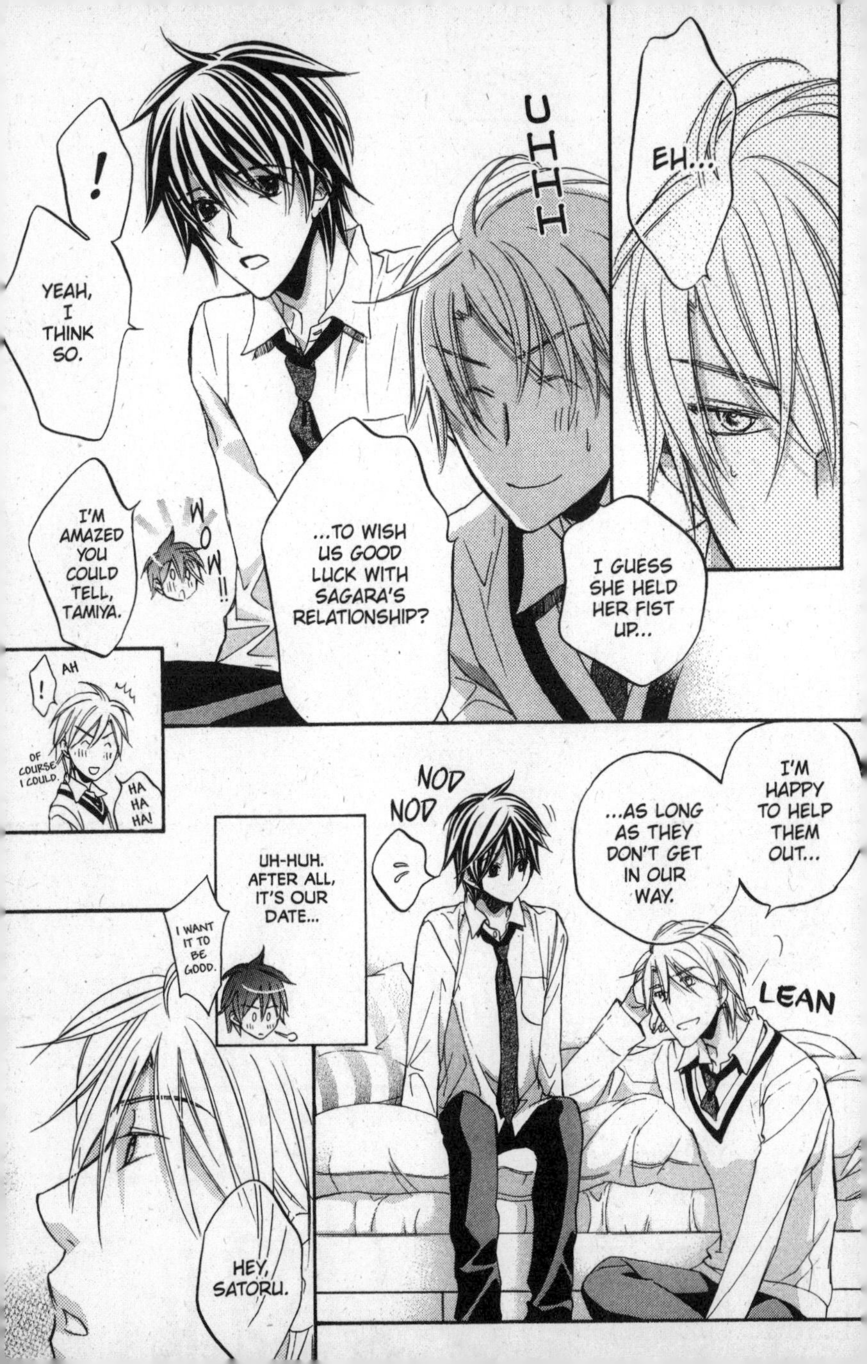
EH...
UHHH
I GUESS SHE HELD HER FIST UP...
...TO WISH US GOOD LUCK WITH SAGARA'S RELATIONSHIP?
!
YEAH, I THINK SO.
I'M AMAZED YOU COULD TELL, TAMIYA.
WOW!!
AH
!
OF COURSE I COULD.
HA HA HA!
I'M HAPPY TO HELP THEM OUT...
...AS LONG AS THEY DON'T GET IN OUR WAY.
LEAN
NOD NOD
UH-HUH. AFTER ALL, IT'S OUR DATE...
I WANT IT TO BE GOOD.
HEY, SATORU.

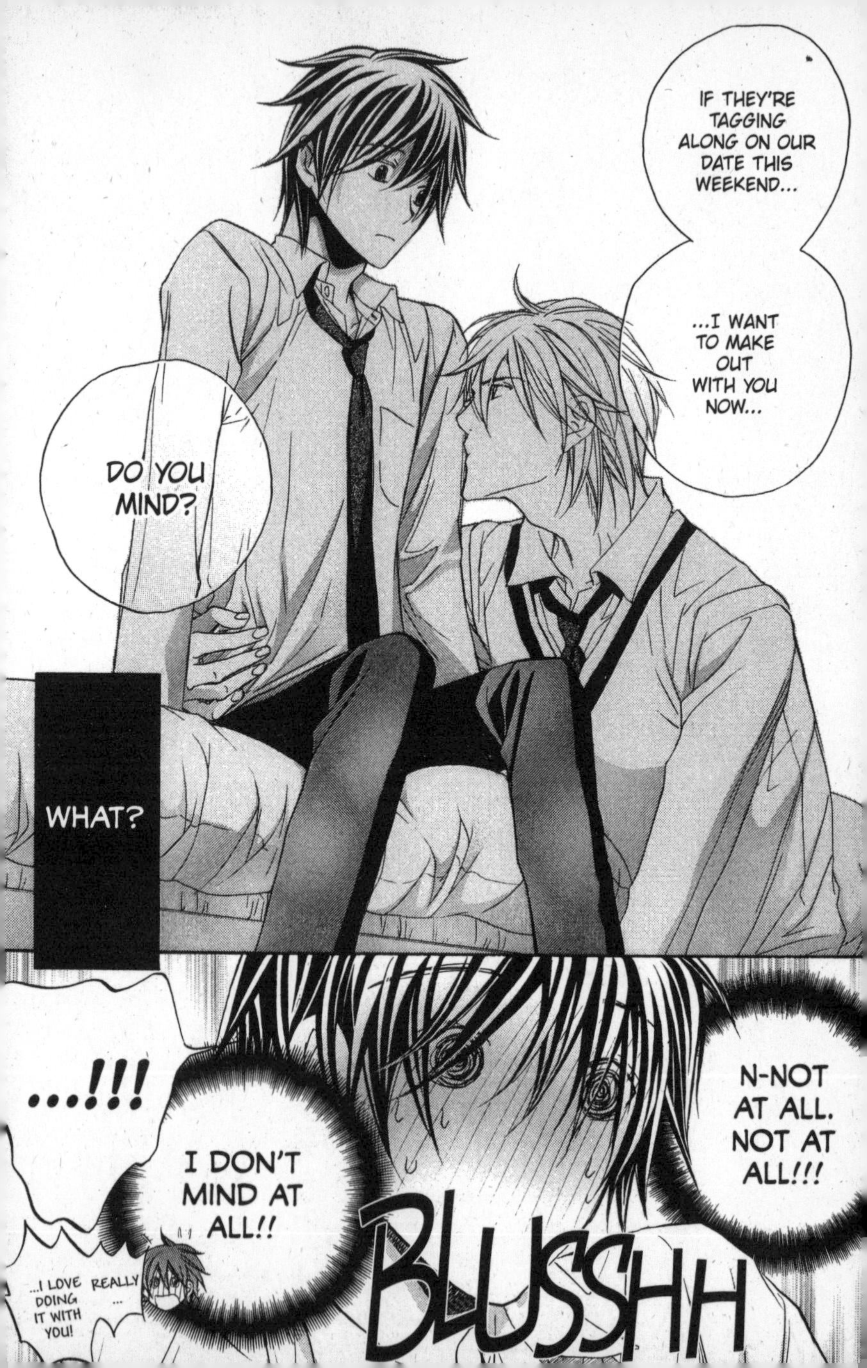
IF THEY'RE TAGGING ALONG ON OUR DATE THIS WEEKEND...
...I WANT TO MAKE OUT WITH YOU NOW...
DO YOU MIND?
WHAT?
N-NOT AT ALL. NOT AT ALL!!!
BLUSSHH
I DON'T MIND AT ALL!!
...!!!
REALLY ...
...I LOVE DOING IT WITH YOU!

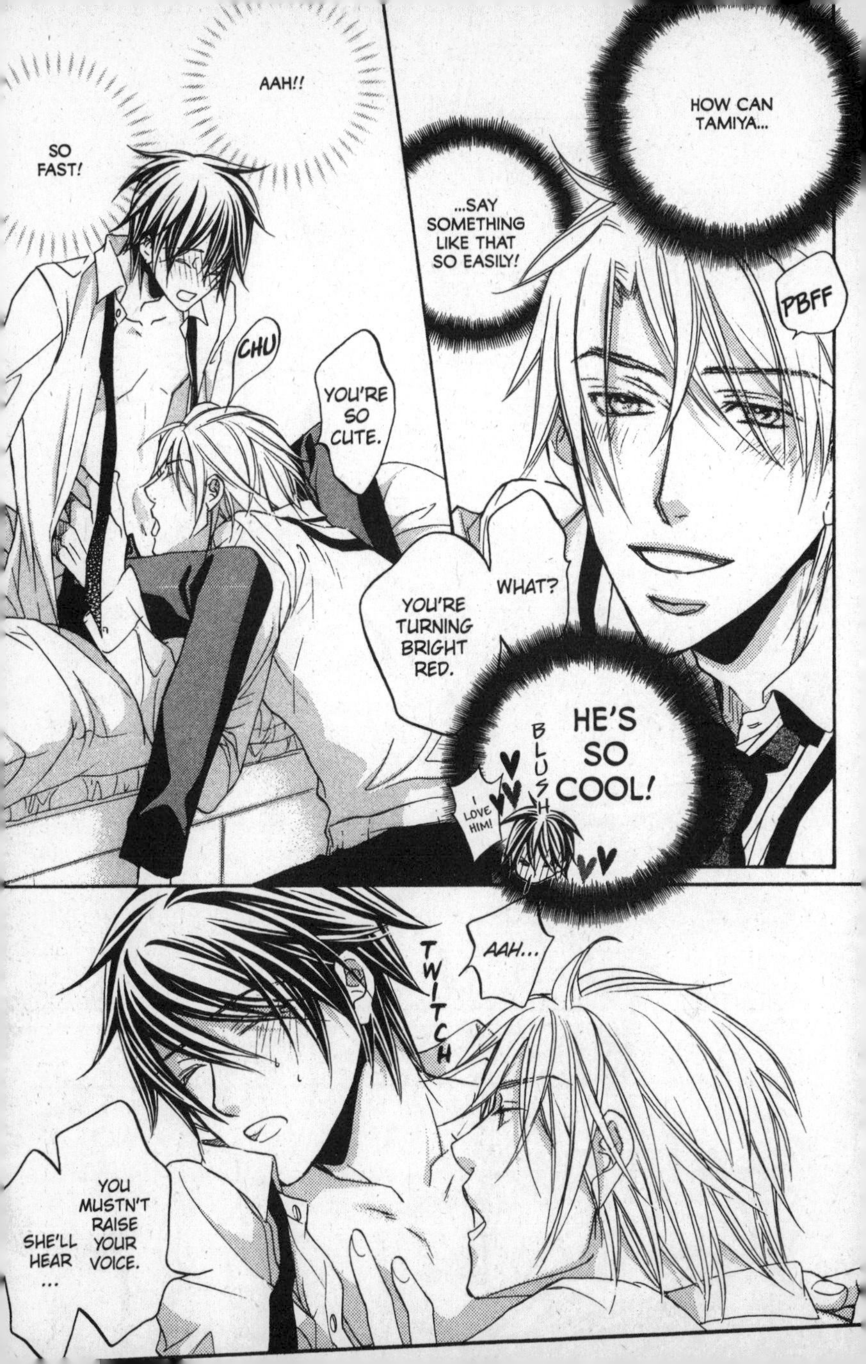
HOW CAN TAMIYA...
...SAY SOMETHING LIKE THAT SO EASILY!
PBFF
WHAT?
YOU'RE TURNING BRIGHT RED.
HE'S SO COOL!
BLUSH
I LOVE HIM!
AAH!!
SO FAST!
CHU
YOU'RE SO CUTE.
AAH...
TWITCH
YOU MUSTN'T RAISE YOUR VOICE.
SHE'LL HEAR ...

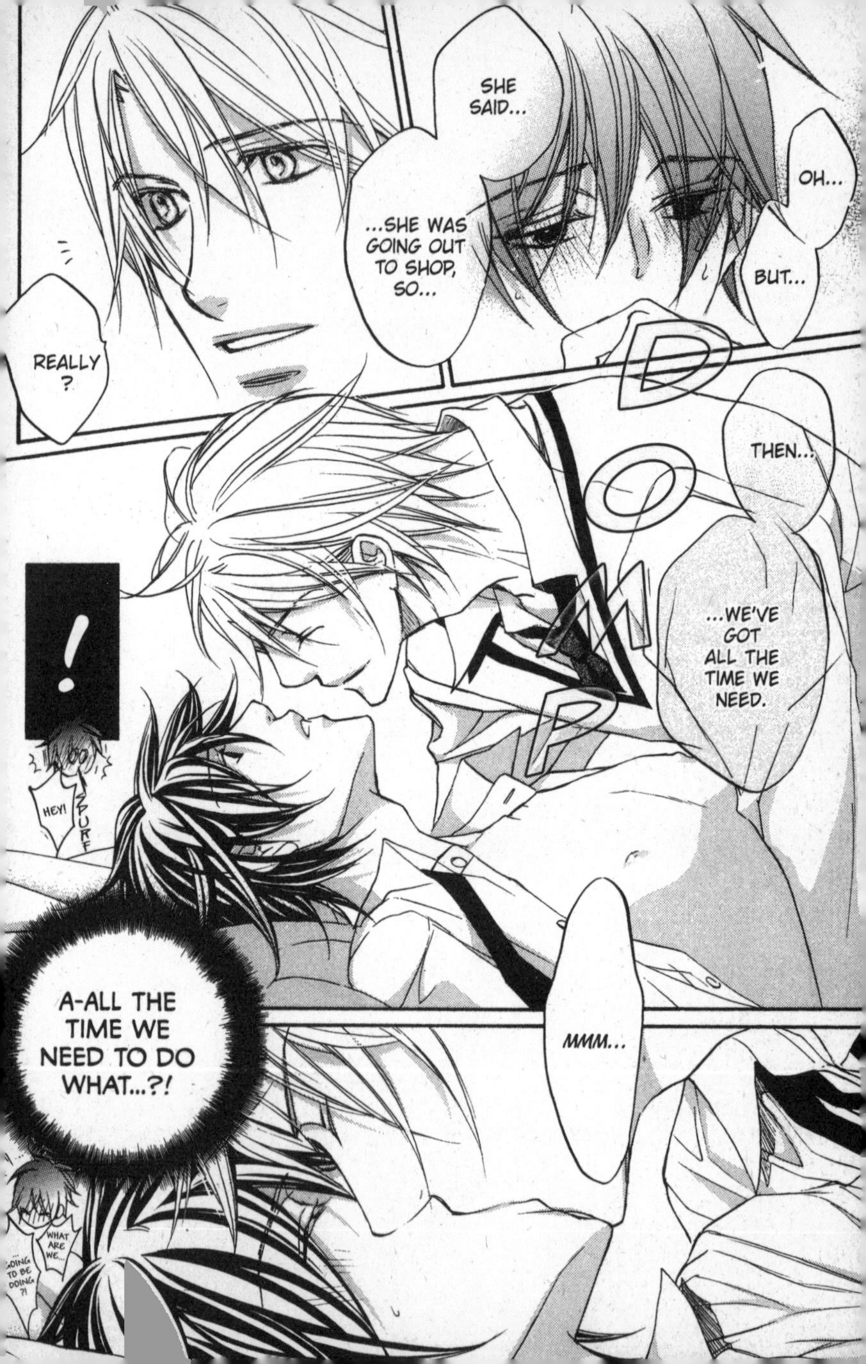
SHE SAID...
...SHE WAS GOING OUT TO SHOP, SO...
OH...
BUT...
REALLY?
THEN...
...WE'VE GOT ALL THE TIME WE NEED.
DOMP
!
HEY!
SPURF
A-ALL THE TIME WE NEED TO DO WHAT...?!
MMM...
WHAT ARE WE...
...GOING TO BE DOING?!

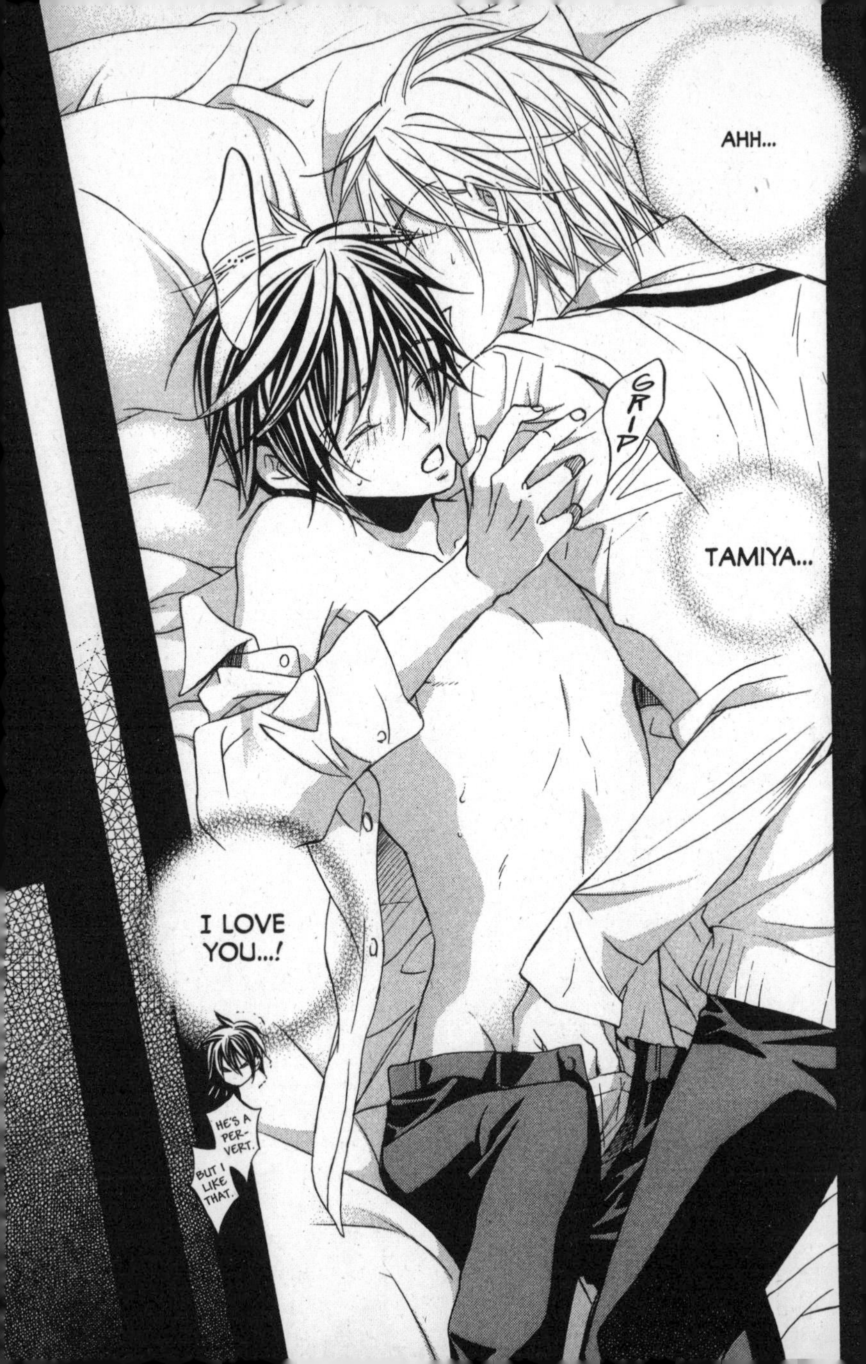
AHH...
GRIP
TAMIYA...
I LOVE YOU...!
HE'S A PER-VERT.
BUT I LIKE THAT.

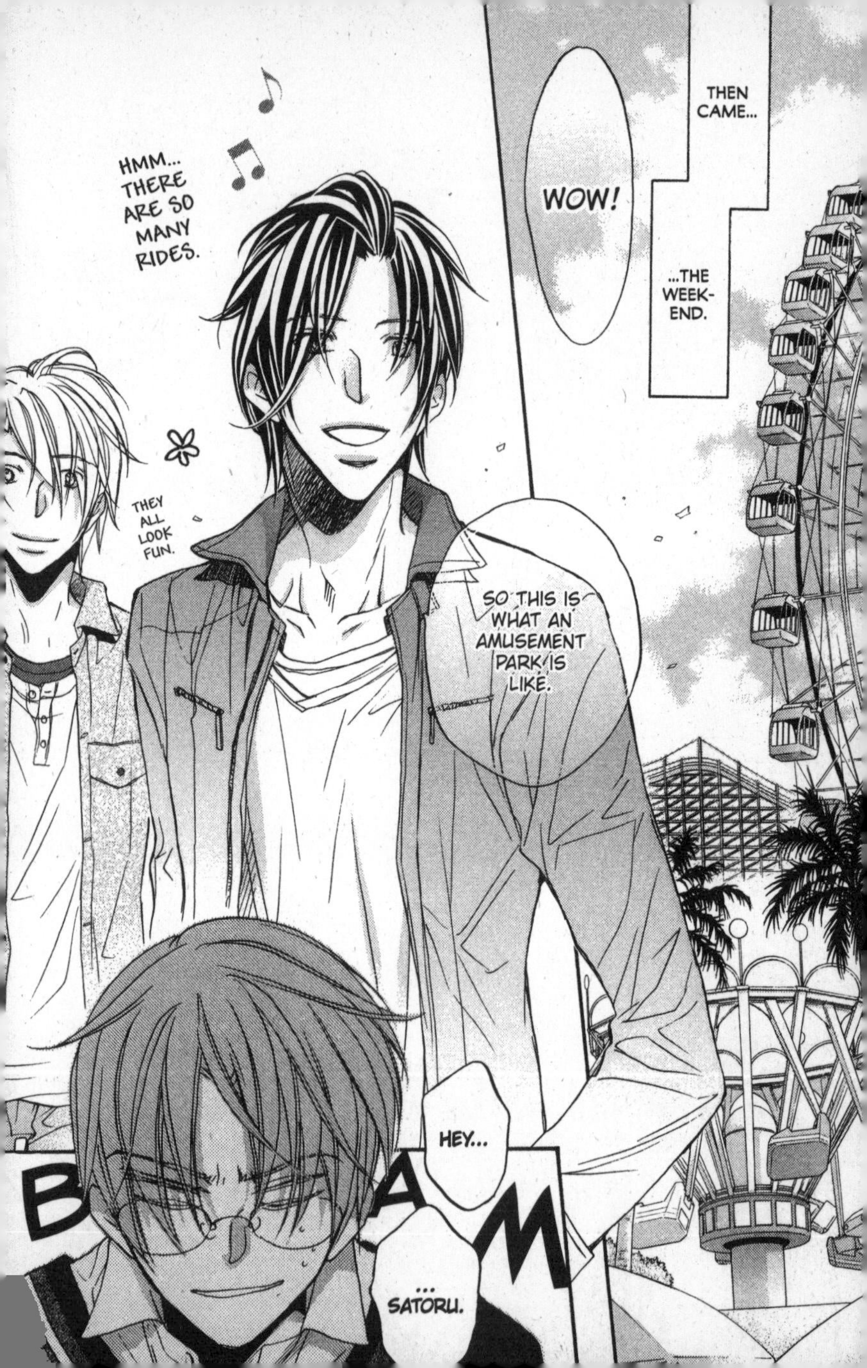
THEN CAME...
...THE WEEK-END.
WOW!
SO THIS IS WHAT AN AMUSEMENT PARK IS LIKE.
HMM... THERE ARE SO MANY RIDES.
THEY ALL LOOK FUN.
HEY...
...SATORU.
BAM

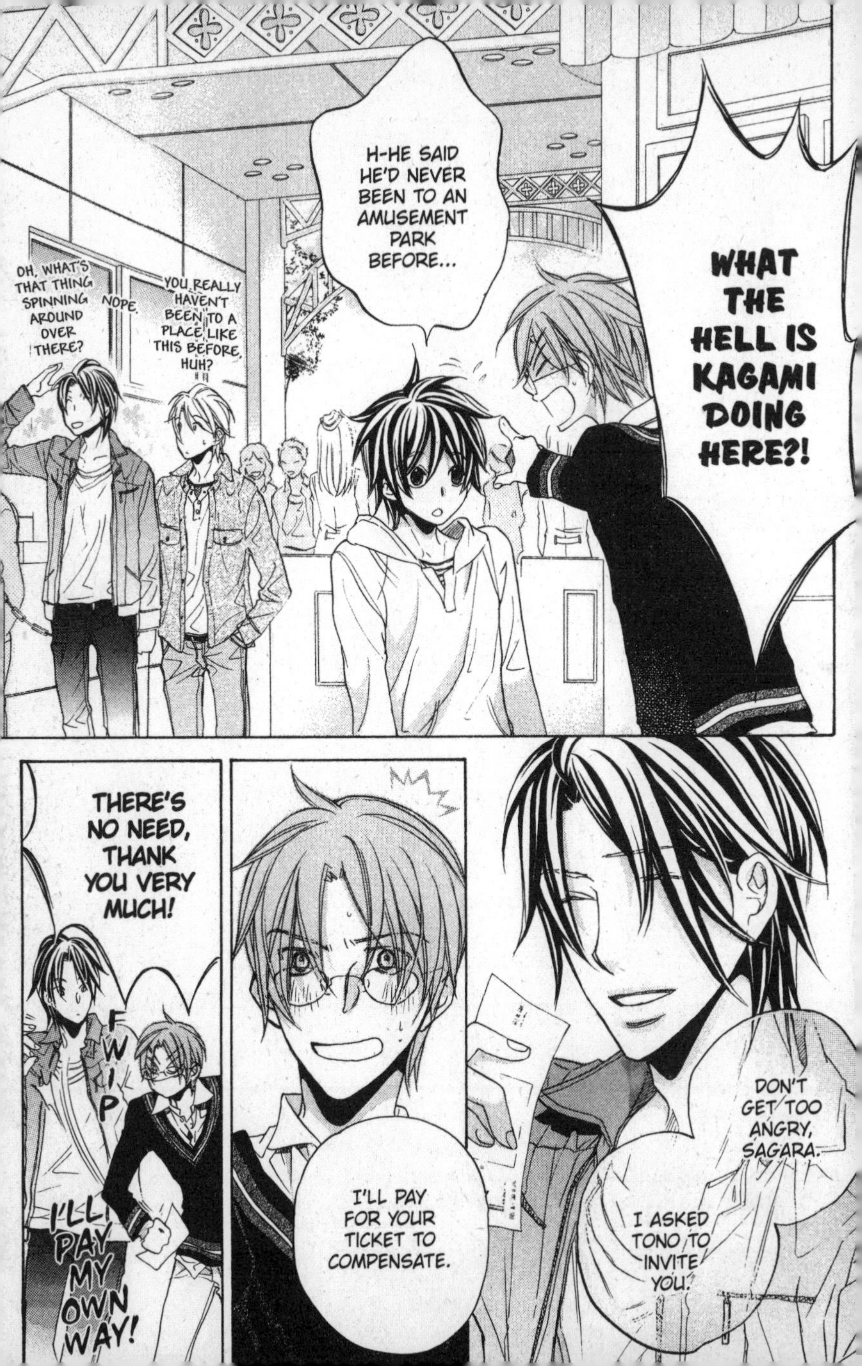
WHAT THE HELL IS KAGAMI DOING HERE?!
H-HE SAID HE'D NEVER BEEN TO AN AMUSEMENT PARK BEFORE...
YOU REALLY HAVEN'T BEEN TO A PLACE LIKE THIS BEFORE, HUH?
NOPE.
OH, WHAT'S THAT THING SPINNING AROUND OVER THERE?
DON'T GET TOO ANGRY, SAGARA.
I ASKED TONO TO INVITE YOU.
I'LL PAY FOR YOUR TICKET TO COMPENSATE.
THERE'S NO NEED, THANK YOU VERY MUCH!
FWIP
I'LL PAY MY OWN WAY!

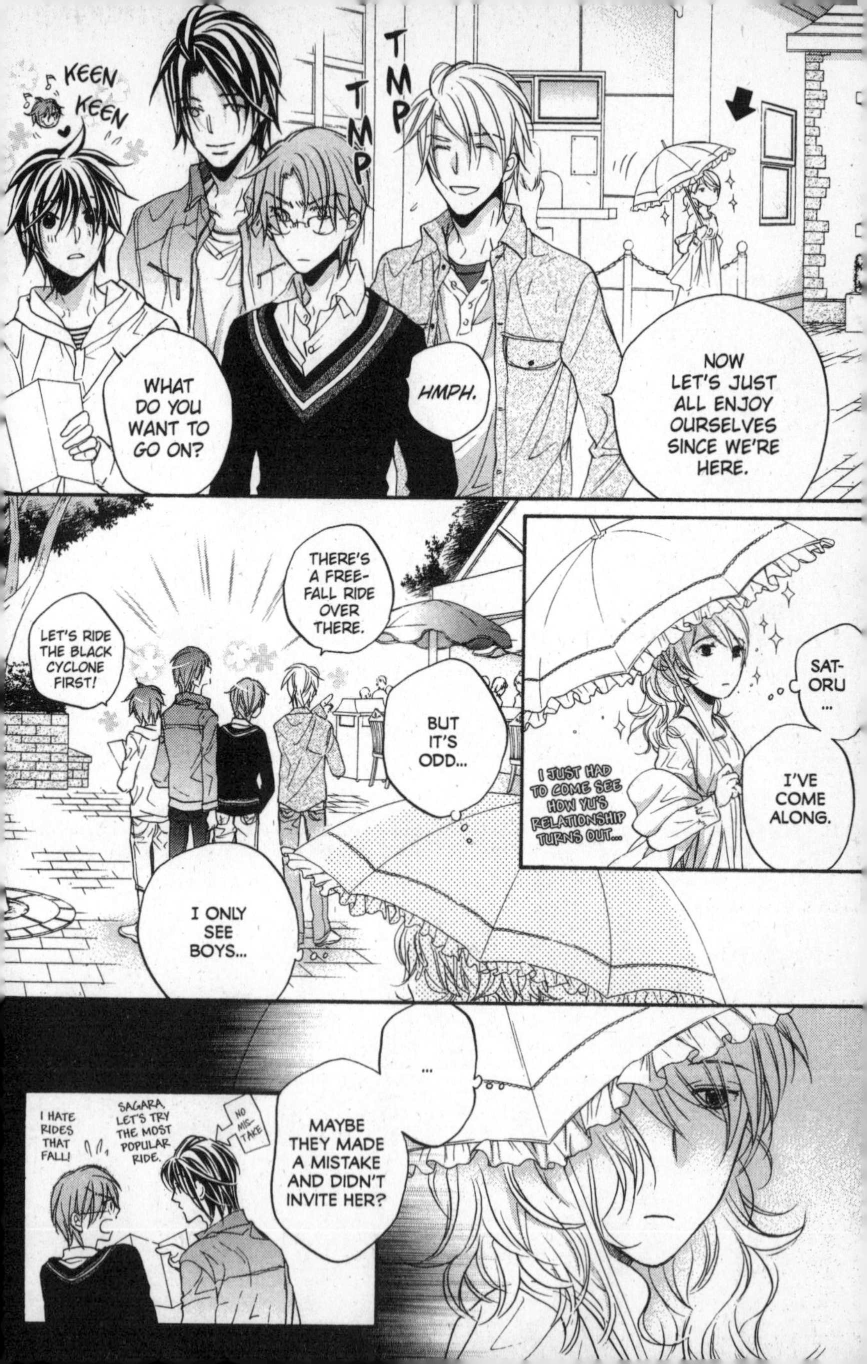
NOW LET'S JUST ALL ENJOY OURSELVES SINCE WE'RE HERE.
TMP TMP
TMP TMP
HMPH.
WHAT DO YOU WANT TO GO ON?
KEEN KEEN
SAT-ORU ...
I'VE COME ALONG.
I JUST HAD TO COME SEE HOW YU'S RELATIONSHIP TURNS OUT...
THERE'S A FREE-FALL RIDE OVER THERE.
LET'S RIDE THE BLACK CYCLONE FIRST!
BUT IT'S ODD...
I ONLY SEE BOYS...
...
MAYBE THEY MADE A MISTAKE AND DIDN'T INVITE HER?
NO MIS-TAKE
SAGARA, LET'S TRY THE MOST POPULAR RIDE.
I HATE RIDES THAT FALL!

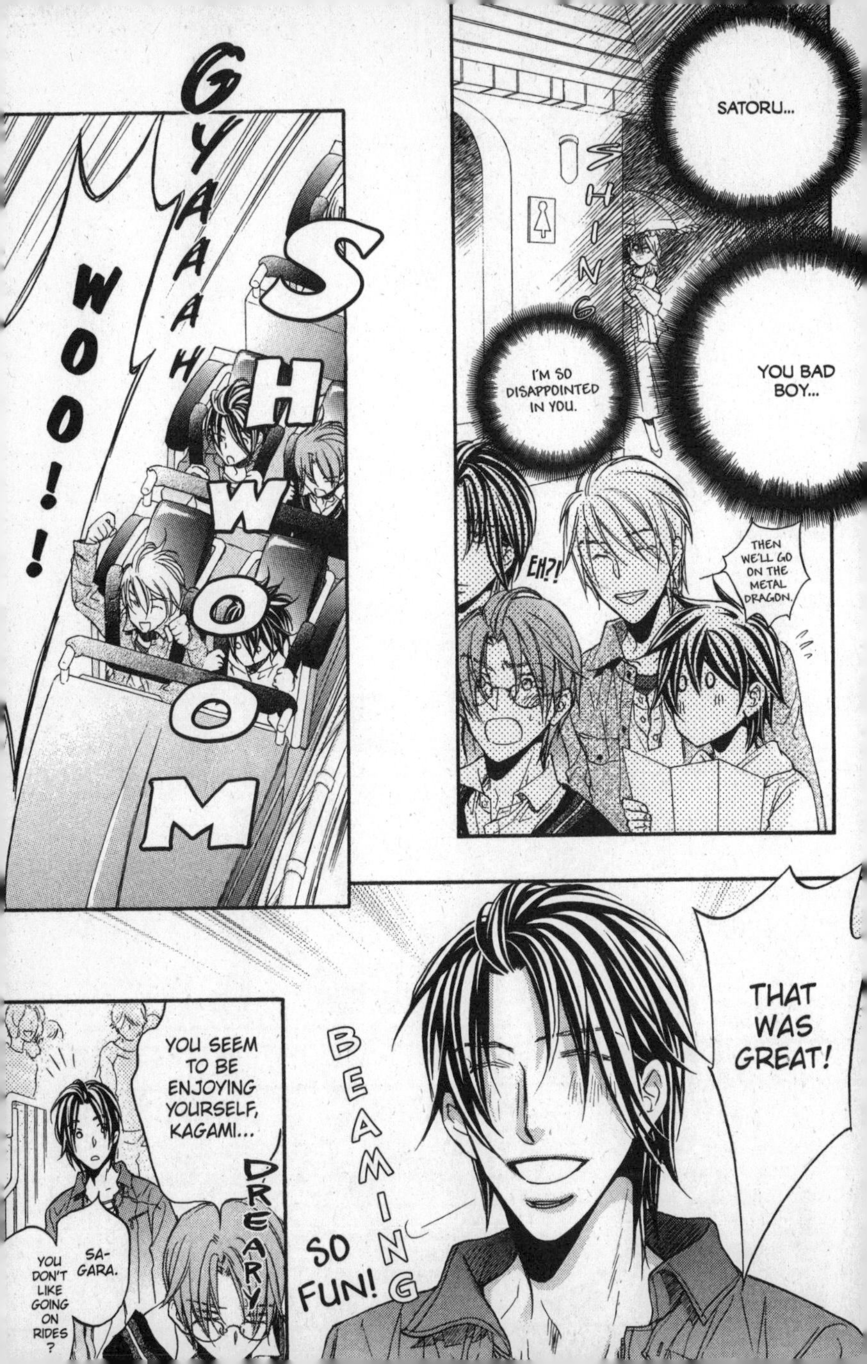
SATORU...
YOU BAD BOY...
SHING
I'M SO DISAPPOINTED IN YOU.
THEN WE'LL GO ON THE METAL DRAGON.
EH?!
GYAAAH
WOOO!!
SHWOOM
THAT WAS GREAT!
BEAMING
SO FUN!
YOU SEEM TO BE ENJOYING YOURSELF, KAGAMI...
DREARY
SA-GARA.
YOU DON'T LIKE GOING ON RIDES?

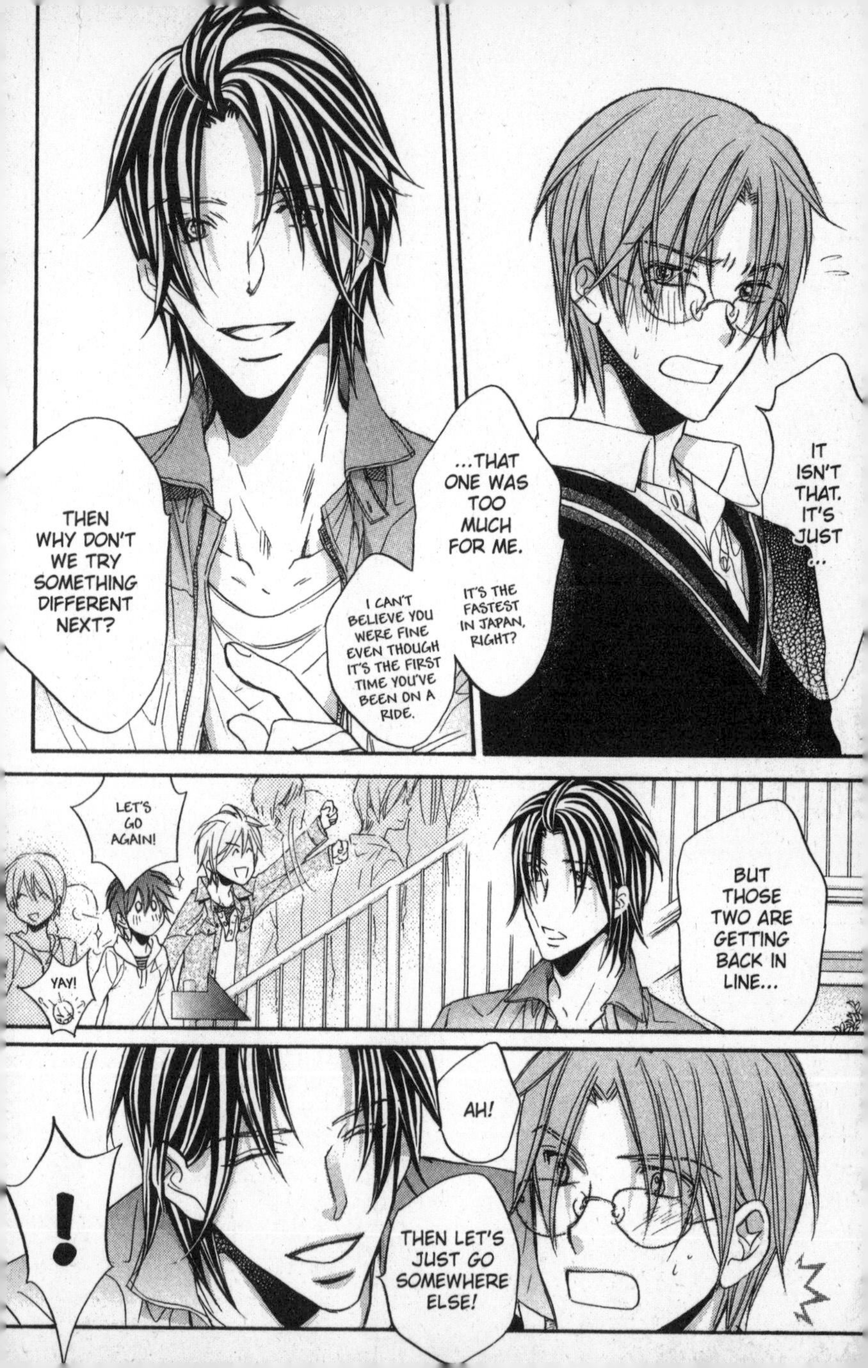
IT ISN'T THAT. IT'S JUST ...
...THAT ONE WAS TOO MUCH FOR ME.
IT'S THE FASTEST IN JAPAN, RIGHT?
I CAN'T BELIEVE YOU WERE FINE EVEN THOUGH IT'S THE FIRST TIME YOU'VE BEEN ON A RIDE.
THEN WHY DON'T WE TRY SOMETHING DIFFERENT NEXT?
BUT THOSE TWO ARE GETTING BACK IN LINE...
LET'S GO AGAIN!
YAY!
AH!
THEN LET'S JUST GO SOMEWHERE ELSE!
!

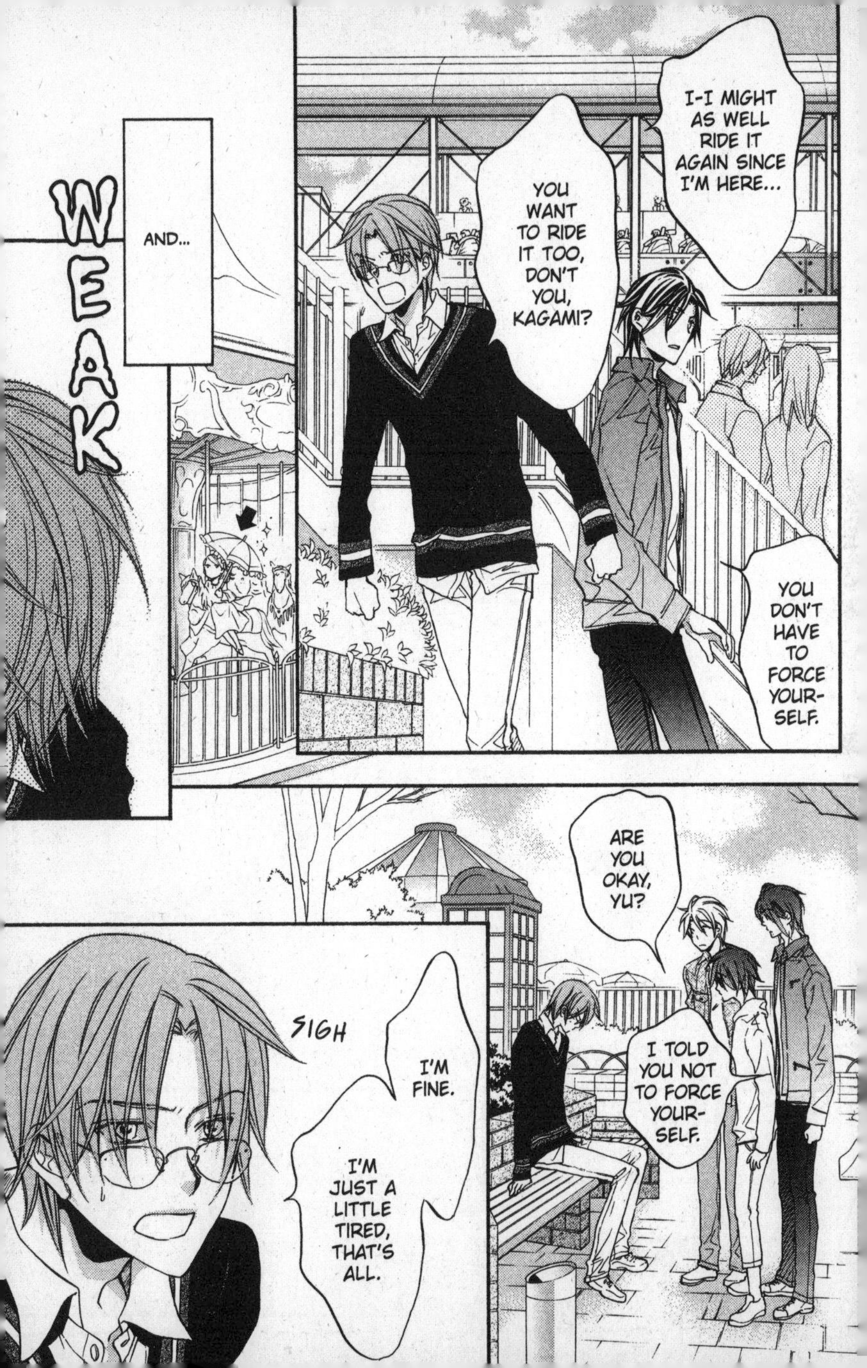
I-I MIGHT AS WELL RIDE IT AGAIN SINCE I'M HERE...
YOU WANT TO RIDE IT TOO, DON'T YOU, KAGAMI?
YOU DON'T HAVE TO FORCE YOUR-SELF.
AND...
WEAK
ARE YOU OKAY, YU?
I TOLD YOU NOT TO FORCE YOUR-SELF.
SIGH
I'M FINE.
I'M JUST A LITTLE TIRED, THAT'S ALL.

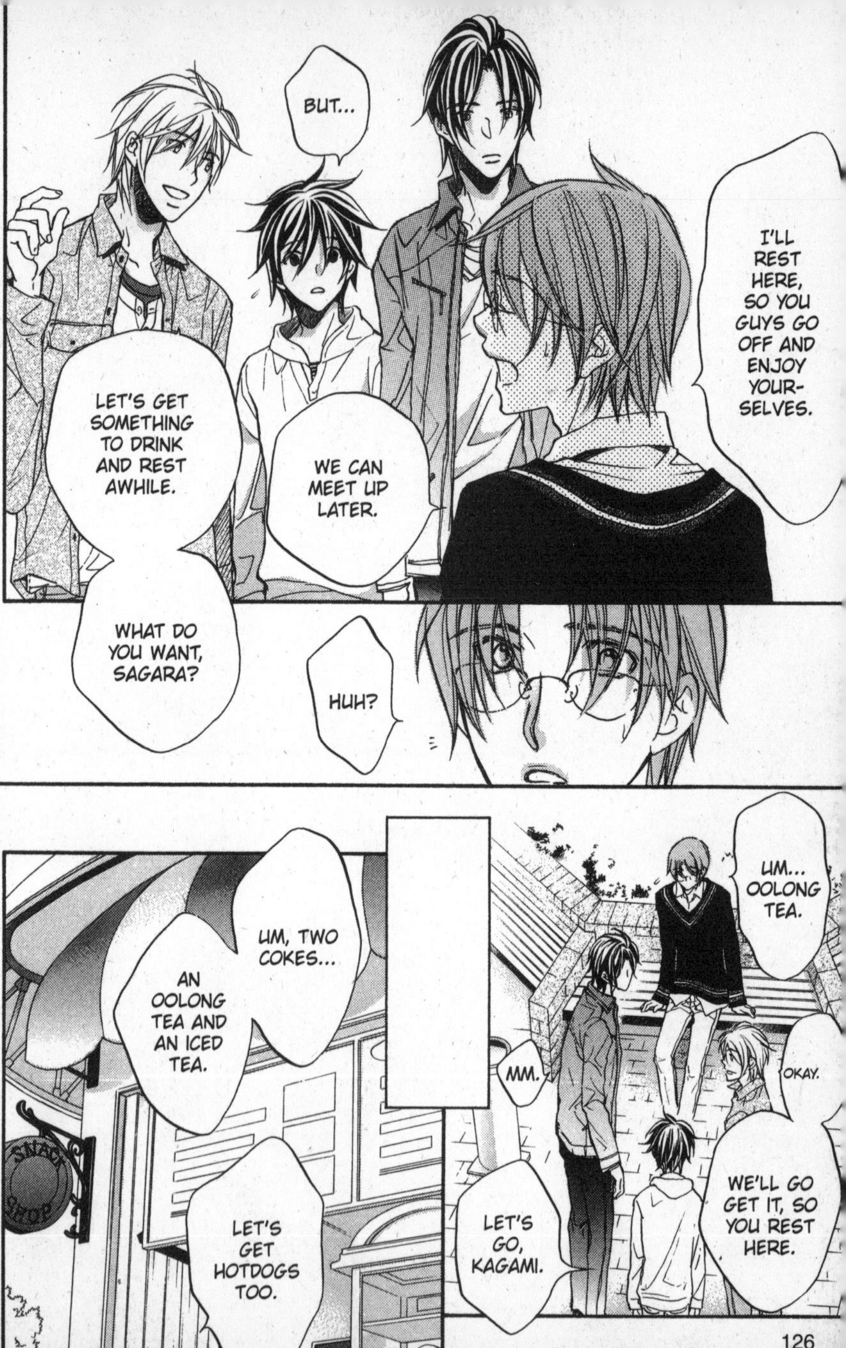
I'LL REST HERE, SO YOU GUYS GO OFF AND ENJOY YOUR-SELVES.
BUT...
WE CAN MEET UP LATER.
LET'S GET SOMETHING TO DRINK AND REST AWHILE.
WHAT DO YOU WANT, SAGARA?
HUH?
UM... OOLONG TEA.
OKAY.
MM.
WE'LL GO GET IT, SO YOU REST HERE.
LET'S GO, KAGAMI.
UM, TWO COKES...
AN OOLONG TEA AND AN ICED TEA.
LET'S GET HOTDOGS TOO.
SNACK SHOP

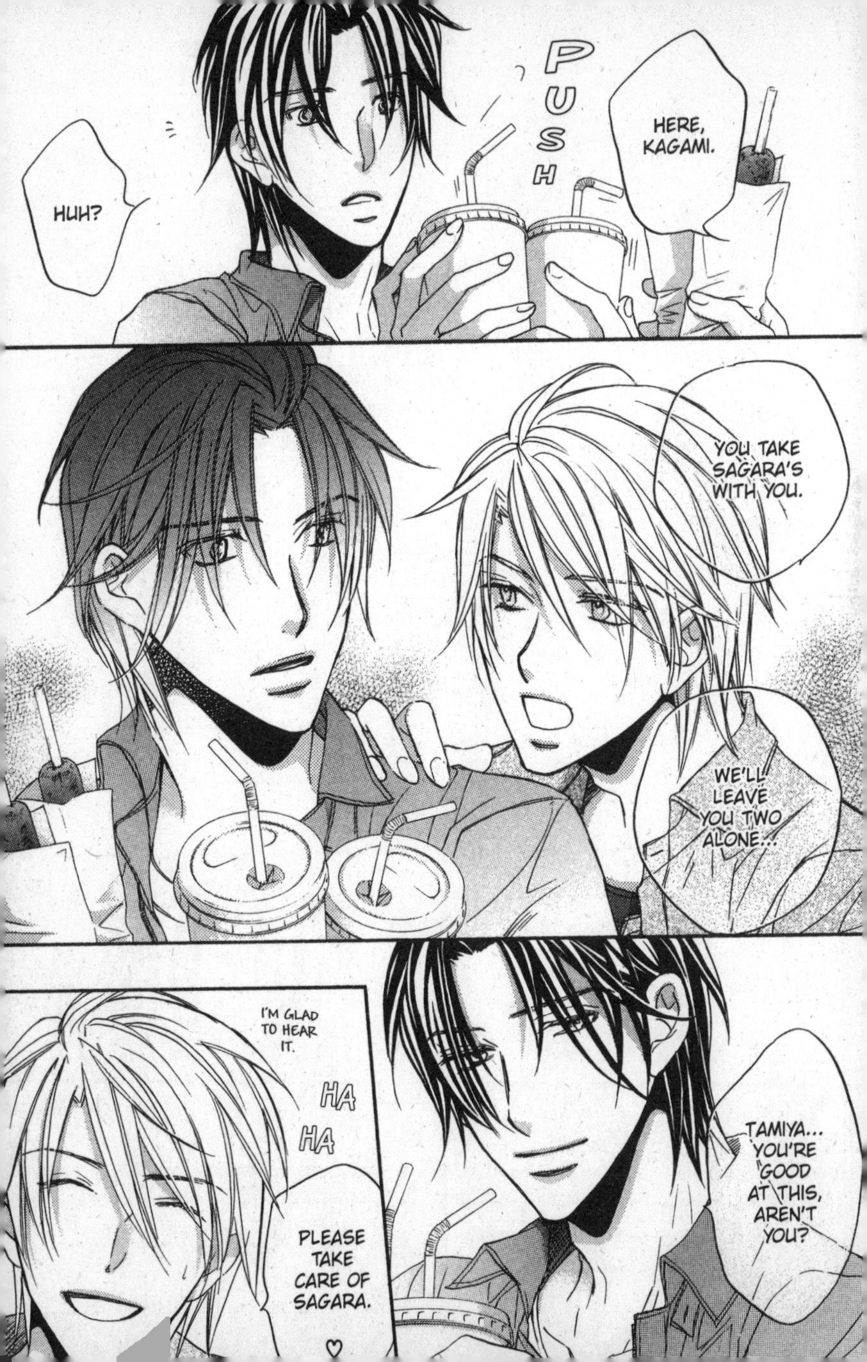
HERE, KAGAMI.
PUSH
HUH?
YOU TAKE SAGARA'S WITH YOU.
WE'LL LEAVE YOU TWO ALONE...
TAMIYA... YOU'RE GOOD AT THIS, AREN'T YOU?
I'M GLAD TO HEAR IT.
HA HA
PLEASE TAKE CARE OF SAGARA. ♡

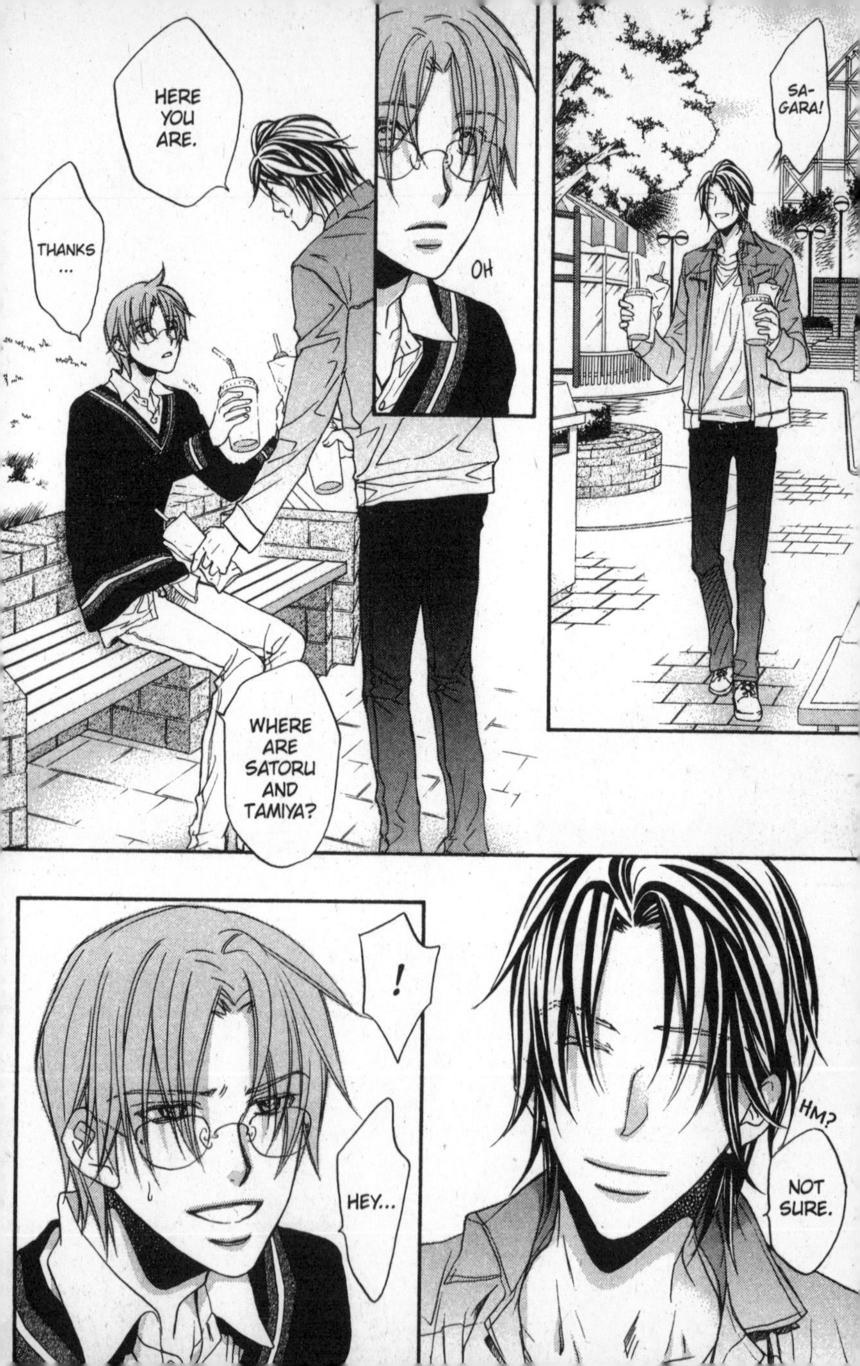
SA-GARA!
OH
HERE YOU ARE.
THANKS...
WHERE ARE SATORU AND TAMIYA?
HM?
NOT SURE.
!
HEY...

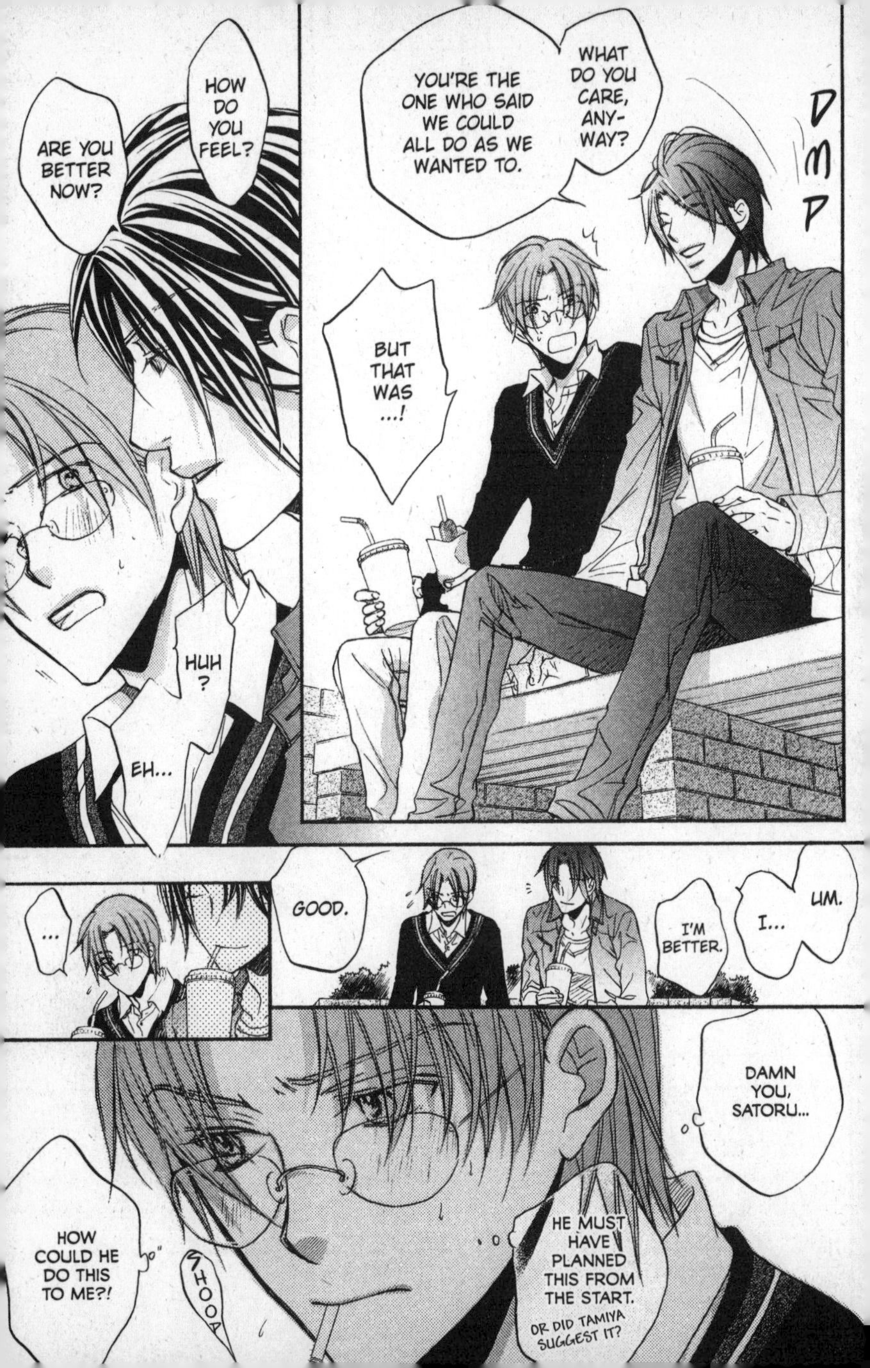

WHAT DO YOU CARE, ANY-WAY?
YOU'RE THE ONE WHO SAID WE COULD ALL DO AS WE WANTED TO.
DMP
BUT THAT WAS ...!
HOW DO YOU FEEL?
ARE YOU BETTER NOW?
HUH?
EH...
UM.
I...
I'M BETTER.
GOOD.
...
DAMN YOU, SATORU...
HE MUST HAVE PLANNED THIS FROM THE START.
OR DID TAMIYA SUGGEST IT?
SHOOA
HOW COULD HE DO THIS TO ME?!

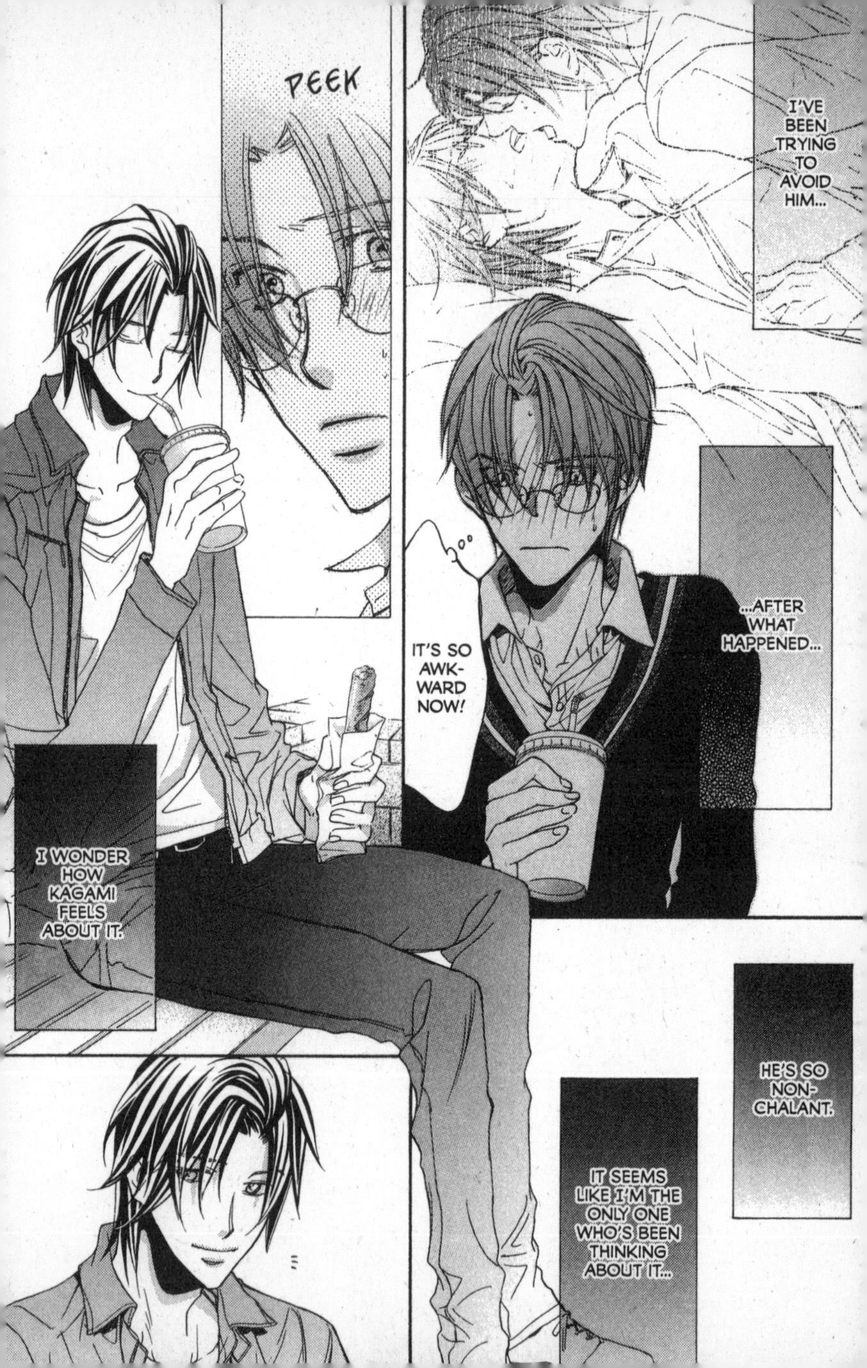
I'VE BEEN TRYING TO AVOID HIM...
PEEK
...AFTER WHAT HAPPENED...
IT'S SO AWK-WARD NOW!
I WONDER HOW KAGAMI FEELS ABOUT IT.
HE'S SO NON-CHALANT.
IT SEEMS LIKE I'M THE ONLY ONE WHO'S BEEN THINKING ABOUT IT...

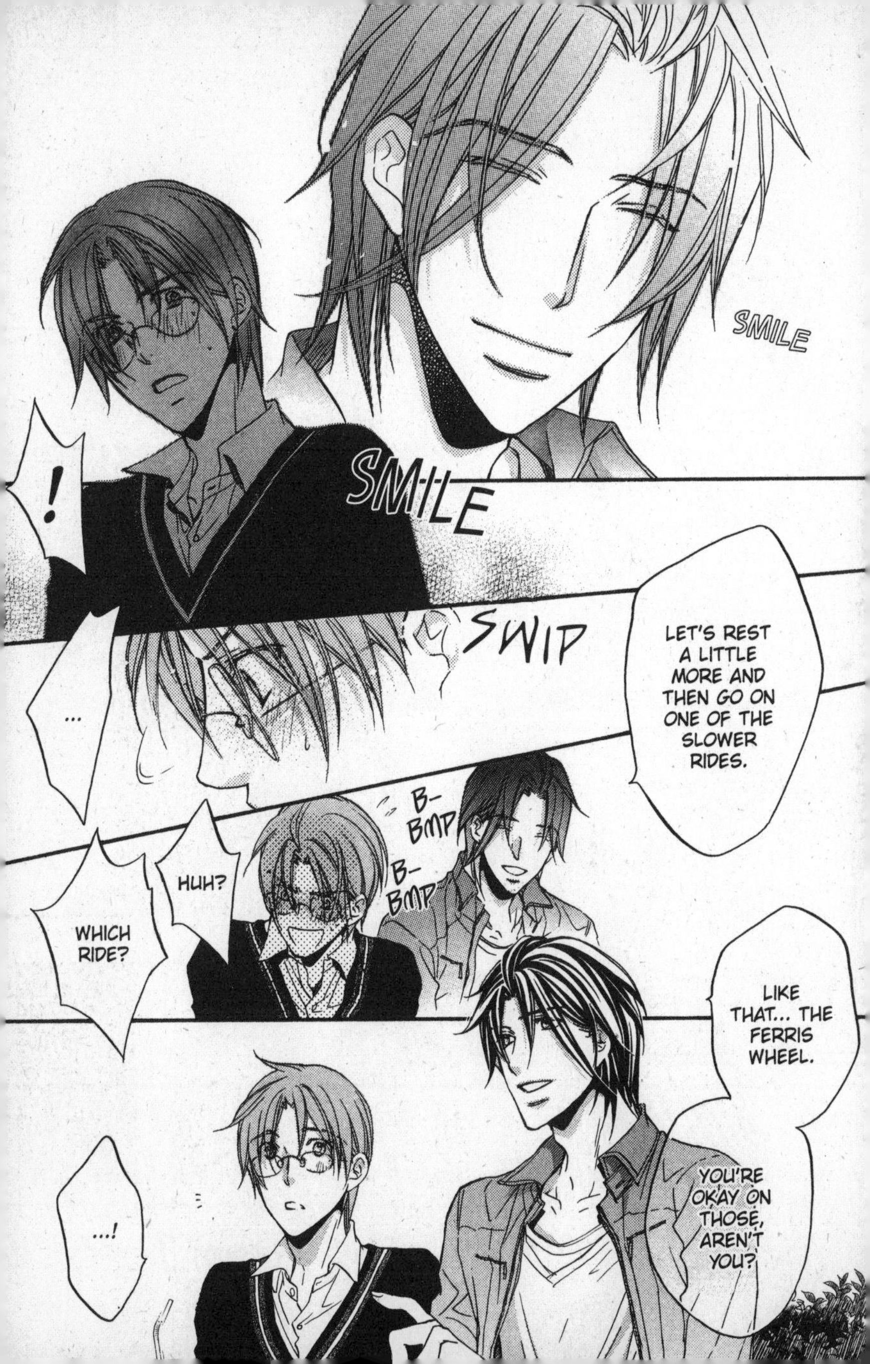
SMILE
SMILE
!
LET'S REST A LITTLE MORE AND THEN GO ON ONE OF THE SLOWER RIDES.
SWIP
...
B-BMP
B-BMP
HUH?
WHICH RIDE?
LIKE THAT... THE FERRIS WHEEL.
YOU'RE OKAY ON THOSE, AREN'T YOU?
...!

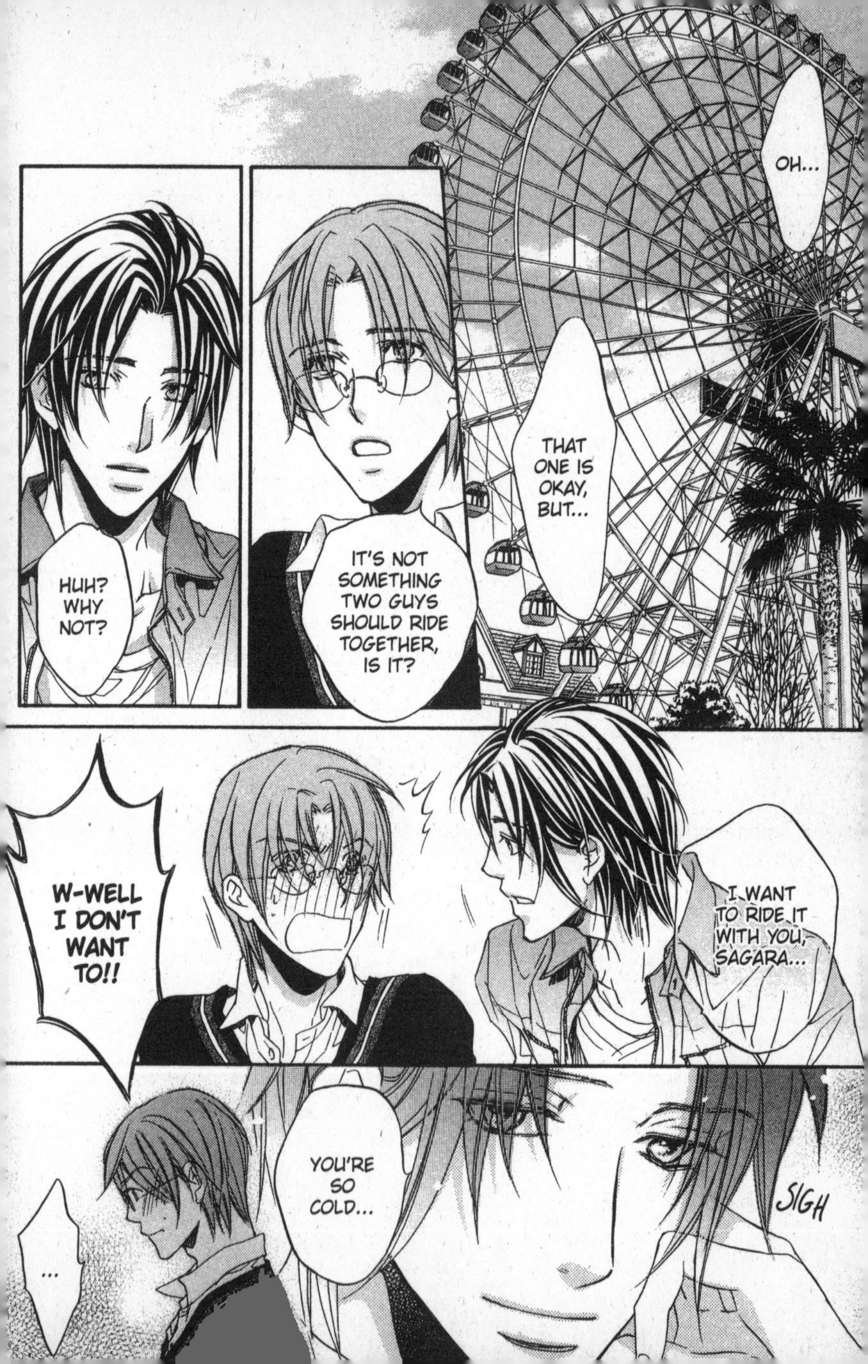
OH...
THAT ONE IS OKAY, BUT...
IT'S NOT SOMETHING TWO GUYS SHOULD RIDE TOGETHER, IS IT?
HUH? WHY NOT?
I WANT TO RIDE IT WITH YOU, SAGARA...
W-WELL I DON'T WANT TO!!
SIGH
YOU'RE SO COLD...
...

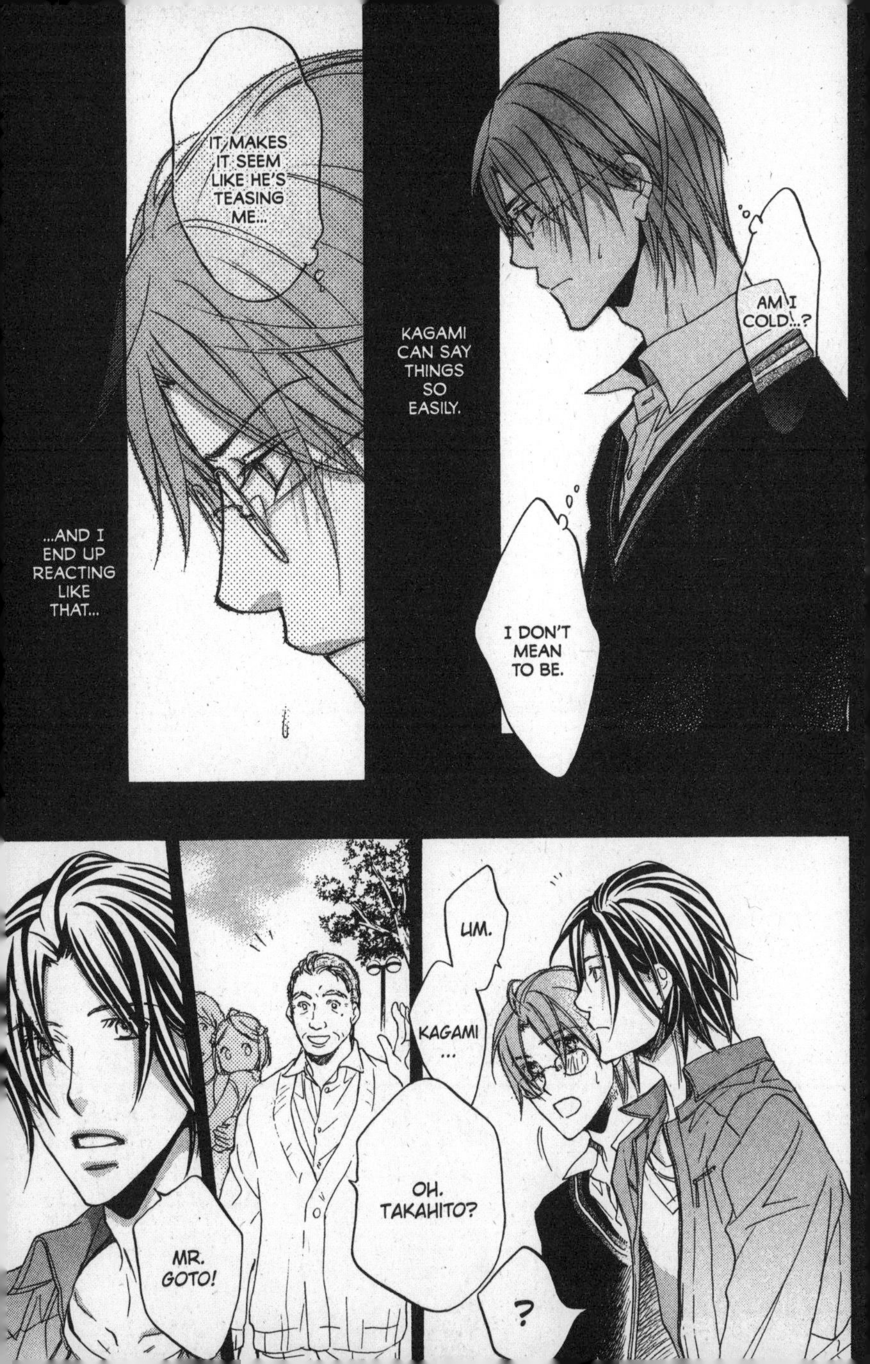
AM I COLD...?
I DON'T MEAN TO BE.
KAGAMI CAN SAY THINGS SO EASILY.
IT MAKES IT SEEM LIKE HE'S TEASING ME...
...AND I END UP REACTING LIKE THAT...
UM.
KAGAMI...
OH. TAKAHITO?
?
MR. GOTO!

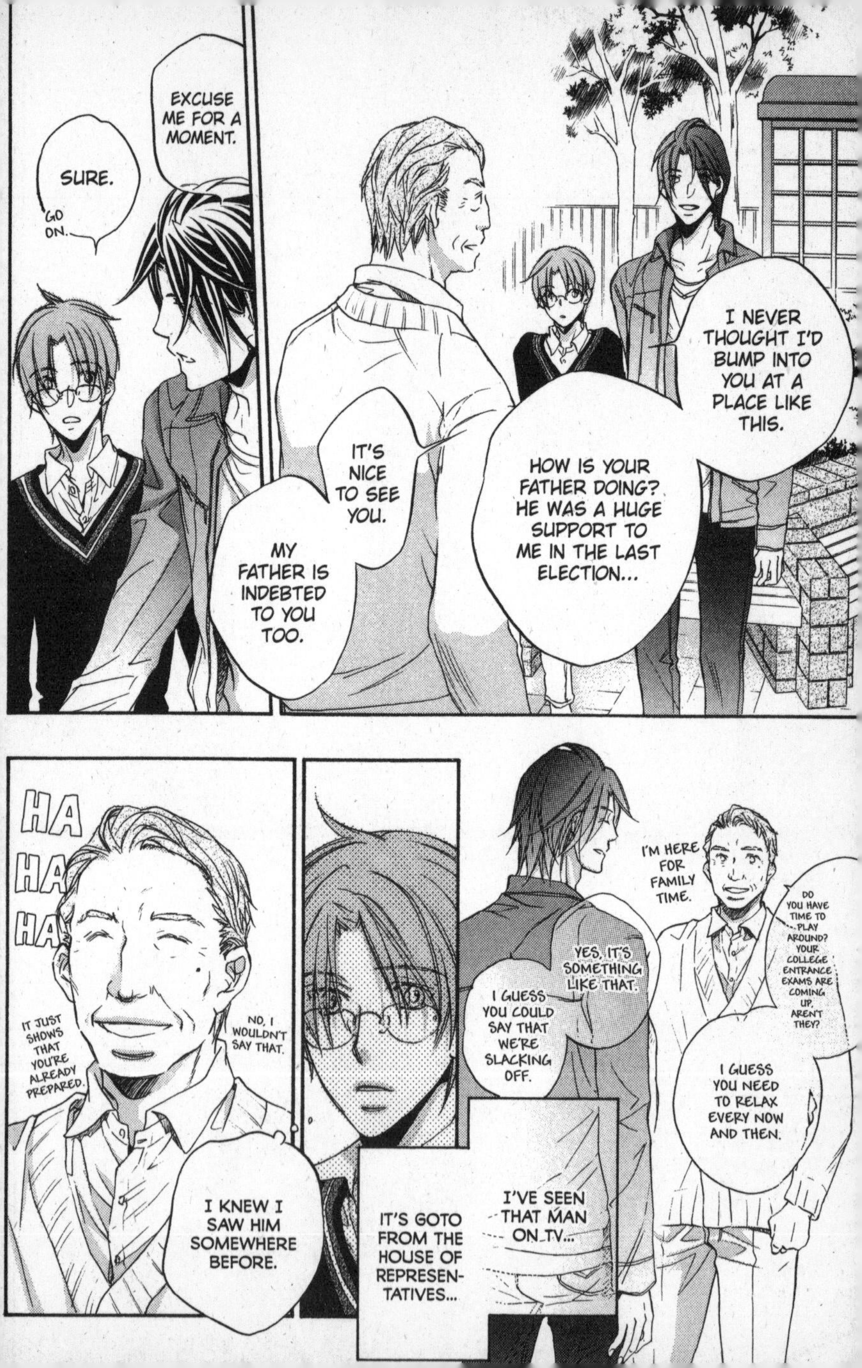
I NEVER THOUGHT I'D BUMP INTO YOU AT A PLACE LIKE THIS.
HOW IS YOUR FATHER DOING? HE WAS A HUGE SUPPORT TO ME IN THE LAST ELECTION...
IT'S NICE TO SEE YOU.
MY FATHER IS INDEBTED TO YOU TOO.
EXCUSE ME FOR A MOMENT.
SURE.
GO ON.
I'M HERE FOR FAMILY TIME.
DO YOU HAVE TIME TO PLAY AROUND? YOUR COLLEGE ENTRANCE EXAMS ARE COMING UP, AREN'T THEY?
YES, IT'S SOMETHING LIKE THAT.
I GUESS YOU COULD SAY THAT WE'RE SLACKING OFF.
I GUESS YOU NEED TO RELAX EVERY NOW AND THEN.
I'VE SEEN THAT MAN ON TV...
IT'S GOTO FROM THE HOUSE OF REPRESEN-TATIVES...
I KNEW I SAW HIM SOMEWHERE BEFORE.
HA HA HA
NO, I WOULDN'T SAY THAT.
IT JUST SHOWS THAT YOU'RE ALREADY PREPARED.

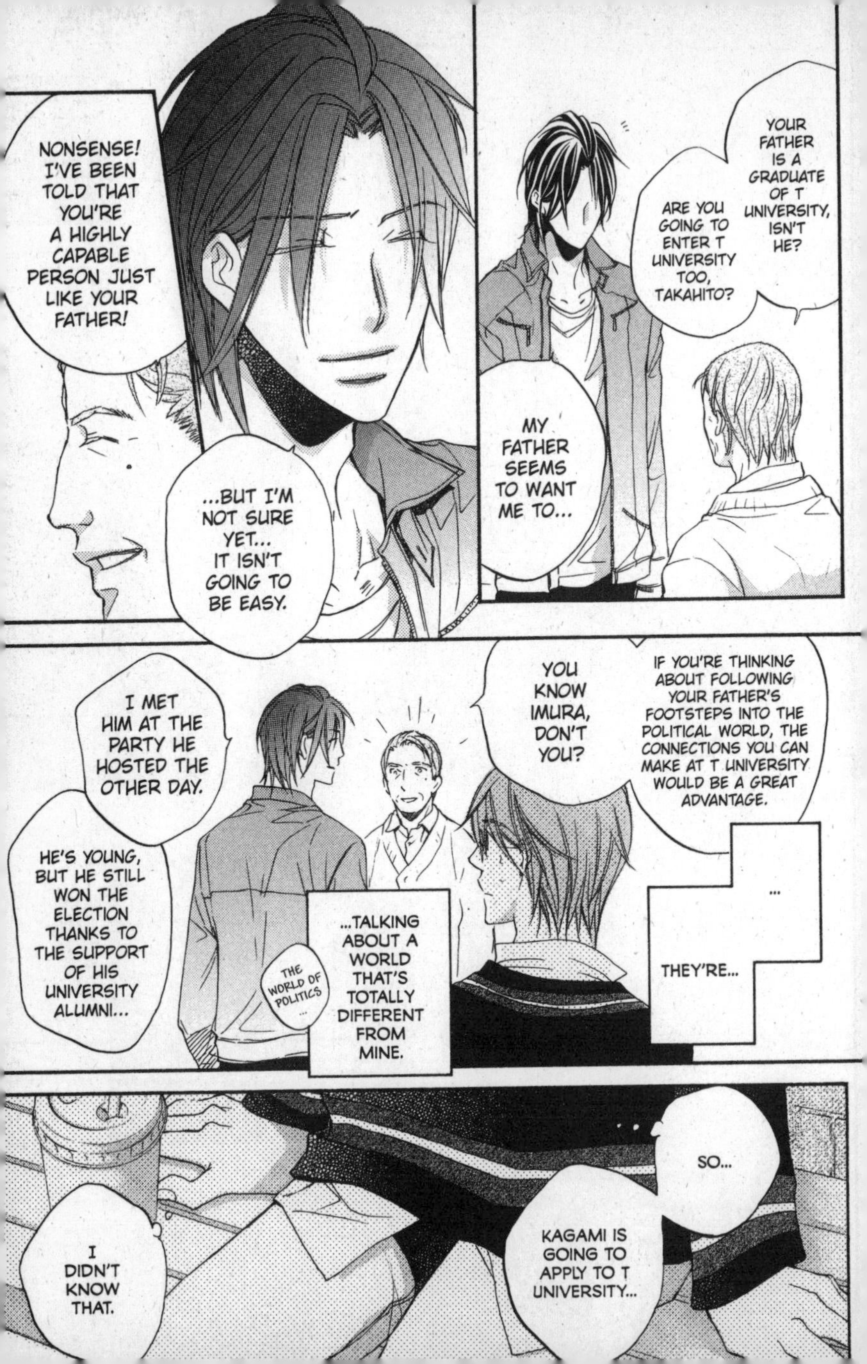
YOUR FATHER IS A GRADUATE OF T UNIVERSITY, ISN'T HE?
ARE YOU GOING TO ENTER T UNIVERSITY TOO, TAKAHITO?
MY FATHER SEEMS TO WANT ME TO...
...BUT I'M NOT SURE YET... IT ISN'T GOING TO BE EASY.
NONSENSE! I'VE BEEN TOLD THAT YOU'RE A HIGHLY CAPABLE PERSON JUST LIKE YOUR FATHER!
IF YOU'RE THINKING ABOUT FOLLOWING YOUR FATHER'S FOOTSTEPS INTO THE POLITICAL WORLD, THE CONNECTIONS YOU CAN MAKE AT T UNIVERSITY WOULD BE A GREAT ADVANTAGE.
YOU KNOW IMURA, DON'T YOU?
I MET HIM AT THE PARTY HE HOSTED THE OTHER DAY.
HE'S YOUNG, BUT HE STILL WON THE ELECTION THANKS TO THE SUPPORT OF HIS UNIVERSITY ALUMNI...
...
THEY'RE...
...TALKING ABOUT A WORLD THAT'S TOTALLY DIFFERENT FROM MINE.
THE WORLD OF POLITICS...
SO...
KAGAMI IS GOING TO APPLY TO T UNIVERSITY...
I DIDN'T KNOW THAT.

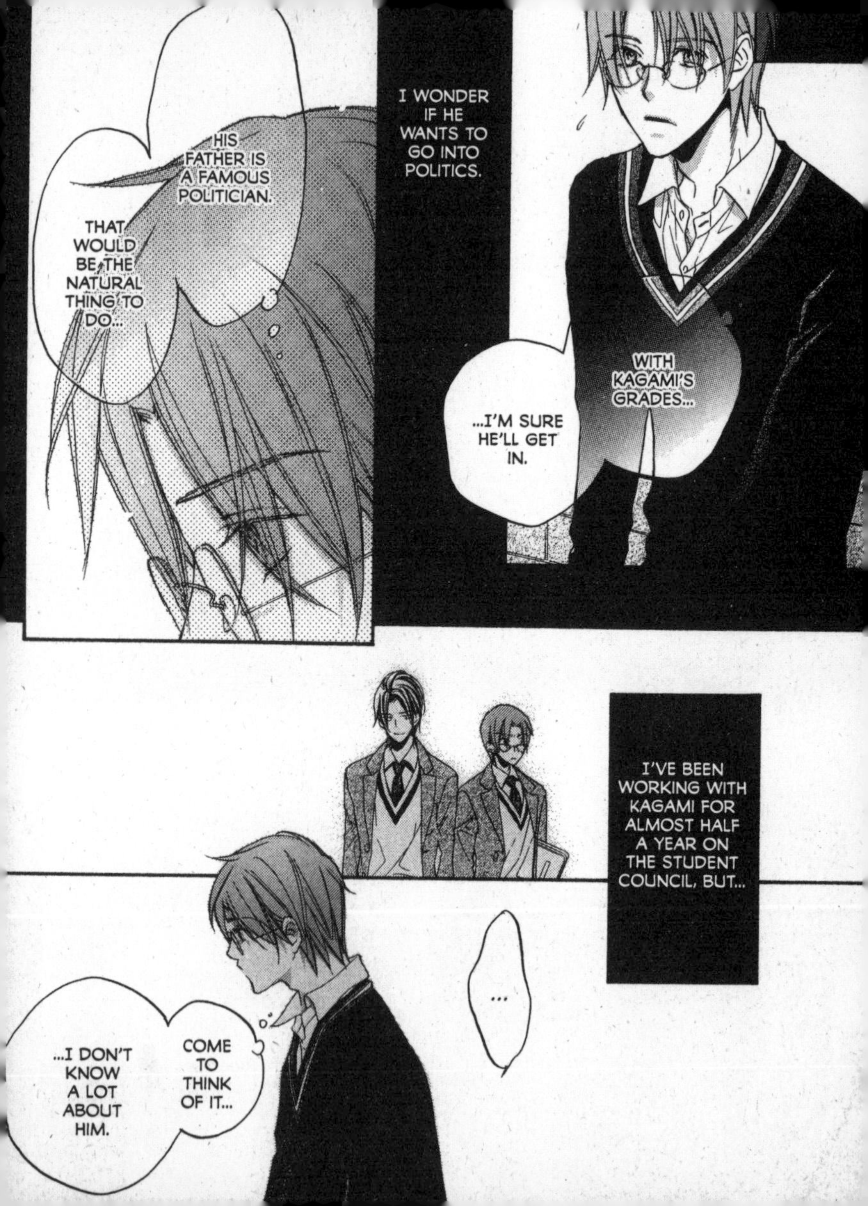
WITH KAGAMI'S GRADES...
...I'M SURE HE'LL GET IN.
I WONDER IF HE WANTS TO GO INTO POLITICS.
HIS FATHER IS A FAMOUS POLITICIAN.
THAT WOULD BE THE NATURAL THING TO DO...
I'VE BEEN WORKING WITH KAGAMI FOR ALMOST HALF A YEAR ON THE STUDENT COUNCIL, BUT...
...
COME TO THINK OF IT...
...I DON'T KNOW A LOT ABOUT HIM.

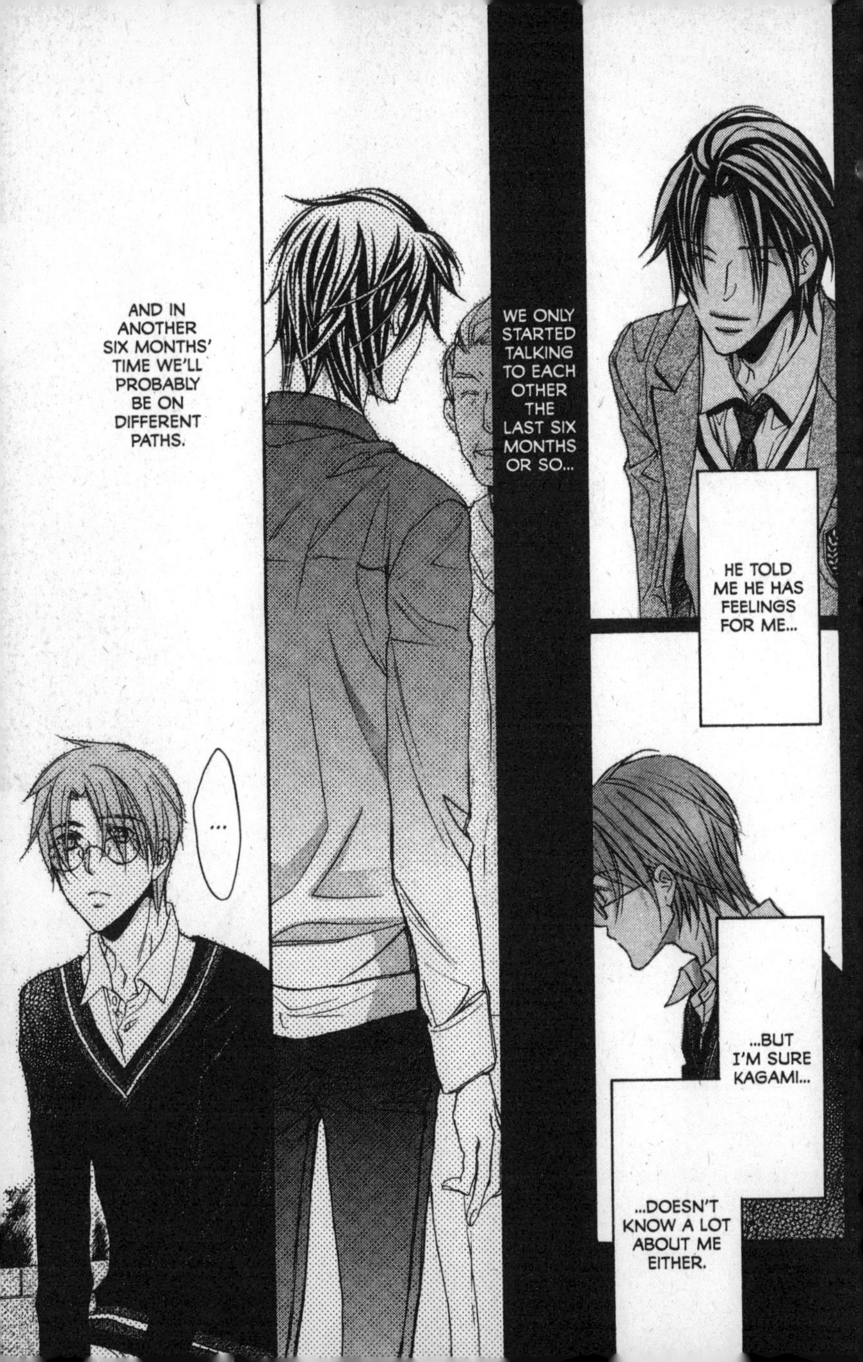
HE TOLD ME HE HAS FEELINGS FOR ME...
...BUT I'M SURE KAGAMI...
...DOESN'T KNOW A LOT ABOUT ME EITHER.
WE ONLY STARTED TALKING TO EACH OTHER THE LAST SIX MONTHS OR SO...
AND IN ANOTHER SIX MONTHS' TIME WE'LL PROBABLY BE ON DIFFERENT PATHS.
...

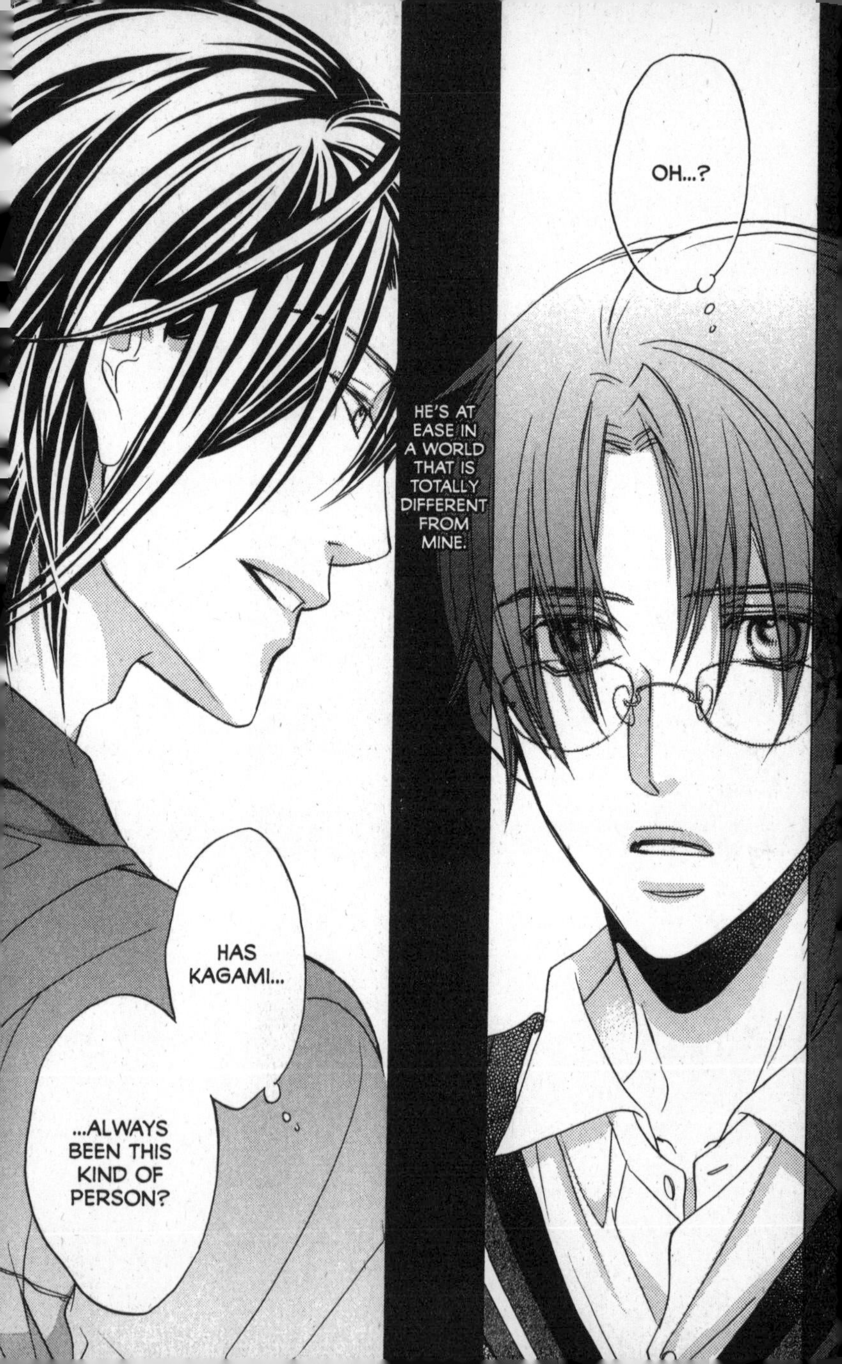
OH...?
HE'S AT EASE IN A WORLD THAT IS TOTALLY DIFFERENT FROM MINE.
HAS KAGAMI...
...ALWAYS BEEN THIS KIND OF PERSON?

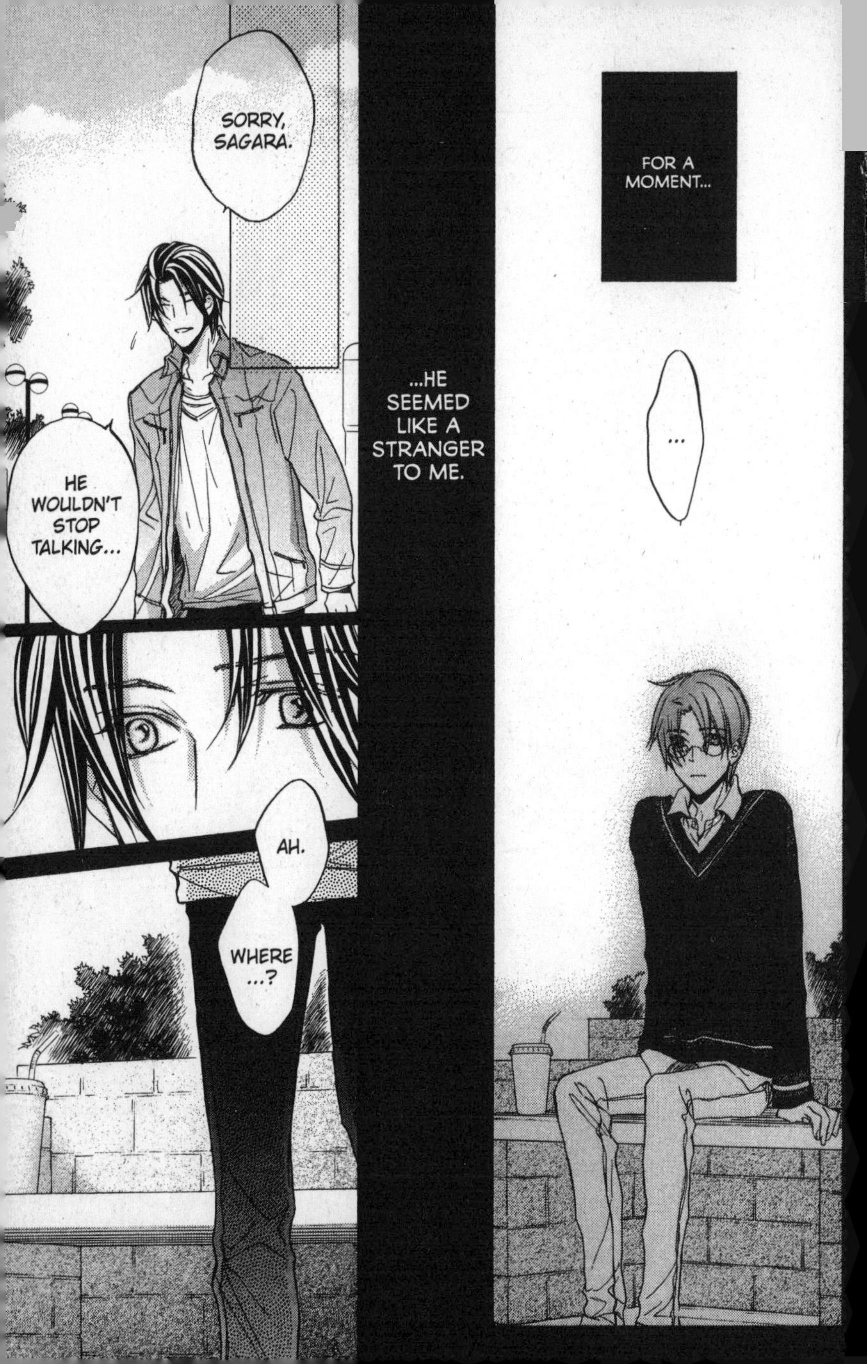
FOR A MOMENT...
...
...HE SEEMED LIKE A STRANGER TO ME.
SORRY, SAGARA.
HE WOULDN'T STOP TALKING...
AH.
WHERE ...?

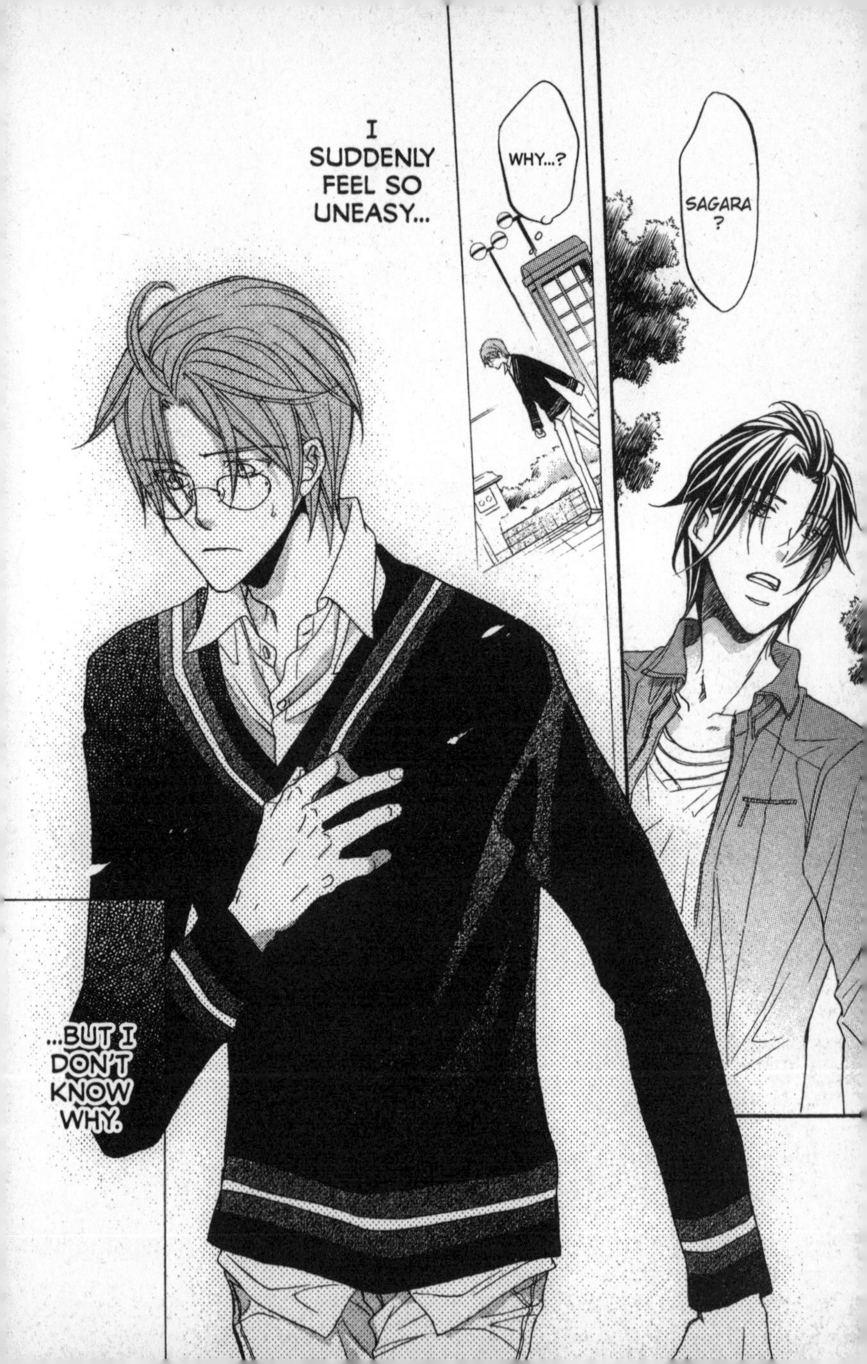
SAGARA ?
WHY...?
I SUDDENLY FEEL SO UNEASY...
...BUT I DON'T KNOW WHY.

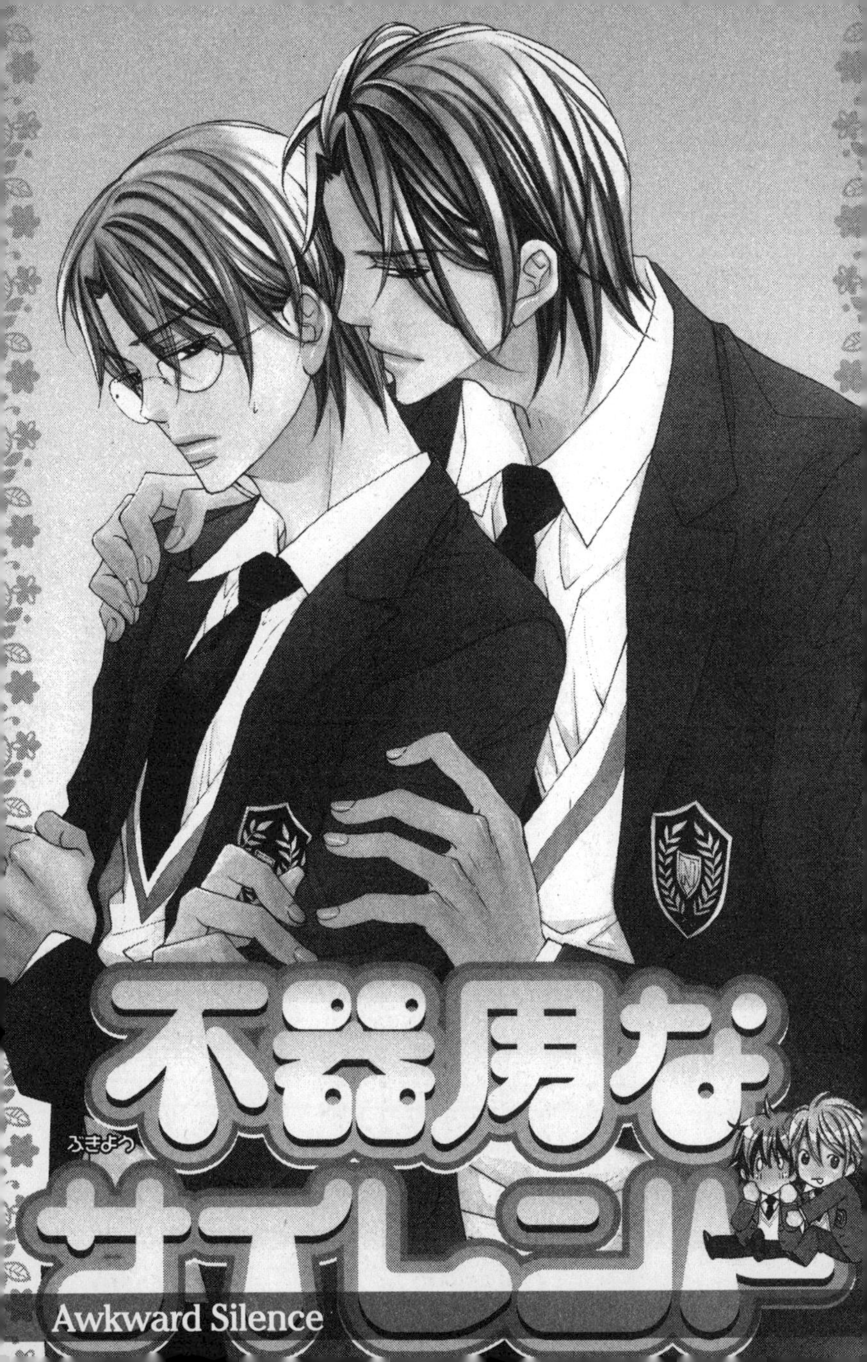

ぶきよう
不器用なサイレント
Awkward Silence

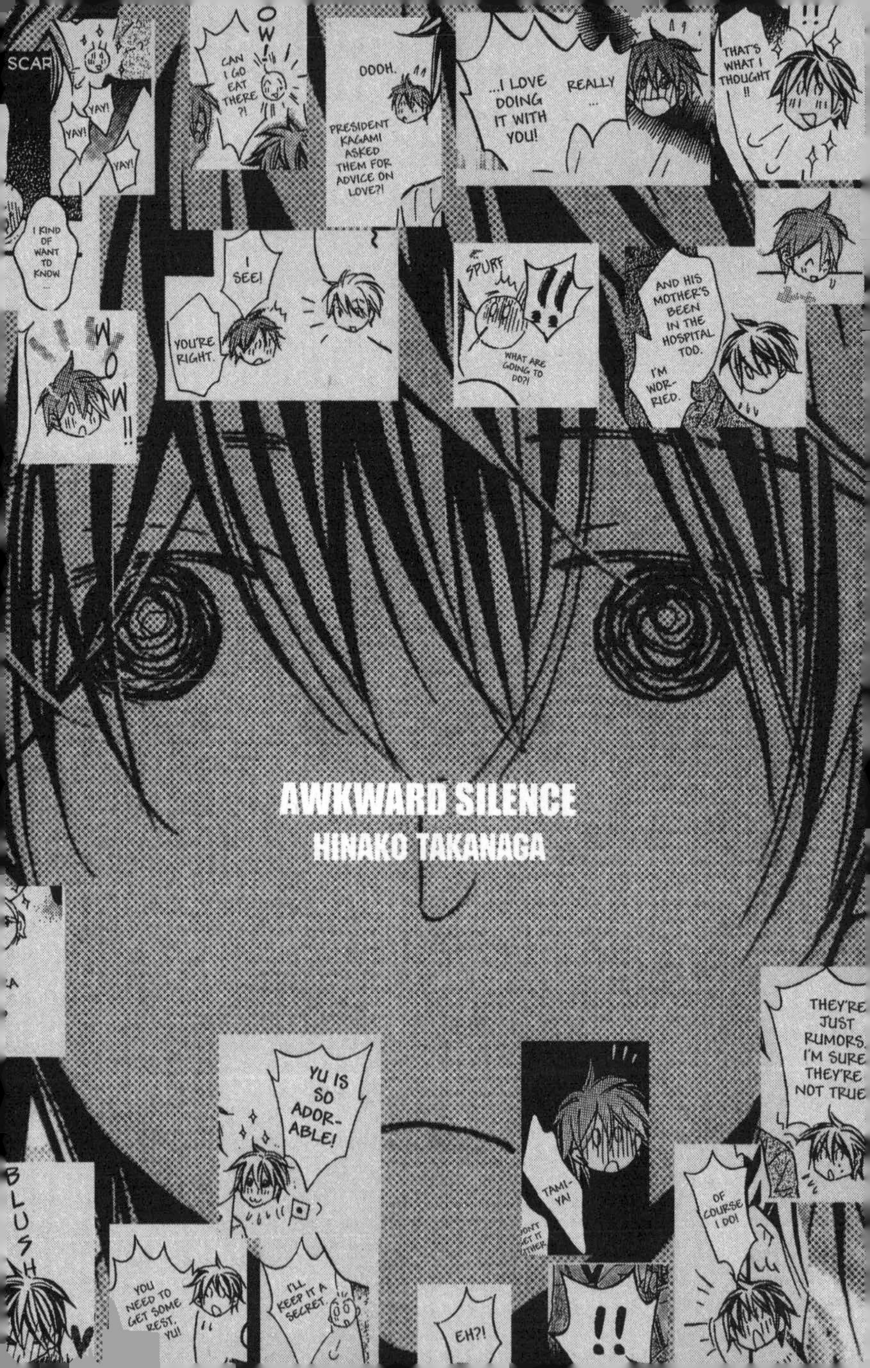
!!
THAT'S WHAT I THOUGHT !!
REALLY ...
...I LOVE DOING IT WITH YOU!
OOOH.
PRESIDENT KAGAMI ASKED THEM FOR ADVICE ON LOVE?!
OW!
CAN I GO EAT THERE ?!
SCAR
YAY!
YAY!
YAY!
AND HIS MOTHER'S BEEN IN THE HOSPITAL TOO.
I'M WOR-RIED.
SPURF
!!
WHAT ARE GOING TO DO?!
I SEE!
YOU'RE RIGHT.
I KIND OF WANT TO KNOW ...
WOW !!
AWKWARD SILENCE
HINAKO TAKANAGA
THEY'RE JUST RUMORS. I'M SURE THEY'RE NOT TRUE
OF COURSE I DO!
TAMI-YA!
!!
EH?!
YU IS SO ADOR-ABLE!
I'LL KEEP IT A SECRET.
YOU NEED TO GET SOME REST, YU!
BLUSH

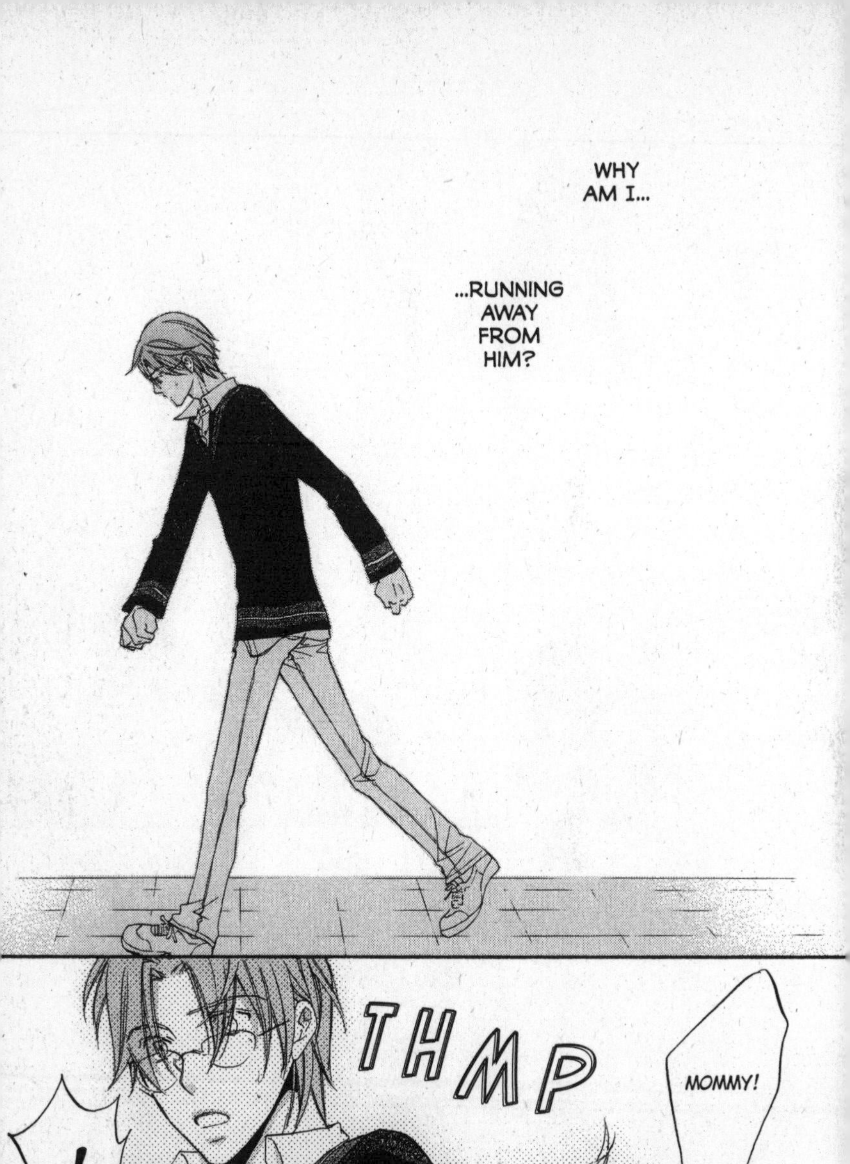
WHY AM I...
...RUNNING AWAY FROM HIM?
MOMMY!
THMP
!

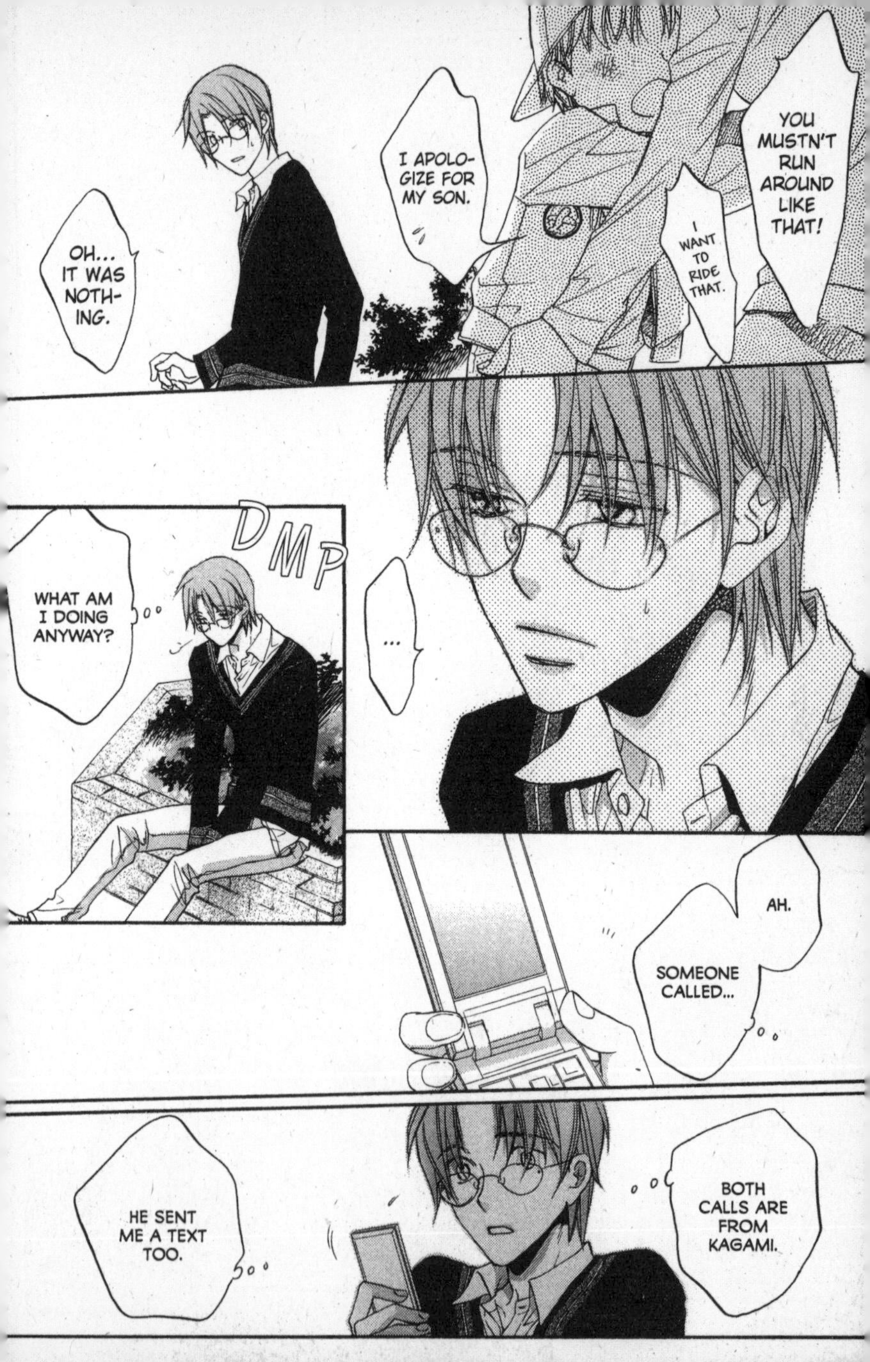
YOU MUSTN'T RUN AROUND LIKE THAT!
I WANT TO RIDE THAT.
I APOLOGIZE FOR MY SON.
OH... IT WAS NOTHING.
...
DMP
WHAT AM I DOING ANYWAY?
AH.
SOMEONE CALLED...
BOTH CALLS ARE FROM KAGAMI.
HE SENT ME A TEXT TOO.

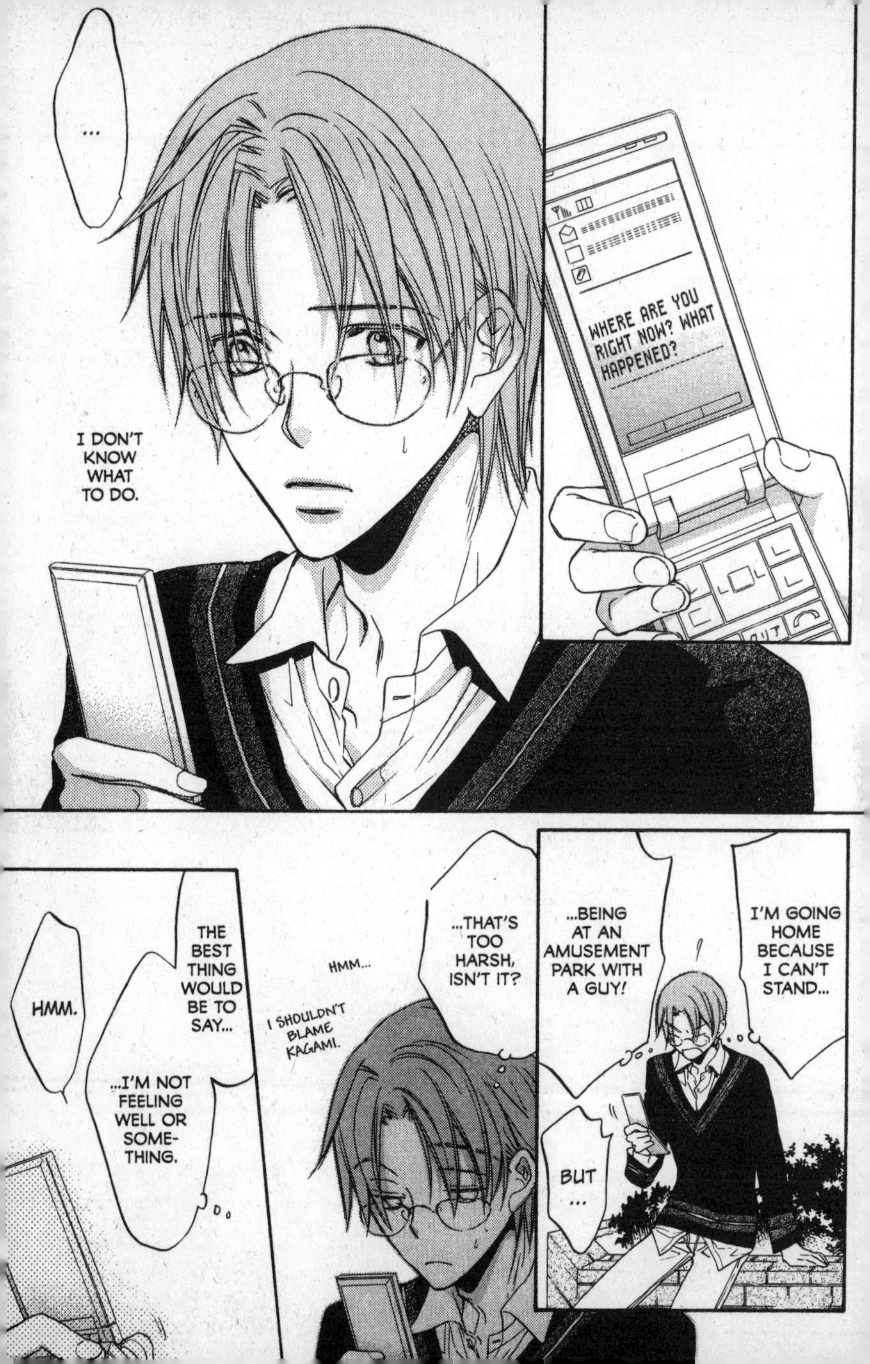
WHERE ARE YOU RIGHT NOW? WHAT HAPPENED?
...
I DON'T KNOW WHAT TO DO.
I'M GOING HOME BECAUSE I CAN'T STAND...
...BEING AT AN AMUSEMENT PARK WITH A GUY!
BUT ...
...THAT'S TOO HARSH, ISN'T IT?
HMM...
I SHOULDN'T BLAME KAGAMI.
THE BEST THING WOULD BE TO SAY...
...I'M NOT FEELING WELL OR SOME-THING.
HMM.

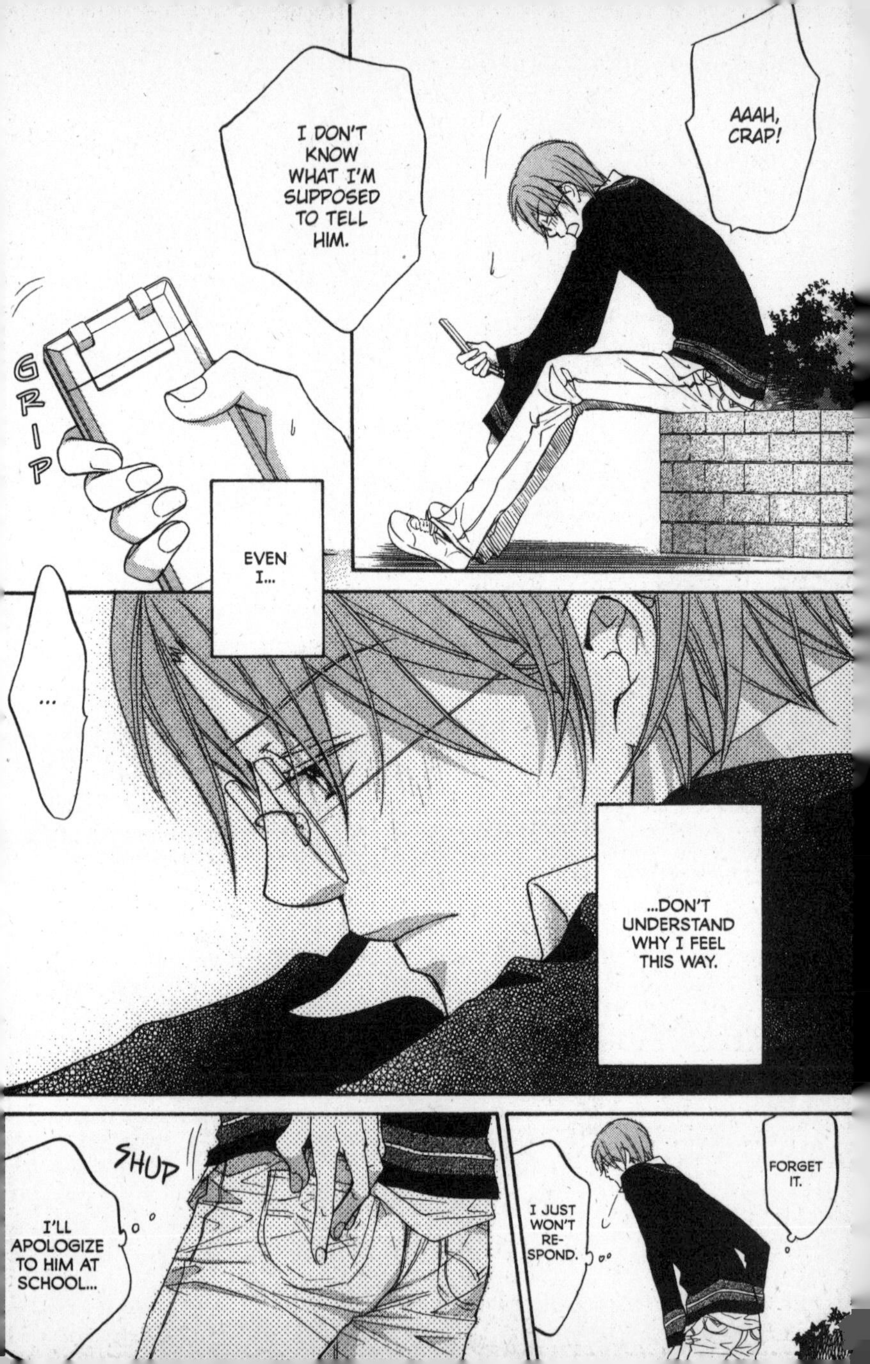
AAAH, CRAP!
I DON'T KNOW WHAT I'M SUPPOSED TO TELL HIM.
GRIP
EVEN I...
...DON'T UNDERSTAND WHY I FEEL THIS WAY.
...
FORGET IT.
I JUST WON'T RE-SPOND.
SHUP
I'LL APOLOGIZE TO HIM AT SCHOOL...

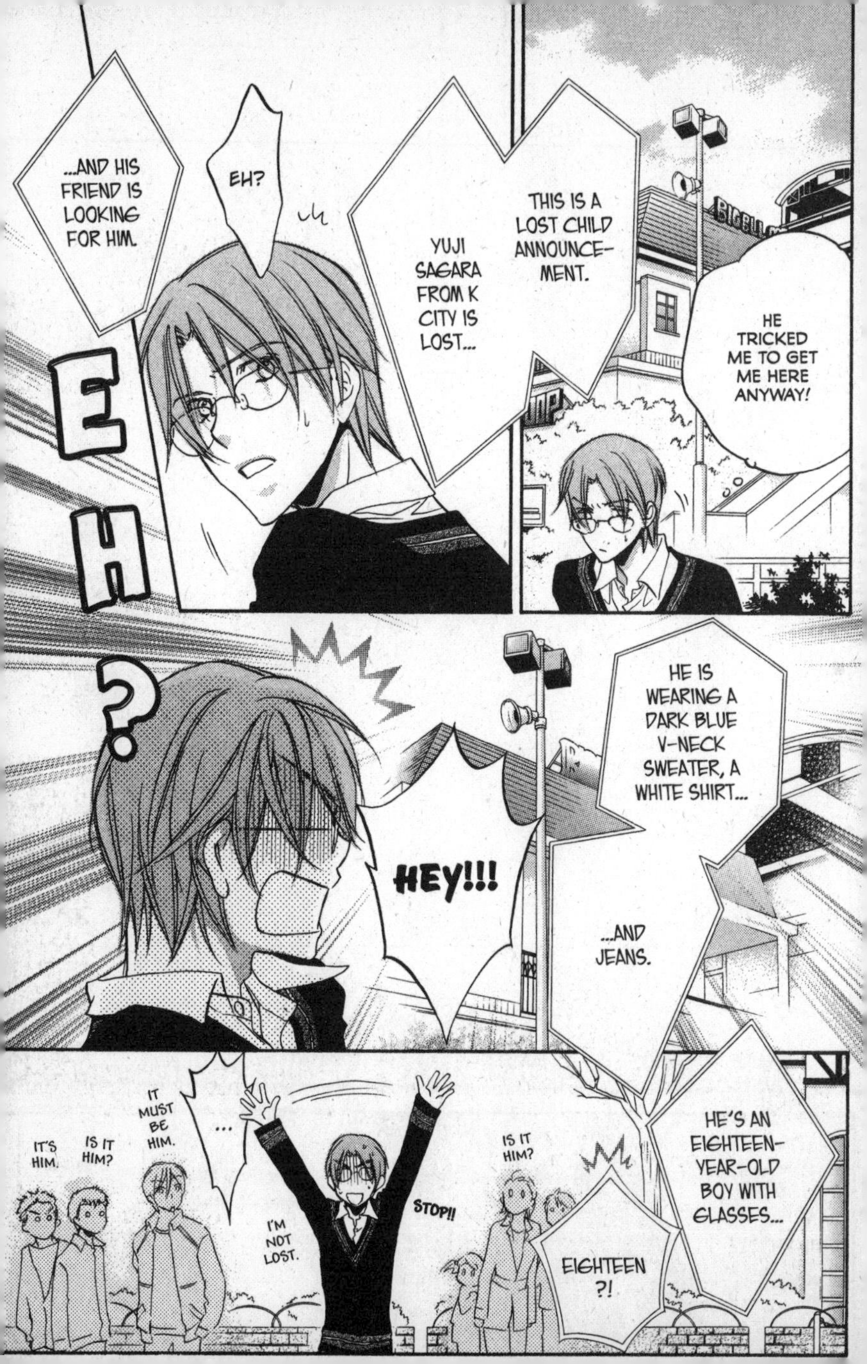
HE TRICKED ME TO GET ME HERE ANYWAY!
THIS IS A LOST CHILD ANNOUNCEMENT.
YUJI SAGARA FROM K CITY IS LOST...
EH?
...AND HIS FRIEND IS LOOKING FOR HIM.
EH
?
HE IS WEARING A DARK BLUE V-NECK SWEATER, A WHITE SHIRT...
...AND JEANS.
HEY!!!
HE'S AN EIGHTEEN-YEAR-OLD BOY WITH GLASSES...
EIGHTEEN?!
IS IT HIM?
STOP!!
I'M NOT LOST.
...
IT MUST BE HIM.
IS IT HIM?
IT'S HIM.

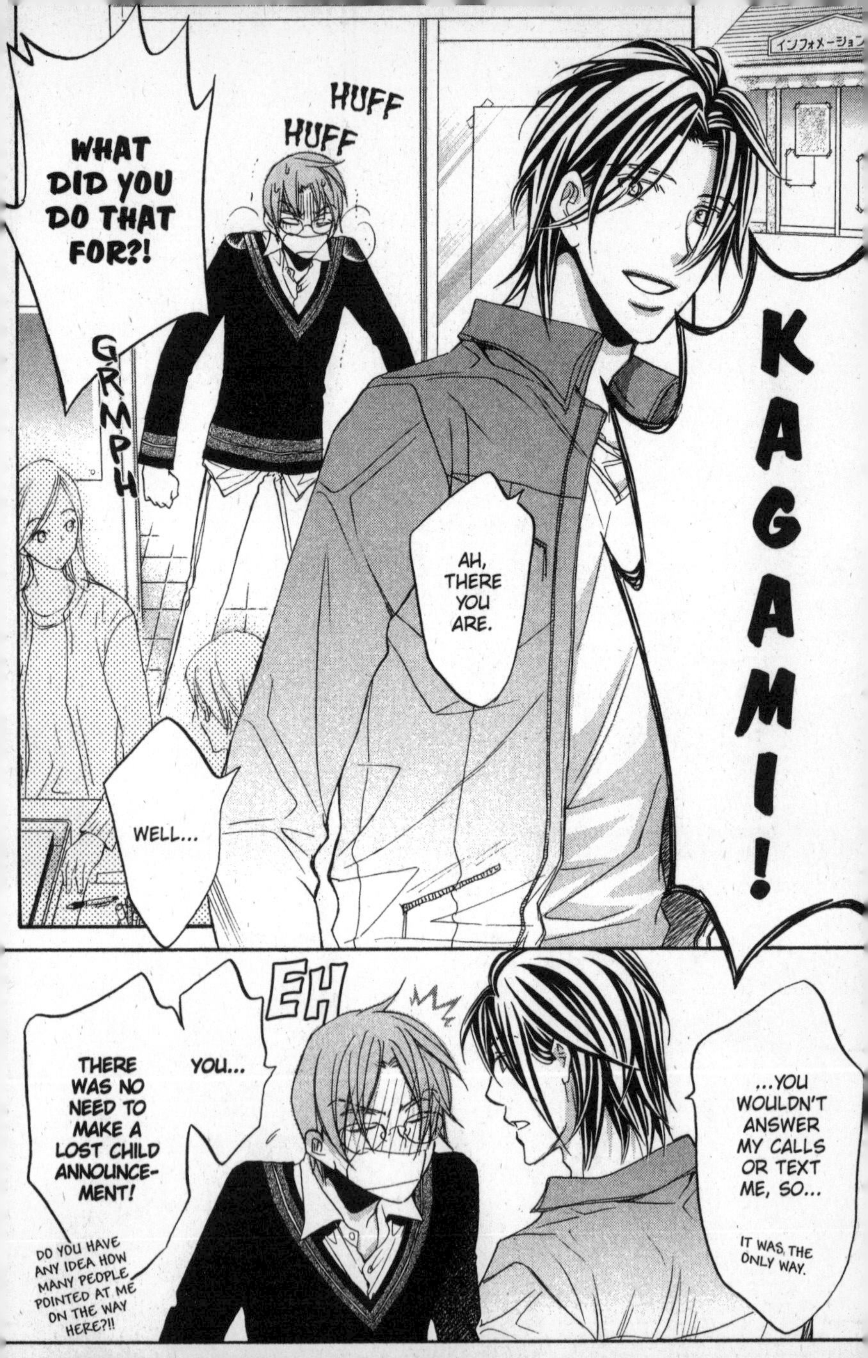
インフォメーション
KAGAMI!
HUFF
HUFF
WHAT DID YOU DO THAT FOR?!
GRMPH
AH, THERE YOU ARE.
WELL...
...YOU WOULDN'T ANSWER MY CALLS OR TEXT ME, SO...
IT WAS THE ONLY WAY.
EH
YOU...
THERE WAS NO NEED TO MAKE A LOST CHILD ANNOUNCE-MENT!
DO YOU HAVE ANY IDEA HOW MANY PEOPLE POINTED AT ME ON THE WAY HERE?!!

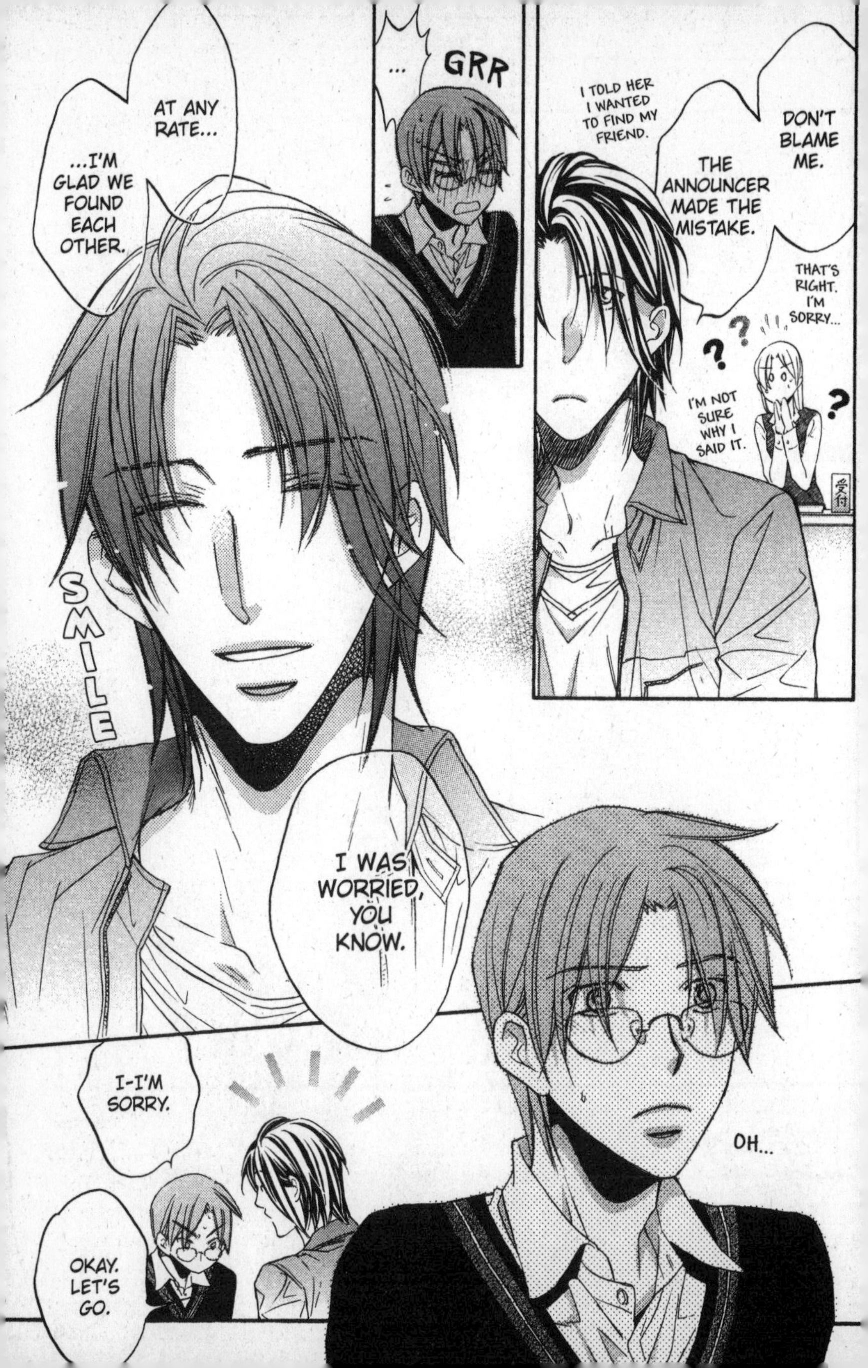
DON'T BLAME ME.
THE ANNOUNCER MADE THE MISTAKE.
I TOLD HER I WANTED TO FIND MY FRIEND.
THAT'S RIGHT. I'M SORRY...
I'M NOT SURE WHY I SAID IT.
受付
...
GRR
AT ANY RATE...
...I'M GLAD WE FOUND EACH OTHER.
SMILE
I WAS WORRIED, YOU KNOW.
OH...
I-I'M SORRY.
OKAY. LET'S GO.

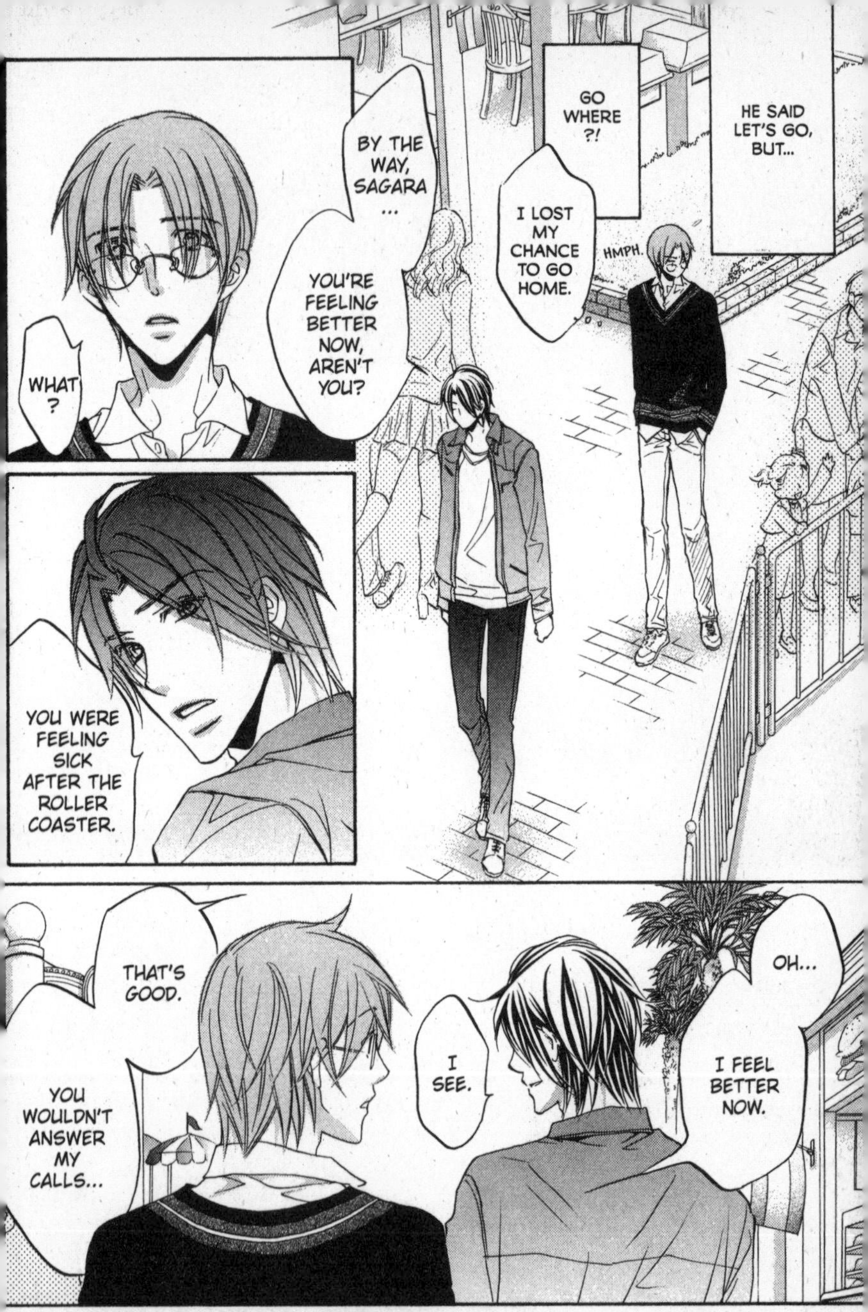
HE SAID LET'S GO, BUT...
GO WHERE ?!
I LOST MY CHANCE TO GO HOME.
HMPH.
BY THE WAY, SAGARA ...
YOU'RE FEELING BETTER NOW, AREN'T YOU?
WHAT ?
YOU WERE FEELING SICK AFTER THE ROLLER COASTER.
OH...
I FEEL BETTER NOW.
I SEE.
THAT'S GOOD.
YOU WOULDN'T ANSWER MY CALLS...

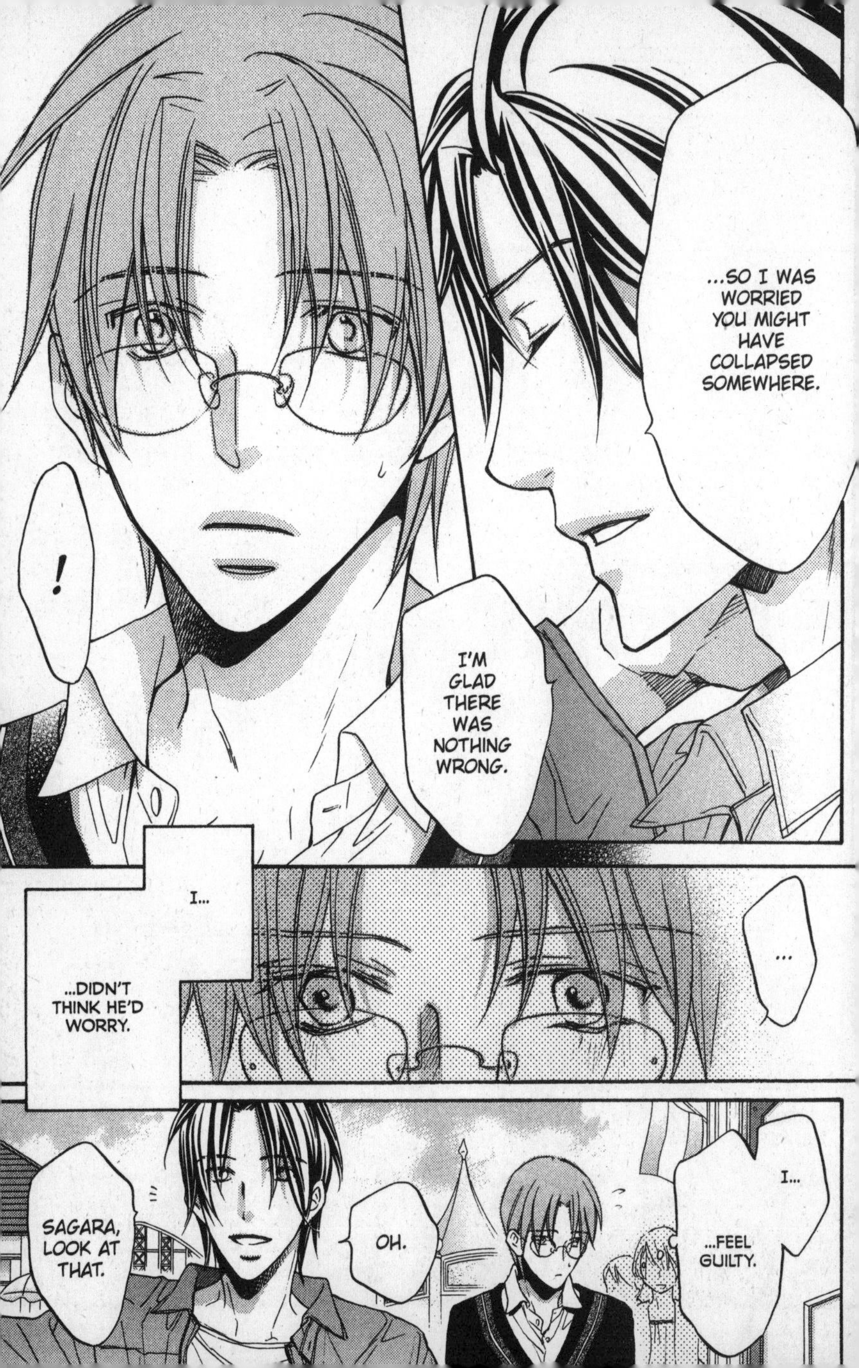
...SO I WAS WORRIED YOU MIGHT HAVE COLLAPSED SOMEWHERE.
I'M GLAD THERE WAS NOTHING WRONG.
!
...
I...
...DIDN'T THINK HE'D WORRY.
I...
...FEEL GUILTY.
OH.
SAGARA, LOOK AT THAT.

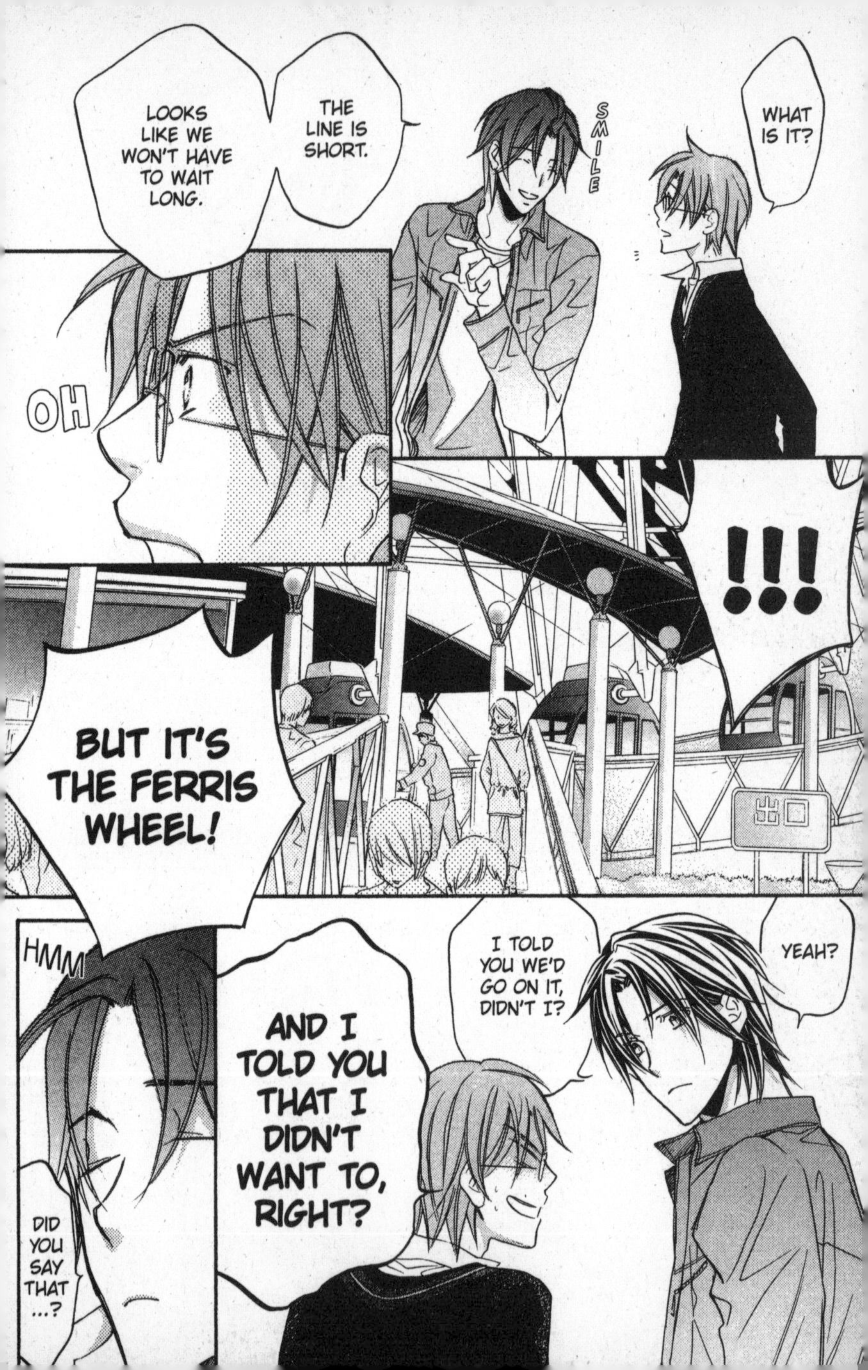
WHAT IS IT?
SMILE
THE LINE IS SHORT.
LOOKS LIKE WE WON'T HAVE TO WAIT LONG.
OH
!!!
BUT IT'S THE FERRIS WHEEL!
YEAH?
I TOLD YOU WE'D GO ON IT, DIDN'T I?
AND I TOLD YOU THAT I DIDN'T WANT TO, RIGHT?
HMM
DID YOU SAY THAT ...?

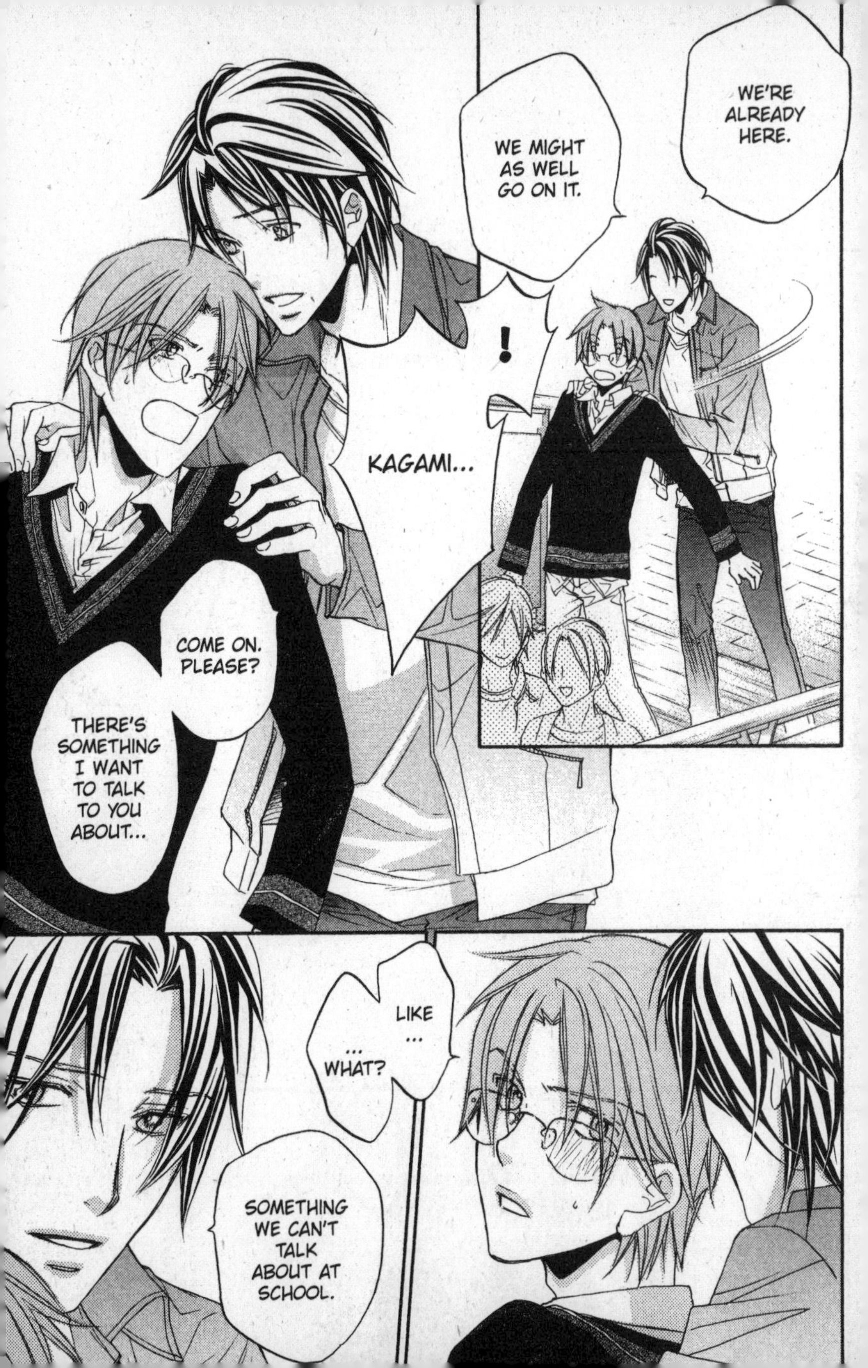
WE'RE ALREADY HERE.
WE MIGHT AS WELL GO ON IT.
!
KAGAMI...
COME ON. PLEASE?
THERE'S SOMETHING I WANT TO TALK TO YOU ABOUT...
LIKE ... ... WHAT?
SOMETHING WE CAN'T TALK ABOUT AT SCHOOL.

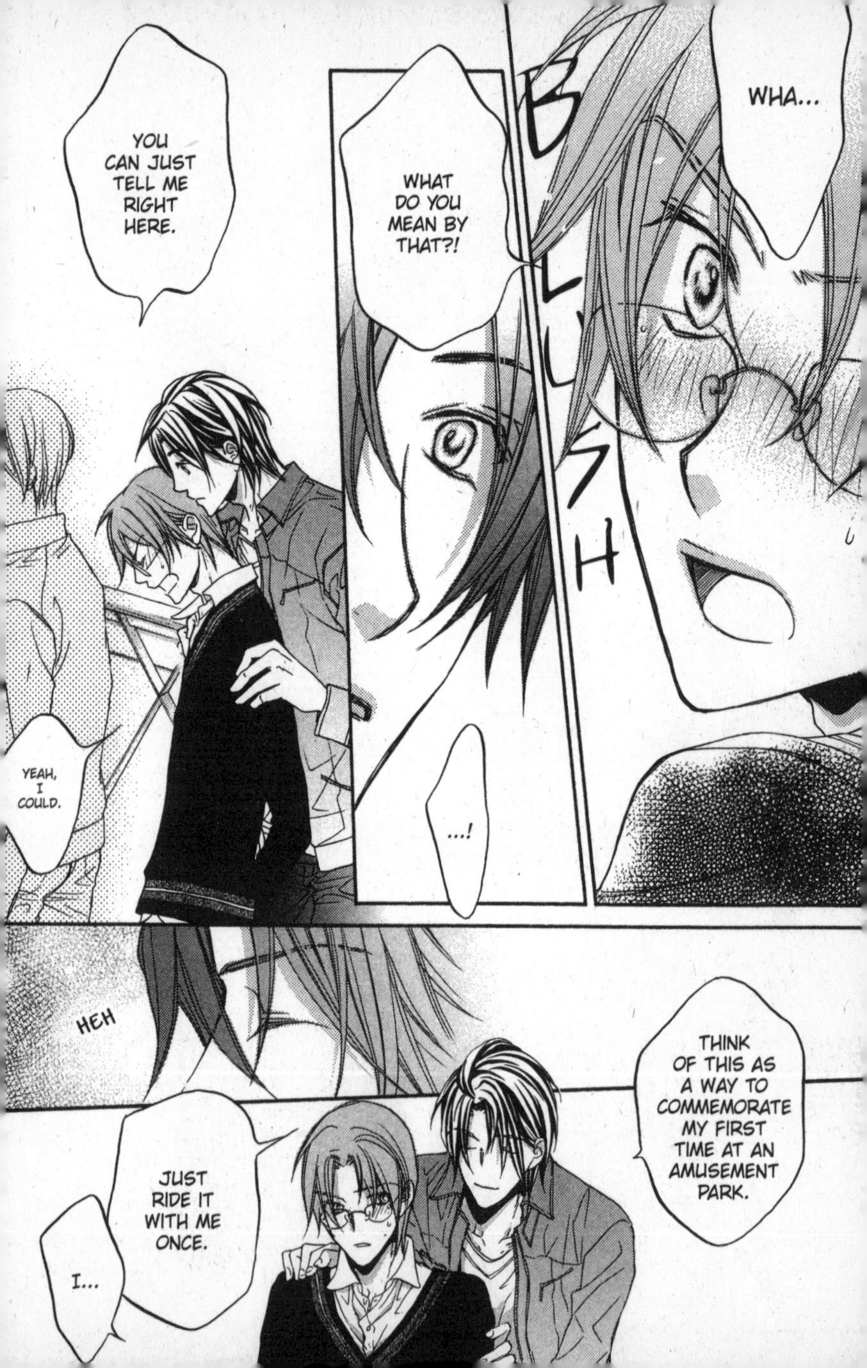
WHA...
BLUSH
WHAT DO YOU MEAN BY THAT?!
...!
YOU CAN JUST TELL ME RIGHT HERE.
YEAH, I COULD.
HEH
THINK OF THIS AS A WAY TO COMMEMORATE MY FIRST TIME AT AN AMUSEMENT PARK.
JUST RIDE IT WITH ME ONCE.
I...

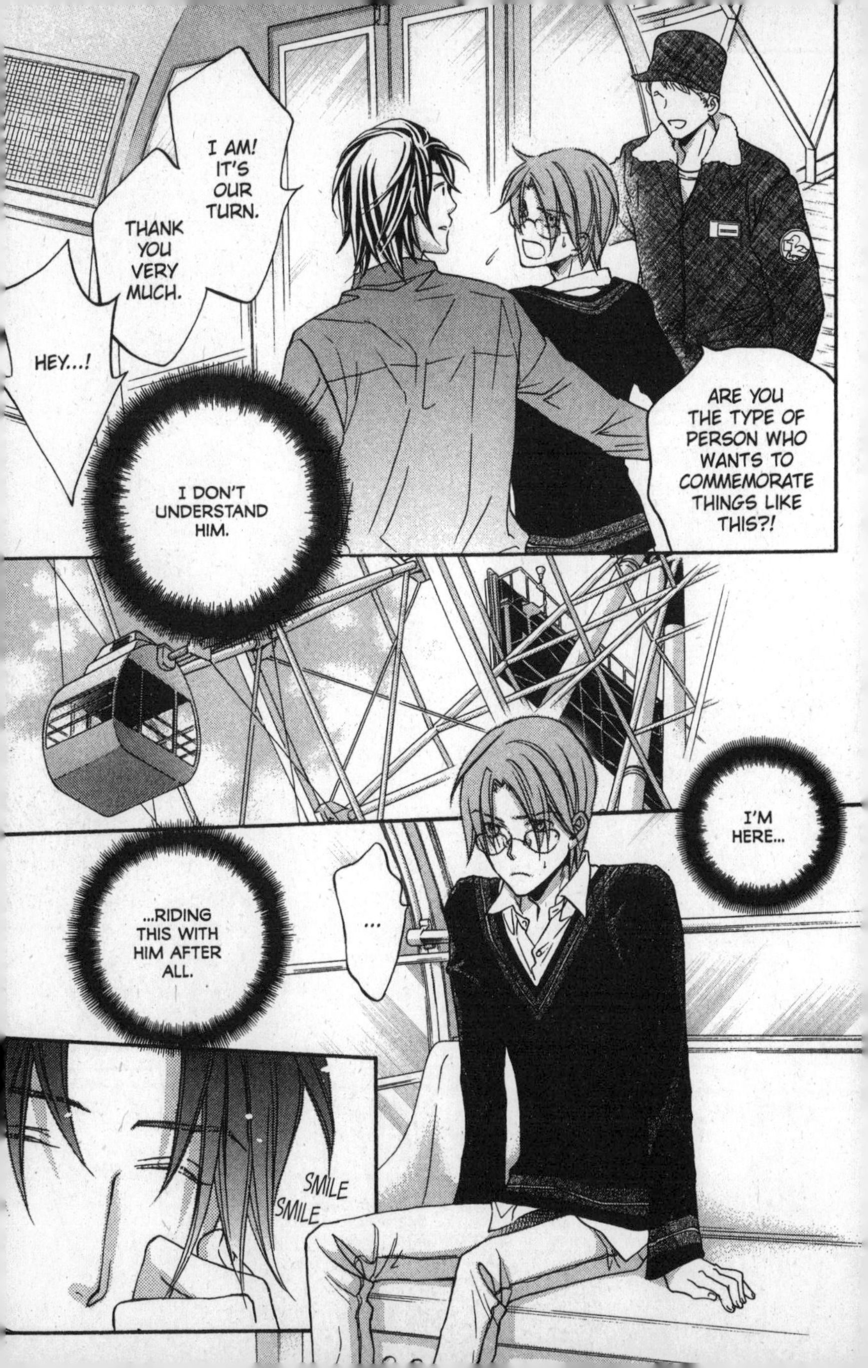
ARE YOU THE TYPE OF PERSON WHO WANTS TO COMMEMORATE THINGS LIKE THIS?!
I AM! IT'S OUR TURN.
THANK YOU VERY MUCH.
HEY...!
I DON'T UNDERSTAND HIM.
I'M HERE...
...RIDING THIS WITH HIM AFTER ALL.
...
SMILE
SMILE

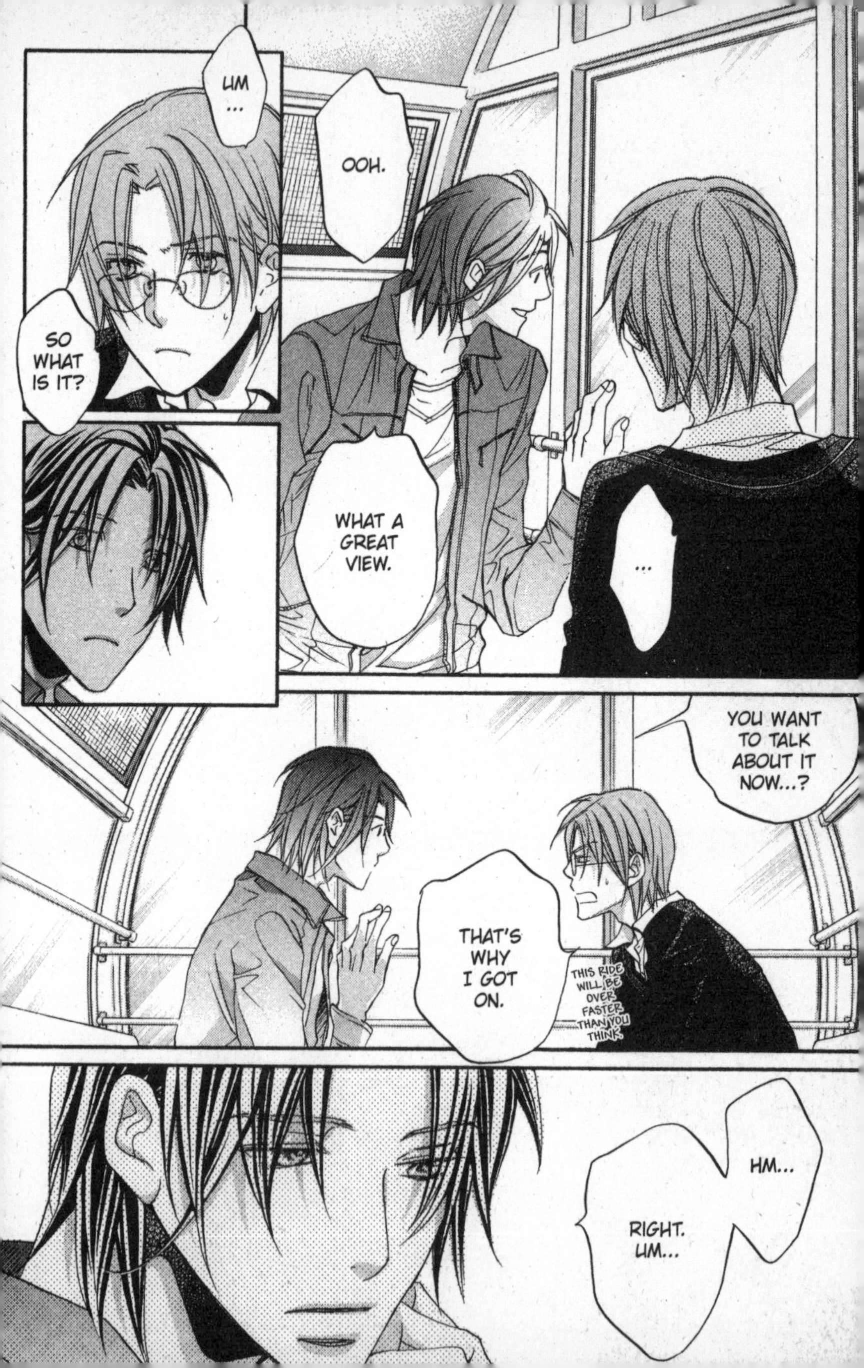
OOH.
WHAT A GREAT VIEW.
...
UM ...
SO WHAT IS IT?
YOU WANT TO TALK ABOUT IT NOW...?
THIS RIDE WILL BE OVER FASTER THAN YOU THINK.
THAT'S WHY I GOT ON.
HM...
RIGHT. UM...

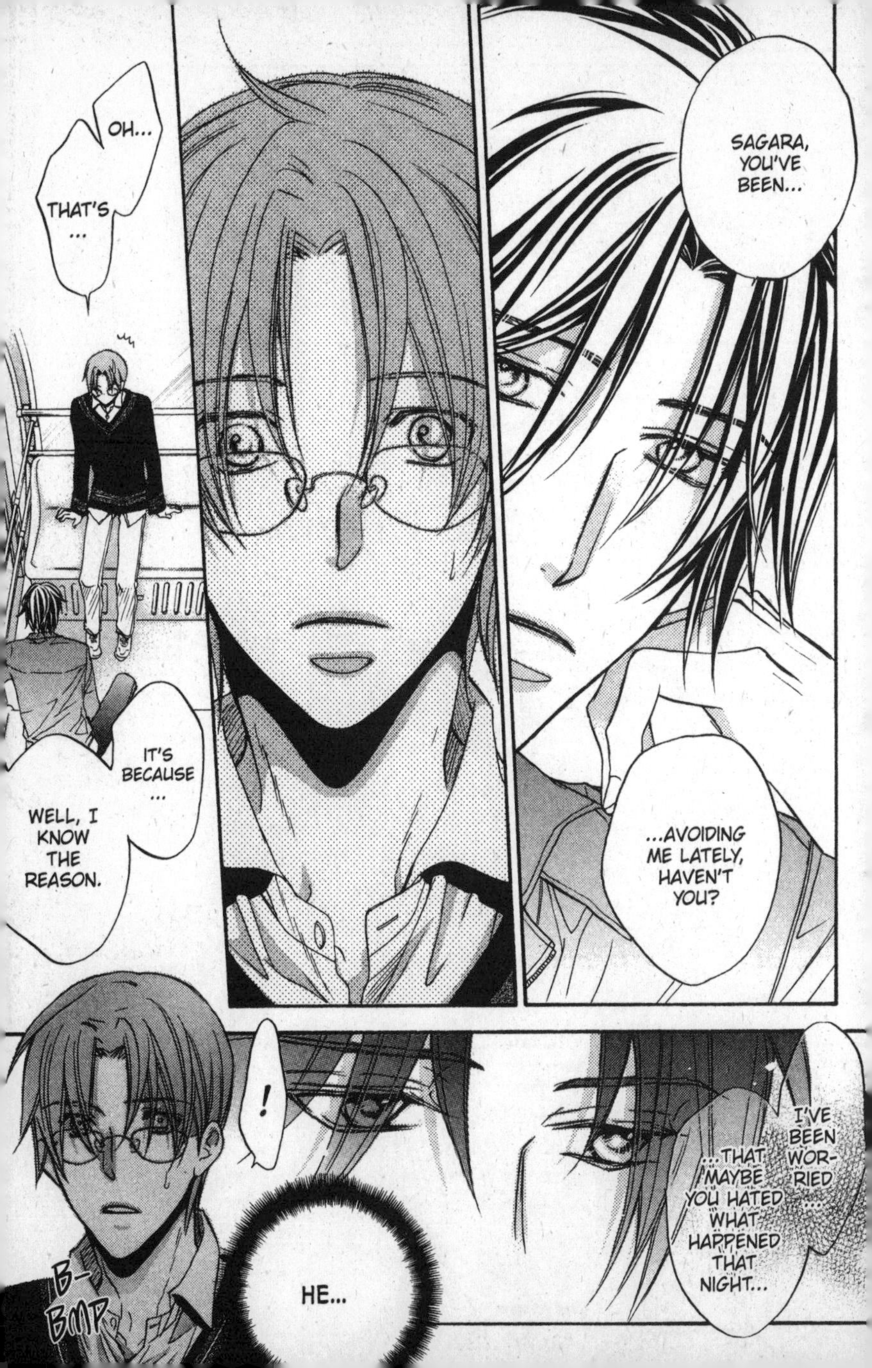
SAGARA, YOU'VE BEEN...
...AVOIDING ME LATELY, HAVEN'T YOU?
OH...
THAT'S ...
IT'S BECAUSE ...
WELL, I KNOW THE REASON.
I'VE BEEN WOR-RIED ...
...THAT MAYBE YOU HATED WHAT HAPPENED THAT NIGHT...
!
HE...
B-BMP

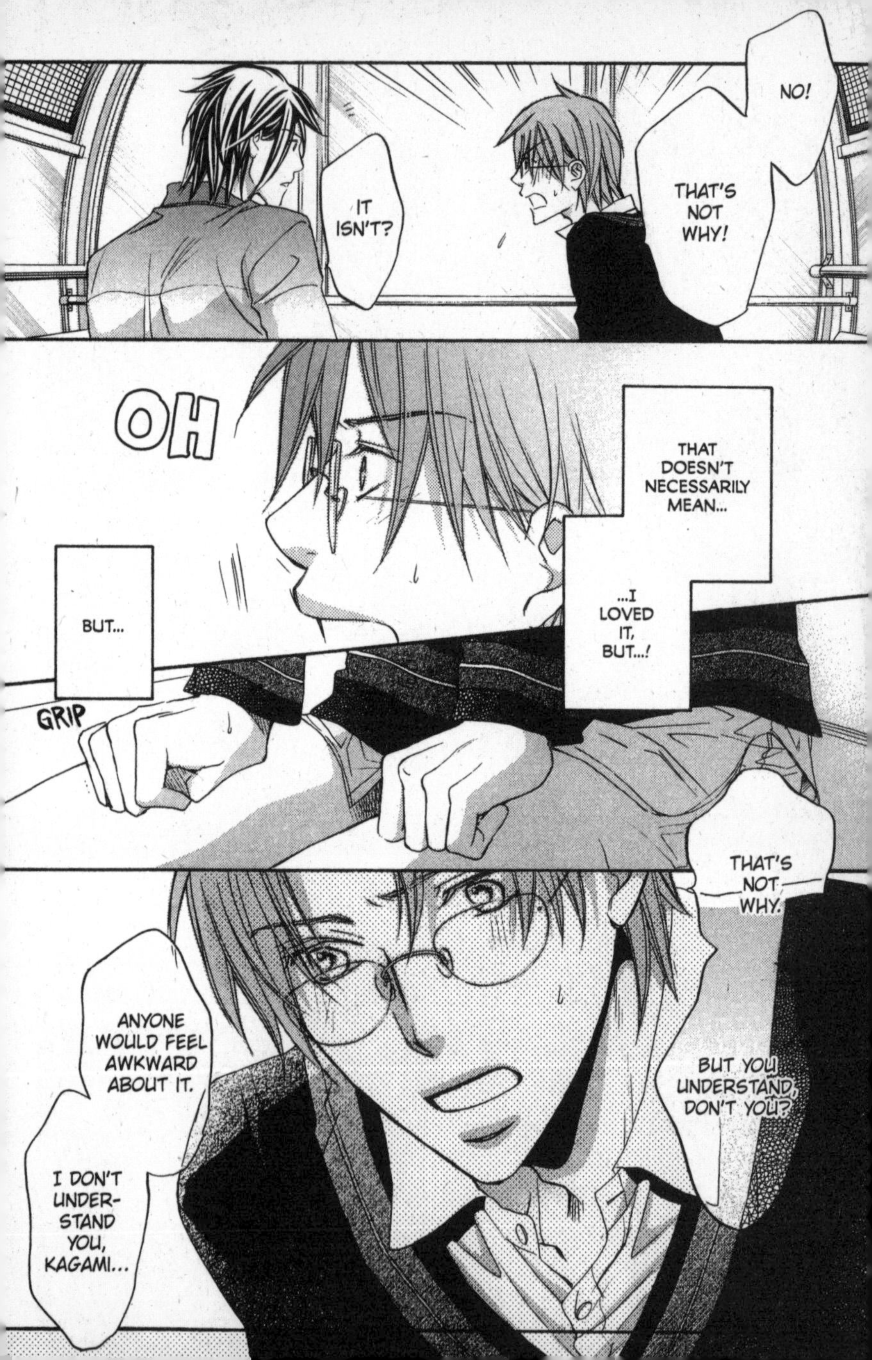
NO!
THAT'S NOT WHY!
IT ISN'T?
THAT DOESN'T NECESSARILY MEAN...
OH
...I LOVED IT, BUT...!
BUT...
GRIP
THAT'S NOT WHY.
BUT YOU UNDERSTAND, DON'T YOU?
ANYONE WOULD FEEL AWKWARD ABOUT IT.
I DON'T UNDER-STAND YOU, KAGAMI...

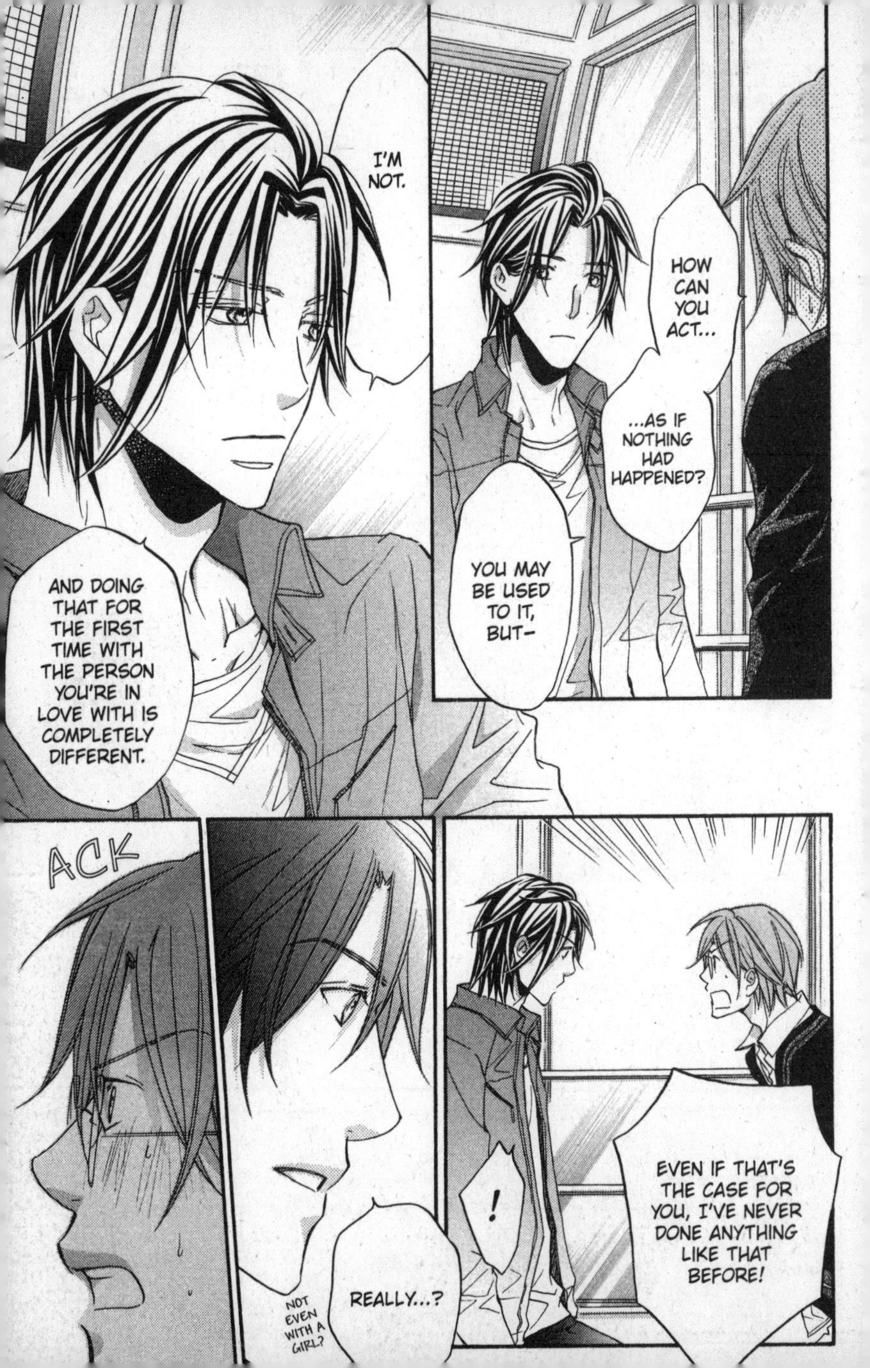
HOW CAN YOU ACT...
...AS IF NOTHING HAD HAPPENED?
YOU MAY BE USED TO IT, BUT-
I'M NOT.
AND DOING THAT FOR THE FIRST TIME WITH THE PERSON YOU'RE IN LOVE WITH IS COMPLETELY DIFFERENT.
EVEN IF THAT'S THE CASE FOR YOU, I'VE NEVER DONE ANYTHING LIKE THAT BEFORE!
!
REALLY...?
NOT EVEN WITH A GIRL?
ACK

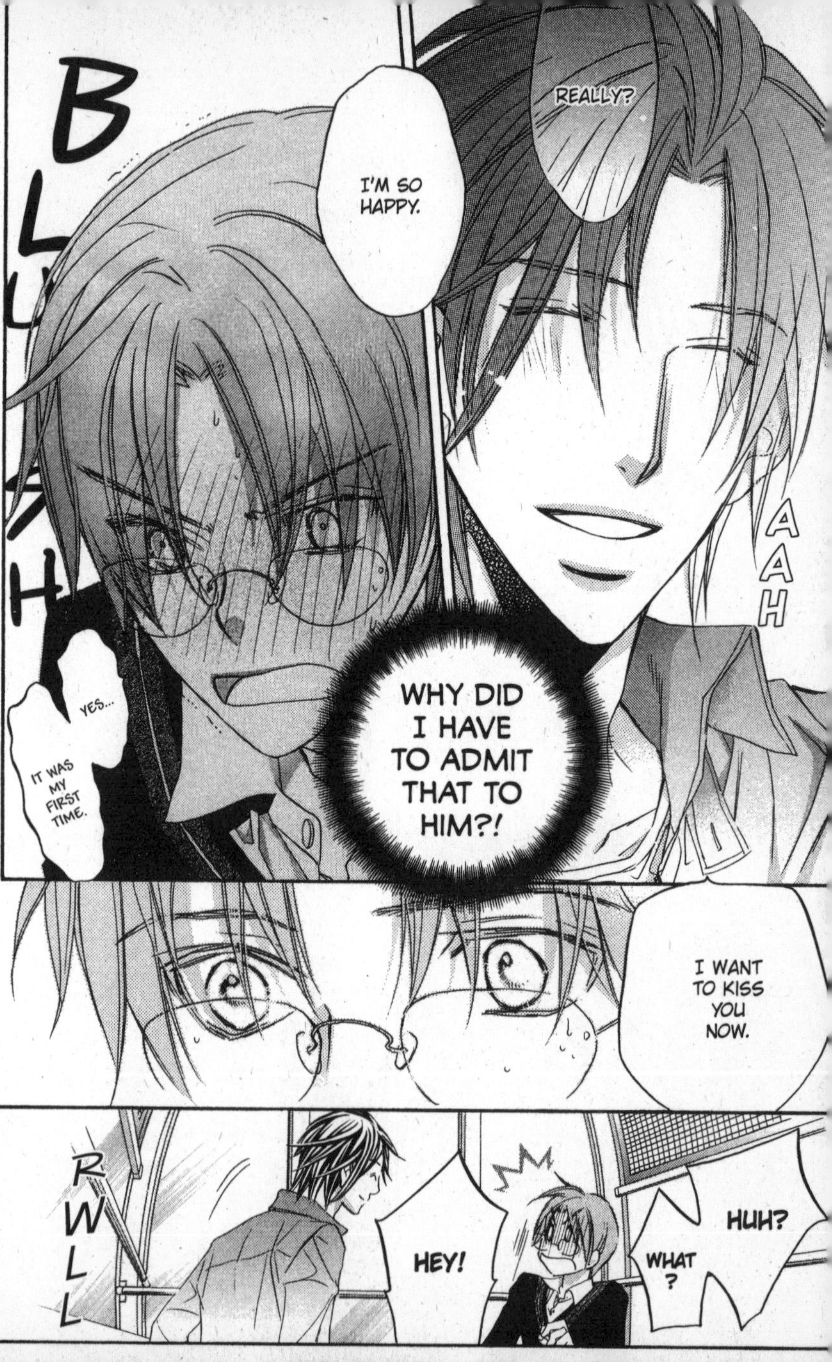
REALLY?
I'M SO HAPPY.
AAAH
BLUSH
YES...
IT WAS MY FIRST TIME.
WHY DID I HAVE TO ADMIT THAT TO HIM?!
I WANT TO KISS YOU NOW.
HUH?
WHAT?
HEY!
RWLL

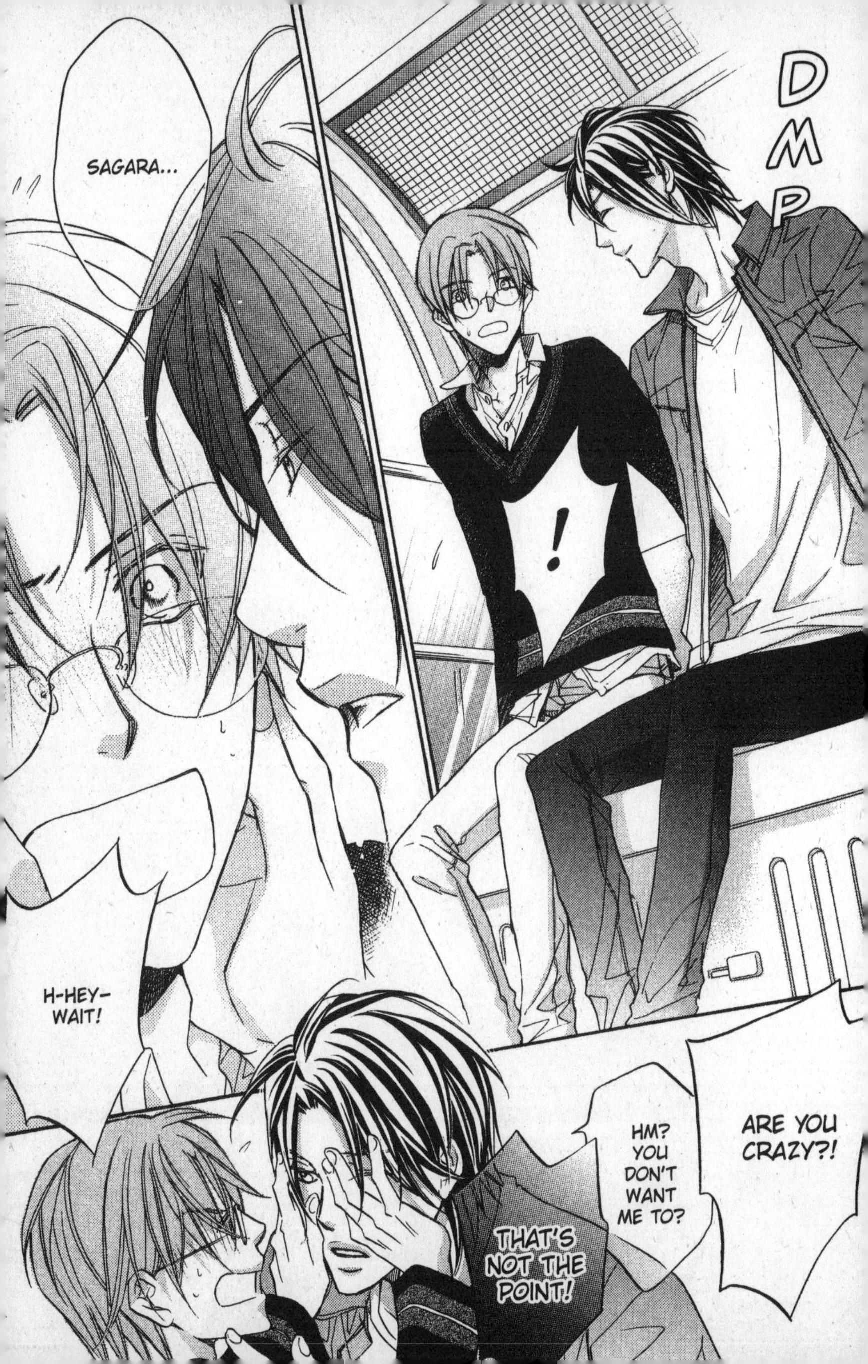
DMP
!
SAGARA...
H-HEY- WAIT!
ARE YOU CRAZY?!
HM? YOU DON'T WANT ME TO?
THAT'S NOT THE POINT!

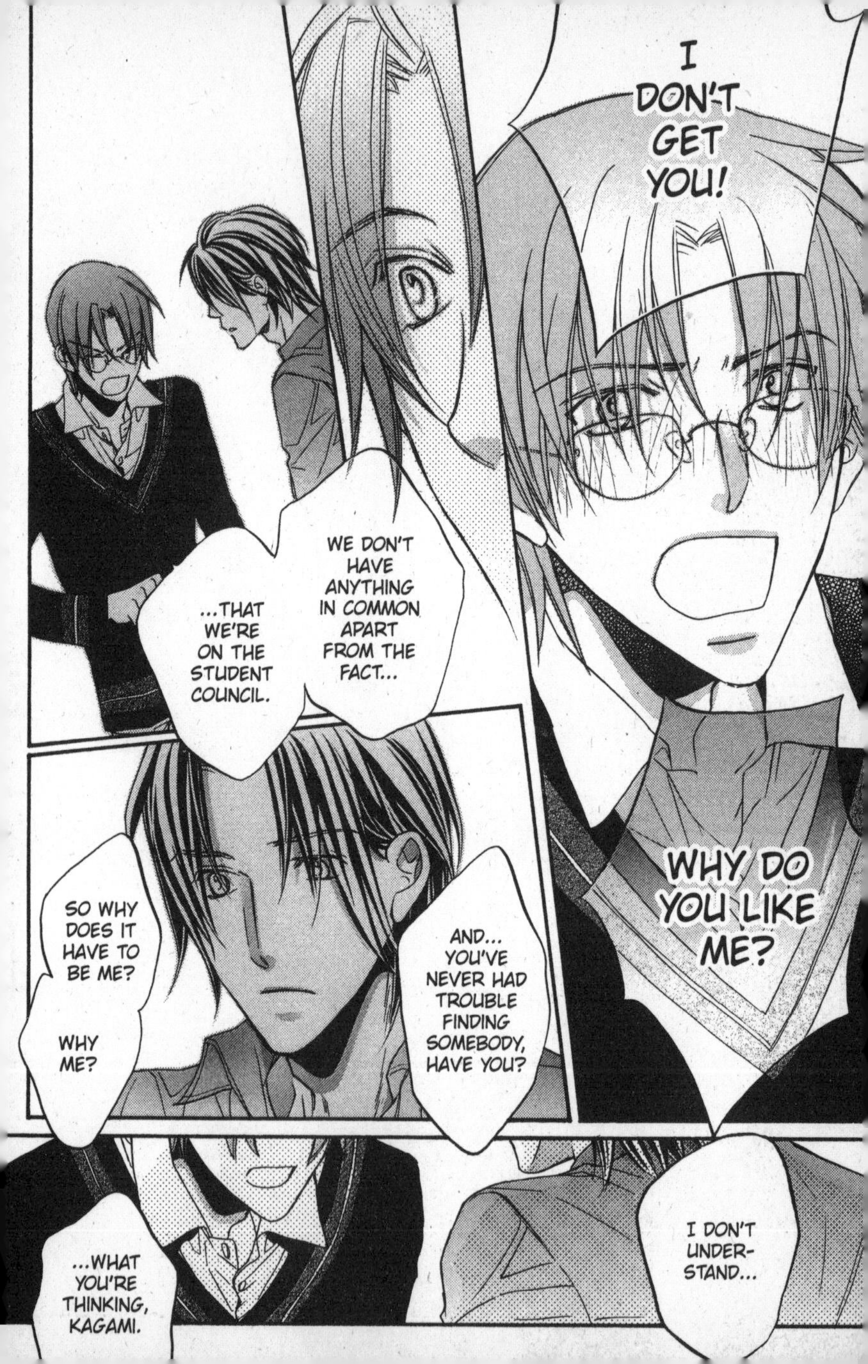
I DON'T GET YOU!
WHY DO YOU LIKE ME?
WE DON'T HAVE ANYTHING IN COMMON APART FROM THE FACT...
...THAT WE'RE ON THE STUDENT COUNCIL.
AND... YOU'VE NEVER HAD TROUBLE FINDING SOMEBODY, HAVE YOU?
SO WHY DOES IT HAVE TO BE ME?
WHY ME?
I DON'T UNDER-STAND...
...WHAT YOU'RE THINKING, KAGAMI.

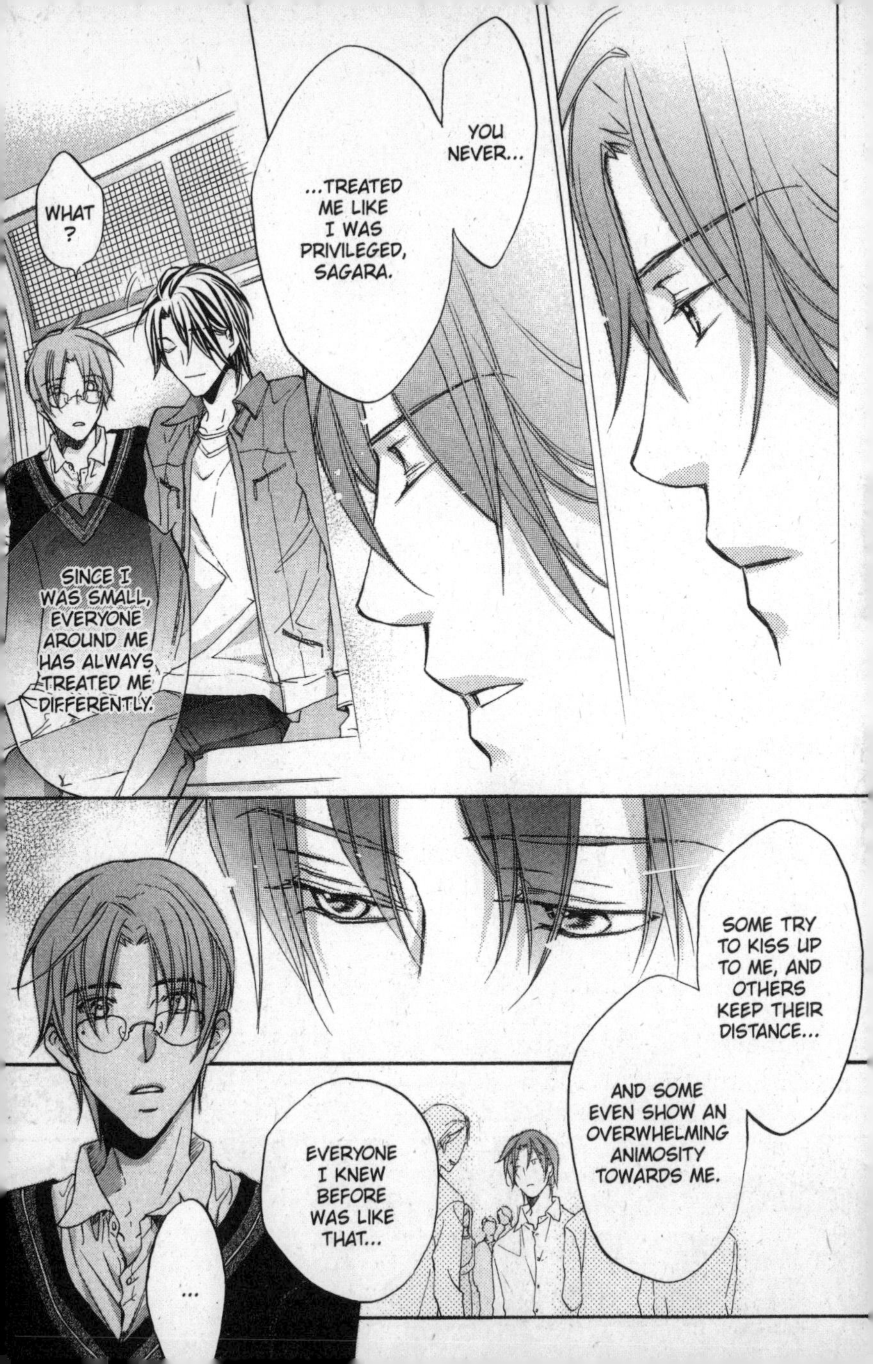
YOU NEVER...
...TREATED ME LIKE I WAS PRIVILEGED, SAGARA.
WHAT?
SINCE I WAS SMALL, EVERYONE AROUND ME HAS ALWAYS TREATED ME DIFFERENTLY.
SOME TRY TO KISS UP TO ME, AND OTHERS KEEP THEIR DISTANCE...
AND SOME EVEN SHOW AN OVERWHELMING ANIMOSITY TOWARDS ME.
EVERYONE I KNEW BEFORE WAS LIKE THAT...
...

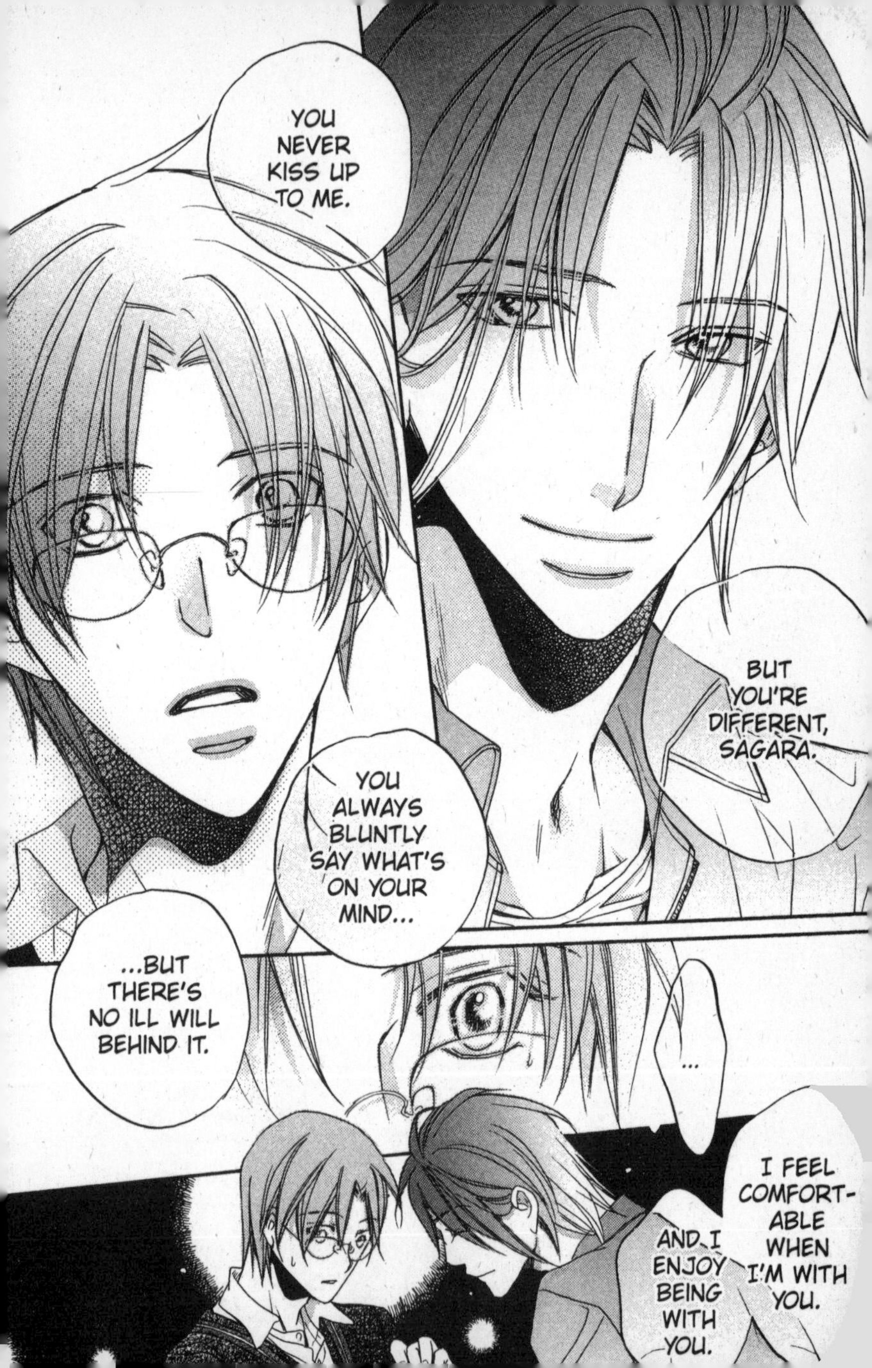
YOU NEVER KISS UP TO ME.
BUT YOU'RE DIFFERENT, SAGARA.
YOU ALWAYS BLUNTLY SAY WHAT'S ON YOUR MIND...
...BUT THERE'S NO ILL WILL BEHIND IT.
...
I FEEL COMFORT-ABLE WHEN I'M WITH YOU.
AND I ENJOY BEING WITH YOU.

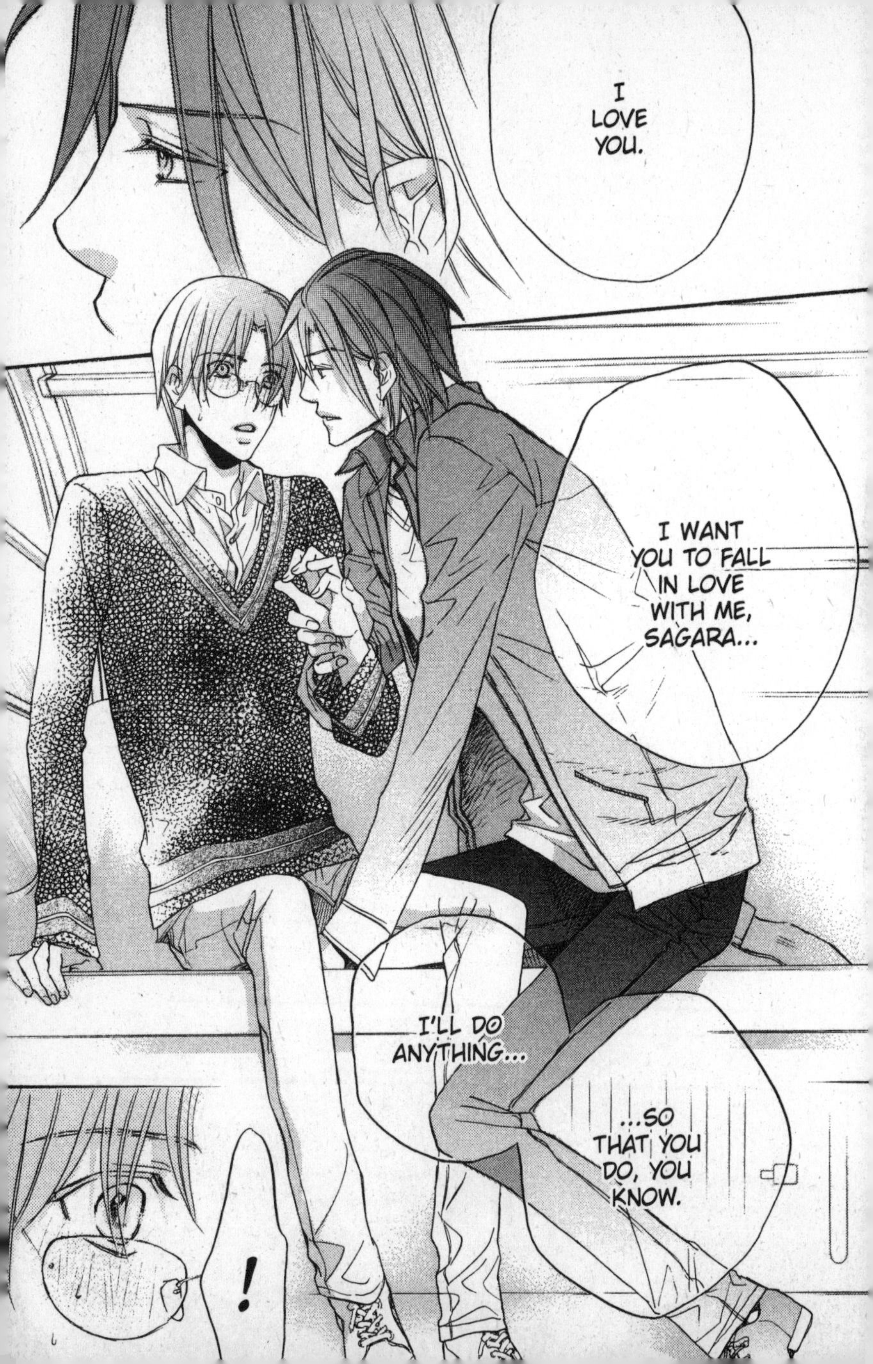
I LOVE YOU.
I WANT YOU TO FALL IN LOVE WITH ME, SAGARA...
I'LL DO ANYTHING...
...SO THAT YOU DO, YOU KNOW.
!

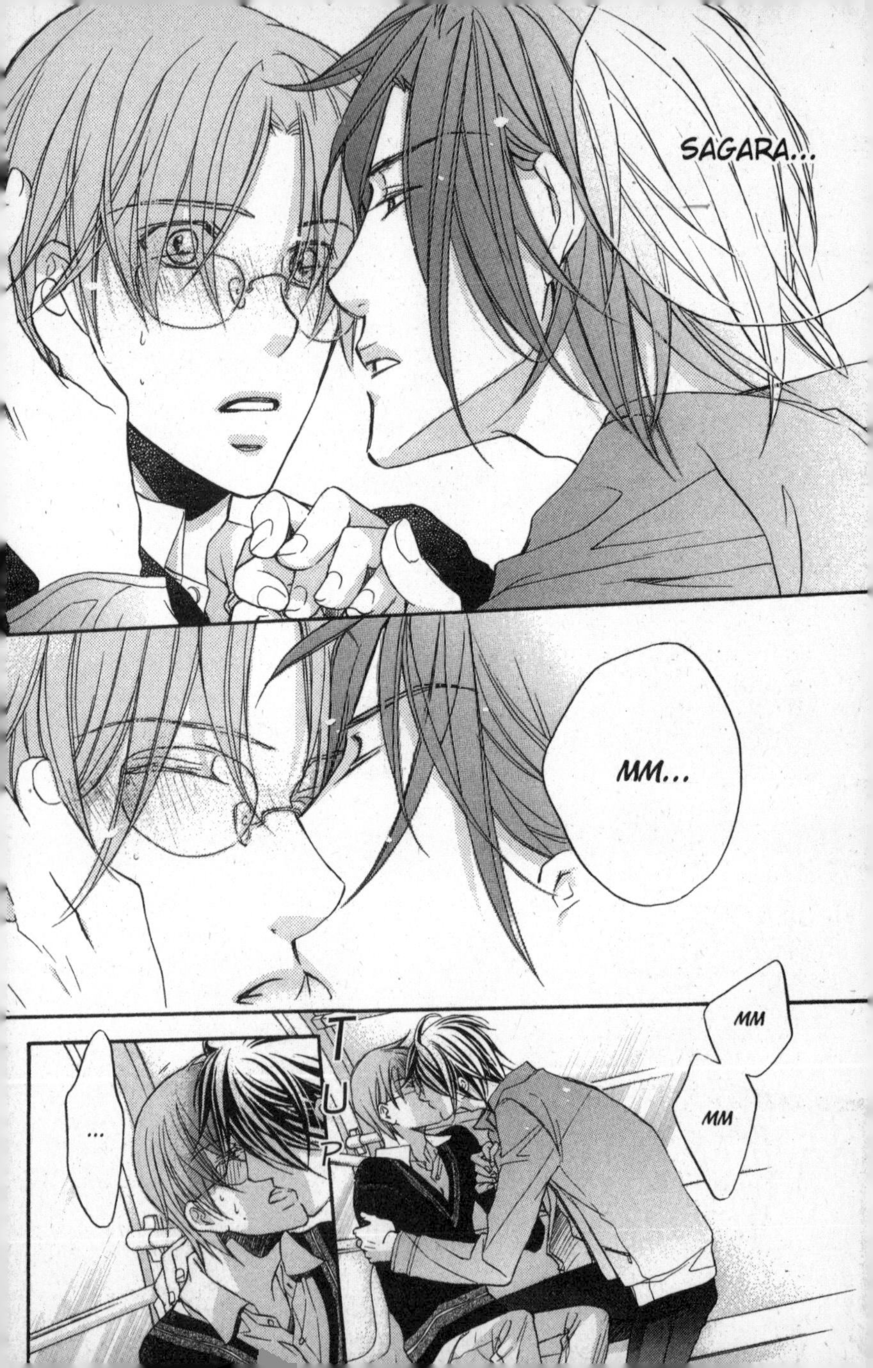
SAGARA...
MM...
MM
MM
TUP
...

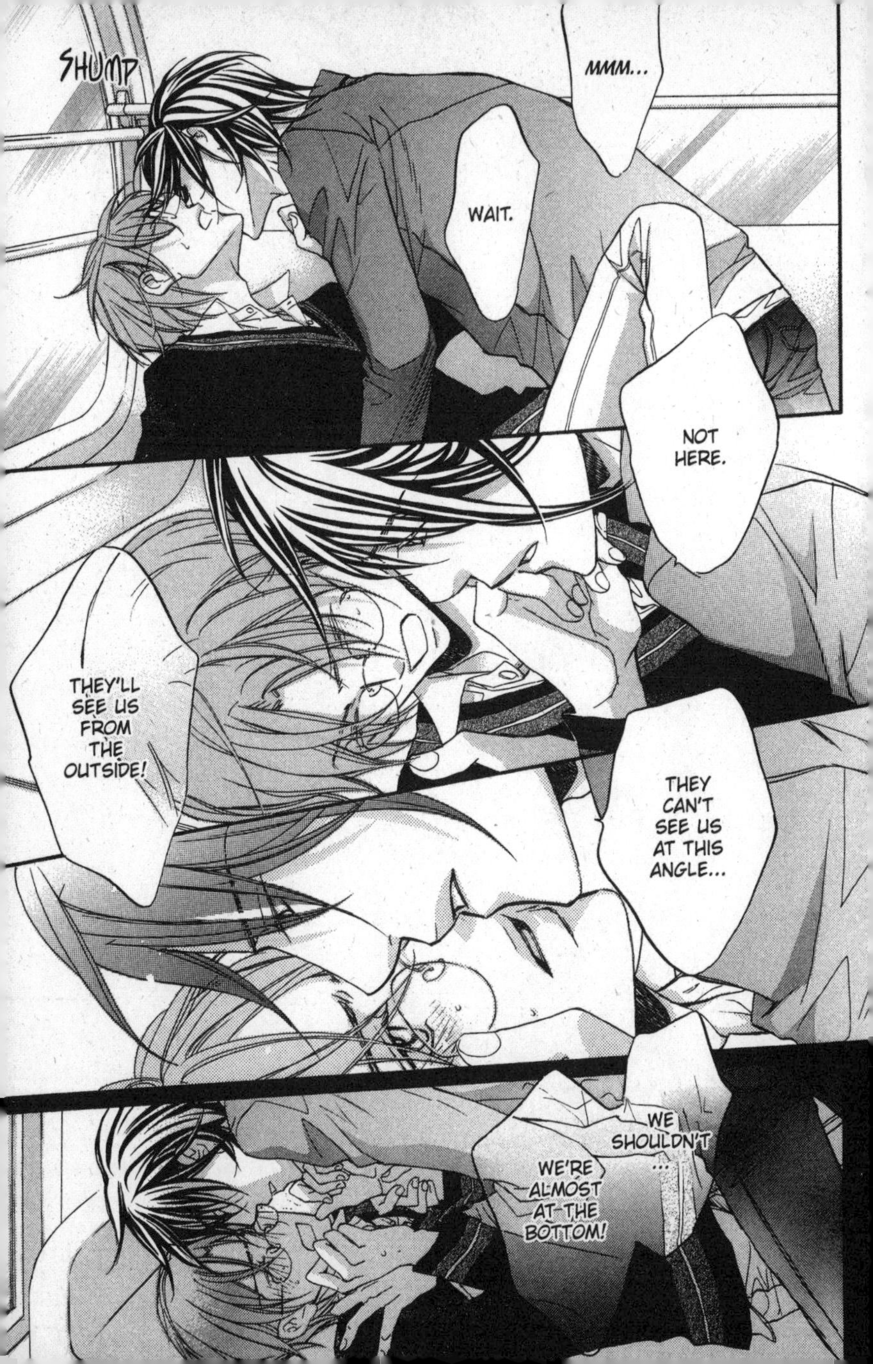
MMM...
WAIT.
SHUMP
NOT HERE.
THEY'LL SEE US FROM THE OUTSIDE!
THEY CAN'T SEE US AT THIS ANGLE...
WE SHOULDN'T ...
WE'RE ALMOST AT THE BOTTOM!

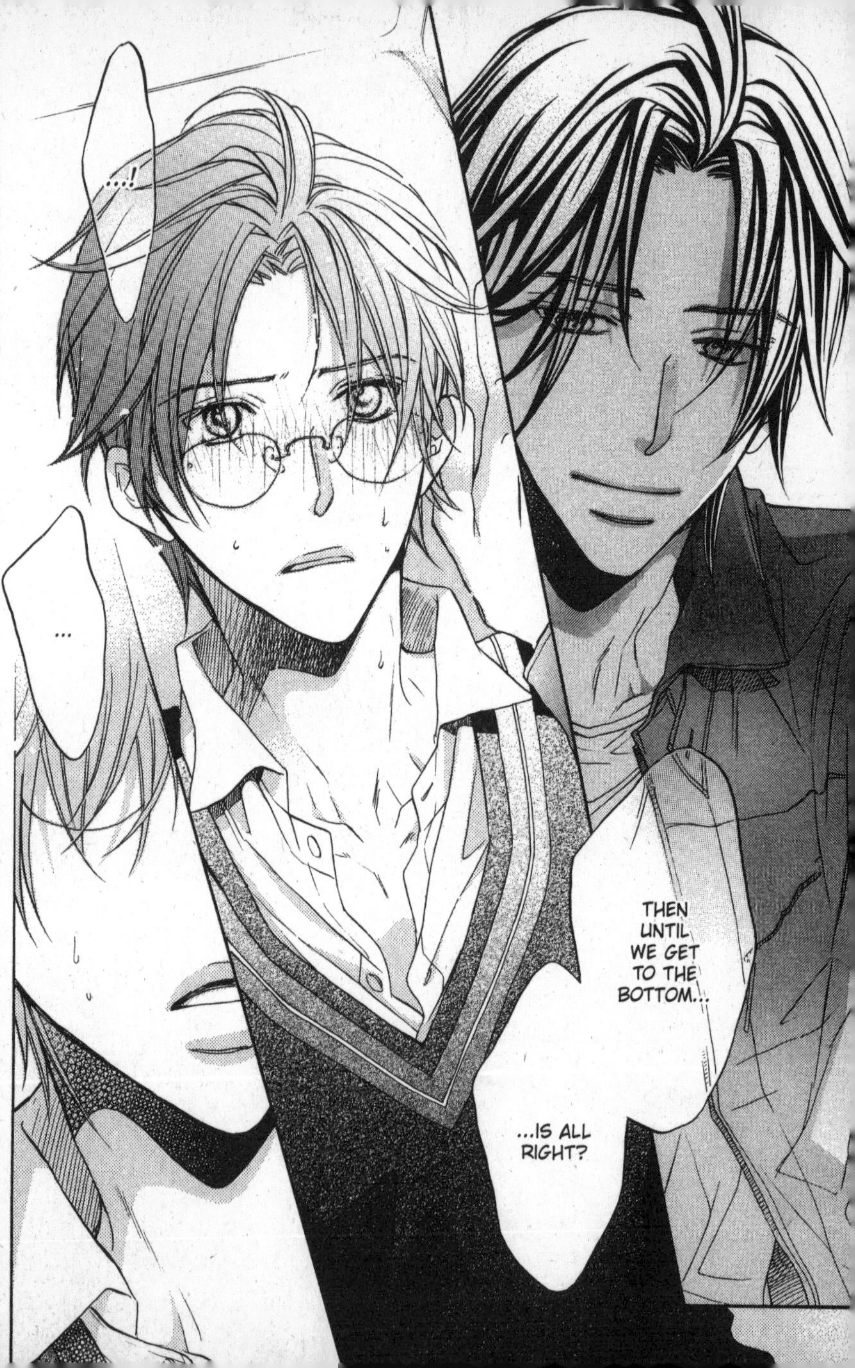
THEN UNTIL WE GET TO THE BOTTOM...
...IS ALL RIGHT?
...!
...

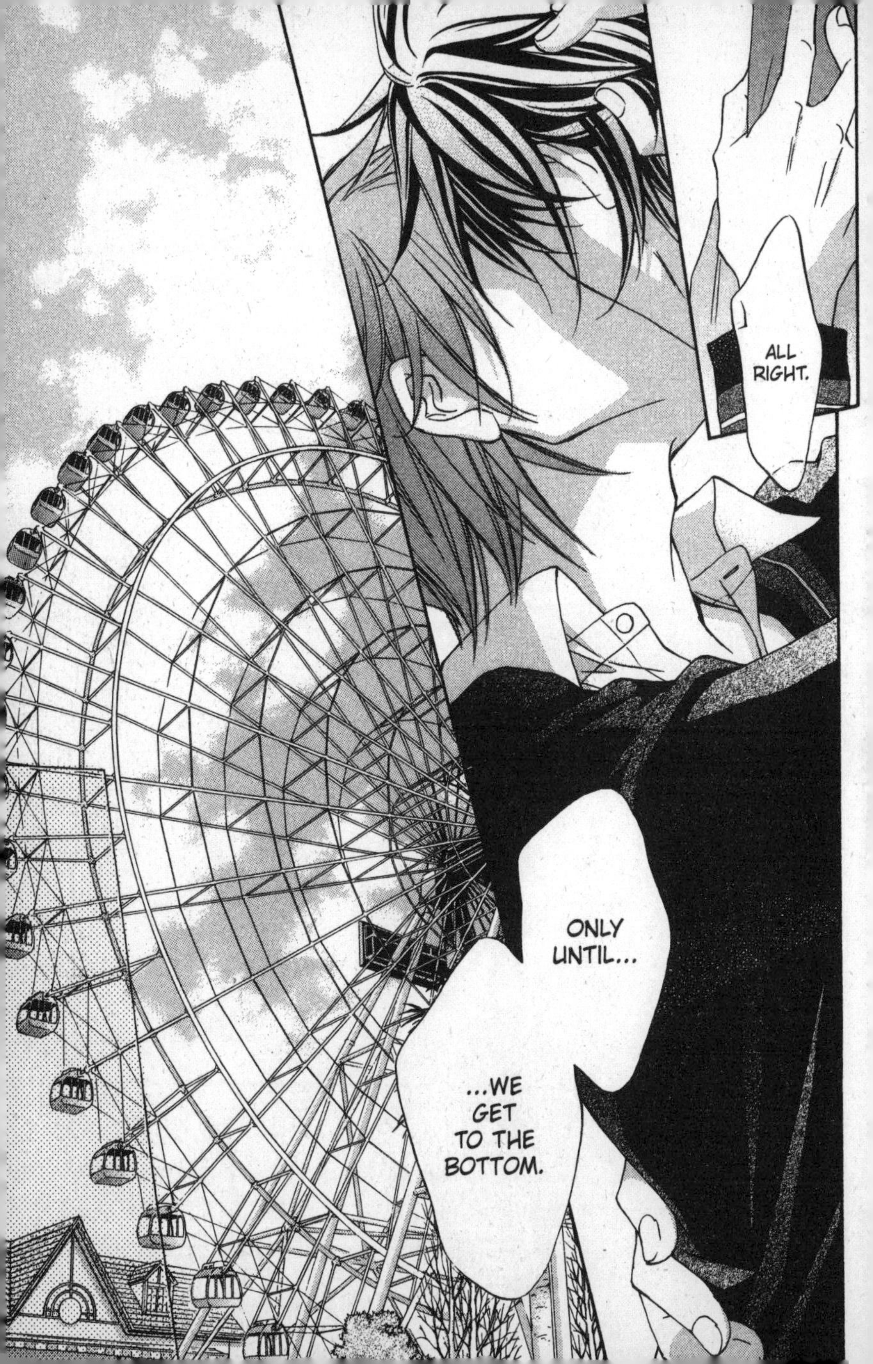
ALL RIGHT.
ONLY UNTIL...
...WE GET TO THE BOTTOM.

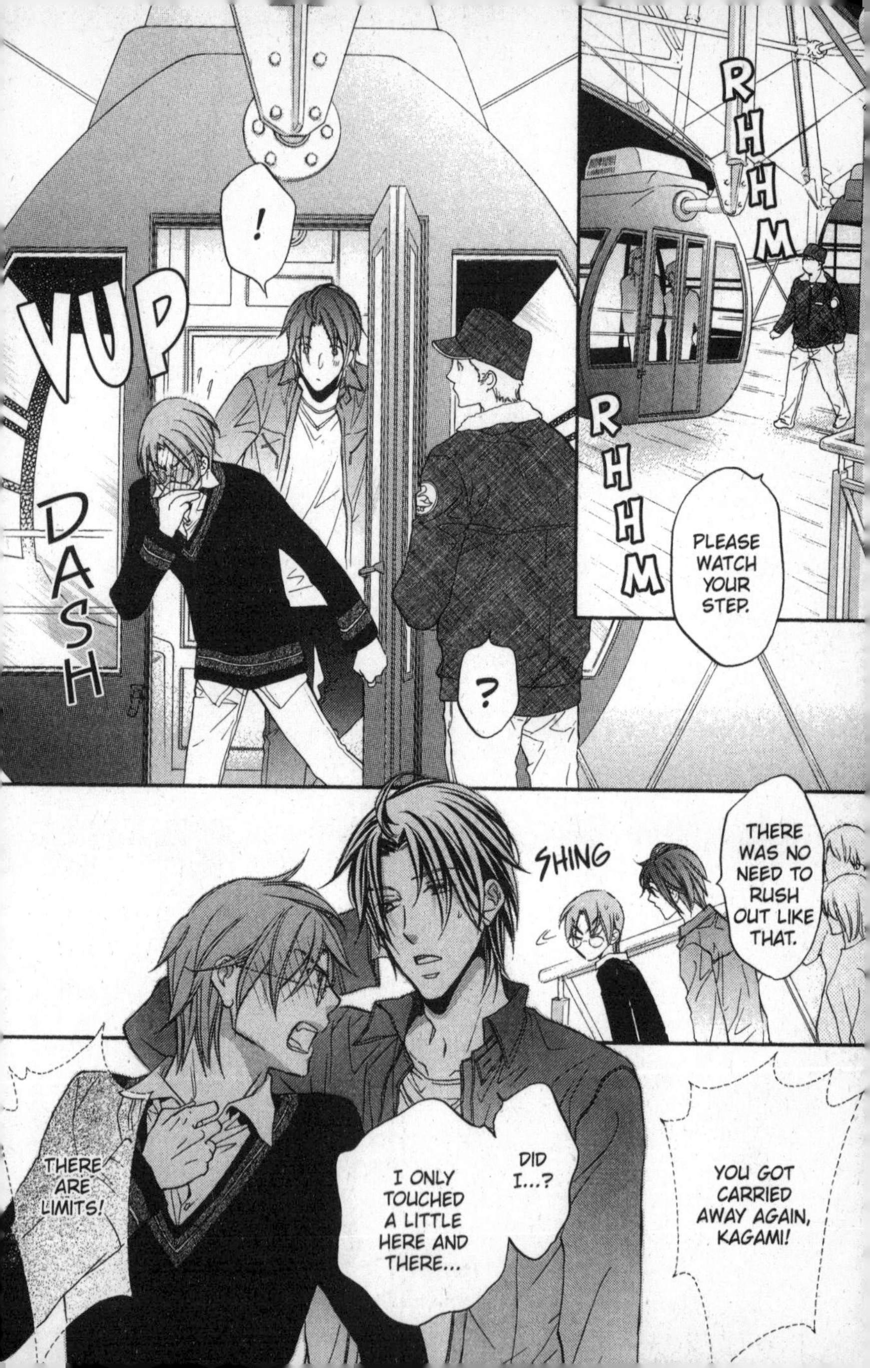
RHHM
RHHM
PLEASE WATCH YOUR STEP.
!
VUP
DASH
?
THERE WAS NO NEED TO RUSH OUT LIKE THAT.
SHING
YOU GOT CARRIED AWAY AGAIN, KAGAMI!
DID I...?
I ONLY TOUCHED A LITTLE HERE AND THERE...
THERE ARE LIMITS!

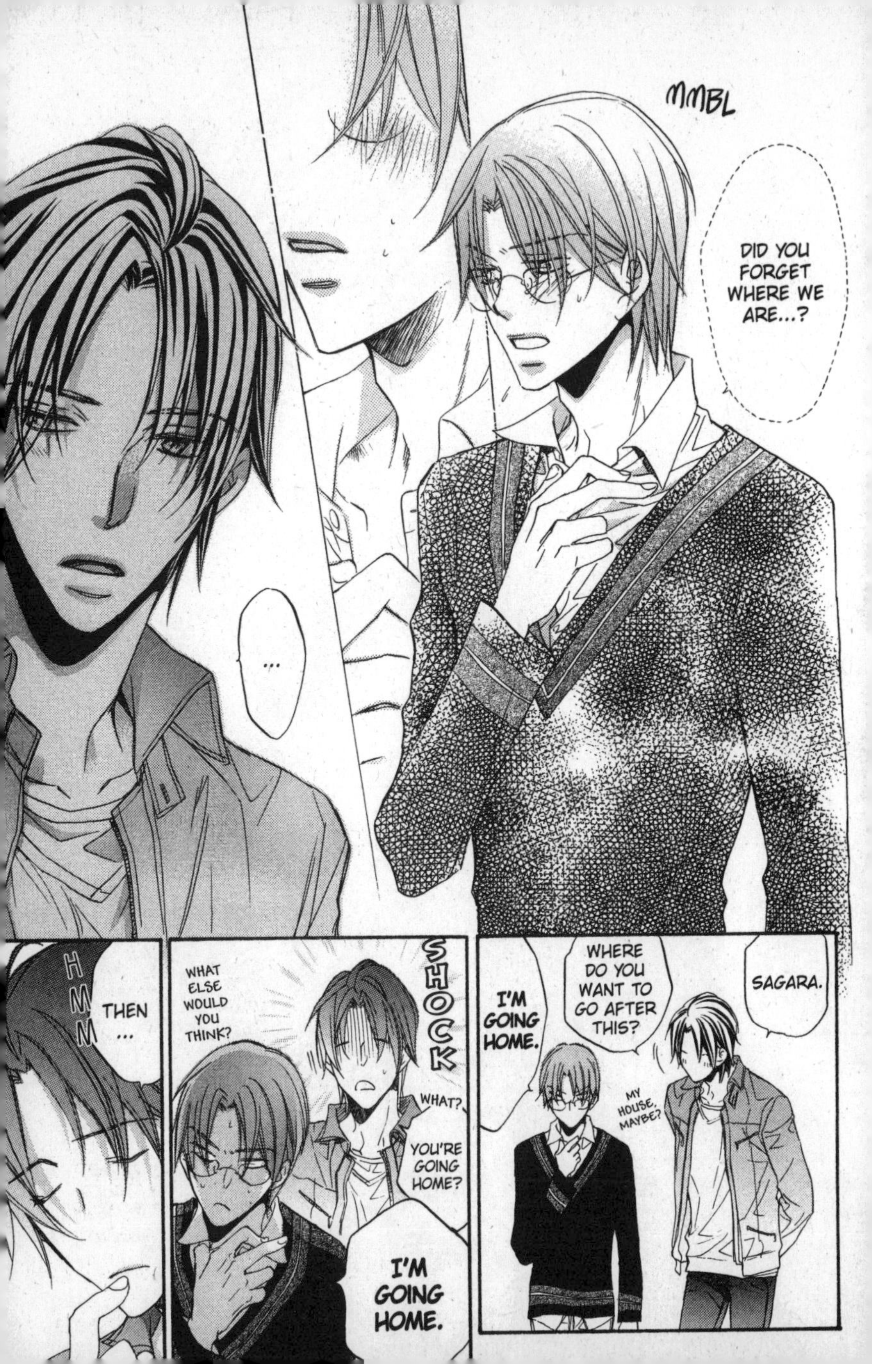
MMBL
DID YOU FORGET WHERE WE ARE...?
...
SAGARA.
WHERE DO YOU WANT TO GO AFTER THIS?
MY HOUSE, MAYBE?
I'M GOING HOME.
SHOCK
WHAT?
YOU'RE GOING HOME?
WHAT ELSE WOULD YOU THINK?
I'M GOING HOME.
HMMM
THEN ...

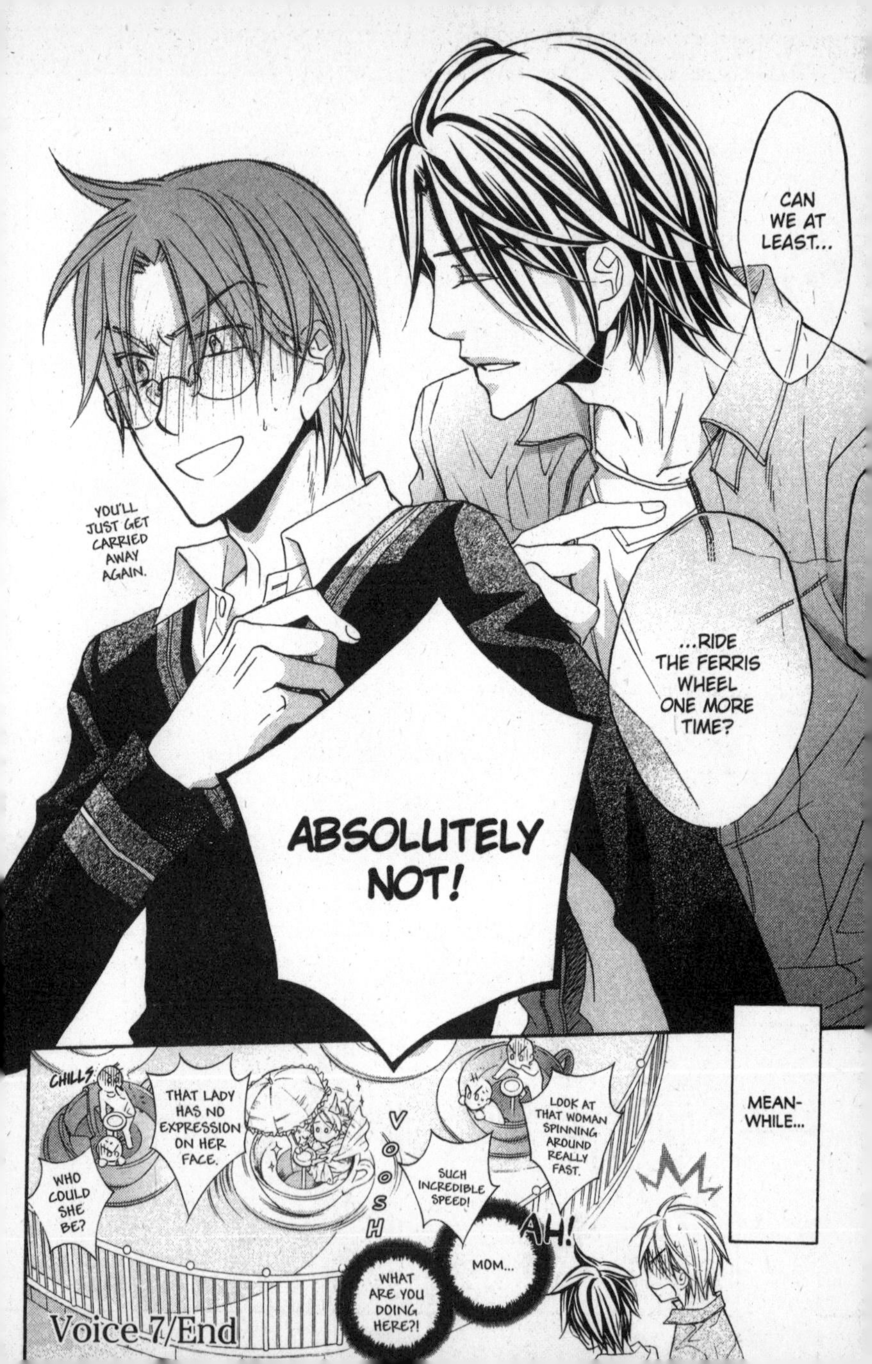
CAN WE AT LEAST...
...RIDE THE FERRIS WHEEL ONE MORE TIME?
YOU'LL JUST GET CARRIED AWAY AGAIN.
ABSOLUTELY NOT!
MEAN-WHILE...
LOOK AT THAT WOMAN SPINNING AROUND REALLY FAST.
SUCH INCREDIBLE SPEED!
VOOSH
THAT LADY HAS NO EXPRESSION ON HER FACE.
CHILLS
WHO COULD SHE BE?
AH!
MOM...
WHAT ARE YOU DOING HERE?!

Voice 7/End

Awkward Silence: Side Voice

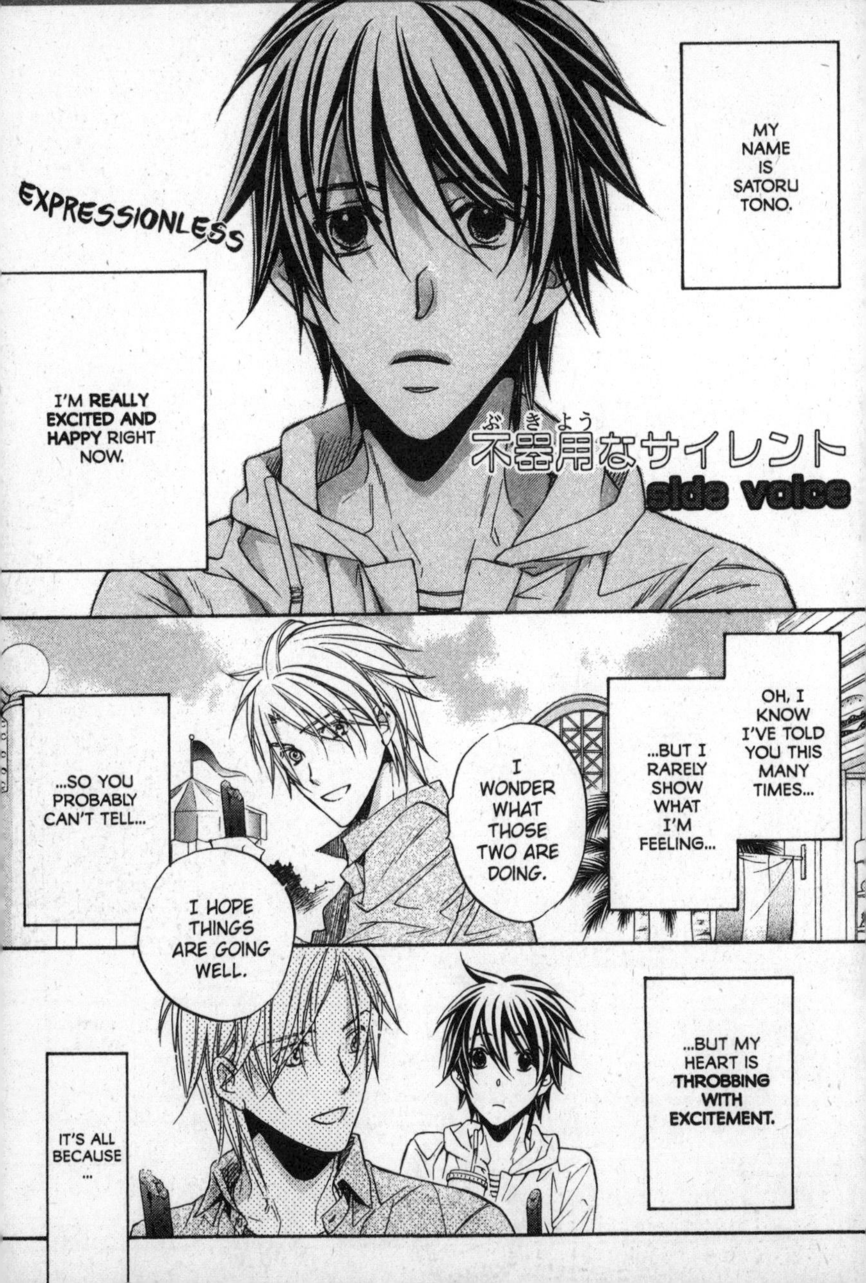
MY NAME IS SATORU TONO.
EXPRESSIONLESS
不器用なサイレント
side voice
I'M REALLY EXCITED AND HAPPY RIGHT NOW.
OH, I KNOW I'VE TOLD YOU THIS MANY TIMES...
...BUT I RARELY SHOW WHAT I'M FEELING...
I WONDER WHAT THOSE TWO ARE DOING.
...SO YOU PROBABLY CAN'T TELL...
I HOPE THINGS ARE GOING WELL.
...BUT MY HEART IS THROBBING WITH EXCITEMENT.
IT'S ALL BECAUSE ...

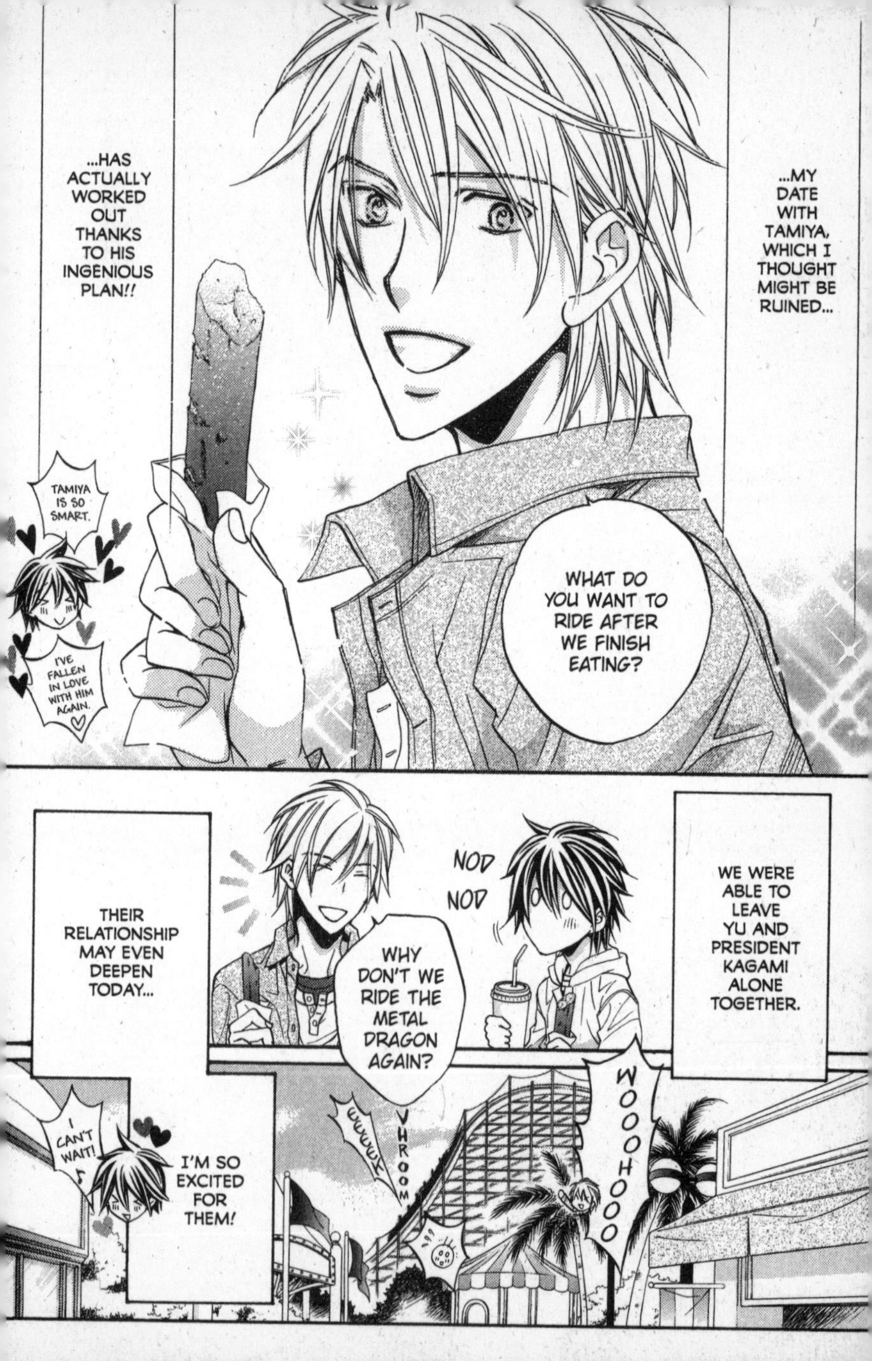
...MY DATE WITH TAMIYA, WHICH I THOUGHT MIGHT BE RUINED...
...HAS ACTUALLY WORKED OUT THANKS TO HIS INGENIOUS PLAN!!
WHAT DO YOU WANT TO RIDE AFTER WE FINISH EATING?
TAMIYA IS SO SMART.
I'VE FALLEN IN LOVE WITH HIM AGAIN. ♡
WE WERE ABLE TO LEAVE YU AND PRESIDENT KAGAMI ALONE TOGETHER.
NOD
NOD
WHY DON'T WE RIDE THE METAL DRAGON AGAIN?
THEIR RELATIONSHIP MAY EVEN DEEPEN TODAY...
WOOOOHOOOO
VHROOM
EEEEK
I'M SO EXCITED FOR THEM!
I CAN'T WAIT! ♪

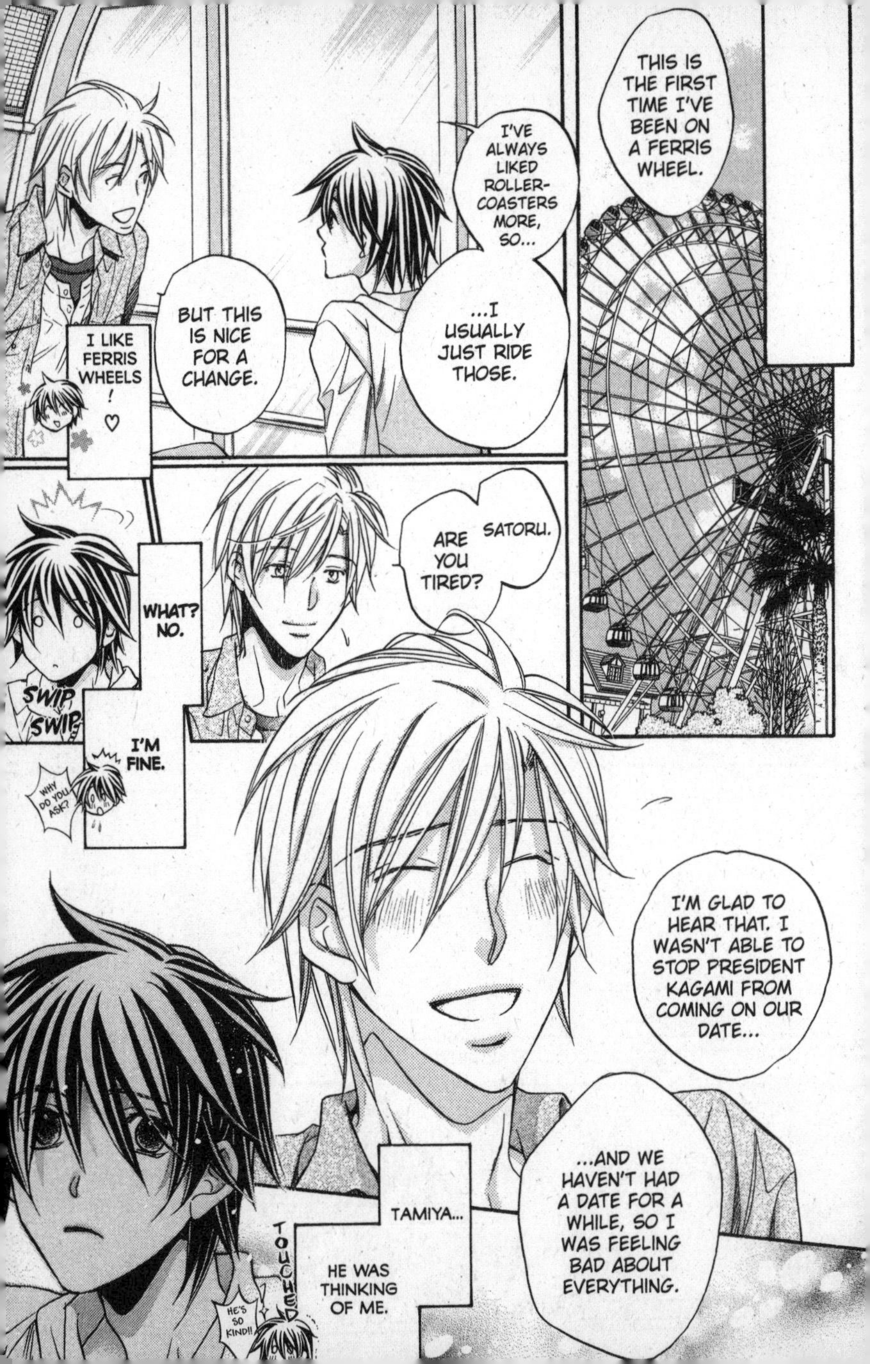
THIS IS THE FIRST TIME I'VE BEEN ON A FERRIS WHEEL.
I'VE ALWAYS LIKED ROLLER-COASTERS MORE, SO...
...I USUALLY JUST RIDE THOSE.
BUT THIS IS NICE FOR A CHANGE.
I LIKE FERRIS WHEELS! ♡
SATORU.
ARE YOU TIRED?
WHAT? NO.
SWIP SWIP
I'M FINE.
WHY DO YOU ASK?
I'M GLAD TO HEAR THAT. I WASN'T ABLE TO STOP PRESIDENT KAGAMI FROM COMING ON OUR DATE...
...AND WE HAVEN'T HAD A DATE FOR A WHILE, SO I WAS FEELING BAD ABOUT EVERYTHING.
TAMIYA...
HE WAS THINKING OF ME.
TOUCHED
HE'S SO KIND!!

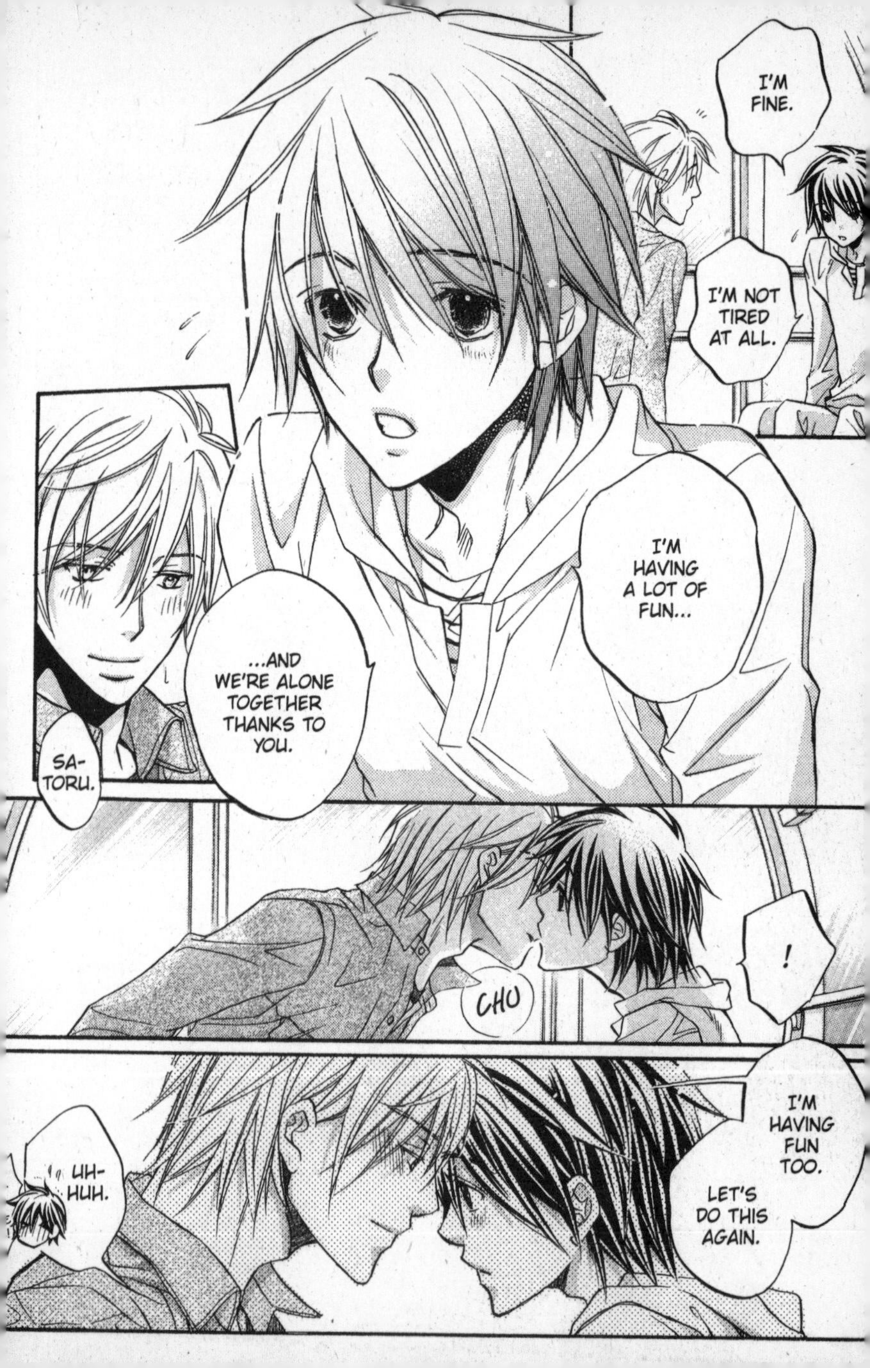
I'M FINE.
I'M NOT TIRED AT ALL.
I'M HAVING A LOT OF FUN...
...AND WE'RE ALONE TOGETHER THANKS TO YOU.
SA-TORU.
!
CHU
I'M HAVING FUN TOO.
LET'S DO THIS AGAIN.
...UH-HUH.

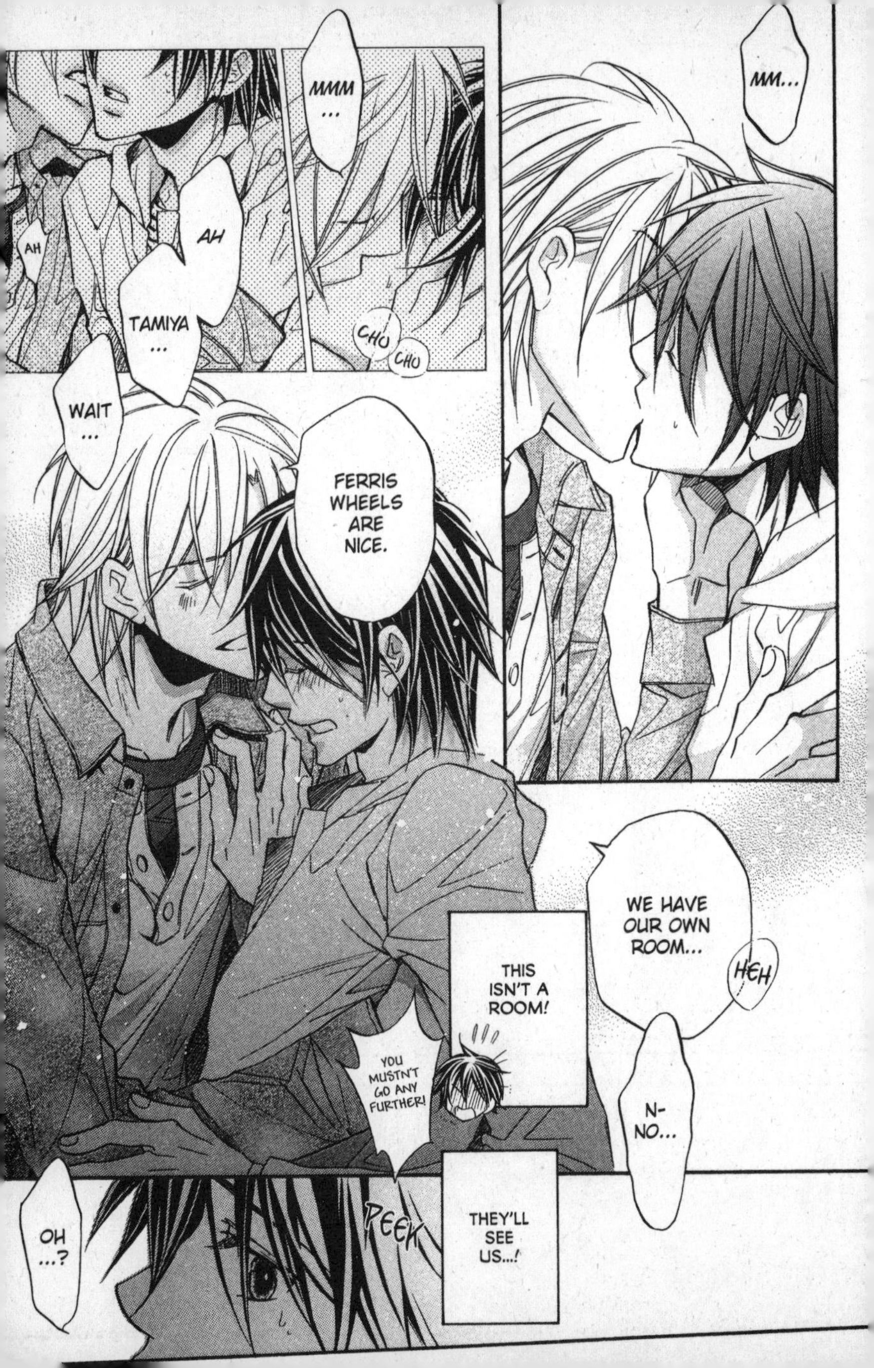
MM...
MMM ...
CHU
CHU
AH
AH
TAMIYA ...
WAIT ...
FERRIS WHEELS ARE NICE.
WE HAVE OUR OWN ROOM...
HEH
N- NO...
THIS ISN'T A ROOM!
YOU MUSTN'T GO ANY FURTHER!
THEY'LL SEE US...!
PEEK
OH ...?

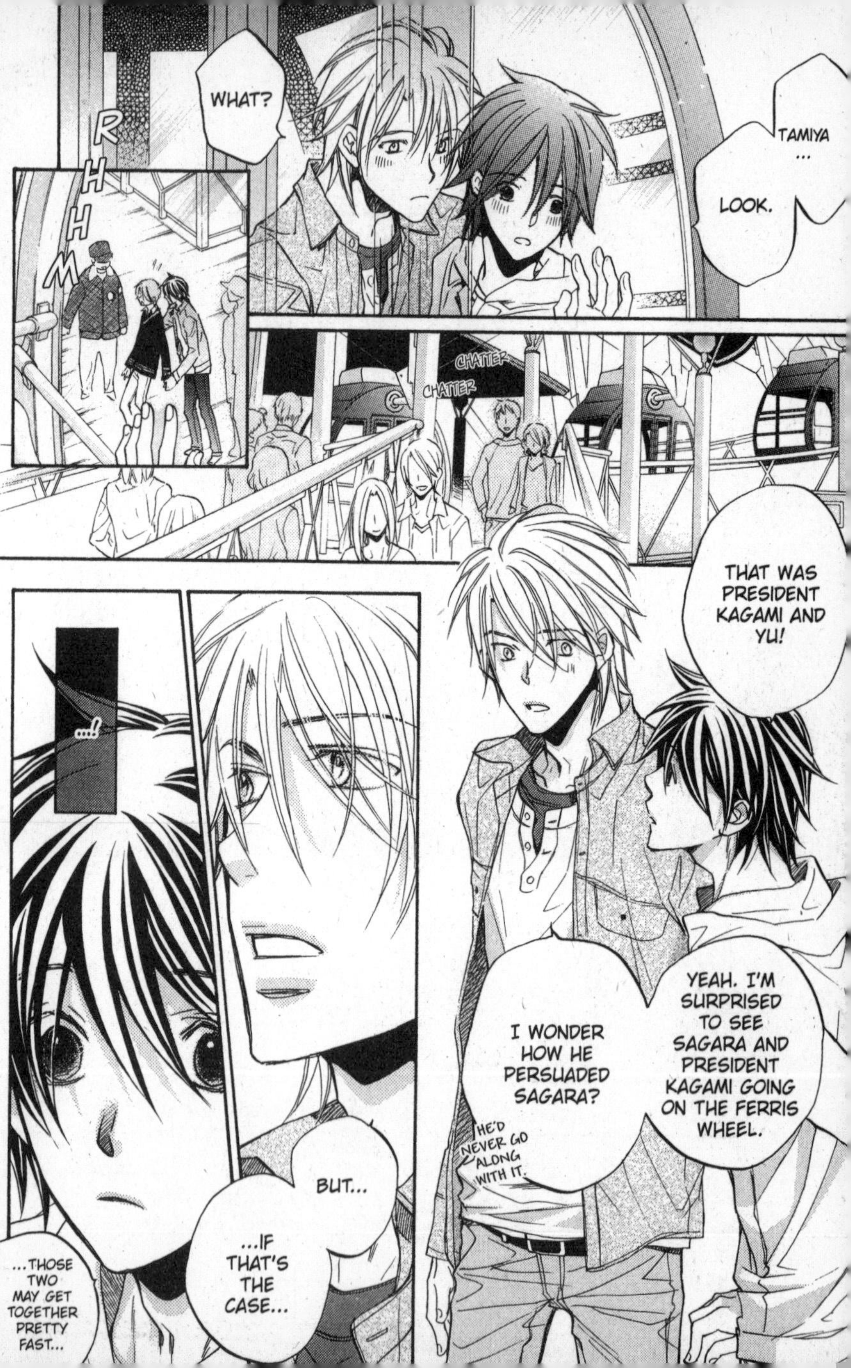
TAMIYA ... LOOK.
WHAT?
RHHHM
CHATTER
CHATTER
THAT WAS PRESIDENT KAGAMI AND YU!
YEAH. I'M SURPRISED TO SEE SAGARA AND PRESIDENT KAGAMI GOING ON THE FERRIS WHEEL.
I WONDER HOW HE PERSUADED SAGARA?
HE'D NEVER GO ALONG WITH IT.
BUT...
...IF THAT'S THE CASE...
...!
...THOSE TWO MAY GET TOGETHER PRETTY FAST...

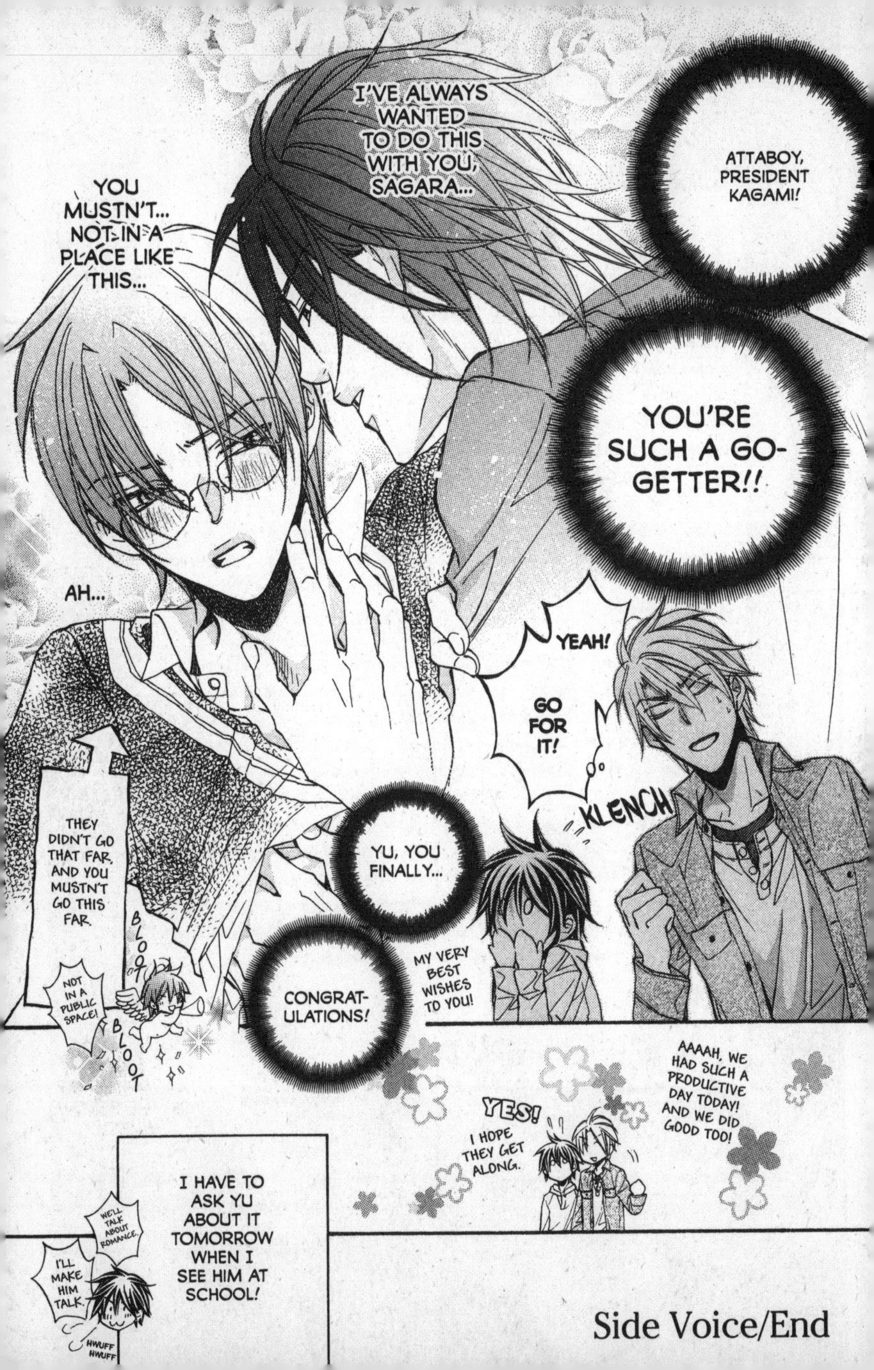
ATTABOY, PRESIDENT KAGAMI!
I'VE ALWAYS WANTED TO DO THIS WITH YOU, SAGARA...
YOU MUSTN'T... NOT IN A PLACE LIKE THIS...
YOU'RE SUCH A GO-GETTER!!
YEAH!
GO FOR IT!
KLENCH
AH...
YU, YOU FINALLY...
MY VERY BEST WISHES TO YOU!
CONGRATULATIONS!
THEY DIDN'T GO THAT FAR, AND YOU MUSTN'T GO THIS FAR.
BLOOT
NOT IN A PUBLIC SPACE!
BLOOT
AAAAH, WE HAD SUCH A PRODUCTIVE DAY TODAY! AND WE DID GOOD TOO!
YES!
I HOPE THEY GET ALONG.
I HAVE TO ASK YU ABOUT IT TOMORROW WHEN I SEE HIM AT SCHOOL!
WE'LL TALK ABOUT ROMANCE.
I'LL MAKE HIM TALK.
HWUFF HWUFF
Side Voice/End

🌸 Hello! Hinako Takanaga here. Thank you very much for picking up *Awkward Silence* Volume 3. 🌸 There are now three volumes in this series, which started out as a one-shot. This is all thanks to the readers who have been supporting this series... 🌸 This comes out at a very slow pace, so the manga volumes take time to be published. I am very grateful to all the people who still continue to read it! Thank you very much. ☺

🌸 To those who have read this, almost all of this volume is about the side characters, President Kagami and Yu. I apologize to the fans of Tamiya and Tono, the main characters... They have such a stable relationship, you see... Come to think of it, I get the feeling that Tono's mother is stealing all the good scenes. Who are the main characters of this series...?! So I decided write the short side story about the two main characters. How did you like it? This side story connects to the main story in this volume. I hope you enjoyed it.

🌸 As you can see, President Kagami and Yu have not exactly gotten together yet. So... I have a feeling that the next volume will be filled with stories that revolve around President Kagami and Yu. Of course I want you to support the main couple, but I would like you to cheer on the side characters as well. I'll do my best so everyone has a nice relationship.

🌸 And last but not least, to my dear editor... I'm very sorry for causing you so much trouble all the time. 😅 Thank you to all the assistants who helped me and to all my friends who support me. Thank you very much!! And of course, I would like to thank everybody who supports this series from the bottom of my heart! Thank you very, very much! I think I'll end here for now. I hope we'll see each other again somewhere.

🌸 Hinako Takanaga 🌸

About the Author

Hinako Takanaga was born on September 16th in Nagoya, Japan. She is the creator of many popular series, including *The Tyrant Falls in Love*, which was also adapted into an anime series. She is a Virgo, blood type O, and a self-proclaimed coffee addict who can get violent if she doesn't get her daily dose. A fortune-teller once told her she wasn't suited to be a manga artist, but she doesn't believe in fortune-telling anyway. She currently lives with her lovely cats Choro and Mame.

Awkward Silence
Volume 3
SuBLime Manga Edition

Story and Art by **Hinako Takanaga**

Translation—**Tetsuichiro Miyaki**
Touch-up Art and Lettering—**NRP Studios**
Cover and Graphic Design—**Fawn Lau**
Editor—**Nancy Thistlethwaite**

Bukiyou na Silent ③ © 2010 Hinako Takanaga
Originally published in Japan in 2010 by Libre Publishing Co.,
Ltd. Tokyo.
English translation rights arranged with Libre Publishing Co.,
Ltd. Tokyo.

Printed in Canada

Published by SuBLime Manga
P.O. Box 77010
San Francisco, CA 94107

10 9 8 7 6 5 4 3 2 1
First printing, February 2013

www.SuBLimeManga.com

For more information

on all our products, along with the most up-to-date news on releases, series announcements, and contests, please visit us at:

 SuBLimeManga.com

 twitter.com/**SuBLimeManga**

 facebook.com/**SuBLimeManga**

SUBLIME
MANGA

Downloading is as easy as:

1